THE BLACK DAHLIA FILES

ALSO BY DONALD H. WOLFE

The Assassination of Marilyn Monroe

The BLACK Dahlia Files

The Mob, the Mogul, and the Murder That Transfixed Los Angeles

Donald H. Wolfe

TIME WARNER
BOOKS

First published in the US in 2006 by Regan Books,
an imprint of HarperCollins Publishers
First published in Great Britain in May 2006 by Time Warner Books
Reprinted 2006

Grateful acknowledgement is made for permission
to quote from the following:

The Cases That Haunt Us by John Douglas and Mark Olshaker. Copyright
2000 by Mindhunters, Inc. Reprinted by permission of Scribner.

Childhood Shadows: The Hidden Story of the Black Dahlia Murder by
Mary Pacios. Copyright 1999 by Mary Pacios. Reprinted by permission
of Mary Pacios.

Severed: The True Story of the Black Dahlia Murder by John Gilmore.
Copyright 1994 by John Gilmore. Reprinted by permission of John
Gilmore.

A CIP catalogue record for this book
is available from the British Library.

ISBN-13: 978-0-3167-2726-6
ISBN-10: 0-3167-2726-1

Printed and bound in Great Britain by
Clays Ltd, St Ives plc

Time Warner Books
An imprint of
Little, Brown Book Group
Brettenham House
Lancaster Place
London WC2E 7EN

A Member of the Hachette Livre Group of Companies

www.littlebrown.co.uk

Time Warner Books is a trademark of Time Warner Inc. or an affiliated
company. Used under licence by Little, Brown Book Group, which is
not affiliated with Time Warner Inc.

To Vince Carter . . .
and all the honest cops who took the oath and kept it.

It was that name, <u>Black</u> <u>Dahlia</u>, that set this one off . . .
just those words strung together in that order.
<u>Black</u> is night, mysterious, forbidding; the <u>Dahlia</u>—
an exotic, mysterious flower. Any other name and it
wouldn't have been the same.

Det. Sgt. Harry Hansen, LAPD
HOMICIDE DIVISION

CONTENTS

CONTENTS

PREFACE

THE BLACK DAHLIA murder occurred in Los Angeles more than fifty years ago, and the heinous crime was never solved. Often referred to as "a riddle wrapped in a mystery inside an enigma," the puzzling homicide has continued to mystify many of us through the decades. A number of books have been written about the subject, with each author attempting to put together the pieces of the murder puzzle; however, after years of speculation, the Black Dahlia case remains stamped "Open and Unsolved."

Time is often the enemy of truth and justice—evidence disappears, memories fade, witnesses die—and today the Black Dahlia murder is a cold, cold case. In our kinetic age the headlines of the day are soon forgotten and major stories, scandals, and unsolved mysteries are buried in civilization's scrap heap as the time machine rolls on and the public becomes immersed in the next scandal, the next war, the next cataclysm—the next murder.

But time can also be the friend of truth. The twentieth century is literally a storehouse of documentation once hidden from public view, and many of these yellowed documents hold the answers to yesterday's mysteries: After more than five decades, the evidence files and research material of the Kefauver Crime Commission are being indexed and slowly becoming available; under the Freedom of Information Act, more and more FBI and CIA files are being released; and although Chief Justice Warren had stated "Not in your lifetime" when he sealed the Warren Commission investigation papers more than forty years ago, many of the documents continue to become available.

In 2002, Los Angeles District Attorney, Steve Cooley, began establishing an archive of historic twentieth century crime investigations culled from the immense LAPD warehouse and the files of the district attorney's office. Included in the archive of notable cases were the Black Dahlia files, containing a wealth of testimony, documented evidence, and information that had never before been made public. For the first time, the district attorney's files reveal the bizarre modus operandi of the crime, establish a time-line of where the victim lived in the last years of her life, identify the people she knew, and provide a list of all the suspects—many of whom were never previously mentioned by the police or the press. Most importantly, the files document the hidden motivation of the psychopathic killer—the dark secret hidden from the public for more than half a century. The files also reveal the Herculean effort by the upper echelons of the Los Angeles Police Department to cover up the nature of the crime. None of this extensive material had been available to former investigative journalists and researchers who spent years attempting to solve the baffling Black Dahlia murder with the limited information that was then accessible.

If the district attorney's archives had been available to John Gilmore when he wrote *Severed: The True Story of the Black Dahlia Murder*, he would have known just how close he was to solving the crime; Mary Pacios, who had known the Black Dahlia as a child and painted such an insightful portrait of her in *Childhood Shadows: The Hidden Story of the Black Dahlia Murder*, may have elected to eliminate some of the people on her suspect list; James Ellroy could have written a nonfiction book about the case, rather than a novel; and Janice Knowlton, author of *Daddy Was the Black Dahlia Killer*, would have been spared the anguish of believing her father was the murderer.

Steve Hodel, author of the most recent book on the case, *Black Dahlia Avenger*, also accused his father, George Hodel, of being the killer. Had he not completed his book just prior to the opening of the district attorney's archives, he could have learned that his father neither knew the Black Dahlia, nor had anything to do with the crime.

Born and raised in Los Angeles, I was fifteen years old when the Black Dahlia murder took place, and all the screaming headlines landed on our doorstep. Early on, I began collecting pieces of the Black Dahlia puzzle, and through the years I encountered reporters and police officers who had worked the case, including Will Fowler, the first reporter on the scene; Aggie Underwood, the ace Hearst crime reporter; Homicide detective Finis Brown; and "Badge # 1"— John St. John.

I met former LAPD officer Vince Carter in 1992 while researching *The Last Days of Marilyn Monroe*. Having worked Administrative Vice at the time of the murder, Vince had a unique insight into the crime, as well as the depths of corruption within the upper echelons of the LAPD; and it was Vince who led me to the two LAPD intelligence officers who had discovered where the Black Dahlia murder took place and knew the identity of the killer.

I was first alerted to the district attorney's historical archives by Steve Lopez, a columnist for the *Los Angeles Times*. Lopez had heard rumors about the D. A.'s Black Dahlia files and was the first to view them. After receiving permission from the district attorney's office to study and copy the documents, I soon realized they were a treasure trove of new and significant evidence. Some of the most valuable information was contained in the handwritten notes and memos of

Lieutenant Frank Jemison, who had been the investigator when the Black Dahlia case was placed before the Grand Jury in 1949.

It was while studying Jemison's notes, more than half a century after they were written, that I knew I had found the pieces that were missing from the Black Dahlia puzzle. With all the pieces in place, I soon realized that they created a monstrous murder mosaic that was far more sinister than ever surmised. And clearly identifiable within the shadows of the assembled picture was the image of the killer himself—the psychopath who had wandered the labyrinthine corridors of power and greed that crisscrossed the dark underworld of Los Angeles in 1947.

—*Donald H. Wolfe*

in other w...... ..... didn't double date, they didn't run
aroun ....er, but she said that she did have lo
.... with this one and that one, and there
.... say, no steady boyfriend.

....gh. .ou have completed your substance of your
...on as to Hansen?
.. that's the highlights on Hansen.

.l, give us the highlights on the next situation, which
b. ..ne of the two.
t ..s Dillon.

.us abou. .hat.
.irst I knew there was a person by the name of Dillo.
...ceived a .hone call at home, I believe I was on a day o.
.. d a phone call at home fr. Capt. Kearney, who was
.. ....me in charge of the Hom..... Division, Captain
.... "How soon can .c.. .... I may ...
....

PART I:

A Riddle Wrapped
in a Mystery...

.....th fix the date in this wa. ..t was the same da. .hen
Dillon was bo... ....

Q And that would have been the 10th of January, according
my recollection?
A The 10th of January, if the records so show, that's when
was, I was told...

Q That was the first date, January 10, 1949, that you ever
heard of Dillon?
A That's correct.

Q And you got downtown as you told us?
A Capt. Kearney said he was in custody of our officers, an
he was being brought to Los Angeles, from up north. I beli
he had been to San Francisco, that's hearsay on my part, I
didn't know. However, I was instructed to go to Highland P
Station and there await the arrival of officers from our
Department who had Dillon in custody. Sgt. Brown was also
called a. home by Capt. Kearney and told to get down as soc
he coul. .e came down, and I went to Highlan. ..k Statio
.. ....ed .here and at about 2:30, as I reca.., in the aft

THE MONSTER

THERE WASN'T MUCH nightlife in Los Angeles back in the 1940s. Most people went to bed early. Even in Hollywood the streets were empty, and the town was pretty dead by 10:00 P.M. But as the city slept, the monster would come to life. The hulking behemoth invariably awoke around midnight, its flames jetting into the inky blackness. Every time they pushed the red button, it would jolt into action. The gears would begin to rotate, the wheels turn, and the platens clank into position. As the steely colossus pulsed into motion, the cavernous depths would begin to vibrate, and the roar became deafening—the rollers turning faster and faster as the leaden plates whirled in a rhythmic crescendo of sound and motion.

The gigantic press was as tall as a two-story building. Rows of flames dried the ink as huge rolls of paper were consumed by the revolving plates that fed the printed pages to the cutter. Smoke from the flames would mingle with the solvent stench of ink and oil, filling the pressroom with its acrid odor.

Before they could roll the press, dozens of people would gather and edit the daily news about war and rumors of war, weddings, births,

funerals, sports, movie stars, society, kidnappings, robberies, politics—
and murder. And every twenty-four hours, at about midnight, they'd
press the red button once again, and the monster would come to life,
devour it all, and spit out the news through the flames that dried the
ink and singed the truth, the lies, and *Felix the Cat*. Then the monster
would fold it, bundle it up, and throw it down the chute, where the
trucks waited in the night to distribute the *Los Angeles Examiner*.

When the Black Dahlia murder hit the headlines on January 15,
1947, it led to one of the biggest press runs in the history of the
newspaper. More copies of the *Los Angeles Examiner* were printed
and sold on that day than any edition during World War II. It was the
beginning of a rabid running war between the L.A. newspapers to
scoop their rivals in the Dahlia case, a bitter battle fought with words,
ink, payoffs, and news pulp from day-to-day, for weeks and weeks—
right down to the daily deadline.

Back in those days you could "read all about it" for a nickel,
though there were those in the City of the Angels who knew what
was printed in the L.A. newspapers about the Black Dahlia case
wasn't worth two cents.

Extra! Extra!

I WAS RAISED on the wrong side of the tracks in Beverly Hills. The Pacific-Electric Railway bisected the city, and people like Gary Cooper, Betty Grable, Louis B. Mayer, Mary Pickford, and Marlene Dietrich lived north of the tracks. We lived on the south side on Camden Drive, where some of our neighbors were strictly name-below-the-title "B" movie folks. Joe E. Brown and Billy Gilbert lived down the street, Anne Revere across the way, and J. Carol Naish around the corner.

The south side had its compensations, however. I used to roller skate with Elizabeth Taylor before she became a child star. She and her brother, Howard, lived nearby on Charleville, and she was a member of what some of the neighborhood kids called "The Beverly Hills Skating Club." With the onset of adolescence, we changed the name to "The Beverly Hills Kissing Club;" but before Elizabeth Taylor could be initiated she was taken away from us by MGM.

Although I was from the lower depths of the south side, I attended El Rodeo Grammar School, which was to the north in the land of the majors. Some of my friends and schoolmates were children of the rich and famous. I first saw *Gone with the Wind* in David O. Selznick's living room on the occasion of Jeffery Selznick's twelfth birthday. Jeffery and I were friends at school and Tenderfoot Scouts in Troop 33. Our Boy Scout house was donated by Will Rogers and stood near the wilds of the L.A. Country Club. While learning to light campfires by rubbing sticks together on the manicured greens of the fourteenth tee, the Selznicks' chauffeured limousine would be waiting outside the rustic scout house to drive Jeffery home to his Summit Drive mansion.

Whenever my older brother, Robert, and I drove with my mother and father through the north side streets of Beverly Hills, with all the imposing mansions, my father would inevitably say, "Behind those mansion doors, there's often a great deal of unhappiness." And my mother would inevitably respond, "Behind the doors of most dumps, there's also a lot of unhappiness, but a lot less room."

After my parents divorced in 1943, my mother married Jeffrey Bernerd, a movie producer, and we moved north, across the tracks to the land of the majors, where we lived behind one of those mansion doors where "there's often a great deal of unhappiness." But I had it good compared to many of my friends who suffered grievously from material riches and emotional want, and I soon learned that my dad was right; in some of those big homes, I observed a lot of unhappiness—broken hearts, drunks, neurotics, psychotics, suicides, and an occasional murder. Many of my pals at El Rodeo and Beverly Hills High School were driven directly from school to their analyst's office on Bedford Drive, and early on, I learned there was a dark side to money, power, and influence and that the truth and what was printed in the newspapers were not necessarily the same.

Beneath appearances and the public image, there was the whispered story, and beneath the whispered story, there was the cover story; and somewhere beneath the cover story lay the genuine rumor—while the body of truth often lay entombed within the corridors of intrigue. I was a sophomore at Beverly Hills High School when the Black Dahlia murder occurred, and all the cover stories and genuine rumors began, but I had reason to suspect that the truth lay sealed in the catacombs of money, power, and influence—in a carefully guarded crypt that has not been violated until this day.

A jovial, smiling figure of Charlie McCarthy wearing his monocle, boutonnière, and funny top hat sat on the rim above the speaker of my bedside radio. In the 1940s you could listen to Red Skelton, Jack Benny, Gang Busters, Fibber McGee and Molly, Edgar Bergen and Charlie McCarthy, and a host of highly entertaining radio shows, but by 10:00 P.M., the entertainment came to an end, and you knew it was time to go to sleep when the fruit frost warnings came on. If the temperature dropped below 35°F in the San Fernando and San Gabriel Valleys, the ranchers had to go out and light their smudge pots to ward off the frost that could damage the citrus crops.

On the night of Tuesday, January 14, 1947, the fruit frost warning had been posted and broadcasted on the ten o'clock news. At that hour few people were out on the streets. There were only those who worked late, those who were coming home from the movies or the wrestling matches at Legion Stadium, and the inveterate night people: the sleepless, the homeless, the inebriated. Downtown at the Hearst Examiner Building on Eleventh Street and Broadway, they were preparing the presses for the midnight run of the *Examiner*—casting the lead plate matrixes, mounting the giant paper rolls, filling the ink vats, and oiling the rollers.

In the small hours after midnight, Bobby Jones, a young man in his early teens, wheeled his bicycle through a vacant lot near Thirty-ninth Street and Norton Avenue in Leimert Park. He had gotten up long before dawn to fold and prepare the newspapers for delivery on his route along Crenshaw Boulevard. In those days Leimert Park was a nice, middle class neighborhood on the fringe of the more fashionable Adams District west of downtown Los Angeles. But the construction of homes had been stopped by the war, and the area north of Thirty-ninth Street was still an extension of vacant lots with driveways leading to nothing but weeds and wild bushes.

Although it was quite dark when Bobby pushed his bicycle through the weeds, he noticed a black sedan with its lights off as it parked next to the sidewalk. The street lighting was dim, and he could not see the occupants of the car. Assuming they might be neckers, Bobby thought little of what he had observed as he continued on to his Crenshaw newspaper route.

Sunrise was at 6:53 A.M. on Wednesday, January 15, 1947, but the sun was shrouded in mist, and the dampness and dew remained on the grass and weeds until late that morning when the sun finally burned through. At about 10:30 A.M., a Leimert Park resident, Betsy Bersinger, was pushing her three-year-old daughter in a baby stroller down the sidewalk bordering the vacant lots on Norton Avenue when she noticed what she thought to be an undressed department store mannequin lying in the weeds near the sidewalk. The discarded mannequin appeared to be broken. The legs were disconnected from the waist, and the top of the torso lay in the grass not far from the legs and a section of the hips. The breasts seemed to have become detached, and the arms were raised above the head, which faced the street.

Mrs. Bersinger noticed that the head had been badly damaged and that there were red marks on the face. She suddenly stopped pushing the baby stroller and stared at the broken head in frozen disbelief as she realized that the red marks were congealed blood and that the broken store dummy was actually the mutilated nude remains of a young woman. Hurrying to a neighbor's house, she called the police and tried to give a coherent report of what she had seen before lapsing into shock.

At about 10:45 A.M., *Los Angeles Examiner* reporter Will Fowler and photographer Felix Paegel were returning to the downtown *Examiner* building from a story they had covered earlier that morning at the Beverly Hills Hotel when they heard the call go out over the police band on their short-wave radio:

"A 390 W—415—down in an empty lot on Norton, one block east of Crenshaw—between 39th and Coliseum Streets . . . Proceed to investigate—Code Two."

"Code Two" meant that police cars in the vicinity should proceed as quickly as possible, but without a red light or siren. A "390" meant a drunk, a "390 W" was a drunk woman, and a "415" designated indecent exposure. Fowler and Paegel were only blocks from the location when they heard the Code Two, and Fowler recalled that they decided to drive by and see what it was all about. Paegel, who was driving, turned east onto Thirty-ninth Street, and when they arrived at Norton, they found that they were the first to arrive at the scene. As Paegel drove along the row of vacant lots looking for the disrobed drunken woman, they glimpsed someone lying in the weeds near the sidewalk. Fowler looked more closely and exclaimed, "God, Felix, this woman's been cut in half!"

Recalling that horrifying moment, Fowler said, "It took a few minutes to get used to looking at this mutilated woman lying there like a discarded marionette that had been separated from itself—the torso was about a foot away from the legs and pelvis. Both halves were facing upward. Her arms were extended above her head. Her eyes were still half-open. There was no blood on the grass and her body was white as marble."

Fowler had observed a number of gruesome murder scenes in his career, but nothing like this. The victim's mouth had been slit open from ear to ear, and her face and head had been badly beaten. He noted that the blows to the head were characteristic of someone who had been pistol-whipped.

While Fowler was studying the gruesome remains of the victim and taking notes, Paegel took out his 4 × 5 Speed Graphic and began taking pictures. Within minutes an L.A. police car pulled up to the curb, and two uniformed officers stepped out—William Fitzgerald and Sgt. Frank Perkins. Seeing Fowler and Paegel hovering around the mutilated body, Officers Fitzgerald and Perkins released the safety straps on their holsters as they approached, and Fitzgerald pulled out his revolver.

"I'm a reporter on the *Examiner* and this is my photographer," Fowler explained as he showed them his press ID.

"Hell, someone's cut this girl right in half!" Sgt. Perkins exclaimed as Officer Fitzgerald stared at the body with disbelief. "Get on the radio," Perkins said, "and put this right through to the watch commander. Get them over here fast!"

Returning to the patrol car, Fitzgerald grabbed the microphone and requested to speak to Lt. Paul Freestone, the watch commander on duty at the University Station on Jefferson Boulevard.

In the days before scanners, CB radios, and cell phones, reporters always carried extra nickels in their pockets to phone in the news, and while the police were preoccupied in examining the body and reporting to the station, Fowler hurried to the nearest payphone on Crenshaw, dropped in a nickel, and dialed his editor, James Richardson, at the *Examiner* city desk. Richardson was incredulous at the description of the murder victim, but when Fowler insisted that the body was cut in half, Richardson told him to hurry in to the editorial office with the photos and start preparing a front-page story.

The city room was already buzzing about the grotesque murder when Fowler and Paegel arrived. Fowler began typing out his initial copy while Paegel's photo negatives were quickly processed. When the first large eleven-by-fourteen print of the victim's severed body came out of the lab, Richardson called the city room people together and held up the photo.

"Take a good look," Richardson said. "This is what a lot of you will be working on today!" And he informed them they were going to beat the afternoon papers out on the street with the story and put out an *EXTRA*.

By the time Fowler returned to Leimert Park, the scene on Norton was crowded with reporters, photographers, and uniformed officers who were having difficulty keeping back the growing crowd of curious spectators. Reporters from the *Los Angeles Times*, the *Hollywood Citizen News*, and the *Daily News* were there, and Fowler spotted Hearst reporter Agness "Aggie" Underwood, one of the few women who had scaled the gender barrier and climbed to the heights as one of Hearst's key reporters. Aggie Underwood worked for the Hearst evening paper, the *Los Angeles Herald Express*, and she had a reputation of being hard as nails. But when Aggie first viewed the victim's remains, Sgt. Perkins recalled, "You could see the color drain right out of her like you'd opened a spigot on her bottom side." Although Aggie had seen many murder victims in her career, the sight of the mutilated body lying in the weeds near the sidewalk knocked her off balance, and Perkins remembered that she "staggered backwards, almost right off the edge of the curb—and almost fell down on her keester. . . ." Aggie had recovered her composure by the time Fowler returned to the scene, but she didn't realize that he had been there earlier, and Aggie derisively remarked, "How come you let the *Times* beat you here, Fowler?"

It wasn't until the *Examiner EXTRA* with Fowler's story and Paegel's photos beat the *Herald Express* onto the street that Aggie realized Fowler had been there much earlier.

When Officer Fitzgerald informed Watch Commander Paul Freestone at University that the 309 W was a severed corpse, Freestone sent Homicide Detective Jesse Haskins to the scene. Observing the condition of the body, Lt. Haskins noted that the body was cold and alabaster white. The remains had been drained of blood and seemed to have been soaked in water. There was little or no blood to be seen on the grass beneath the two sections of the corpse, and it was obvious that the murder had taken place some place else.

Haskins soon realized that what he was viewing was unlike any homicide he had encountered before. This was a crime of another dimension—outside the realm of his experience—and he was somewhat relieved when he received a call from Captain Jack Donahoe, chief of Homicide in the Central Division, informing him that homicide detectives Harry Hansen and Finis Brown from Central would be taking over the case from University. Det. Sgt. Harry Hansen had been with the LAPD since 1926 and was the senior officer supervising most of the homicide investigations in Central's metropolitan district. Hansen was investigating a crime in downtown Los Angeles with his partner, Finis Brown, when he received the call that morning from Capt. Donahoe telling him to proceed to Thirty-ninth Street and Norton as quickly as possible.

It was almost noon before Hansen and Brown reached the Norton crime scene, and from the beginning, Hansen was unhappy with the way University had handled it. Hansen was the author of the police handbook on the protection of crime scene evidence, and what he saw when he arrived at Norton violated all the rules. Reporters had been allowed to roam the area, possibly obliterating tire tracks and footprints, and they had littered the crime scene with cigarette butts and burnt flash bulbs. The street had not been blocked off and was rapidly filling with cars of the curious, and some of the spectators had converged onto the vacant lot.

Hansen had a somewhat mystical approach to homicide; in his police handbook, he had decreed a murder scene as a "sacred setting." "Homicide is a union that never dies," Hansen stated. He maintained that the murder forever bonds together the murderer and the victim. "Like marriage, murder is an irreversible act. It can never be changed, or the circumstances altered. The murderer and the victim are tied together in a bond that goes on into infinity. That's why I say it's sacred, and every murder scene has its sacred ground which should not be touched."

The Norton Avenue crime scene. The victim's remains are center, left. (BRUCE HENSTELL COLLECTION)

Hansen believed that evidence and clues regarding the victim as well as the murderer could be found in what may appear to the casual observer as insignificant detail. Every minute shred of evidence, he felt, was a tessera in a large mosaic picture —even if the body was disposed of in a different location than the scene of the actual murder.

Dismayed that the Norton Avenue crime scene had been disturbed, Hansen told the uniformed officers to clear the area and call in Ray Pinker, who was head of the LAPD Crime Lab. "Get him over here!" Hansen commanded as he kneeled down at the edge of the sidewalk and stared at the victim. Hansen was known for his scientific objectivity in investigating a murder case, but in his twenty years of police work, he had never seen a victim so brutally mutilated as the victim on Norton. According to Finis Brown, Hansen's stolid wall seemed to crumble a little when he first viewed the bisected body. Hansen noted that there were rope marks on the victim's neck, wrists, and ankles, and there were a number of severe bruises to the face and the right side of the forehead, as though she had been repeatedly struck by a blunt instrument. Both cheeks had been slashed open from the corners of the mouth to the ear lobes. Her breasts had been partially mutilated, and her arms were bruised and bent at right angles and extended back above the shoulders. Hansen noted that the body had been meticulously bisected at the waist—neatly and surgically. Some of the inner organs had been removed. The legs were spread apart, and there were strange knife marks in the pubic area and on the upper legs. Unlike most rage murders, the victim's body had been displayed—not dumped. Hansen and Brown observed that the perpetrator had deliberately arranged the bisected body near a public sidewalk, where the killer apparently wanted it to be discovered.

Noting that there was dampness from the dew on the grass beneath the body, Hansen concluded that the remains had probably been placed in the lot sometime between midnight and dawn. On the grass not far from the upper torso was an empty cement sack that appeared to have watery blood stains. A watery blood spot was also visible on the sidewalk near the body—along with a man's bloody heel print near the victim's head.

Hansen silently studied the body and the "sacred setting" for some time before he stood up and said to Finis, "We won't know what we're really dealing with here until we get a post mortem." He requested that the body be covered until Ray Pinker of the crime lab arrived.

When Pinker appeared at the scene shortly after noon, he examined the body and made the preliminary determination that the victim had been dead for at least ten hours—possibly longer. Pinker found there was post-mortem lividity on the front side of both parts of the body, indicating the victim had lain face down for some period of time following death. The multiplicity of bruises, wounds, and lacerations made it impossible to determine the exact cause of death, which would have to be determined at the autopsy. Discovering some small bits of bristle-like fragments on the victim's face and pubic region, Pinker believed that they may have been from a scrub brush. He noted that there was a four-inch incision in the lower abdomen and that flesh had been removed from the left leg above the knee. Pinker concurred with Hansen that the lower section of the body had been transported from the vehicle on the empty cement sack found near the body. The contours of the cement sack indicated that it might have been carried by more than one person.[1]

Detectives knocking on doors in the surrounding area found a witness who corroborated the newsboy's story of seeing a black sedan at the Norton Avenue site. Robert Meyer, who lived at 3900 South Bronson, said he saw a black 1936 or 1937 Ford sedan drive up and park at the site in the hours before dawn. "It stayed about three or four minutes, then drove off," Meyer told the police. He explained that he had not seen anything to arouse his suspicions at the time because the weeds obscured his view.

Meyer believed it was approximately 6:30 A.M. when he saw the old black Ford sedan; but the newsboy, Bobby Jones, stated that he had seen the black sedan at around 4:00 A.M. One of the witnesses was incorrect regarding the time, or it's possible that the vehicle had been at the site twice in the early morning hours. Investigators found a man's wristwatch in the weeds near the body. It was determined that the watch had only recently been lost, as it did not appear to be weathered. Identified as a military watch, the *Hollywood Citizen News* described it as a "17-jewel Croton with a leather bound, steel snap band." Engraved on it were the words, "Swiss-made, waterproof, Brevet, stainless-steel back."

The person, or one of the persons, who disposed of the body, may

---

1. See Appendix A on pages 325 and 326 for a digest of the LAPD files regarding the crime scene.

have discovered that his watch was missing and suspected it had been lost at the site. Perhaps concerned that a fingerprint could be found on the face or the back of the steel casing, the owner might have returned in the black sedan in an attempt to retrieve it. Though it was stated by the press that "Police chemists were checking ownership of the military watch," no follow-up stories appeared regarding results of the examination for prints.[2]

When Pinker concluded his examination of the crime scene, he turned to Hansen and said, "This is the worst crime I've ever seen committed upon a woman." Hansen did not respond, but stood in silence as he stared at the "sacred setting."

No one at the scene on Norton Avenue that day—Betsy Bersinger, the reporters, the detectives, the crime lab people, the uniformed officers, or the spectators—would ever forget what they had seen, nor would they ever be quite the same. All of them sensed it was the worst murder in the history of Los Angeles, perhaps the worst crime of the century. Something singularly depraved.

It was close to 2:00 P.M. when the California Hearse Service arrived to take the remains of the body to the Los Angeles County Morgue, located in the basement of the Hall of Justice in downtown Los Angeles. There the remains were unloaded, wheeled up the rear ramp, and tagged "Jane Doe #1."

The *Examiner EXTRA* hit the streets at 3:00 P.M., beating the rival newspapers to the newsstands with the murder story by one hour. The *EXTRA* was sold out by 5:30 P.M., and a second run of the *EXTRA* was sold out by 10:30 P.M. One of the Paegel photos of Jane Doe #1 was printed on the front page, but staff artists retouched the victim's face and removed the gruesome knife slashes on either side of the

---

2. In *Black Dahlia Avenger* by Steve Hodel (Arcade Publishing, NY, 2003), Hodel claims that his father, George Hodel, murdered Elizabeth Short and that the watch belonged to his father. However, he offers no tangible evidence that his father was the murderer or that the watch found near the body belonged to his father. (See "The Hodel Hypothesis" in Appendix B.)

mouth. A blanket covering the bisected body was airbrushed in, concealing the brutal mutilation. It would be decades before unretouched pictures of the victim were published, and the full horror of the killer's butchery became apparent.

The weather had turned warmer during the day, and there was no fruit frost warning that night on the ten o'clock news. Back in those days few people had television. The one Los Angeles television station, KTLA, was only on the air for three hours in the evening, and

A blanket has been painted over the bisected body and the face has been retouched by *Examiner* artists. (LAPL PHOTO COLLECTION)

Los Angeles Examiner

CHARACTER · QUALITY · AMERICA · ENTERPRISE

AN AMERICAN PAPER FOR THE AMERICAN PEOPLE · PREMIER NEWSPAPER OF THE GREAT SOUTHWEST

Examiner Telephone Richmond 1212 — Examiner Building—1111 S. Broadway

LOS ANGELES, THURSDAY, JANUARY 16, 1947 — Two Sections—Part I—FIVE CENTS

BRITISH REJECT RUSS CLAIM TO SPITSBERGEN

Foreign Office Denies Soviet Not Party to 1920 Treaty

By Thomas C. Watson

LONDON, Jan. 15.—The British Foreign Office announced today it will not recognize Soviet arguments presented to invalidate the 1920 pact which gives Norway sole sovereignty over the Spitsbergen archipelago.

A Government spokesman denied the Soviet claim that Russia was not a party to the pact and refuted the Russian contention the treaty no longer was effective because enemy states were signatories.

Both arguments were advanced by Tass, official Soviet agency, to justify the Russian move to share defense of the strategic islands with Norway.

The British official asserted Russia first gave recognition to the treaty in 1924 and 14 years later reaffirmed its recognition when she voluntarily accepted the obligations of the pact.

NOT NOTIFIED

In rebuttal to the argument concerning enemy states as signatories, he pointed out that numerous other treaties, including the Montreux convention governing the Dardanelles, were in a similar category.

He stated that the British government had not been notified by either Russia or Norway of any proposal to revise the treaty.

He said that as far as Britain is concerned, Norway's sovereignty over Spitsbergen and the power of the treaty can be altered with the consent of the signatories.

Tass, in presenting the Russian viewpoint, claimed that Russian concern over security and Soviet economic interests led to an understanding with the Norwegian government for the joint defense of the island chain.

Lord Ashley Divorced by Wife

LONDON, Jan. 15 (U.P)—An additional decree of divorce was granted today to Lady Ashley, heir of the Earl of Shaftesbury and formerly Francoise Soulier of Paris.

The decree was on grounds of infidelity by her husband, involving a French woman at a Paris hotel.

Lady Ashley was given custody of her two children. Lord Ashley's first wife, divorced in 1935, later married Film Actor Douglas Fairbanks.

King of Denmark Has Heart Attack

COPENHAGEN, Jan. 15.—(INS)—Government announcement said tonight that 76-year-old King Christian X of Denmark had suffered a heart attack.

The monarch was stricken Tuesday. First announcement of illness said he was suffering from a slight cold and congestion in the lungs. Tonight's bulletin said possible is being administered continuously to the king.

Mercury, Winds to Rise in L.A. Area, Forecast

Slightly rising temperatures, but strong northeasterly winds were predicted by the Weather Bureau for Los Angeles today and Friday.

Fiend Tortures, Kills Girl; Leaves Body in L.A. Lot

SLAYER'S PREY—The body of a teen-age girl was found yesterday in a vacant lot on Norton ave. She apparently had been bound, tortured and strangled before being mutilated.—*Los Angeles Examiner Photo*

ARTIST'S DRAWING OF VICTIM—Using police ideas and photographs, Examiner Artist Howard Burke drew this likeness of the victim of the slaying. The hair was discovered yesterday in a vacant lot.

New York State Revokes Mrs. FDR's Driving License

ALBANY, N.Y., Jan. 15.—(U.P)—New York State tonight revoked the automobile license of Mrs. Eleanor Roosevelt as the result of an accident at Yonkers last August, but an official pointed out that the license could be reinstated after 30 days.

Howard P. Miles, Deputy Commissioner of Motor Vehicles, announced that notice of revocation had been sent to Mrs. Roosevelt yesterday.

The decision to revoke the license followed a hearing January 8 at White Plains.

Mrs. Roosevelt was injured in the accident involving the

First Lady's automobile and her other men.

Police said Mrs. Roosevelt reported at the time that she had been slightly and her car turned over to the opposite lane in an accident somewhat at the intersection. However, she made no mention of damage.

Miles said Mrs. Roosevelt would have to pass a driver's test to get her license back.

Evidence Shows Teen-Age Victim Bound, Gagged During Slaying

Slain by a fiend, the body of a 'teen-age girl' was found in a vacant lot here yesterday.

The nude body was severed at the waist.

The girl had been killed elsewhere and her body taken to the lot and left in plain view, not three feet from the sidewalk.

Death came to the girl, police scientists said, after hours of torture.

Her slayer, they said, had trussed her hands and feet in ropes and had similarly bound her head. Rope burns and bruises on ankles and wrists supported their theory.

And from clinical evidence, Dr. Frederick Newbarr, Coroner's chief autopsy surgeon, deduced that the slaying possibly occurred while the girl was in a bathtub.

Woman's Call Leads to Discovery

The body was found by Radio Officers W. E. Fitzgerald and P. S. Perkins in a lot on Norton avenue between 39th street and Coliseum avenue.

They had been sent to the vicinity after a woman called University Police Station. Describing herself as a motorist, she said:

"I think a drunken man is lying in the weeds in a lot on Norton avenue near the intersection of Crenshaw and Santa Barbara boulevard."

Preliminary investigation at the scene brought few promising clews. All pointed to the sadistic nature of the slayer rather than to his identity or the identity of his victim.

The body was that of a young girl, 15 or 16—possibly older—whose dark brown hair had been hen-aned, and whose toenails were tinted rose.

She had been a good-looking girl, with a pert up-turned nose and a high forehead and gray-green eyes.

But aside from an inventory of small identifying scars and marks, police knew only one other thing about her—that she chewed her finger nails.

Donahue Takes Charge of Case

"This may be an important clew in her identification," said Captain Jack Donahue, chief of the homicide squad.

Taking personal charge of the investigation, Donahue assigned Detective Lieutenants Harry Hansen and S. A. Brown to the case.

They quickly eliminated a bundle of women's clothing at first believed to belong to the victim.

The bundle had been found by Joe Weaver, 1500 West Adams boulevard.

Tracing a laundry mark, police learned the clothing belonged to Clora Bryant, 951 East 46th street, and had been stolen from her car last Saturday.

Meanwhile, search was being made for a 1936 black Ford sedan seen at the Norton av. site site early yesterday by Bob Meyer, 3900 South Bronson avenue.

"I saw a car drive up and park about 6:30 a. m.," Meyer told police. "It stayed about three or four minutes then drove off."

He explained tall weeds obscured his view and that he had seen nothing to induce his suspicions at the time.

But police studied stains on the curbing and tire tracks in the mud, both of which strengthened the belief the slayer had used the black sedan.

In this belief, they were corroborated by the police Chemist Ray Pinker, identified as one of small bristles as coming from an automobile floor mat.

Once, for a few brief hours, prospect of identifi-

Ford Prices Will Be Cut

Decreases as Much as $50 Planned

DETROIT, Jan. 15.—(U.P)—Ford Motor Company announced its current models. The decrease amounts to as much as $50 on some models.

The cut apparently forecast increased expectations of greatly increased production volume this year.

Henry Ford II, president of the company, said:

"This is our 'down payment' toward a continued high level of production and employment in the months ahead.

"We believe that the stark treatment of prompt action is needed to halt the insane spiral of mounting costs and rising prices and to restore a sound basis for the hopeful period of postwar production we are now entering."

The price reductions are as follows:

- Super deluxe six sedan, four-door and sedan coupe $50 each.
- Super deluxe tudor $33.
- Super deluxe eight sedan eight coupe $35.
- Tudor, fordor and convertible club coupe $10 each.

4 Jets Fly 700 Mi. Luzon-Okinawa, in 1-Hr., 40 Min.

MANILA, Jan. 15 (Thursday.—(U.P)—Four Shooting Star jet fighters planes flew the 700 miles from Luzon to Okinawa in 1 hour and 40 minutes the Far Eastern Air Forces Command announced today.

The first demonstration of long-distance patrolling of the jet planes in the Pacific, under command of Brig. Gen. Benel commander Lieutenant General Keith C. Whitehead.

The flight "demonstrates that our newest planes and aircraft are conquering new horizons in the development of air power," General Whitehead said.

The planes took off from Luzon, at Luzon's southernmost coast, and landed at Kadena airbase on Okinawa, averaging 420 miles an hour.

91 Thefts Top City's Crime Total of 177 for 24 Hours

In the last 24 hours 177 crimes were committed in Los Angeles. They were:

91	thefts
47	burglaries
18	robberies
6	assaults
4	morals offenses
3	murders
3	suicides
1	attempted attack on a woman
13	automobile thefts

the news still belonged to paper and ink and the radio waves. Because of a Boy Scout meeting that Wednesday, I had not seen the newspapers and first heard about the bizarre murder of "Jane Doe #1" and some of the gruesome details on my bedside radio, where a jovial, smiling figure of Charlie McCarthy sat on the rim of the speaker, wearing his monocle, boutonnière, and funny top hat.

THE *LOS ANGELES* *Examiner's* headline story had a staccato quality that reflected the brutal reality of the murder:

> Slain by a fiend, the body of a teenage girl was found in a vacant lot here yesterday.
>
> The nude body was severed at the waist.
>
> The girl had been killed elsewhere and her body taken to the lot and left in plain view, not three feet from the sidewalk.
>
> Death came to the girl, police scientists said, after hours of torture.

The evening *Herald Express* referred to the murder as the diabolical act of a "werewolf fiend." In its ten-star final edition, the *Daily News* ran a four-column photo of the crime scene with an arrow pointing to the body under the headline: YOUNG L.A. GIRL SLAIN; BODY SLASHED IN TWO. The *Los Angeles Times* put the murder story on the front page in the morning edition of January 16; the headline was less lurid, yet the article vividly described the mutilated victim.

It was the Hearst papers that gave the Black Dahlia story the biggest play—the *Los Angeles Examiner* and the *Herald Express* outdid themselves in sensationalizing the sensational, and in the exploitive way it was reported in the press, the hideous murder took on a surreal quality that seemed to hang over the city like the hovering smog.

To a kid of fifteen, the Dahlia case was unspeakably bizarre. Though I didn't talk about it, I probably knew more about the Black Dahlia case than most of my classmates at Beverly Hills High. It was because of my "Uncle" Vern. Vern wasn't really my uncle, but that was how my mother referred to him. Vern was consorting with my grandmother, whom I called "Little Tah." My grandmother's real name was Bessie Harkins, and she lived in the old chauffeur's quarters attached to our garage. Little Tah drank too much, and I tried to avoid her whenever possible, but when I went to bed at night, she would often come up to my room and tell me whiskey-sodden bedtime tales. I'd feign falling asleep, but she'd go on and on, regardless. Uncle Vern was always hanging around the house with Little Tah, and I guess my mother thought that calling him "Uncle" would make a questionable arrangement more palatable to an impressionable teenager and the nosey neighbors. Vern's real name was Vernon Hamilton, and he had been an assistant district attorney in Los Angeles before resigning in 1938 under a cloud of scandal, along with Mayor Frank Shaw and District Attorney Buron Fitts.

Frank Shaw had been elected Mayor of Los Angeles in 1933 and ran what was considered to be the most corrupt administration in the city's history, which was saying a lot. In 1938 a Grand Jury investigating Shaw's corrupt regime found evidence of 1,800 bookie joints, 600 brothels, and 200 gambling dens operating within the County of Los Angeles—all protected with payoffs from the underworld to District Attorney Buron Fitts, the LAPD, and His Honor, Mayor Frank Shaw. The evidence of corruption was overwhelming and led to the recall of Shaw, the first mayor of a major city in the nation to be so honored, and it resulted in the resignation of Police Chief James E. "Two-Gun" Davis and the removal of Uncle Vern's pal, Buron Fitts.

Fitts had been the Los Angeles District Attorney since 1928, and the key component in the triad of corruption that ruled the city during the 1930s. Mayor Shaw, Police Chief Davis, and Fitts had all been protégés of the publisher of the *Los Angeles Times*, Harry Chandler, who ruled the political life of the city with a hand of iron and the molten lead of the *Times* Linotype machine.

Before the days of tabloid scandal sheets, Buron Fitts had covered up enough crimes and scandals to decimate forests of tabloid pulp. One of the notorious scandals had involved the alleged suicide of Jean Harlow's husband, Paul Bern, whom many believed had been murdered by mobster Longy Zwillman. Another cover-up had been the murder of actress Thelma Todd. Best remembered for her comedic roles in Marx Brothers movies and Charlie Chase comedies, Thelma Todd, the "Ice Cream Blonde," had been a popular actress in the late twenties and early thirties. On December 16, 1935, her mink-clad corpse had been found sitting behind the wheel of the actress's Lincoln Phaeton in the garage behind Thelma Todd's Sidewalk Café, a popular nightspot on the oceanfront of Castellammare near the Pacific Palisades. The Phaeton's motor had been left running in the closed garage, and it was ruled that the actress died of asphyxiation. The autopsy, however, disclosed that Thelma Todd had been badly beaten, her nose smashed, her body bruised and bloody, two ribs broken, and her teeth knocked loose and chipped. Nevertheless, D. A. Buron Fitts insisted that her death was a suicide, though there were rumors among the movieland cognoscenti that Thelma Todd had been murdered by one of her intimate acquaintances—a mob boss who suddenly left town on the night of Thelma's "suicide."[3]

---

3. Many have speculated that the "mob boss" who murdered Thelma Todd was Lucky Luciano; however, in 1935, Luciano had been in New York City living in suite 39C at the Waldorf Towers until the murder of Dutch Schultz on November 13, 1935. Five days later Luciano fled to Florida and was known by New York authorities to be in Hot Springs, Arkansas, at the time of Thelma Todd's murder.

In 1932 Thelma had a whirlwind romance with Pasquale "Pat" DiCicco, who had been an associate of the mob in New York during the bootleg days of the roaring twenties. Married in July 1932, DiCicco and the Ice Cream Blonde opened Thelma Todd's Sidewalk Café, which became a popular nightspot frequented by filmland celebrities and high-rollers who were admitted into the Joya Room, a clandestine Syndicate gambling den on the third floor. Thelma Todd had never wanted the gambling room, nor did she care for DiCicco's underworld friends, among whom were Longy Zwillman and Benjamin "Bugsy" Siegel. In the mob's efforts to set up new avenues of illicit revenue after the end of Prohibition, Bugsy Siegel had become a frequent visitor to the West Coast, and in 1935 he rented an apartment on the Sunset Strip. While it is popularly believed that Bugsy Siegel did not move to Los Angeles until 1936 or 1937, his FBI files establish that he became a resident of Los Angeles in 1934. The 1935 Los Angeles Telephone Directory places Benjamin Siegel's residence at 8421 Sunset Boulevard, which was the Piazza Del Sol Apartments next to the Clover Club—where only a select Hollywood crowd was admitted by Siegel's mob maître d' into the fashionable Clover Club casino.

It wasn't long after Thelma Todd's marriage to Pat DiCicco that she began to realize her husband and the mob were using her and the Sidewalk Café as a front for their gambling operations, and her marriage to DiCicco proved to be stormy and short-lived. Divorcing him in 1935, she tried to evict DiCicco and his mob friends from the casino operation, but she began receiving threats and was told that she better cooperate with the Syndicate gangsters. Without explaining the nature of her growing fears, Thelma wrote a family member in Massachusetts that she was worried because she had fallen in with a bad crowd and was being intimidated.

Angry about the threats she was receiving if she didn't cooperate with Bugsy Siegel and his pals, on December 11 Thelma made the mistake of going to District Attorney Buron Fitts's office and lodging a complaint against the mobsters who had muscled in on her café. She had no knowledge, of course, that the District Attorney of Los Angeles was on the mob payroll and that word would soon get back to the very people who had threatened her.

On the night of Saturday, December 14, she went to a party at Billy Wilkerson's Trocadero nightclub on the Sunset Strip, which was attended by Sid Grauman, Spyros Skouras, Zazu Pitts, Ida Lupino, and a number of film stars. Sometime after midnight, she was told by the headwaiter, Alex Hounie, that a gentleman wanted to see her in the nightclub office. Whoever the "gentleman" might have been, Thelma became frightened, fled the office, and abruptly left the party. Telling her chauffeur to drive "faster, faster!", she hurried back to Castellammare and her apartment above the Sidewalk Café. The chauffeur maintained that he dropped her off at the café door before returning the Phaeton to the garage. Two days later, on Monday morning, her body was found behind the wheel of the car.

When the Trocadero headwaiter was questioned at the inquest as to the identity of the "gentleman" who had frightened Thelma in the nightclub office, Hounie mumbled that he could not remember before breaking down and blurting out that he had been warned not to talk. "I can't speak out of fear I'll be kidnapped and killed," Hounie stammered. He then produced a post card addressed to: "MR. ALEX . . . CAFÉ EMPLOYEE . . . TROCADERO CAFÉ." The message on the back read: "WITHHELD TESTIMONY OR KIDNAP TRIP." The paste-up words had been clipped from the *Los Angeles Times*. When District Attorney Buron Fitts was asked by reporters if he thought the underworld was behind the threats, he merely remarked, "Witnesses before the Grand Jury are not being as helpful as they might be," and he insisted that Thelma Todd's death was an "accident or probable suicide," despite evidence to the contrary.

Uncle Vern had been working in the D. A.'s office at the time, and in later years, he remembered much about the Thelma Todd case. One

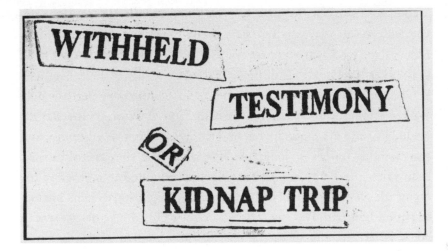

night he talked about it with Little Tah when they were in their cups. Vern said that the man in the Trocadero office who had frightened Thelma Todd was Bugsy Siegel. Siegel had become enraged when he learned that the Ice Cream Blonde had gone to the D. A., and according to Vern, it was Bugsy Siegel who had beaten and murdered Thelma Todd, put together the suicide scenario, and paid off Buron Fitts.

Vern was rather circumspect when he was sober, but a loquacious gabber when intoxicated—which was oft. To my mother's aggravation, he would spend hours on the phone in the taproom yakking with his pals, and I couldn't help but overhear some of Vern's conversations. Perhaps he thought he could talk freely around me because I was quiet and withdrawn. I was so shy in those days that Vern may have assumed I was mentally deficient. But I would hear things—things I didn't want to hear. Things I didn't want to understand. But I understood.

Early on I perceived that Vern was connected to the mob. During the period of time he was consorting with my grandmother, he was one of Bugsy Siegel's lawyers. Bugsy and the Syndicate operated an increasing number of casinos, brothels, and race wires in the Hollywood area that catered to the movie crowd, and I gathered Vern was the "fixer" for the mob, the go-between with the D. A.'s office and the police to keep things nice and quiet—the "bag man." After moving north to the land of the majors, we lived at 803 North Roxbury Drive, and Bugsy Siegel and his girlfriend, Virginia "Sugar" Hill, lived just behind us at 810 North Linden Drive. In 1946 Bugsy and Virginia were spending a good deal of time in Las Vegas preparing for the opening of the Flamingo Hotel, and Vern had a key to their Moorish mansion on Linden and looked after it when they were out of town.

In December 1946, Bugsy Siegel staged the elaborate grand opening of the Flamingo Hotel in Las Vegas, which proved to be a disaster. In the early months of 1947, he was struggling to keep his dream of a Las Vegas gambling empire afloat. He often came to L.A. and stayed at the Linden Drive house while on his cash-hunting forays. The Flamingo venture was being financed with laundered Syndicate money along with other devious sources, and if there were things that Vern and Bugsy couldn't talk about over the taproom phone, it was only a short walk across the alley for a chat over the back fence.

On the night Bugsy Siegel was shot to death while sitting on the sofa in his living room reading the *Los Angeles Times* of June 20, 1947, Vern and one of his pals lugged a large padlocked steamer trunk over to our house and stashed it in the garage. It contained something that belonged to Bugsy and remained in the garage for a number of months. Around the house my brother and I referred to it as "Bugsy's trunk." Though I wasn't supposed to talk about it, I'd show it off to the neighborhood kids, and we'd speculate as to what— or who—was inside. By the end of 1947, "Bugsy's trunk" disappeared along with Uncle Vern and Little Tah.

Uncle Vern also knew a lot about the Black Dahlia case. When the news first broke about the murder of Jane Doe #1, the police were knocking on doors around Norton Avenue, trying to pick up clues to the victim's identity. Vern talked about the murder with Little Tah and other people on the phone, referring to the victim as though he knew her, and I got the impression that the murdered woman was somehow associated with the mob and Bugsy Siegel.

Through the years there had been many Jane Does brought into the Los Angeles County Morgue, but establishing the identity of Jane Doe #1 of January 15, 1947 was difficult. The body had been mutilated to such a degree that photos taken at the morgue could not produce a true likeness. The description in the Unknown Dead Ledger stated:

JANE DOE #1

Weight:	115 pounds
Complexion:	Light
Eyes:	Green-gray
Age:	Between 15 and 30
Height:	5' 5"
Hair:	Hennaed

According to Det. Finis Brown, the extent of the disfigurement had led Harry Hansen to conclude that there had been a deliberate attempt to conceal the victim's identity. The knife slash through the mouth from ear to ear made the face unrecognizable, and the fingerprints had been partially obliterated because the remains had been immersed in water for an extended period of time. As a result, the whorls and ridges of the fingers had become grooved and shrunken; nevertheless, Ray Pinker's crime lab team inked the fingers and attempted to transfer the prints to a fingerprint card.

Capt. Donahoe of Homicide requested that Brown keep him informed of every aspect of the investigation. When Donahoe learned that *Examiner* staff artist Howard Burke had been allowed into the morgue to make a sketch of the murder victim for identification purposes, Donahoe became angry and questioned the merits of the procedure. Brown explained, "You can't tell much from the original

photo, her face is badly cut, bruised, and puffed out of shape . . . so identification is difficult without the artist working on her likeness—hopefully it will be recognized by someone."

Newspaper reporters and police investigators had a different relationship back in the forties. They were less adversarial and recognized the need to cooperate with one another in a crime investigation. While today there is only one daily metropolitan newspaper in Los Angeles, back in 1947 there were five, and all were zealous competitors—especially on a major murder case that had captured the public's attention. The force of highly motivated investigative reporters out on the streets trying to dig up scraps of information by their daily deadline was much larger and more aggressive than the investigative force of the LAPD, and there was a cooperative tradeoff of information between the police and the press—as well as a cooperative silence regarding facts and information that the LAPD wanted to keep under wraps.

According to reporter Will Fowler, when the *Examiner* learned that the crime lab had sent the fingerprint card of Jane Doe #1 to Washington, editor Jim Richardson had managing editor Warden Woolard call Capt. Donahoe and request that the LAPD supply the *Examiner* with a copy of the prints. Pointing out that winter storms had closed the airports in Washington and it might take days before the FBI could examine the prints, Woolard suggested sending a copy to the FBI via the Hearst electronic Soundphoto service, which was a new system for transmitting photos instantly to Hearst editorial offices across the country.

"We have this new Soundphoto machine," Woolard said. "What about sending the prints over the Soundphoto? It's never been done before, but I don't see why it wouldn't work. Until we get an identification, we'll all be stymied with the investigation."

Convinced that the impaired prints would not be sufficient to lead to an identification and the Soundphoto system was problematic, Donahoe felt there was no harm in cooperating and sent a copy of the prints to the *Examiner*'s editorial office. And, for the first time in the history of crime investigation, at 4:00 A.M. on January 16, 1947, a fingerprint card was transmitted to the FBI via Soundphoto. Waiting to take the prints off the machine was Ray Richards, head of the Hearst Newspapers Washington Bureau, who immediately handed them over to the cavernous FBI fingerprint file room. But as Donahoe had suspected, the FBI fingerprint experts were initially unable to work with the Soundphoto prints, which lacked clarity.

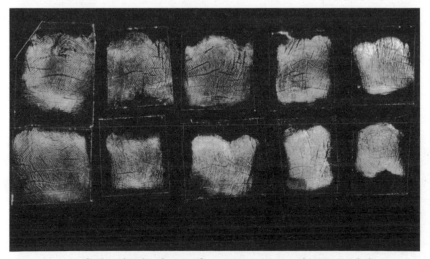

Negatives of Elizabeth Short's fingerprints sent by Soundphoto to the FBI

Undaunted, the *Examiner* photo lab made a new photocopy, blew the prints up to a larger size, and transmitted enlarged negatives rather than positives. It proved to be a success. Within an hour, FBI experts were able to identify Jane Doe #1. The victim was Elizabeth Short, age twenty-two, born in Hyde Park, Massachusetts, on July 29, 1924.

Elizabeth Short had been arrested on September 23, 1943 with a group of soldiers and other girls who were drinking and causing a disturbance near Camp Cooke, an army base north of Santa Barbara, California. Because she had been a minor and unaccompanied by a parent or legal guardian, she'd been taken into custody, booked, and fingerprinted. The prints of Elizabeth Short were on file with the FBI in Washington and clearly matched those of Jane Doe #1.

By midmorning, Thursday, January 16, the *Examiner* knew the victim's identity and broke the headline story in the morning edition of Friday, January 17. In an extraordinary coup, the *Examiner* had succeeded in scooping its rivals.

"This scoop put the *Examiner* so far ahead of its opposition, they were never able to catch up," Will Fowler stated. "Hours before other papers had a clue that the body had ever been identified, our crew of reporters and photogs were digging into Elizabeth Short's life. The competition actually had to read our paper before they knew what step to take next in the investigation. Richardson's crew worked so effectively with the clues we were digging up on our own that we were able to start making deals with LAPD Homicide. This made Capt. Donahoe fume, but he had to go along."

"Richardson shared William Randolph Hearst's penchant for sensational news and was highly skilled in beating the competition out on the street with the latest scoop," Fowler recalled. "He could be merciless, and there were many reporters at the *Examiner* that didn't like him. Though he was respected for his news-gathering genius, Richardson's demands on his staff were so high that some broke under the pressure. He could be inhuman from the moment he walked into the city room in the morning, until after deadline and the next day's edition was locked up. But if he had won the scoop war, he could be human from deadline to dawn, and he'd break into his lazy-eyed grin and glide around the newsroom with his hands behind his back as if he were on ice skates, making figure skating moves learned as a champion skater when he was a kid in Canada."

On January 16, at 10:30 A.M., at the approximate time that Jane Doe #1 was identified, the autopsy began in the dank, rat-infested basement of the Los Angeles Hall of Justice. The autopsy was to be conducted by Dr. Frederick Newbarr, the Chief Autopsy Surgeon for the County of Los Angeles. Dr. Victor Cefalu had been assigned as Newbarr's assistant.

Dr. Newbarr concluded that the immediate cause of death was hemorrhage and shock due to the deep knife lacerations of the face and repeated blows by a heavy metal object to the face and right forehead.

"There were deep ridges on her ankles, thighs, wrists, and neck, indicating she had been tied with rope or wire," Dr. Newbarr stated to an INS reporter. "The victim's mouth had been slit at each side to the ear while she was still alive. The excruciating pain of this would bring on shock. . . . The blows to the face and head and the brain concussion came from blows from an iron instrument with a blunt edge." Dr. Newbarr thought this may have occurred after the slitting of the mouth. The ecchymosis surrounding the deep facial cuts and head injuries revealed that these wounds occurred while she was still alive; such discoloration and bruising only occurs when the circulation of blood is unimpaired. But all the other indices of mutilation to the corpse were without ecchymosis, which was a clear indication that she was already dead when they occurred. One of the deep lacerations on the left leg eventually proved to be the surgical removal of a tattoo, which could have aided in the identification process. Dr. Newbarr was quoted by the press as saying that he believed the victim was "killed and mutilated while tied in a bath tub."

What was clear to Dr. Newbarr and those who had studied the condition of the corpse on Norton Avenue was that the deep cuts were not brought about by the same instrument that was used to severe the corpse. The slashed mouth and cheek areas exhibited the ragged cuts of a knife, while the mutilation and bisection of the body was accomplished methodically with a surgical instrument by someone who was proficient in surgical procedure—two different cutting instruments, two MO's. One instrument was employed before death, and the other was employed after death. The fact that the body had been bisected by someone with advanced surgical knowledge was never disclosed at the time, and the withholding of this vital information led to a misconception of the crime by both the press and the public that has been perpetuated for decades.

The slashed mouth and the blows to the head were characteristic of a rage murder, while the meticulous mutilation and bisection of the corpse with a surgical instrument were indices of a more methodical pathology, suggesting that more than one person may have been involved in the murder and disposition of the body. An examination for spermatozoa showed no results, and there was no indication that the victim had been raped.

Autopsy reports are ordinarily part of the public record; however, Elizabeth Short's autopsy report has never been made available to the public. The original explanation for the sealed report was Capt. Donahoe's claim that it contained certain information that would be known only to the killer and that Homicide could use this secret information as a "control question" when establishing the credibility of a prime suspect. Although many former LAPD Homicide detectives, including Harry Hansen, long ago conceded that the murderer was deceased, up until the end of the twentieth century, the Los Angeles County Coroner's Office continued to refuse the release of Elizabeth Short's autopsy report, claiming that this public document was being retained because the case was unsolved. Yet, there is not another cold-case homicide on record in Los Angeles in which the autopsy report has not been made available to the public.

Upon making a request for Elizabeth Short's autopsy in September 2003, the Los Angeles Coroner's Office stated, "The Elizabeth Short Autopsy Report has been lost." Yet, in the 1970s, duplicate copies of all autopsy reports in Los Angeles County were put on microfiche; the inevitable question arises—*What secret is contained in the autopsy report that officialdom still does not want the public to know after a lapse of more than half a century?*

An alleged copy of the autopsy report was printed for the first time in Janice Knowlton's book, *Daddy Was the Black Dahlia Killer* (Pocket Books, NY, 1995). But this, too, was suspect and proved not to be the official autopsy report. It was based on a handwritten copy by an ex-officer of the Sheriff's Department who led Knowlton to believe it was copied word for word from the original. But it was a word for word deception that once again hid the dark secret that the authorities did not want the public to know—a secret known at the time only by Capt. Jack Donahoe, Medical Examiner Dr. Newbarr, Finis Brown, Harry Hansen, and the killer or killers.

Through the years, various rumors regarding the secret of the autopsy have been propagated. When *Examiner* editor Jim Richardson approached Capt. Donahoe in an attempt to obtain a copy of the coroner's report, Donahoe outlined why the report and its secret information could not be released. Will Fowler recalled that Donahoe privately informed Richardson of the mysterious secret of the autopsy, on the condition that the information would never be printed in the newspaper.

Fowler disclosed that Richardson was informed by Donahoe that the killer had inserted an earlobe as well as the tattooed flesh cut from the victim's leg into her vagina. However, photos indicate that her earlobes were intact, and if the flesh bearing the tattoo was removed to avoid identification, it was unlikely that the killer would have left it with the body. According to Fowler, Richardson concluded that Donahoe wasn't telling him the truth. Nevertheless, this unpublished information was circulated by hearsay in the *Examiner* pressroom at the time, and similar rumors regarding the dark secret of the autopsy continue to be promulgated to this day.

When Hansen had first viewed the body on Norton Avenue, he had said, "We won't know what we're really dealing with here until we get a post mortem." But the autopsy seemed to pose more questions than answers, and in Hansen's experience, the modus operandi in the death of Elizabeth Short had never occurred before—the deep slashing of the mouth by a knife, the severe blows to the head by a metal object, the methodical mutilation and bisection of the body with a surgical instrument, the draining of blood, the attempt to prevent identification, the prolonged immersion in water, the transport of the remains from a car on an empty cement sack found near the body, and the placement and display of the body near the sidewalk of a public thoroughfare. This strange MO silently screamed its story, but spoke in the alien language of the deranged.

Though there had been a number of brutal unsolved slayings of young women in the past, no similar MO existed in the homicide files of the LAPD, nor would a similar MO ever occur again during the remaining twenty-three years that Hansen was on the force. The indelible image of Elizabeth Short's mutilated body as it lay in the weeds on Norton Avenue would stay with Det. Harry Hansen until he understood the dark secret contained in the autopsy report. And with the passage of time, Hansen would eventually translate the silent scream of the "sacred setting."

aka the "Black Dahlia"

ALTHOUGH WE HAD moved north to the land of the majors, my stepfather, Jeffrey Bernerd, was a producer at Monogram Pictures, which cranked out Bowery Boys movies, Charlie Chans, and cheap B-Westerns on Hollywood's "poverty row." It took me a while to accept Jeff as my stepfather, but in time I grew to understand and greatly admire him. However, it was a long time before I was able to cipher the puzzling Monogram anagram, which had to do with the mob, money, and movies.

I didn't fully realize it at the time, but the mob was entrenched in a number of Hollywood enterprises. In the days of Prohibition, bootleggers were making so much money they didn't know what to do with it. Hollywood was a natural draw for the mob, and Syndicate money was often placed in the film industry, where the underworld was connected to Joe Schenck, chairman of 20th Century Fox, and his brother Nicholas Schenck, who was an executive at Loews, Inc., the parent company of MGM. Republic Pictures was founded with Syndicate funds, and Harry Cohn, the president of Columbia Pictures, was often bailed out of financial difficulties by Mafioso Johnny Rosselli, who was once Cohn's bodyguard.

Monogram Pictures was a Syndicate money laundering operation founded in 1925 by former bootlegger Joseph P. Kennedy. The studio was aptly incorporated under the name of Syndicate Pictures, but the name was changed to Monogram Pictures in 1930 when the Syndicate connotation became unpropitious. While many independents on poverty row went bankrupt after several films, those with business acumen observed Monogram's staying power with wonderment. The studio, which was located near the junction of Sunset and Hollywood Boulevard, kept grinding out low-budget celluloid schlock for three decades from 1925 to 1955—RIP. After the end of Prohibition in 1933, the studio's secret of survival was the mob's focus on racketeering, race wires, narcotics, brothels, and gambling; subsequently, the Syndicate cash flow continued to amass in large bundles that were badly in need of laundering.

During the 1940s, Jack Dragna, Johnny Rosselli, Bugsy Siegel, and Mickey Cohen were the Mafia bosses and Syndicate chiefs in Los Angeles. At the time, many people were under the impression that Bugsy's mistress, Virginia "Sugar" Hill, was just another voluptuous girlfriend. She was known around Hollywood for throwing lavish nightclub parties and tipping waiters and maître d's with fifty-dollar bills. Hill was referred to in the gossip columns as a "Southern Heiress"; however, Virginia was the cash courier and money laundress for the Syndicate. She traveled from city to city using various aliases as she collected and distributed laundered cash for Joseph "Joey Ep" Epstein, the mob's trusted exchequer in Chicago.

Some of the mob money out of New York was laundered through "The Club," which was an affiliation of Frank Costello and other Syndicate investors who held their ill-gotten gains in a fund at Morgan Guarantee Bank in New York City. Money from The Club was often distributed to George Burrows, the vice president and treasurer of Monogram, who was an old crony of Joe Kennedy's.

Johnny Rosselli, who had been a friend of Kennedy's going back to their early days together in Hollywood, became an associate producer

at Monogram on several films, and one of the studio's more successful pictures in the 1940s was *Dillinger*, which was produced by the
King Brothers, a family of Hollywood gangsters who made the film as
a tribute to one of their fallen idols.

My stepfather, Jeff, was the odd man out at Monogram, where
everyone seemed to speak out of the corner of their mouths with either a Bostonian East Dock accent or a western twang. Jeff was a
highly sophisticated British gentleman who had been an important
figure in the London film industry prior to World War II. As the vice
president and executive in charge of production at Gaumont British
Studios, he had taken Alfred Hitchcock out of the cutting rooms and
made him a director. It was at Gaumont British that Jeff was the executive producer of such cinema classics as *The Lady Vanishes*, *The
39 Steps*, and *Pastor Hall*.

When the former bootlegger Joseph P. Kennedy was appointed ambassador to England and moved to London in 1937, Jeff became a social acquaintance. Both were members of London's Screen Golfing
Society and mutual admirers of Constance Bennett, who appeared in
several of Jeff's Gaumont British films. It was through Joe Kennedy
that Jeff ultimately became a producer at Monogram, where he lent
the studio an air of respectability while producing some excellent
program pictures that actually made money.

Hollywood Mafioso Johnny Rosselli, along with the studio's vice
president and treasurer, George Burrows, were occasional guests at
our home. My mother knew that Bugsy Siegel was a gangster, and she
wouldn't allow him in our house, but we first learned that Rosselli
was a Mafia figure when he was indicted along with Willy Bioff and
Joe Schenck for racketeering and extortion. The story of how Rosselli
had been receiving protection money from the major studios made the
front pages of the L.A. newspapers in 1943, and the Rosselli story
was hard to miss. Because Jeff liked to keep up with all the latest Hollywood news and gossip, we subscribed to all the major metropolitan

newspapers—including the *Los Angeles Times* and the Hearst publications, the *Evening Herald* and the *Examiner*.

Shortly before the Black Dahlia case made the headlines, there had been a number of front page stories concerning Los Angeles gang warfare—numerous shootings, bombings, and attempted assassinations that culminated in Bugsy Siegel's murder just five months following the murder of Elizabeth Short. The mob warfare stories would break and soon fade, but the Dahlia murder case appeared "above the fold" on the front pages every day for more than a month. There was an element to the Dahlia case that made it unique to its time and place. Somehow, the gruesome crime could not have occurred in any other era or any other place. The Black Dahlia murder uniquely belonged to the postwar months, on the mob-ridden streets in the land of sunshine and shadow—Los Angeles, 1947.

When the *Los Angeles Examiner* identified the victim as Elizabeth Short, editor Jim Richardson sent Will Fowler to Santa Barbara to find out more about her 1943 arrest. The Santa Barbara Police Department's desk sergeant handed Fowler her arrest record, which indicated that Elizabeth Short had been sent back home as a juvenile delinquent to her mother, Phoebe Short, who lived in Medford, Massachusetts, a suburb of Boston. Included in the arrest record were mug shots taken when she was booked. Fowler recalled being struck by Elizabeth Short's eyes, which had a vacant fatalistic stare, yet "reflected a sort of inquisitive innocence." Fowler observed, "Her skin looked as though it had the quality of alabaster. Her dark, curly hair loosely draping this inculpable stare suggested she might have been a beautiful woman."

The *Examiner* headline story of Friday, January 17, included the Santa Barbara police photos and an interview with Santa Barbara policewoman, Mary H. Unkefer. Juvenile Officer Unkefer had been

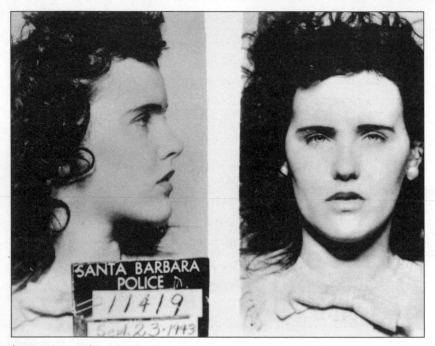

(LADA ARCHIVES)

called into the 1943 case when Elizabeth Short was arrested for drunk and disorderly conduct and was identified as a minor.

"She was living in a bungalow court with Vera Green," Officer Un- kefer recalled. "There were four soldiers from Camp Cooke in their cottage when they were arrested." The Santa Barbara cottage was at 321-C West Montecito Street, and neighbors had complained about wild parties. It was obvious to the arresting officers that the soldiers were staying there over the weekend with the girls and that a good deal of drinking was going on. "Miss Green claimed that one of the soldiers found in her bedroom was her husband," Officer Unkefer re- called. "But we later learned her husband was a soldier overseas. . . . While Miss Short was awaiting action on the juvenile probation in- vestigation, I took her into my home. She was a very nice girl and was most neat about her person and clothes. . . . The Juvenile Court released her on probation finally, and I took her to a bus on which she started back to Massachusetts. The Santa Barbara Neighborhood House gave her ten dollars for expense money."

The *Examiner* story pointed out that Officer Unkefer revealed Miss Short had a rose tattoo on her left leg. "She loved to sit so that it would show," Unkefer recalled. The article went on to note that the murderer had mutilated her left leg, removing this identifying mark.

The *Examiner* story of January 17 also included a significant observation that has eluded the scrutiny of investigative journalists for more than half a century: "'She had the blackest hair I ever saw,' Miss Unkefer recalled yesterday. At the time of her death, the girl's hair was hennaed, but the original dark strands were beginning to regrow."

Henna is a reddish hair dye made from a tropical plant that was popular at the time. But everyone who knew Elizabeth Short prior to her disappearance and murder could only recall her as having jet-black hair. Will Fowler recalled that the corpse had "reddish-brown" hair, and the Jane Doe description at the morgue noted that her hair was "hennaed." If the *Examiner* was correct in stating that "the original dark strands were beginning to regrow," then it can be assumed that the hair was dyed at least a week or two prior to her death, which would indicate that she had tried to change her appearance shortly before she was murdered. It was also observed that bleach had been applied to her eyebrows.

When Will Fowler returned to the *Examiner* city room with copies of the Santa Barbara photos and arrest record, Richardson assigned rewrite man Wayne Sutton to locate Elizabeth Short's mother. Sutton obtained Phoebe Short's home phone number from Medford information, and in an unholy gambit, Richardson told Sutton not to break the news about her daughter's murder until he had obtained as much background information as possible.

"Don't tell her right out," Richardson instructed. "First say Elizabeth won a beauty contest . . . in Santa Barbara. . . . Get what we need in background. . . . I'll give you the sign when to tell her her daughter's dead."

Richardson listened in on an extension line as Sutton dutifully dialed the long distance number.

"Hello," Sutton said, "Mrs. Phoebe Short? Eh . . . Mrs. Short, this is Wayne Sutton on the *Los Angeles Examiner* . . . I called to tell you . . . eh . . ." Sutton stammered as he looked to Richardson, who impatiently motioned for him to continue.

"Eh, I just wanted to be the first to tell you that your daughter, Elizabeth, has won a beauty contest . . . in Santa Barbara."

Sutton recalled that Phoebe was overjoyed to hear the good news about her daughter and went on and on about "Betty's" special beauty and charm and that she had won other beauty contests as well, including one in Medford.

Stricken by what he was doing, Sutton glared at Richardson, cupped his hands over the phone, and said, "You lousy son-of-a-bitch!" But Richardson just leaned over in his chair as he listened intently on the extension and mouthed the words, "Keep going!"

Phoebe told Sutton that many men found Betty to be attractive and commented on a letter she had only recently received from her daughter, dated January 8, 1947: "It had been written while visiting friends in San Diego," she said, and indicated that she was returning to Los Angeles "with a gentleman, Betty referred to as 'Red.'"

"Get the San Diego address!" Richardson urgently whispered.

When Sutton obtained the return address on Elizabeth's letter from San Diego, Richardson finally gave the sign and whispered, "Now." It was time for Sutton to tell Mrs. Short the ghastly truth—that her daughter had been brutally murdered.

After breaking the tragic news, Sutton recalled that Mrs. Short stayed on the line, mostly because she was hoping there was some mistake—that it was not really her daughter—and because she wanted to know "exactly what happened." Sutton tried to enlist her cooperation, telling her that the *Examiner* would pay her airfare and arrange accommodations if she would fly to Los Angeles for the inquest, which had been scheduled for Wednesday, January 22. To Richardson's delight, Phoebe Short agreed to the *Examiner*'s offer, in the hope of being able to help in some way. But Richardson's ruthless gambit was to keep the murder victim's mother in seclusion and away from the police and rival reporters long enough to pump her for additional information.

In the meantime, Richardson was onto another scoop—an address in San Diego where Elizabeth Short had been staying only a week before her body was discovered, and the fact that she planned to leave San Diego with a gentleman she referred to as "Red." Sutton recalled that Richardson had absolutely no intention of sharing the San Diego leads with Capt. Donahoe—not until the *Examiner* had a chance to track down the mysterious man called Red. By the time Sutton concluded his conversation with the victim's mother and hung up the phone, Richardson had already assigned reporters Tom Devlin and George O'Day to head south immediately to San Diego—"Find out where she was staying! And get an ID on Red!"

Reporters working for Richardson were known to be on assignment for seventy-two hours straight, keeping themselves awake on Benzedrine before turning in their story and collapsing in Moran's Bar across the street from the *Examiner*—where Will Fowler could often be found, nursing his exhaustion while Richardson skated around the city room.

William Randolph Fowler was named after William Randolph Hearst by his father, Gene Fowler, the notable author and journalist. Will's father had worked for Hearst in the 1920s on Park Row, where he was the managing editor of the *New York Daily American*. The family moved to Southern California in 1935, when Gene Fowler became a prominent screenwriter at 20th Century Fox. Graduating from Beverly Hills High School in 1940, Will served in the Coast Guard during the war, before joining the *Examiner* in 1945 at the age of twenty-two. As a young man, Will hung around with such notable family friends as John Barrymore, W.C. Fields, who was his godfather, and the prominent author and screenwriter, Ben Hecht.

Hecht, who had been a crime reporter for the Hearst newspapers in Chicago, once said, "A Hearst newspaper is like a screaming woman running down the street with her throat cut." While the Hearst newspapers were known for yellow journalism and took the sensational quick nickel approach to the news, the *Daily News* was more liberal. Originally founded in 1923 by Cornelius Vanderbilt, Jr. as a penny, family newspaper that avoided scandal and sensationalism, the *Daily News* was taken over by Manchester Boddy in 1932. The paper endorsed Franklin D. Roosevelt and the New Deal, and for decades remained the only liberal voice among the Los Angeles metropolitan papers.

Located at Pico Boulevard and Los Angeles Street, the *Daily News* did not have the large staff of the *Los Angeles Times* or the Hearst papers. While the *Examiner* had a dozen reporters working the Black Dahlia story, the *Daily News* had only two, and the city desk was starving for copy. Roy Ringer was a new office employee at the *Daily News* when the Black Dahlia story broke, and he recalled that the *Daily News* was getting hammered by Richardson and the *Examiner* scoops. Because Ringer was new on the job and unknown to rival reporters, the *Daily News* city desk sent him over to the *Examiner* on a spy mission. Ringer recalled that he casually walked into the nearby *Examiner* building and entered the composing room, where he spotted the Dahlia story proofs hanging on spikes for the copy boys. He began filching one copy of the proofs each day and racing back to the *Daily News* city desk, where the Dahlia news story would be rewritten and often out on the street before the *Examiner*. On the fourth day of his enterprising newsgathering from the *Examiner* spikes, he felt a hand clamp down on his shoulder. It was Richardson. "Nice try," he scowled, as Ringer was kicked out of the building and told not to come back.

The *Los Angeles Times* was the more conservative of the metropolitan papers and did not engage in the lurid sensationalism of the Hearst papers, nor did it care to lead an active investigation into the murder of Elizabeth Short. The *Times* had been owned and operated by the Chandler dynasty since the 1880s, and under the family's inflexible patriarch, Harry Chandler, the dynasty literally ran the city—making appointments to the Chamber of Commerce and nominating and seeing to the election of mayors and appointments of police chiefs, sheriffs, and city commissioners. During the first half of the twentieth century, the Chandlers were *the* dominant political and social voice of Southern California, and they spoke through the *Los Angeles Times*. Candidates for political office in Los Angeles knew that the support of Harry Chandler and the *Times* was a prerequisite if they expected to win. No mayor could possibly be elected unless he was a Chandler choice. And, as insurance, Chandler always made sure he had a majority of the fifteen city councilmen in his back pocket—a city council majority could always override an uncooperative mayor.

While the mayor's office and the city council were Chandler's central power-hold on the city, full control of Los Angeles depended on domination of the police department. Chandler accomplished this through the five-member police commission, and it was Chandler's man, the mayor, who appointed the police commissioners. Chandler only needed three commissioners for a majority, but he usually controlled all five—therefore, Chandler controlled the LAPD.

It was the police commission that appointed the police chief, and Chief Clemence B. Horrall had been a Chandler choice. Although it was common knowledge on the top floors of City Hall that the upper echelons of the police department and the mayor's office were receiving payoffs from Bugsy Siegel, Jack Dragna, and the underworld, this was something that did not concern Chandler as long as discretion was employed.

Both William Randolph Hearst and Harry Chandler had relied on the Red Squad within the LAPD to break the labor strikes that often plagued the newspapers, the studios, and major city industries; and the Red Squad had often recruited goons from the underworld who were known to threaten, kidnap, and beat troublesome labor leaders.

As additional insurance that he had control of the police department, Chandler circumvented the city charter provisions and had Mayor Bowron appoint an assistant police chief. Prior to 1939 there had never been an assistant police chief in Los Angeles, but at the behest of Harry Chandler, Bowron appointed Chandler aide, Joe Reed, as assistant chief to Clemence B. Horrall. Reed was placed in power over the heads of the police inspectors and deputy chiefs who would have been rightfully entitled to the newly designated position. Reed was Chandler's key operative within the department, reporting back to Chandler as the liaison with Horrall. Reed remained the Chandler overseer of the LAPD until he resigned in a cloud of scandal in 1949.

With the death of Harry Chandler in 1944, his son Norman became the mogul heir apparent. A handsome debonair man of forty-three when his father died, Norman Chandler enjoyed the good life and the benefits of being the scion of an empire, but he was self-obsessed, indulgent, and lacked his father's drive and ruthless ambition. Norman Chandler became the publisher of the *Los Angeles Times* in 1945, but the newspaper that Norman published in the forties and early fifties was merely the ultra-capitalist voice for the property holdings and political interests of the Chandlers and their coterie of cronies and influential friends.

When the Black Dahlia case broke, the editors at the *Times* would have preferred to keep the hideous murder story on the back pages; however, they were compelled to put the story on the front page for a period of time to compete with the sensational Hearst coverage. Primarily printing Donahoe's handouts, the *Times* had few investigative reporters working the case, and much of what appeared in the morning *Times* was simply a rehash of what had appeared in Hearst's *Evening Herald Express* or the previous day's *Examiner*.

Perhaps in a moment of pique, on January 17, 1947, the *Times* publicly took credit for identifying the murder victim as Elizabeth Short with the announcement on page one that "Capt. Jack A. Donahoe, given the identification by the *Times*, launched an immediate

investigation to trace the movements of the girl before she fell prey to the perverted sadism of a person who apparently tortured her before she died." However, many Angelenos were aware that the identification story had already appeared in the *Examiner* on the previous day, and Richardson had his revenge by running an interview with FBI Bureau Chief J. Edgar Hoover the following day, congratulating the *Examiner* for assisting the FBI in the "spectacular identification achieved under extraordinary circumstance."

While Richardson, in his ruthless way, was far ahead of his competition

View from the city editor's desk at the *Los Angeles Times*. (WESSELMAN COLLECTION)

on the Black Dahlia story, Aggie Underwood at the *Herald Express* had a reputation as a formidable crime reporter and was working her own leads. Although Aggie didn't like to think of herself as a crime reporter, she had covered most of the major murder cases in Los

Angeles since 1936 and had the gift of total recall. Having stashed away all the cases in her mental murder file, she agreed with Det. Harry Hansen that there had never been a case in Los Angeles quite like the murder of Elizabeth Short. Yet, there was something about the MO that rang a distant bell and had Aggie searching her murder memory morgue for a clue.

It was Aggie who was responsible for discovering that Elizabeth Short was known in the shady dives of Hollywood and Long Beach as the "Black Dahlia." In recalling how this discovery came about, Aggie stated, "The 'Black Dahlia' tag which the case assumed was dug out one day when we all were combing blind alleys and I was checking with Ray Giese, Homicide Detective-Lieutenant, for any strange fact that might have been overlooked. Later in the squad room, he said, 'This is something you might like, Aggie, I've found out they called her the "Black Dahlia" around a drugstore where she hung out down in Long Beach.'"

Aggie sent *Herald* reporter Bevo Means out to Long Beach to check out detective Giese's tip, and he discovered that around the bars of Long Beach and the dives of Hollywood, Elizabeth Short was called the Black Dahlia because of her jet-black, flowery hair and the slinky black clothes she wore. The Black Dahlia moniker first appeared in the *Herald Express* of Friday, January 17, and all of the Los Angeles headline-hungry press quickly glommed onto that name. Henceforth, Elizabeth Short would be known as the Black Dahlia. Though few people today know who Elizabeth Short may have been, a passing reference to the Black Dahlia conjures up cinema noir visions of a hauntress of the night stalked by a fiend in the sinister shadow-land of Hollywood in the 1940s.

TRUE
DETECTIVE

October
25¢

The
Black
Dahlia
Murders

"**I WANT NOTHING** to do with this!" Cleo Short told Harry Hansen and Finis Brown. The detectives had found Elizabeth's father living in an apartment in Los Angeles at 1020 South Kingsley Drive— less than two miles from where his daughter's body was discovered. The victim's sixty-two-year-old father had only recently read the news that the mutilated body of Jane Doe #1 was identified as his daughter, but the detectives found Cleo to be strangely cold and indifferent to her brutal murder.

"I broke off with the mother and the family several years ago," Cleo said. "My wife wanted it that way. When I left the family, I provided a trust fund for their support. Five years ago, though, Elizabeth wrote to me. So I sent her some money. She came out here, and she lived at my house when I was living in Vallejo."

It was reported in the metropolitan newspapers that Elizabeth moved to California in 1943 to live with her father, who was working at the Mare Island Naval Base in the San Francisco Bay area. Reportedly, she only lived with her father for a month or two before they had a falling out that led to her departure. It was said that Elizabeth had begun dating a number of servicemen, and Cleo complained that she was seeing a different boyfriend every evening and staying out very late—sometimes all night. A church-going Baptist, Cleo admonished Elizabeth for living a licentious life.

"She wouldn't stay home," Cleo complained. "In 1943 I told her to go her way. I'd go mine. After that she headed south and worked at Camp Cooke, and then she was arrested in Santa Barbara for juvenile delinquency."

Though the police characterized Cleo as "uncooperative," Hansen and Brown eventually concluded that he had no relevance to their investigation, and the full extent of his statements to the police has remained locked within the LAPD Black Dahlia files for more than fifty years. But Cleo had not been exactly forthright regarding the circumstances of his estrangement from his family or the events that occurred when his daughter visited him in California.

In 1930, Cleo had deserted his wife, Phoebe, and their five children. His abandoned car was found on the Charleston Bridge near Boston. Cleo simply disappeared. The police concluded he had jumped from the bridge and drowned in the rushing currents of the Charleston River. It would be years before Phoebe and the children would learn that Cleo was alive and well and living in California.

During the boom years of the 1920s, Cleo Short had been in the business of building miniature golf courses in the Boston area, but with the stock market crash of 1929 and the Great Depression, Cleo's business hit hard times. No longer able to support his family, he chose to abandon them—leaving his wife Phoebe with the foreclosure of his business, angry creditors, and the problem of paying the rent and feeding and clothing their children. There was no trust fund, as Cleo had stated, and life was very difficult for Phoebe and the children. Elizabeth was the third child of five girls born to Phoebe and Cleo Short. Elizabeth's youngest sister, Muriel, was only two when Cleo disappeared, and she recalled, "I didn't have a way of really

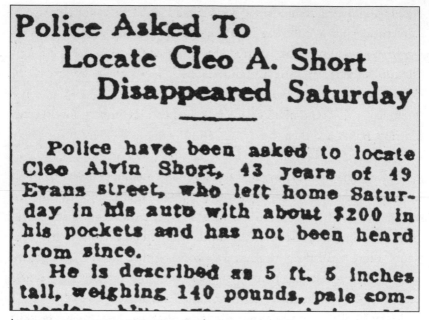

Police Asked To Locate Cleo A. Short Disappeared Saturday

Police have been asked to locate Cleo Alvin Short, 43 years of 49 Evans street, who left home Saturday in his auto with about $200 in his pockets and has not been heard from since.

He is described as 5 ft. 5 inches tall, weighing 140 pounds, pale com-

(MEDFORD MERCURY, OCTOBER 15, 1930)

missing him, but my sisters did, especially Ginnie and Betty [Elizabeth]. Nobody knew what happened."

Elizabeth was eight years old when her father vanished, and according to her mother, it was the beginning of her emotional problems. Unlike her sisters, Elizabeth had mood swings, emotional ups and downs. "She was happy one moment—sad the next," Phoebe said. "I guess she was what you would call a manic-depressive."

Unable to pay the rent, Phoebe moved with the children from their large, pleasant house on Evans Street in Medford to a third-floor walkup at 115 Salem Street, where the children had to share a bedroom. Depending on Mother's Aid and welfare handouts, Phoebe found occasional employment as a bookkeeper. To escape from their problems, she often took the children to the movies. Muriel recalled, "I don't know why, but Betty and I were like Mama—we loved the movies!" Muriel remembered that Elizabeth always liked to make something special out of their trips to the movies and would dress up "as if she was somebody important." Elizabeth especially loved seeing movies in Boston's ornate movie palaces with the huge fancy lobbies, gilded ceilings, and crystal chandeliers. It became part of her dream world, and she talked about going to Hollywood and becoming a movie star.

According to Muriel, Elizabeth and her older sister, Ginnie, frequently fought over using the family radio. "Ginnie wanted to listen to the opera, and since Ginnie was the oldest, that's what we listened to. But Betty would quarrel over the music. She didn't want to *always* hear the longhair stuff—neither did I. Betty liked popular music and show tunes. 'Another Deanna Durbin' is what people said about her. . . . She wanted to dance—she wanted to jitterbug. Betty didn't want to listen to that 'caterwauling,' as she called it."

Mary Pacios, a schoolmate who lived around the corner from the Short's apartment, recalled, "Betty had always been very friendly and kind to me. She reminded me of Snow White because she was very pale, pretty, and had that same dark hair." Mary's younger brother Bob remembers Elizabeth as "by far the prettiest of the five sisters," and she "turned heads" wherever she went. "She liked to tease me," Pacios recalled. "She knew I was bashful, and she liked to see me blush. Betty would say things like, 'We ought to go out dancing together,' and my face would turn crimson. . . . But she was a nice girl."

Elizabeth began having asthma attacks shortly after the family moved to the walkup on Salem Street. Muriel remembered that sometimes the attacks were so bad that their mother would have to call the doctor in the middle of the night to give Elizabeth an adrenalin shot. In February 1939, she had to be sent to Boston Hospital for an operation to clear her lungs. The doctors told Phoebe that it would be better for her daughter to be in a milder climate during the wintry months; and in 1940, when Elizabeth was sixteen, Phoebe made an arrangement for her to stay with "friends" in Miami Beach during the winter. In Miami, she obtained a part-time job at a beach resort and wrote that she hadn't had an asthma attack or cold during the entire winter.

Very little is known about Elizabeth's time in Miami. The family did not reveal where she stayed, what she did, or who her acquaintances had been. There were only the photos found in Elizabeth's memory book of unidentified companions and servicemen she met. Finis Brown went to Miami in the course of the homicide investigation to trace her activities—where she stayed, where she worked, and who she knew—but his report was withheld in the homicide files, and little of what he learned was passed on to the press or the public.

ELIZABETH SHORT as she looked while a student at the Roberts Junior High School, Medford.

(MEDFORD HISTORICAL SOCIETY)

A former Miami police officer believes Elizabeth may have initially stayed in the home of a relative of the Short family—Philip Short, who was a lieutenant in the Miami Police Department in the early 1940s and was said to be connected with Meyer Lansky and Syndicate operations in the Miami area.[4]

After her sophomore year, Elizabeth dropped out of high school and began spending more than just the winter months in Miami. She was in Florida when the Japanese bombed Pearl Harbor, and she began dating servicemen stationed in the Miami area and obtained occasional

---

4. In 1948 Philip Short became the Miami police chief. In his 1950 testimony before Senator Kefauver and the Committee to Investigate Organized Crime, it became evident that Chief Short allowed Meyer Lansky and the Syndicate to openly operate betting parlors and gambling casinos in the Miami area without police interference.

modeling jobs. Returning to Medford in the spring of 1942, Elizabeth worked as an usherette at the Tremont, one of her favorite Boston movie palaces, where she replaced a young man who had been drafted.

When Elizabeth returned to Medford, she was no longer the innocent schoolgirl who had reminded Mary Pacios of Snow White. Eleanor Kurz, a friend of Elizabeth's older sisters, Dottie and Ginnie, remembered that when Elizabeth returned from Miami, she wore heavy makeup and would often hang around a popular cafeteria on Salem Street owned by Donald Griffin. Elizabeth had only recently returned from Florida in 1942 when Eleanor spotted her in Mr. Griffin's cafeteria. "I remember I hadn't seen Betty in a while, and she was sitting very straight on a counter stool furthest from the door, dressed to the minute in a leopard fur coat and hat," Eleanor recalled. "Betty had her legs crossed, and she wore dark stockings and suede pumps and a lot of makeup by Medford standards. She was in her teens, but looked older—sophisticated. She made me feel like a country bumpkin. I thought to myself, Dottie's kid sister sure has grown up!"

Although Mr. Griffin was quite a bit older than Elizabeth, Eleanor recalled there were rumors circulating in Medford that Mr. Griffin and Elizabeth were having an affair. "Some people said that Mr. Griffin was Betty's boyfriend," Eleanor stated, "but I think it was just that he wanted to help her in a fatherly way."

When Elizabeth told Eleanor that she was doing some modeling in Miami, Eleanor told her, "You could go far with your looks—maybe get in the movies!"

"I would like to," Elizabeth said. "Mr. Griffin thinks I can certainly do it!"

Mary Pacios recalled that Elizabeth had a distinctive walk, and heads would turn when she walked down the streets of Medford: "Everyone always stopped what they were doing to watch Betty, and the women laughed about the way men looked at her and fell all over themselves."

"Betty doesn't miss a step, even in platform shoes," Pacios recalled her aunt remarking. "She carries herself straight and tall just like a model, swinging and swaying all the way up Salem Street."

A dozen years after Cleo had vanished and was presumed dead, Phoebe received a letter from him. She was shocked to learn that Cleo was alive and working in the shipyards in Northern California. In the letter, he tried to explain that he left because he hadn't been able to face up to their financial problems, and he hoped that Phoebe might forgive him and allow him to return to his family. Phoebe angrily responded that she no longer considered Cleo to be her husband, and she could never forgive him. He was still dead as far as she was concerned.

However, when Elizabeth learned that her father was living in California, she was overjoyed and began writing to him about her dreams of moving to sunny California and obtaining employment there. Cleo suggested that Elizabeth could stay with him at his house in Vallejo until she could find a job, and if that was what she wanted to do, he would send her the money for the train fare. According to Muriel, Phoebe had mixed feelings about the arrangement, but Elizabeth was insistent. Mary Hernon, a girl who lived next door to the Shorts, remembered that all Elizabeth could talk about during the week before she left for California was Hollywood. "I asked her if she was going to be a movie star," Mary recalled. "She laughed and told me that's what she hoped to do, and if you wanted to be a movie star, it wasn't going to happen to you in Medford. She'd have to go to Hollywood." And so, on an icy day in December 1942, Elizabeth Short boarded a train in Boston and departed for the land of sunshine—and shadow.

Elizabeth found that the sunshine in Vallejo, California, was often obscured by fog, and the Bay area was a long way from the glittering glamour of movieland. She tried to persuade her father to take her south to Los Angeles for a visit, but Cleo thought her movie star dreams were foolish. According to his statements in the press, they had their falling out in January 1943; Elizabeth headed south to

Camp Cooke, and there had been no trip to Hollywood. However, according to the Black Dahlia files recently discovered in the Los Angeles District Attorney's Office, Cleo had not told the whole story. Found among the archives of historic cases established by D. A. Steve Cooley was the testimony of Det. Harry Hansen before the 1949 Grand Jury investigator, Lt. Frank B. Jemison. In his statement, Hansen recalled that several days after the murder, the police had located Cleo's Los Angeles address, and he and Finis Brown had gone to Cleo's Kingsley Drive apartment to question him. "We knocked and knocked and knocked on the door, and finally aroused him," Hansen stated. "We found him to be in a drunken stupor—found wine bottles all over the place. He was very uncooperative, especially in view of the fact that, after all, his daughter had just been murdered."

Hansen related to the Grand Jury that they decided to return the next day when Cleo was sober and question him at some length. They found that he had been living off and on with a Mrs. Yanke on Nebraska Street in Vallejo, California, where Elizabeth had journeyed to visit her father in December 1942. Mrs. Yanke revealed to the investigators that Cleo's daughter had stayed at the Nebraska Street house for only several days before Elizabeth, Cleo, and Mrs. Yanke traveled south to Los Angeles, where they stayed at 1028½ West Thirty-sixth Street for approximately three weeks in January 1943. And, according to the D. A.'s Black Dahlia files, when detectives checked with a Mrs. Monte, who still lived in the rear of that address, she confirmed their visit and had a clear recollection of seeing Elizabeth Short there with Cleo and Mrs. Yanke. According to Mrs. Monte, Cleo was an alcoholic and was drunk most of the time, and he and his daughter had many arguments over money and his drinking. While in Los Angeles, Elizabeth had met "Chuck," a sergeant in the Sixth Armored Division stationed at Camp Cooke, north of Santa Barbara. Mrs. Monte recalled that on January 29, 1943, following an argument over her father's drunkenness, Elizabeth had left word that she was heading north to Camp Cooke with the sergeant.

When Cleo spoke to the police and the press in 1947, alcohol might have impaired his memory of the visit to Los Angeles with his daughter in January 1943 and the circumstances of Elizabeth's departure.

Although Cleo had permanently relocated to Los Angeles in 1945, he insisted that he had never seen or spoken to Elizabeth in the four years since she left for Camp Cooke; nevertheless, in Harry Hansen's statements to Grand Jury investigators, he made it clear that at one time Cleo had been a suspect in the Black Dahlia murder. "We found that Mr. Short was working as a refrigeration repairman or engineer in a store in Hollywood on Santa Monica Boulevard when the murder took place," Hansen recalled. "However, we were satisfied, after going to the store, seeing the employment records, the time sheets—checking up on various bars where he would go and drink after he was through [with] work—we were satisfied that he could be eliminated as a suspect."

When it was discovered that Elizabeth Short had been working at a Camp Cooke Post Exchange when she was arrested in 1943, reporters interviewed several Camp Cooke employees who had known her. Inez Keeling, an employee of PX #1, remembered that Elizabeth had a "childlike charm and beauty. She was one of the loveliest girls I had ever seen." Popular with many GIs at the camp, Elizabeth was voted "Cutie of the Week," and an item in the camp newspaper cited her as "the main reason for the steady increase of business at PX #1."

Investigators learned that Elizabeth had been living at Camp Cooke with "Chuck," the sergeant she had met in Los Angeles, and Chuck had threatened and beaten her. Elizabeth had filed a complaint with his commanding officer, and she tried to attach Chuck's paycheck and obtain damages. But damages were denied, and the sergeant was shipped overseas. Elizabeth then moved from the army base to Vera Green's apartment on Montecito Street in Santa Barbara, where the incident took place that led to her arrest on September 23, 1943, and the subsequent fingerprints and mug shots that led to her identification.

While Jim Richardson was waiting in the *Examiner* city room to hear from the reporters he had sent to Santa Barbara and San Diego, he was trying to get a fix on Elizabeth Short's life in Hollywood before she left the city. Where did she live? Who did she know? Did she have a job? How long had she lived in Los Angeles?

Will Fowler recalled that the *Examiner* was tipped that Elizabeth Short had been living in an apartment near Hollywood Boulevard shortly before she suddenly left the city in December 1946. Richardson sent out a team of reporters to work the Hollywood bars and nightclubs for leads; the *Examiner* soon learned that the Black Dahlia had been a familiar figure in a number of Hollywood cocktail lounges, and she had been living at the Chancellor Apartments at 1842 North Cherokee Avenue—just north of Hollywood Boulevard.

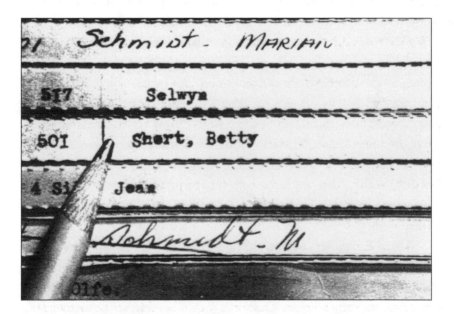

Reporters found Elizabeth Short's name still on the mailbox of apartment 501. There were five other girls sharing the apartment, which was on the top floor overlooking the street below. The building was managed by Glenn Wolfe, a suspected narcotics dealer who recruited girls for the Syndicate brothels. The landlady, Mrs. Juanita

Ringo, told the *Examiner* that Elizabeth Short had moved into the apartment on November 13, 1946, just two months prior to her murder, and she left so abruptly that it seemed she was afraid of something or someone. "She looked tired and worried," Mrs. Ringo said. "I felt sorry for her, even when she got behind on the weekly rent. When I went up for the rent last December 5, she didn't have it. I don't think she had a job. That night she got the money somewhere, but she suddenly left the next morning."

Sherryl Maylond, one of the girls who lived with Elizabeth Short in apartment 501, told reporters that Miss Short "loved to roam Hollywood Boulevard," and "she'd be out with a different man every night." Linda Rohr, another twenty-two-year-old roommate, who worked in the makeup room at Max Factor, said that Elizabeth—whom she knew as Beth—seemed to be worried or afraid. "She had a lot of telephone calls, mostly from a man named Maurice, and she was out almost every night. The morning she left, she was very anxious about something. Beth said to me, 'I've got to hurry! I've got to get out of here!'" Linda recalled that Elizabeth told her that she was leaving town to live with her sister in Berkeley. But her older sister, Ginnie, who had moved to Berkeley after marrying university professor Adrian West, told investigators that she hadn't heard from her sister for some time and had no knowledge of an impending visit. Instead, Elizabeth headed south—for San Diego.

When *Examiner* reporter Wayne Sutton spoke to Elizabeth's mother on the phone about the letter that her daughter had mailed from San Diego on January 8, he had learned that the return address was 2750 Camino Padero in Pacific Beach. *Examiner* reporters Tom Devlin and George O'Day, who had been instructed by Richardson to check out the address and learn the identity of Red, discovered that the address was the residence of Elvera French. Elvera lived there with her twenty-one-year-old daughter, Dorothy, and her twelve-year-old son, Corey. Dorothy worked as a cashier at the Aztec Theatre in downtown San Diego on Fifth Street, not far from the Greyhound bus depot. On the night of December 9, 1946, the Aztec was playing *The Jolson Story*, and Dorothy recalled that she was preparing to close up the theater after the end of the last show when she noticed a young woman who had fallen asleep in one of the front rows. Upon waking her, the girl apologized and told Dorothy that she had just arrived on the bus from Hollywood, was broke, and had no place to sleep. As they walked out to the street, she told Dorothy that her name was Beth Short. She said she'd been an usherette at a theater in Boston, and she wondered if she could get a temporary job at the Aztec.

"When she said 'temporary,' I thought it meant she wasn't looking for a permanent job," Dorothy recalled, "and that she didn't intend on staying in San Diego. I suggested she talk to the manager the next day. There was something so sorrowful about her—she seemed lost and a stranger to the area, and I felt I wanted to help her. I wasn't sure how. She apparently had no place to stay. I suggested she come home with me and get a good night's sleep, if that would help. She said she was thankful for my generosity."

Taking the local bus to Pacific Beach, Dorothy and Elizabeth got off at the intersection of Balboa and the Pacific Coast Highway and walked up the hill to the French's small housing project home, where Dorothy's mother, Elvera, was still awake, having a snack in the kitchen. Introducing the unexpected guest, Dorothy explained that Elizabeth had no place to stay. Elvera remembered that she was pale and didn't look well. She brought Elizabeth a pillow and a blanket and suggested that she sleep on the sofa.

The next morning, Dorothy's younger brother, Corey, went to the Greyhound bus depot and brought back the suitcases Elizabeth had left at the checkroom. He recalled that the suitcases were so heavy that he was sure "they were filled with rocks"—until Elizabeth opened them, and he saw they were crammed with fancy clothes.

Mrs. French's husband had been killed in the war, and Elizabeth told her that she, too, was a war widow—that her "husband," Major Matt Gordon, had been killed in a plane crash in India while flying for the army's air force. "She mentioned that she had a baby boy by him, but that the baby had died," Elvera recalled. "She showed me a newspaper clipping she'd been keeping in her purse. She said it told about her and the Major." Elizabeth's sad story engendered sympathy from Elvera and Dorothy French, and initially the Frenches believed that their houseguest often wore black because she was in mourning for her dead husband and baby. But her frequent late night dates and frivolous lifestyle seemed to belie that conclusion. It wasn't until the news about the murder of their former houseguest appeared in the newspapers that they learned she had never been married or given birth to a child.

Elizabeth told the Frenches she had been working in Hollywood as a movie extra and was expecting some money to be sent to her at the Western Union office. She said she was hoping to get a job in San Diego, and if she could stay over a day or two, she would be "happy to pay for the inconvenience." Dorothy said, "I told her that was not necessary. A lot of people were having a hard time—the housing and apartment shortage was bad, and my mother also told her not to worry about putting us out, and whatever she needed we'd be able to take care of it." But the "day or two" soon became a week, and the week soon became a month. The expected money-wire never seemed to arrive, and instead of getting up in the morning to look for employment, Elizabeth would stay out late at night—sometimes until two or three in the morning—and then sleep until noon. Her late dates, she said, were "with prospective employers."

Elvera worked as a civil employee at the San Diego Naval Hospital, and when she came home for lunch, she'd often find Elizabeth still sleeping on the sofa with her fancy clothes strewn around the living room and her exotic lingerie hanging over the furniture. "There was a strong, sweet-smelling, flowery scent in the house from her perfume," Elvera recalled. "It was as though she had sprinkled perfume everywhere. She hadn't, of course, it was just her way of using it. Her clothes were quite expensive, especially the lingerie. There were brand new black silk stockings. I could tell they weren't nylon—but silk."

Because Elizabeth slept until noon, Elvera found herself tiptoeing around the house as she prepared herself breakfast and got ready for work. Soon she began wondering why she had to tiptoe around her own house when Elizabeth should have been out seeking employment instead of sleeping in late. It wasn't long before Elvera began slamming the door on her way out, and as the days went on, Elvera and Dorothy French would have arguments over the merits of sheltering Elizabeth. She had overstayed her welcome as far as Elvera was concerned, but Dorothy felt sorry for her and kept persuading her mother to "be patient for a little longer." Dorothy and Elvera both sensed that Elizabeth was in some kind of precarious limbo—almost as if she were hiding out. She was in the habit of chewing her fingernails down to the quick, and at times she seemed despondent and fearful, as though she had been in some kind of trouble before she left Hollywood.

The Frenches recalled that Elizabeth had bad teeth that needed filling, but she didn't have the money to see a dentist. Instead, she kept a supply of paraffin candles and used the melted candle wax to disguise her dental problems before going out on a date or a "job interview."

As a matter of economy, there was no phone in the French's house, and Elizabeth often used the neighbor's telephone or walked down the hill to the payphone at the corner drugstore. She frequently talked about jobs she was pursuing and told the Frenches that she hoped to get a job at Western Airlines or perhaps at the Naval Air Station. She told Dorothy that the manager of the Aztec Theatre was considering giving her a job as an usherette. One afternoon she had an appointment with the theater manager, and Elizabeth told Dorothy she would meet her afterwards, but Elizabeth never showed up. She had dinner with Dorothy's boss instead and stayed out most of the night. The next day, Dorothy noticed that she had long red scratches on her upper arms. Elizabeth explained she had gone to the theater manager's home for dinner. "He had too much to drink," Elizabeth said, "and he started grabbing for me and scratched my arms." Dorothy recalled that Elizabeth never got a job at the theater, but despite the manager's behavior, she dated him again, along with other men she had met in the brief time she stayed with the Frenches.

Elvera and Dorothy noted that the "sad soul" who had seemed "so lost and a stranger to the area" was quite adept at quickly gathering a large coterie of male acquaintances. One of the acquaintances was Red—the mystery man who was to drive Elizabeth back to Los Angeles.

When *Examiner* reporters Devlin and O'Day questioned Elvera and Dorothy French about the identity of Red, they recalled that one day in mid-December, Elizabeth had brought to their home an "old acquaintance" she had bumped into near the Western Airlines office in downtown San Diego. Elizabeth said he was an ex-Marine Corps flyer and referred to him as Red. She had told them that Red was now flying for Western Airlines and was helping her get a job there as a stenographer. According to Elvera, Elizabeth dated Red every night from December 16 to the 21, and then he suddenly left town. Elvera remembered that Elizabeth went out with other men almost every night until Red returned in the first week of January to drive Elizabeth back to Los Angeles. Elvera and Dorothy both described him as a tall, red-haired, freckle-faced man in his mid-twenties. They recalled that his first name may have been Bob, but they didn't know his full name.

Dorothy revealed that when Elizabeth suddenly decided to leave San Diego, she seemed disturbed and agitated, and Dorothy attributed it to an incident that had occurred on January 6. Dorothy recalled that two days before Elizabeth packed up and moved out, "Some people came to our door and knocked. There was a man and a woman, and another man was waiting in a car parked on the street in front of the house. Beth became very frightened—she seemed to get panicky and didn't want to see the people or answer the door. They finally went back to the car and drove away. Even our neighbors thought all of this was very suspicious. . . ."

Aware that Elizabeth had been frightened by the mysterious visitors, the Frenches tried to ask Elizabeth who they were, but she didn't want to discuss it. Elvera believed it was after this incident that Elizabeth contacted Red, who subsequently sent a telegram indicating he would be there on the following afternoon. In checking at the San Diego Western Union office, the reporters found that Red had sent the telegram from Huntington Park, a suburb of Los Angeles, on January 7—eight days before Elizabeth Short's mutilated body was found on Norton Avenue.

When the *Examiner* reporters phoned in their story, Richardson knew he had his scoop—Red may have been the last person to see Elizabeth Short alive. Knowing he had secured his exclusive, Richardson took two of the little, white nerve pills he was in the habit of taking when the scoop-cooker was coming to a boil, and then picked up the phone to clue in Capt. Donahoe about Red and Elizabeth Short's stay in San Diego. Donahoe agreed that "Red" was the prime suspect in the Black Dahlia murder, and Richardson set the *Examiner* headline for Saturday, January 18.

In checking the origins of the telegram to Elizabeth Short sent from Huntington Park, Det. Hansen found that the sender had declined to give his full name or address. In checking with the San Diego office of Western Airlines, Det. Brown was told they had no employee in the San Diego area that matched the description of Red given by Elvera and Dorothy French. After interviewing the Frenches, Hansen and Brown proceeded to question the neighbors. Forrest Faith, who lived

Police Hunt Flyer in Torture Death; Telegram New Clew

Girl's Father Found Here

Search started in Los Angeles and San Diego yesterday for, a former Marine Corps flyer called "Red" as the No. 1 suspect in the slaying of Elizabeth Short, whose mutilated body was found here last Wednesday.

Concentration of the manhunt on "Red's," a former lieutenant whose first name is Bob, was based on a telegram it was discovered he had sent the girl when she was still in San Diego.

The message, dispatched from Huntington Park, January 7, one day before Miss Short left San Diego for Los Angeles and eight days before her body was found, read:

"Be there tomorrow afternoon late. Would like to see you. Red."

If the girl complied with this suggestion and Red kept his promise, then he may have been the last person to see her alive, police reasoned.

LIVED AT HOME—

Police, eager to obtain a specimen of "Red's" handwriting, were chagrined to discover that, in filing the telegram he had printed the message on the Western Union form.

Also, he refused to provide the

ELIZABETH SHORT
Victim of Mutilation Slaying

opposite the Frenches' home, recalled seeing the mysterious man and woman who had frightened Elizabeth when they knocked on the Frenches' door several days before her departure. He also observed Red when he picked up Miss Short in the late afternoon of January 8. Faith said that he saw a "tall fellow with red hair" park near his home at about 6:00 P.M. "The man put the girl's bags in the car's turtleback," Faith recalled. "She didn't seem to be afraid then. They were laughing and joking together." Faith gave Hansen and Brown a detailed description of the car, and the detectives sent out an all-points bulletin for Red—the number one suspect in the murder of the Black Dahlia:

Suspect described as white male, American, approximately 25 years, 6 feet, 175 pounds, red hair, blue eyes and light complexion.

He is known as "Red" or "Bob."

Car is described as being possibly a 1940 Studebaker coupe, cream or light tan in color, bearing California license number with one digit preceding letter "V."

> If car is located hold for fingerprints and all oc-
> cupants, and notify Sergeants F.A. Brown or Harry
> Hansen, homicide division.

But by the time the all-points police bulletin had been broadcast, Richardson had already succeeded in finding Red—the suspected "Werewolf Killer of the Black Dahlia."

IF RED HAD driven Elizabeth Short back to Los Angeles, and they had left late in the day, Richardson believed they may have stopped off along the way. He instructed reporters Devlin and O'Day to check every likely stopover along the Pacific Coast Highway. They were to talk to gas station attendants, café waitresses, hotel and motel clerks—anyone who might give them a lead to an ID on Red.

Initially, Devlin and O'Day were unable to discover anyone who had seen a tall, redheaded man with a woman matching the description of Elizabeth Short. But at the Mecca Motel, known to be a "hot pillow joint," located less than twelve miles north of Pacific Beach, the clerk recalled a couple that matched the description; however, they had not registered in January. The clerk recalled them registering back in mid-December. "Yes, the man was tall, freckle-faced, had red hair, and was in his mid-twenties," the clerk recalled, "and he was with a striking young woman with jet-black hair."

"Are you sure he had red hair?"

"Oh, yes," the motel clerk responded.

Examining the register for mid-December, Devlin discovered that the couple had checked in on December 16, and he was amazed to find that they had not checked in as the proverbial "Mr. and Mrs. Smith;" Elizabeth Short's name was on the register along with the name of the man with whom she had shared the room. There on the register, next to Elizabeth Short's name, was Red's full name and address—"Robert Morris Manley, 8010 Mountain View Avenue, Huntington Park, California."

Back in those days, cooperative ace reporters were given Los Angeles County Sheriff courtesy badges to help them out in scrapes with the law and to gain entry into restricted crime scenes. Without saying he was an officer of the law, reporter Will Fowler flashed his sheriff's courtesy badge when Robert "Red" Manley's wife, Harriet, answered the door at 8010 Mountain View Avenue. Fowler recalled that she was an attractive, young blonde and was holding a baby in her arms. When Harriet learned that her husband was being sought by the police, she became nervous, but cooperative. She told Fowler that she had just heard from her husband, who had telephoned from San Francisco. She said her husband worked as a salesman for a hardware company that manufactured pipe clamps, and he was traveling with his boss, J. W. Palmer, on a business trip to the Bay area. Red had told his wife that he would be returning home the next day, Sunday, January 19, after he stopped off at Palmer's house in Eagle Rock to pick up his car.

Under the impression that Fowler was a police investigator, Harriet confided that she had known Red for several years before their marriage. They had been married for fifteen months and had only recently become parents of a baby boy, and she knew in her heart that her husband "couldn't have done anything wrong." Electing not to inform Mrs. Manley that her husband was the number one suspect in the murder of Elizabeth Short, Fowler cautioned her not to talk to anyone about her husband—especially "any nosey reporters who may come knocking at your door."

Nailing the name, address, and whereabouts of the number one suspect in the Dahlia case was another extraordinary coup for Richardson. When he informed Capt. Donahoe of the *Examiner*'s discovery, the LAPD detectives questioned Harriet Manley and staked out J. W. Palmer's house at 5048 Mount Royal Drive in Eagle Rock.

It was hours be-
fore Palmer's car
finally showed up,
and Robert "Red"
Manley stepped out.
Dressed in a heavy,
gray overcoat and
broad-brimmed hat
that partially con-
cealed his red hair,
he briefly stood
near the curb talk-
ing to Palmer. As
he turned toward
his tan Studebaker
parked in the drive-
way, the police de-
tectives jumped out
of their car with
guns drawn and
closed in on the

(LAPL PHOTO COLLECTION)

fugitive suspect. Spotting the detectives, Manley quickly raised his arms high in the air and said, "I know why you're here, but I didn't do it."

Examiner photographer Ferde Olmo flashed pictures with his Speed Graphic as Manley was handcuffed, placed in the detectives' car, and driven to Hollenbeck Station, where Hansen, and Brown, and Capt. Donahoe were waiting. Donahoe informed the press that he was confident that the police had apprehended the fiendish killer. But Hansen had his doubts.

Before the enactment of the Miranda Rules, police were not required to inform detainees of their rights, and often suspects were mercilessly grilled at great length without benefit of legal representation. Such was the case for Robert Morris Manley that Sunday night at Hollenbeck. Before being booked, he was permitted one call, which he made to his wife. She hurried to her husband's side. Manley stood at a distance and looked at Harriet in silence for a moment before rushing forward to embrace her. Kissing and hugging with tears in their eyes, they were allowed to be together for five minutes before the booking and interrogation began.

Manley was repeatedly questioned by Hansen and Brown all Sunday night and subjected to two lie detector tests before becoming incoherent and collapsing with fatigue. He admitted knowing Elizabeth Short and acknowledged that he had driven her from San Diego to Los Angeles on January 9, but steadfastly maintained that he had not seen her since and had nothing to do with the murder. Manley stated that he first became aware that she had been the victim of the gruesome crime when he read about it in the newspaper. "When I saw the newspaper in San Francisco on Friday with Beth's picture on the front page, I read the story, and I got sick at my stomach."

"I called my wife that night, but I didn't mention it to her, of course, because she didn't even know I knew the girl," Manley recalled. "Saturday afternoon when I was out on calls with Palmer, my wife called me. I returned the call Saturday night, and when I finally got through to her, she told me the cops had been at our house that afternoon and told her I was connected with Elizabeth Short. Then I knew I was in for it, and I said to Palmer, 'I'm in a heck of a mess, and I don't know what to do.'"

Photographers for the *Examiner* and the *Herald Express* used the

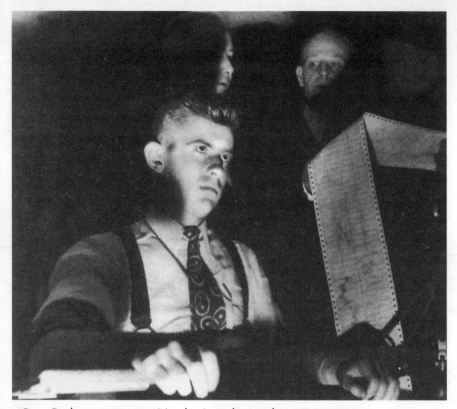

Ray Pinker examines Manley's polygraph test. (UCLA SPECIAL COLLECTIONS)

standard Hearst horror-lighting in the photos taken of Manley as he was undergoing the lie detector tests. The Draculan lighting effect was achieved by placing the flashgun near the floor and casting weird elongated shadows across the suspect's face. When the pictures appeared in the Hearst newspapers, there was little doubt in the viewer's mind that Manley was the fiendish killer.

According to practice, the official record of Manley's full statement to the police was sealed within the LAPD Dahlia file, which remains locked in the Los Angeles Police Department warehouse; but in an unusual procedure, Capt. Donahoe allowed reporter Aggie Underwood to visit the suspect. As the *Examiner*'s blazing headlines about Red Manley's capture landed on thousands of Los Angeles doorsteps on Monday morning, January 20, Aggie Underwood of the *Herald Express* was escorted by Harry Hansen to Manley's cell for an exclusive interview with the exhausted suspect.

Knowing that he had been through a rough night of hard questioning, Aggie decided to take advantage of her gender and use a sympathetic, motherly approach in coaxing out Manley's story. Upon entering his cell, Aggie recalled that she sized up the haggard suspect and remarked, "You look like you've been on a drunk."

"This is worse than any drunk I've ever been on," Manley replied.

Offering Manley a cigarette and a light to relax her subject, Aggie said, "Look fella, you're in one hell of a spot. If you're as innocent as you say you are, tell the whole story; and if you haven't anything to hide, people can't help knowing you're telling the truth. That way, you'll get it over with all at once, and it won't be kicking around to cause you more trouble."

"She's right," Hansen said, "Tell her everything that happened. I've known this lady for a long time—on a lot of cases—and I can tell you she won't betray your trust."

Aggie recalled that she primed Manley with a few casual queries before he began to open up and tell the whole story, which was printed in the *Herald Express* that evening. But according to Administrative Vice officer, Sgt. Vincent Carter, who was at Hollenbeck when Manley was interrogated, the story Manley told Underwood for public consumption wasn't exactly the same story he had told detectives Hansen and Brown during the interrogation. Desperately trying to save his marriage, Manley publicly denied having an affair with the murder victim, while privately admitting to detectives under questioning that he had indeed been intimate with Elizabeth Short. Manley told Aggie Underwood for the *Herald Express*:

> I knew Beth Short—sure. I saw her twice. I even kissed her
> a couple of times. But that was it. And, believe me, knowing

her has taught me to walk the straight and narrow. If ever a guy found himself in a mess—I'm it.

Relating the story of his encounter with Elizabeth Short, Manley told Aggie:

A week or ten days before Christmas, my company sent me to San Diego on business. I drove into downtown San Diego after hitting all my sales spots, and arrived there about 5:00 P.M. I decided to take it slow and see everything I could . . . I saw Miss Short standing on a corner across from the Western Airlines office. I looked at her and decided to pick her up. [Manley said he drove around the block before pulling his car up to the curb where Miss Short was standing.]

My wife and I had just had a baby, and we had to go through sort of an adjustment period. We had lots to iron out. It was nothing important—but just lots of little things. I decided to pick up Miss Short to make a real test for myself and see if I loved my wife or not.

I asked Miss Short if she wanted a ride. She turned her head and wouldn't look at me. I talked some more. I told her who I was and what I did, and so forth. Finally she turned around and asked me if I didn't think it was wrong to ask a girl on a corner to get in my car.

I said, "Yes, but I'd like to take you home." So she got in the car. I drove her to a housing project in Pacific Beach, where she was staying with some friends [Elvera and Dorothy French]. When we got there we sat in the car and talked, and I asked her if she would go to dinner with me.

She said she would, but was worried about how she

would tell the people she was staying with just who I was; so she decided to tell them that I worked with her. She said she worked for Western Airlines.

Apparently, the Black Dahlia lived in a world of white lies. She had told Manley that she worked at Western Airlines because it was convenient—as convenient as the Western Airlines office that was just across the street from where she stood when Manley picked her up. The capricious fantasy/lie, which Elizabeth Short seemed to pluck out of the air with great dexterity, became compounded when she told the Frenches that she happened to run into Red in downtown San Diego near the Western Airlines office; she described him as an old friend who was once a pilot in the Marines and was now a pilot with Western Airlines. But the truth was that Red Manley had never been a pilot—least of all in the Marines. During the war, he had been a musician in an army band before being given a Section Eight—an early discharge from the service due to psychiatric problems. The army found him to be high-strung and nervous under pressure and the routine restrictions of military discipline.

Elizabeth told the Frenches that she and Red were going out that evening to talk over old times, and it was understood that Red would return that evening to pick her up. In relating what happened after he left the Frenches, Manley told Aggie:

After I left her, I drove down the highway until I found a room. I registered for myself, went to the corner and got a beer. Because I was a stranger in town, I asked the people where I bought the beer where would be a good place to get dinner and maybe dance. They told me the Hacienda Club, out on University Avenue in Mission Valley.

I went back to my room then. I'll admit I was a little worried about my wife, because, you see, we were just married in November, 1945, and I had never "stepped out" on her before.

I cleaned up a little bit and picked up Miss Short at seven o'clock, and we left and tried to find. . . .

At this point Manley hesitated in his story. Correcting himself, he said, "No—we started to drive to the Club, and it took us two and a half or three hours to find it. . . . Boy, it's sure easy to get lost in San Diego!"

Before correcting himself, Manley may have been about to say that they left and tried to find a motel. Though Manley told Aggie that he had left Elizabeth Short at the Frenches, and then found a "room" up the coast, and registered "for myself," the *Examiner* reporters had discovered that both Manley and Elizabeth Short had registered together at the Mecca Motel on the day in question— December 16. The "two and a half or three hours" supposedly spent trying to find the Hacienda Club were more than likely spent at the motel where they had both registered before going to the club, which was only a fifteen-minute drive from the French residence in Pacific Beach and only ten minutes from the Hacienda Club. Manley continued: "When we got to the Hacienda Club, we had a few drinks and danced a few times. Then it was twelve o'clock. We went to a drive-in, had a sandwich, and I took her home."

When Aggie asked if he had taken her to his motel room, Manley replied: "No, I didn't ask her to stop at my room. We did sit in the car and talk for a short time, and I kissed her a couple of times, but she was kind of cold, I would say."

Manley said that he told Elizabeth he was married, and she had told him that she had once been married to a "Major Matt somebody . . . who had been killed in the war." Continuing his story to Aggie, Manley recalled the following:

When I walked her to the door, I told her I might be down that way again, and I asked her if it would be all right to wire her when I was arriving. She said, "Yes," but that she did not like San Diego and might not be there.

I went to my room with a guilty conscience, and the next morning I made my San Diego calls. As I left town I drove through Pacific Beach and stopped where she lived, but they told me she was at work. [According to the Frenches, Elizabeth was never employed during her stay in San Diego—more than likely she was still sleeping.]

In his public statements, Manley gave the impression that he had only seen Elizabeth Short on December 16, before heading back to Los Angeles. But according to the Frenches, their houseguest had been "out with Red every night from the 16th through the 21st." Manley continued his story to Aggie:

When I got home I didn't tell my wife I'd been out with her. I found out I had to make another trip to San Diego, and on January 7th, I sent Miss Short a wire that I was arriving the next day. . . . I drove to the place at Pacific Beach and she was there to greet me at the door.

We walked outside and she asked me if I'd take her down to a telephone. She said she wanted to make a call. But en route she said she decided not to make the call after all. We started back to where she lived and she asked me if I was going to drive her to Los Angeles. I said, "Yes," but told her I couldn't leave until the next day.

According to the Frenches, when Beth became frightened after the strangers knocked on their door on the night of January 6, she was anxious to leave San Diego as quickly as possible. Though Manley said he had a business appointment and couldn't drive to Los Angeles until Wednesday, January 9, she packed her things on Tuesday, January 8, and moved out that afternoon—the day she had written her mother and mentioned she was driving to Los Angeles with Red.

As observed by Forrest Faith, the Frenches' neighbor across the street, Manley parked his tan Studebaker coupé in front of the Frenches' residence in the late afternoon of January 8. Manley recalled:

> She decided to put her bags in my car that night, so I helped her load them. Then she got in the car and we drove down the highway. I decided it was about time for me to find a place to sleep, so we stopped at a motel.

Manley's statement gave the impression that they may have traveled some distance "down the highway" before it was "time for me to find a place to sleep." But according to the Frenches' neighbor, Forrest Faith, they had driven off from the Frenches at about 6:00 P.M. They checked into a motel in the immediate area—about a fifteen-minute drive from the Frenches' home and not far from the nearby Hacienda Club in Mission Valley: "We went to the motel cabin, and I washed my face and shaved and changed my shirt. She combed her hair."

When Aggie Underwood asked if he had made love to Miss Short after they checked into the motel, Manley strongly denied it:

> We decided to go eat. So we ate, then went back to the Hacienda Club—and again it took us a couple of hours to find it.
>
> En route, she wanted to stop at a big hotel in San Diego—the U.S. Grant—that was it. We went in the room where the music and everything was, but it was dead so we had one drink and then went on to the Hacienda Club. We

danced several times and had several drinks. She was gay and happy and seemed to be having a swell time. We left at twelve, and . . . we went to a drive-in. I got a couple of hamburgers and we went back to the room.

When we got in she said she was cold, and she grabbed an overcoat and put it around her. She said she wanted a fire, so I lit it. We ate the sandwiches and there was no affection between us. We talked for a while and she said she didn't feel good—said she was very cold and pulled a chair up in front of the fire, and I threw a couple of blankets over her.

Pretty soon I looked at my watch and it was late. With her back to me, I took off my trousers, my coat, my shirt, and climbed into bed and went to sleep.

When I woke up the next morning, she was propped up on the other side of the bed, awake. She said she'd had chills all night long. I hopped out and dressed and told her I had to make some calls in San Diego that morning. I did, then at 12:20—12 noon was checkout time at the motel—I went back and picked her up.

Manley described Elizabeth as being smartly dressed. She was wearing a black, collarless suit, a fluffy white silk blouse, and white gloves accented by a large, black handbag and a pair of black suede high-heel shoes. Manley recalled: "We stopped at a small restaurant and had another sandwich. Then we drove to Laguna Beach. There we stopped and got gas."

In his interview with Aggie Underwood, Manley did not discuss an occurrence that he had apparently revealed to Hansen and Brown; this significant information was recently discovered among the Los Angeles District Attorney's Black Dahlia files—in Manley's testimony to investigator Frank B. Jemison during the 1949 Grand Jury investigations into the Black Dahlia case:

Jemison: During the course of your conversation with her, during that five or six hours when you were driving to Los Angeles . . . what did you talk about?

Manley: Things we talked about were so unimportant, I don't even remember them. In fact, she talked very little on the way to Los Angeles. I don't know what was the matter with her. I don't know if she was worried about something or what.

Jemison: You said that she was apparently looking for or noticing automobiles both behind your car and coming from the opposite direction.

Manley: Cars that passed on the right, and then, if I'm not mistaken, cars that would pass us, but I noticed mainly on cars I would pass. She would strain her neck and look, like this (turning head, looking back) toward the rear of the car.

Jemison: For the record then, after you would pass automobiles proceeding in the same direction as yours, she would turn her head to the rear to see the occupants of the car?

Manley: Yes, and take a good look at the occupants.

Jemison: When did she first start that?

Manley: Gosh, that's hard to say. I noticed a few times that happened and I made some remark about it.

Jemison: What was her answer to that remark? Now, really think deep on that if you will please. When you made the remark about looking, did she say anything about she was expecting any friends to come to Los Angeles, or that there were other people coming she knew, to Los Angeles, or anything like that?

Manley: No, I just was curious about it, you know, and it seems like I made some remark, something about my company, I imagine.

Jemison: What you really said was "Don't you like my company?" Is that it?

Manley: Well, I made some remark, I know. She just passed it off and said, "It isn't that" but she didn't give any reason or anything, I'm sure, but I was curious, you see. That's how I happened to remember it.

Jemison: Did you think she was afraid of someone?

Manley: I didn't know what to think.

Jemison: Did this first—peering backwards—was this when you first left San Diego, before you stopped for the night—her looking back at those cars?

Manley: That was on the way into Los Angeles. After she wanted to come to Los Angeles, when I picked her up that night from out at the Frenches.

In his *Herald Express* interview with Aggie Underwood, Manley said it was in Laguna that Elizabeth told him that she had to make a phone call to somebody in Los Angeles. He waited in the car until she returned. Manley stated he didn't know who the call was to, but thought it may have been to her sister, Mrs. Adrian West (Ginnie), who Elizabeth said she was supposed to meet in L.A.

> I asked where she was going to meet her, and she said, 'The Biltmore Hotel'. . . . When we got into Los Angeles, she wanted me to take her to the Greyhound bus station so she could check her bags before she met her sister. I drove her to the bus station and carried her bags in. I had to go out to move my car, but told her I would drive around and pick her up and take her to the Biltmore.

The Greyhound bus station was on Sixth and Los Angeles Street— just four blocks from the stately Biltmore, a fashionable luxury hotel on Olive between Fifth and Sixth Streets that had been built in 1929 by Harry Chandler and a group of wealthy Los Angeles businessmen.

> When we got to the Biltmore she said she had to go to the restroom and asked me if I would check at the desk on whether her sister had arrived. I checked information and they had no Mrs. West registered. She had told me her sister was short and blonde.[5] I went up to a couple of short, blonde women in the lobby and asked whether they were Mrs. West—but they weren't.
>
> It was getting late and I told her I had to leave. I had to get home. I was worried about my wife. Miss Short said she had to wait there, and I left her there.

As Manley walked toward the Olive Street door, he glanced back to wave at Elizabeth, but she had already turned and was talking to the clerk at the tobacco stand and getting telephone change. She was still standing there when Robert "Red" Manley exited the hotel at approximately 6:30 P.M. on Wednesday, January 9, 1947.

"That is the last time I ever saw Miss Short," Manley told Aggie Underwood. "I'll take truth serum, or anything they want to give me. And I'll swear on a stack of Bibles, and tell my minister, too—that was the last time I saw Beth Short. I did not kill her!"

Biltmore Hotel employees recalled noticing Elizabeth Short in the lobby, and the ladies room attendant remembered seeing her at the ladies' room mirror, where she had lit a paraffin candle and applied the melted paraffin to her teeth. Bellboy Captain Harold Studholme told the police that he saw her make several telephone calls and wait

---

5. Mrs. Adrian West, who was Elizabeth's older sister, "Ginnie," had dark brown hair. Ginnie denied to the police that there had been any plans to meet her sister at the Biltmore.

in a chair near the bell station for some time before crossing the lobby and walking out of the Olive Street door at about 10:00 P.M.—approximately three-and-a-half hours after her arrival. The doorman remembered greeting her as she exited the hotel and walked toward Sixth Street before vanishing into the night.

One week later, Elizabeth Short's mutilated and dismembered body would be found amongst the weeds on Norton Avenue in Liemert Park.

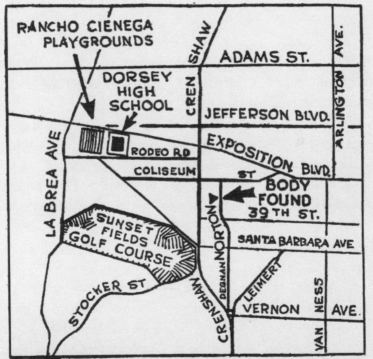

DEATH AREA—The girl's body was discovered in vacant lot on Norton avenue between 39th street and Coliseum avenue (arrow) at right). Scene of crime is near Dorsey High School and Rancho Cienega Playgrounds (arrows at left).

(HEARST NEWSPAPERS)

ALTHOUGH CAPT. DONAHOE expressed confidence that the LAPD had apprehended the Black Dahlia killer, Harry Hansen became convinced that Robert "Red" Manley had not attended the "sacred setting." Manley's wife, Harriet, along with several additional witnesses, established his whereabouts on the critical days in question—January 14 and 15. He had repeatedly passed polygraph examinations, and no bloodstains were found in his car, which did not match the description of the 1936 or 1937 black Ford sedan seen parked at the site on Norton Avenue where the body was discovered. Manley may have been guilty of being a fool, but he wasn't guilty of murder. Nonetheless, the newspapers had a field day with the prime suspect, and Donahoe allowed the press to squeeze every drop of ink out of Manley before announcing his release and probable innocence. "Most of the evidence seems to be on Manley's side," Donahoe ultimately acknowledged.

After an exhaustive search, police investigators and *Examiner* reporters succeeded in finding the luggage that Red Manley insisted Elizabeth Short had checked at the Greyhound bus station on January

9. However, it was quickly confiscated by Capt. Donahoe. Up to that time, newspaper coverage of the Dahlia case had been pictorially weak. There was only the one police mugshot of Elizabeth Short, and the press had to resort to artists' renderings, along with the usual X-marks-the-spot diagrams to illustrate the crime. Richardson implored Donahoe to allow photographs to be taken of the contents of the murder victim's luggage, but Donahoe refused, stating that the contents were "dynamite" and were being held in evidence. To this day, the contents of Elizabeth Short's luggage, checked at the Greyhound bus station on January 9, have never been disclosed to the press or the public.

Undeterred, Richardson learned that Elvera and Dorothy French had mentioned that Elizabeth spoke of another trunk full of personal possessions and "memory books" that had been lost in transit when she traveled from Chicago to Los Angeles in July 1946.

"Find that trunk!" Richardson told reporters Will Fowler and Baker Conrad.

Fowler remembers searching a number of Railway Express offices, freight depots, and train and bus stations before finding Elizabeth Short's lost luggage in the storeroom of a Railway Express agency in downtown Los Angeles. "The luggage turned out to be a suitcase and some bags—not a trunk," Fowler recalled, "but, sure enough, the memory books were inside. After that the Black Dahlia case became the best-illustrated crime story in newspaper history. And it all emanated from the *Examiner*."

Before this new cache of information hit the headlines, Richardson gleefully called Capt. Donahoe and said, "You're welcome to the luggage we found, Donahoe, but I want it understood that the story is ours exclusively." And Richardson laid down the condition that the LAPD detectives would have to come to the *Examiner* offices, where the luggage was to be opened and examined. "Donahoe blew a fuse," Fowler recalled. "But what could he do? If Donahoe refused to cooperate, Richardson told him he'd just have to damn well read about the contents of Beth Short's luggage and the progress of the case in the *Examiner*."

When the luggage was opened in the newspaper's conference room, detectives and reporters scrutinized the memory books, which were found to contain dozens of photographs of Elizabeth in Miami posing with a number of servicemen—including a four-star general.[6]

(MEDFORD HISTORICAL SOCIETY)

---

6. Some of the material found in Elizabeth Short's lost luggage by the *Examiner* was returned to Phoebe Short, but many of the photos of Elizabeth ended up in the *Examiner* Archive, which was donated to the Special Collections Department of the University of Southern California in 1988. Most of these photos vanished from the USC Library in the early 1990s and were eventually auctioned off on eBay in 2002.

Among Elizabeth's belongings was an unsigned telegram that had apparently been sent by an admirer in Washington, D.C. to her Miami address.[7]

A number of love letters tied in red ribbon were also found in Elizabeth's luggage. They reflected the hopes and romantic dreams of a young woman who had been through a number of disappointing wartime romances and had drifted into a desperate existence—while at the same time still dreaming of love, marriage, and fulfillment. In a letter written to Major Matt Gordon in January 1945, she wrote:

My Darling Matt:

I have just received your most recent letter and clippings. And darling, I can't begin to tell you how happy and proud I am. . . .

I'm so much in love with you, Matt, that I live for your return and your beautiful letters, so please write when you can and be careful, Matt for me. I'm so afraid! I love you with all my heart.

Beth

In a letter to her mother, Elizabeth had written that she had become engaged to Major Gordon, and that they planned to marry when he returned from overseas; however, while Elizabeth was writing her love letters to Matt Gordon, she was also writing love letters to other servicemen she was attracted to, including a Stephen Wolak, whom she had also hoped to marry. But in a letter to Elizabeth, Wolak wrote:

---

7. In *Black Dahlia Avenger* (Arcade Publishing, NY, 2003), author Steve Hodel makes the unsubstantiated claim that this telegram was sent to Elizabeth Short by his father, George Hodel, when he was studying the Chinese language in Washington, D.C. (See The "Hodel Hypothesis" in Appendix B.)

When you mentioned marriage in your letter, Beth, I got to wondering about myself. Seems like you have to be in love with a person before it's a safe bet. Infatuation is sometimes mistakenly accepted for true love, which can never be.

Yet, she dreamed. . . .

Found among the love letters were Elizabeth's correspondence with Lt. Joseph Gordon Fickling, an army pilot she had met in September 1944, shortly before he was sent overseas. Although she expressed her hopes of marrying Lt. Fickling, he had written to her "Time and again I've suggested that you forget me as I've believed it's the only thing for you to do to be happy."

In an unmailed letter written to Lt. Fickling from San Diego, dated December 13, 1946, Elizabeth wrote:

Frankly, darling, if everyone waited to have everything all smooth before they decide to marry, none of them ever would be together. . . .

I'll never love any man as I do you. And I should think that you would stop and wonder whether or not another woman will love you as much.

While Elizabeth's expressions of deep longing and future hopes in her letters to Major Matt Gordon were also quite moving, she must have understood the reality of their relationship—that it was merely another wartime brief encounter—because the romantic letters to Major Gordon were signed and sealed but never mailed.

Yet, she dreamed. . . .

In a sealed, unmailed letter written to him on May 8, 1945, she wrote:

My Sweetheart:
I love you, I love you, I love you. Sweetheart of all my
dreams. . . . Oh, Matt, honestly, I suppose when two peo-
ple are in love as we are our letters sound out of this world
to a censor. . . .
Just dreaming and hoping for a letter and now you are
going to be Mine. . . .
It is going to be wonderful, darling, when this is all over.
You want to slip away and be married. We'll do whatever
you wish, darling. Whatever you want. I love you and all I
want is you. . . .

Beth

Although the unmailed letter expresses Elizabeth's hope of marriage, there was no indication in Matt's correspondence that marriage was his intention. And Elizabeth's abiding hope that she would one day become Mrs. Matt Gordon abruptly ended with his death in a plane crash in India in November 1945.

Yet she dreamed. . . .

She told Red Manley and the Frenches that she had actually married Major Matt Gordon, but the dream had died, just as Matt and their imagined child had died, and the dream had evolved into a fantasy/lie.

As Jim Richardson observed, "She had been a pitiful wanderer, ricocheting from one cheap job to another and from one cheap man to another in a sad search for a good husband and a home and happiness. Not bad. Not good. Just lost and trying to find a way out. Every big city has hundreds just like her."

Phoebe Short
arrives in
Los Angeles.

The inquest was set for Wednesday, January 22, at 10:30 A.M. Richardson had arranged for Phoebe Short to arrive at Mines Field in Los Angeles on a flight from Boston, on Saturday, January 18. She met briefly with *Examiner* reporter Will Fowler, before making a connecting flight to Berkeley to spend a few days with her daughter and son-in-law, Virginia and Adrian West. Phoebe commented:

> Betty always wanted to be an actress. She was ambitious, and beautiful, and full of life, but she had her moments of despondency. She was gay and carefree one minute, then blue and in the depth of despair the next. . . . She was a good girl. She wrote often—at least once a week. It was

only two weeks ago that I received a letter from San Diego. I can't imagine who did this dreadful thing. I'm anxious to do anything to help in tracking down the fiend.

Following the interview, Phoebe told Fowler she would be returning from Berkeley on Wednesday to attend the inquest.

"I have suffered deeply," she stated, "but the worst is yet to come."

When Phoebe returned to Los Angeles accompanied by Virginia and her husband, Adrian, they were met at the airport by *Examiner* reporters who drove them to the coroner's office at the Hall of Justice. Visual identification of the remains had to be made for the official record prior to the inquest. Cleo Short had refused to identify the body, and Phoebe and Ginnie were aware of the ordeal they had to face. Upon their arrival, Harry Hansen and Finis Brown escorted them to the morgue-viewing window, where they would have to identify the body that was lying on a gurney behind the glass.

Phoebe gasped as the coroner's aide pulled back the sheet and revealed her daughter's mutilated face. There was a moment of stunned silence before Ginnie said, "I can't tell, Momma, I don't know."

Phoebe told Hansen that her daughter had a birthmark on her right shoulder that she could recognize. When the sheet was lowered, Phoebe and Ginnie started sobbing. No question—it was "Betty."

While Phoebe had been brave and resolute from the day she received the call from Richardson's office, the sight of her daughter's mutilated remains broke her heart, and she sobbed uncontrollably. Hansen escorted her to a chair and sat down beside her while trying to reassure her that he would do everything in his power to find the person who had so brutally murdered Elizabeth. Phoebe wondered aloud why the newspapers and the police had painted such a bad picture of her daughter. "She was a good girl," Phoebe kept repeating over and over through her tears—"She was a good girl!"

When Phoebe and Ginnie recovered their composure, they were escorted to the coroner's hearing room in the Hall of Justice, where the

Phoebe Short, center, is shown with her eldest daughter, Virginia West, and Charles West at the Coroner's Office.

inquest into Case # 7569 was scheduled to take place at 10:30 A.M.

The nine inquest jurors were presided over by Coroner Ben H. Brown. Called to testify were Detectives Jesse Haskins, Harry Hansen, Dr. Frederic Newbarr, Phoebe Short, and Robert Manley. Manley was accompanied by his wife, Harriet, along with his father.

In what was an inquest into the most bizarre murder case in the history of Los Angeles, the testimony was rather perfunctory and without surprises.[8] Ordinarily in a homicide case, a full copy of the autopsy report is presented to the jury and read and elaborated upon by the medical examiner on the witness stand; but in the Black Dahlia Case, the jury was not presented with a copy of the report, which had been sealed. And the transcript of the inquest reveals that, as Dr. Newbarr read the report, Coroner Brown interrupted when he approached the most significant part of the autopsy—the description of the organs of the victim that had been removed by the killer.

Coroner Brown stopped Dr. Newbarr and said, "Doctor, I don't believe it will be necessary for you to read all of this. It is rather long, and I don't think we need to read all of it here. The essential findings with regard to the cause of death have already been expressed, and that is the concussion of the brain and lacerations of the face."

Had Dr. Newbarr been allowed to continue, the dark forensic secret sealed within the autopsy report would have become public, and the startling motive and MO in the murder of Elizabeth Short would have become evident to the jurors. But the truth was concealed within the sealed report, where it has remained hidden for more than fifty years.

At the conclusion of the forty-five minute inquest, the coroner's

---

8. For a complete transcript of the inquest, see pages 327 to 338 of Appendix A.

jury confirmed the death in Case # 7569 to be a homicide, and death came as a result of hemorrhage and shock due to deep knife lacerations of the face, blows by a blunt metal object to the head, and concussion to the brain by a "Person or Persons Unknown."[9]

As the witnesses filed out of the coroner's chambers, *Examiner* reporters escorted Phoebe and Ginnie out the back door to avoid the rival press. No longer a suspect, Robert "Red" Manley walked out the front door a free man. Perhaps he believed that the Black Dahlia nightmare was behind him; however, shortly after the murder was reported in the papers, Robert Hyman, the proprietor of a café at 1136 South Crenshaw, reported that someone had put a relatively new pair of high heel shoes and a large handbag in an incinerator behind his café, which was near Pico Boulevard—just twenty blocks north of Thirty-ninth Street and Norton. Suspecting they may be connected to the murder, Hyman removed the items from the incinerator and placed them on top of a trashcan while he called the police. But by the time the police arrived to check out the report, a rubbish truck had made its rounds and removed the shoes and handbag along with the trash.

After a search of the city dump, the shoes and handbag were recovered by the police, and Red Manley was picked up by detectives and brought in to identify the items. As in a lineup, the items were intermingled with twenty other handbags and pairs of high heel shoes. Without hesitation, Manley picked out a pair of high heel, black suede pumps, which he said Elizabeth Short was wearing when he drove her to Los Angeles.

---

9. Author Eliot Paul (*Life and Death in a Spanish Town*, Random House, NY, 1939) was visiting Los Angeles at the time and was one of the few to note that the slashing of the mouth from ear-to-ear was characteristic of an age-old Sicilian mode of murder—connoting the mortal danger for those who violate the code of Omerta (silence). Although the symbolism was apparently lost to the investigators and the press, the morbid message would have been recognized by the Sicilian Capo de Capo of the city—Jack Dragna.

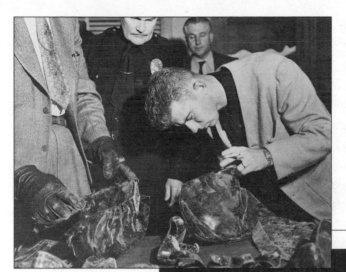

Robert Manley identifies the shoes Elizabeth Short was wearing and the handbag she was carrying when he dropped her off at the Biltmore Hotel.

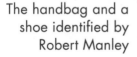

The handbag and a shoe identified by Robert Manley

"Those shoes have double heel caps on them," he told the detectives, "and I remember that she asked me to take her to a San Diego shoe repair shop to have extra caps put on those shoes." Manley also identified a black plastic handbag as the one she was carrying when he last saw her in the lobby of the Biltmore Hotel on January 9. Although the handbag had been emptied, Manley noted that faint traces of Elizabeth's distinctive perfume were still discernible inside.

While Robert Morris Manley was no longer considered a suspect, exoneration didn't bring an end to the problems brought about by his liaison with the Black Dahlia. The adulterous affair with Elizabeth Short ultimately turned his life into a nightmare. Manley's shadowy face had been published along with his shabby story in newspapers nationwide, and his moment of marital infidelity cost him his marriage, his job, his sanity, and ultimately his life. Divorced by Harriet the following year, Manley was plagued by guilt and was in and out of mental institutions before being remanded to the Patton Asylum for the insane where he committed suicide.

Following the inquest, Elizabeth Short's remains were released to Pierce Brothers Mortuary, and Phoebe decided to have her daughter buried at the Oakland Mountain View Cemetery in Berkeley, not far from the home of Virginia and Adrian West.

On Saturday, January 25, 1947, the victim of one of the most notorious crimes of the twentieth century was buried in a brief service with three family members in attendance.

The grave marker simply states:

DAUGHTER
ELIZABETH SHORT
July 29, 1924 – Jan. 15, 1947

But the Black Dahlia's diabolical killer was still at large, and Capt. Jack Donahoe no longer had a solid suspect or a tangible clue.

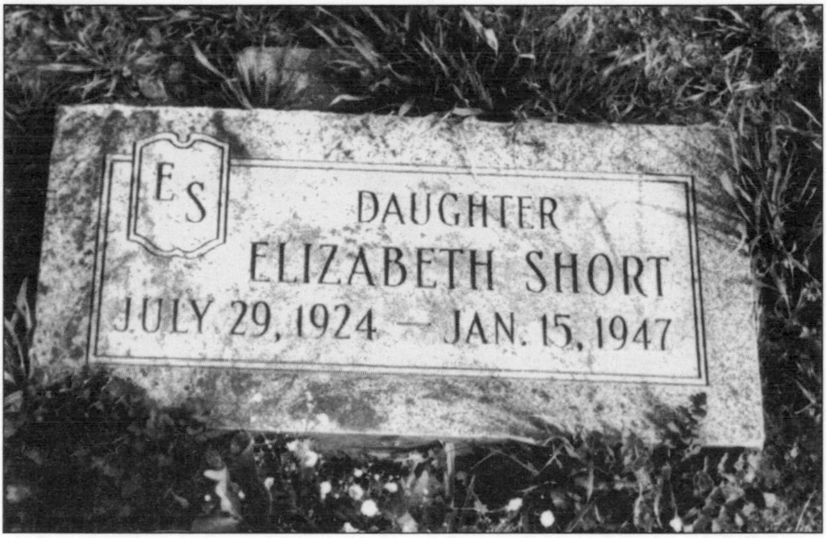
ES
DAUGHTER
ELIZABETH SHORT
JULY 29, 1924 — JAN. 15, 1947

ONE OF THE complications of the Dahlia case was the plethora of crackpots who were eager to confess. After the LAPD released Manley, scores of them came forward to confess to the murder and bask in their luminous moment of fame amidst an explosion of flash bulbs. Homicide received more than fifty confessions within the first weeks of the investigation, and the newspapers played up the choicer confessions with front page photos, fighting fang and claw for all the lurid details before consigning the suspect to the hoax hopper. There were the habitual confessors, known to the LAPD as "confessing Sams," and there were the homeless drunks who merely wanted shelter and a meal for a night; but there were also some confessors who were fairly convincing and necessitated many LAPD man-hours of follow-up investigation.

A young man by the name of Daniel Voorhees said he "couldn't stand it any longer" and had to confess that he killed Elizabeth Short. Although he was quite vivid as he described how he had hacked the victim's body in half, he claimed that he had first met Elizabeth Short at "a Los Angeles bar on Fourth and Hill Street in 1941." But Elizabeth Short wasn't in California in 1941, nor did Voorhees have any knowledge of the control question—the "dark secret" sealed in the autopsy report. According to Harry Hansen, the odds that a false suspect or confessor could come up with the answer to the control question was one in a million.

An army corporal stationed at Fort Dix, New Jersey, by the name of Joseph Dumais, became a suspect when he gave his fifty-page handwritten confession to the murder to his commanding officer, who stated that he was "definitely convinced of Dumais' guilt."

Dumais claimed to have been "bar-hopping with Elizabeth Short in Los Angeles on January 9th or 10th" when he blacked out and later had "flashbacks" of the gruesome murder. But the "flashbacks" did not include knowledge of the control question, and Finis Brown dug up witnesses who placed Dumais in New Jersey on the dates in question. "None of the confessors ever came close to answering the key question that Harry had put together from the confidential files," Finis Brown recalled.

While the police were being inundated with false confessions, they were also receiving numerous false tips and leads from imaginative "witnesses" who had gotten caught up in the sensational Black Dahlia headlines. Many claimed to have spotted Elizabeth Short during the week that she had seemingly vanished after exiting the Biltmore. Among them were a Mr. and Mrs. William Johnson, who managed the Hirsh Hotel at 300 East Washington Boulevard. Perhaps piqued that the Biltmore was getting more publicity than the Hirsh, the Johnsons claimed that Elizabeth Short and a man had checked into their hotel under the name of Mr. and Mrs. Barnes on January 12; but Hansen and Brown quickly discounted their tip, along with many other false leads that involved sightings of the Black Dahlia and her "jet-black hair" after January 9. The detectives' knowledge that her hair had been hennaed or dyed a reddish-brown prior to her return to Los Angeles was overlooked by the disingenuous tipsters and saved the LAPD many excursions down dead-end trails. Ultimately, the Johnsons admitted they had been mistaken.[10]

More than four hundred investigators and officers of the LAPD and the Sheriff's Department were assigned to the Dahlia case, knocking on doors in the Leimert Park area, questioning known sex offenders, and searching storm drains, basements, and attics. They attempted

---

10. In *Black Dahlia Avenger*, author Steve Hodel claimed it was his father, George Hodel, who checked into the Johnson's hotel with Elizabeth Short on January 12. (See "The Hodel Hypothesis" in Appendix B.)

to discover where the victim had been murdered and where she had been between the evenings of January 9 and January 14. Although a number of witnesses came forward insisting that they had sighted the Black Dahlia in Hollywood, downtown Los Angeles, or San Diego between January 9 and January 14, Detectives Hansen and Brown concluded there was no viable identification of her whereabouts during that missing week, and they deduced that she had been abducted and held captive at a secluded location until the murder and subsequent transportation of the body.

"No matter how questionable each lead appeared on the surface," Finis Brown stated, "we had to track it down, and in this case, each lead seemed to open into something else, and it went on and on, and none of them were giving a clue to the missing week, or to the murder itself."

Investigators learned that prior to Elizabeth Short's return to Los Angeles on January 9, 1947 with Red Manley, she had been a resident of Los Angeles on three separate occasions. Her brief initial visit with Cleo and Mrs. Yanke in January 1943 ended when she traveled to Camp Cooke. She was later arrested in Santa Barbara and sent back to her mother's home in Medford.

After spending several weeks in Medford, Elizabeth returned to Miami for the winter season of 1943–1944. She stayed at the El Mar Hotel at 220 Twenty-first Street, which was not far from the Miami Beach front and the Victory Canteen. Miami employment records obtained by Finis Brown indicated that she worked as a waitress for several months at the Rosedale Delicatessen at 1437 Washington Avenue. She then became a part-time waitress at Mammy's, which at that time was located at 2038 Collins Avenue. In letters to her family, Elizabeth said she was also "modeling" for a Miami man named "Duffy" Sawyer.

Elizabeth traveled to Los Angeles for the second time in August of 1944. She stayed briefly at the Clinton Hotel in downtown Los Angeles

'Lost Week' ● The Missing Link

The "missing link?" Where is it? This is the problem which confronts Los Angeles police officers today in their investigation into the "Black Dahlia" murder case that has already degenerated into a weird jumble of "Idiots' Delight," with three confusing "confessions" and a mounting flood of anonymous letters purporting to be

This is Elizabeth Short, 22, the "Black Dahlia," whose nude, mutilated body was found in a "lover's lane" here on Jan. 15.

Among the first persons questioned was Ann Toth, friend of the victim, who provided not more than a scant sketch of the "Dahlia's" background.

Lynn Martin, 16, another acquaintance of the victim, delved more into the "Dahlia's" background with her description of Hollywood's "life among the bars."

Linda Rohr, left, and Marian Schmidt, former roommates of the "Dahlia," provide police with a description of the victim's personal life.

at Eighth and Broadway, where she shared a room with a slim, dark-haired girl named Lucille Varela. The Clinton Hotel was operated by Nate Bass, who owned a number of Syndicate bars in the downtown area, and was referred to as "Mr. Main Street" by the Vice Squad working out of Central. According to Vice Squad officer Sgt. Charles Stoker, Bass was known to run ads in southern states and cities offering girls employment in the movies or as models in Hollywood. "Girls answering these advertisements would be screened as potential B-girls, and some were sent to a hotel in Hollywood [the Hawthorne], where efforts were made to induce them to enter a life of prostitution," Stoker stated.

Elizabeth's roommate at the Clinton, Lucille Varela, was another Hollywood wannabe—among the hundreds who arrived every month—hoping to become a movie star. It was difficult for Hollywood hopefuls to work nine-to-five and still manage to make the casting rounds. While waiting for that "big break," Lucille worked the downtown and Hollywood bars in the evening as a B-girl. B-girls were not prostitutes. They received money from the bars they worked

In Hunt for 'Black Dahlia' Killer

penned by other "killer confessors." So far, all clues have failed and notwithstanding the numerous "confessions," police are still looking for the "missing link" which might be some person or activity that came into the "Dahlia's" life during the "lost week" prior to the slaying. So far, this is what police have on hand in chain of evidence—

A more recent acquaintance of the "Dahlia" is Dorothy French, who told of Miss Short's activities in San Diego.

This is Robert "Red" Manley, the last known person to see the "Dahlia" alive, who drove Miss Short from San Diego to Los Angeles.

What happened during the "lost week" which the "Dahlia" spent in Los Angeles following her arrival from San Diego? This is the "missing link."

The end of the trail for beauteous Elizabeth Short came at a "lovers' lane" on Norton avenue, where her nude body was found.

by pushing drinks on thirsty, lusty "Georges." B-girls made sure that the George's thirsts were quenched, if not their lusts. A professional B-girl would push the drinks, but never sleep with the George. The rule of the game was to get the cash without delivering the merchandise, and upon occasion the George would be slipped a "Mickey" and pass out along with his wallet.

Elizabeth Short met all the requirements to play the B-girl game— she had the look and the flirtatious personality, and she dressed the part. While trying to break into the movies, Lucille and Elizabeth made the B-girl rounds, pushing drinks at Hollywood and downtown bars where the bartenders would measure out just enough cash to get them by from day to day. But it was a dangerous game, and it often ended up in a sudden descent through the tinseltown trapdoor. A number of Hollywood and downtown bars were run by the Syndicate, and many of the B-girls ended up being recruited as prostitutes and descending into a movieland nightmare.

Syndicate Madam, Brenda Allen (née Marie Mitchell), ran a notorious call-girl ring from her spacious apartment in the Wilshire

District. Catering to the lecherous elite, Brenda's girls were attractive and expensive; and she was always on the lookout for new recruits with special talents. Former Hollywood Vice Squad officer Charles Stoker commented, "No broken-down bags worked for Brenda. She procured the best for her Hollywood and Beverly Hills Rolls-Royce trade. There are hundreds of girls who come to Hollywood each year hoping that the lightning of film fame will strike. When it doesn't, and the percentage is strictly against them, some of them wind up working for dames like Brenda in the world's oldest profession."

In a call-girl setup organized under the vice-map of Bugsy Siegel and Mickey Cohen, Brenda Allen had tie-ins with major studio executives who were anxious to keep visiting moguls, movie stars, and masher-moneymen happy. She advertised herself in the Players Directory, which was published by the Academy of Motion Picture Arts and Sciences as a handy guide for Hollywood producers and casting directors seeking "talent."

BRENDA ALLEN

·

HO-2555

THE PLAYERS DIRECTORY   *Page 39*

Sgt. Charles Stoker first ran across Brenda Allen and her activities when he was assigned to the Vice Squad in 1941. At that time she was Marie Mitchell, a streetwalker who plied her trade in the perimeters of the prestigious Ambassador Hotel on Wilshire Boulevard. In those days she was operating within the vice-map territory of Jack Dragna, the Mafia boss who controlled the narcotics and vice operations in the central city and Long Beach. After Stoker returned from active duty in the army during World War II, he rejoined the Vice Squad in 1945 and learned that in the intervening years Marie Mitchell had changed her name to Brenda Allen and had become Bugsy Siegel's Syndicate vice-queen of movieland. Stoker soon discovered that Brenda was as shrewd as they come, and it was rumored at Central that she had entered the big time through her payoffs and liaisons with an officer in Administrative Vice who had become her "business manager."

"Her method of operation was almost foolproof," Stoker recalled. "And I learned that Brenda worked in the following manner: She was a subscriber to a professional telephone exchange similar to those used by physicians, attorneys, and some movie people. A customer, or a prospective customer, would call the telephone exchange number and ask for Brenda. If he was a previous customer, he would identify himself; or if he wasn't, he would tell Brenda the source of his referral. He would then request a specific girl or describe the type of girl he desired, and a price was agreed upon . . . Brenda would then call a girl on the phone and dispatch her after giving her the pertinent information."

Brenda accepted only the wealthiest clients, checked their credit ratings, and permitted no "tricks" to be serviced from her residence, which was primarily a communications center. The call girls would often take a taxi or be chauffeured by one of Brenda's drivers to a drop-off spot near the client's location to avoid vehicle identification. In some instances, the girls had their own plush rendezvous apartments for special clients.

In the course of his investigation into the Brenda Allen call-girl ring, Stoker found that more than a hundred girls were in Brenda's employ. He noted, "She boasted to the girls who worked for her, and to her customers, that she was operating under police protection. And it was a known fact that the type of customer to whom Miss Allen catered had to be reasonably certain that he wouldn't suffer the embarrassment of an arrest."

Only a select few knew Brenda's address or her private phone number, but her Hollywood exchange number had been advertised in the Players Directory, and Stoker was able to obtain her private number and address from an employee at the telephone exchange. He discovered that Brenda was working out of an apartment building on the corner of Ninth Street and Fedora Avenue—an upscale neighborhood in the Wilshire District behind the Ambassador Hotel. Brenda maintained a nearby bungalow court at 836 Catalina Street, where a number of Brenda's girls who worked the Ambassador Hotel stayed—the hotel was just a half-block north of the bungalow. While staking out Brenda's communication center on Fedora, Stoker posed as a deliveryman and mimed ringing her bell while listening at the door. He could hear the phone frequently ringing and Brenda answering.

Several days later, Stoker returned with an independent electronic surveillance expert, James Arthur Vaus, Jr., and they managed to enter the basement of Brenda's apartment building to place a tap on her phone.

"On the second day of surveillance, Brenda called a number that rang a bell in my mind," Stoker recalled. "Then it struck me full force—the number she had called was the confidential number of the Administrative Vice Squad at Central. When someone answered Brenda's call, she asked for Sgt. Jackson and said it was 'Mrs. Johnson calling. She was told that Sgt. Jackson was out, but it wasn't long before Sgt. Jackson returned Brenda's call on her private line and said, 'Hi Honey. How's business?' They then talked about business and private matters, and a rendezvous date was set when Jackson would tell his wife that he had to be in court."

Though he had heard rumors, Stoker was shocked to learn that Brenda's business partner was one of his superiors—Sgt. Elmer V. Jackson, the trusted aide of Lt. Rudy Wellpott, Commander of Administrative Vice, and a confidant of Assistant Chief Joe Reed. Stoker was also shocked to learn that some known Hollywood starlets worked for Brenda and that many of Brenda's customers were famous movie stars, studio executives, and major business and political figures in the city. An honest cop, Stoker tried to bring about an arrest of Brenda Allen for her vice activities but was warned by members of the LAPD's notorious Gangster Squad to cease his unauthorized investigation, and he was soon transferred out of Central.

The Gangster Squad had a dark history within the LAPD. Originally called the Intelligence Unit, it was purportedly a unit that worked closely with the Chief and Administrative Vice in gathering intelligence information regarding criminal elements operating within the city. But, as a matter of practice, under the reign of Chief James E. "Two Gun" Davis, the Intelligence Unit became the enforcers of Chief Davis's corrupt regime and the protectors of the vice-take from the underworld.

When Angelenos learned in 1938 that members of the Intelligence Unit had tried to assassinate Grand Jury investigator Clifford Clinton, who was investigating LAPD corruption and pay-offs to Buron Fitts and City Hall, the Intelligence Unit was disbanded and became replaced by the "Gangster Squad." But under the new regime of Chief Clemence B. Horrall and Chandler's aide, Assistant Chief Joe Reed, only the name had changed. Horrall continued to use the Gangster Squad unit as enforcers and protectors of police corruption.[11]

After being transferred to the Hollywood Division, Stoker soon observed that Brenda's girls would be on call at Hollywood parties or on special house calls to those on the "A" list. One of Brenda's big clients was Columbia Studio boss Harry Cohn, who took Brenda's

11. When the Gangster Squad came under scrutiny by the Grand Jury in 1949 and was found to be enforcing pay-offs from the Syndicate, the name of the Squad reverted back to the "Intelligence Unit," under the regime of Chief William Parker. However, when the Intelligence Unit was put under investigation by the Police Commission in 1974, it was once again learned that only the name had changed.

girls on cruises aboard his luxury yacht, along with his coterie of Hollywood pals and visiting lechers.

One of the Hollywood hopefuls who fell through the tinseltown trapdoor was the curvaceous blonde starlet, Barbara Payton, who became a prostitute on her way down the ladder of success—before literally dying in the gutter from a narcotics addiction. Elizabeth Short met Barbara Payton through Lucille Varela at Al Green's Nightlife Bar and Grill on McCadden. "Al Green" was Albert Louis Greenberg, a former bootlegger for Bugsy Siegel and Meyer Lansky, who had a long rap-sheet and did odd-job robberies and rub-outs on the side for Bugsy.

When Elizabeth met Barbara Payton, Payton had already become a starlet on the casting-couch circuit. She introduced Elizabeth to some movie and radio fringe people and taught her where the "right places" were to be seen by the "right people." One of the right places was the Formosa Café, across the street from Samuel Goldwyn Studios on the corner of Santa Monica Boulevard and Formosa Avenue. Stars and studio executives working on the Goldwyn lot would often dine and drink there, and the Formosa bar was a rendezvous at night for Hollywood lowlife looking for a high. In the 1940s, the backroom was a bookie joint, and the upstairs was Bugsy Siegel's well-guarded office, where he kept his books, ran the Extras Guild, and conducted the vice operations and business of his Syndicate empire.

It was at the Formosa that actor Franchot Tone encountered an alluring young woman with jet-black hair. Tone was starring in *Phantom Lady* with Ella Raines, which was shooting at Goldwyn, when he entered the Formosa and spotted the Black Dahlia sitting at the bar. Tone recalled that he struck up a conversation. "She said she was waiting for someone, and I said, 'Of course you are, you're waiting for me!'" Over a few drinks, Tone told her that a Hollywood associate was looking for young women with "your kind of looks." He suggested they go to the associate's apartment, and Elizabeth agreed to go with him—after all, Tone was a prominent movie star, and he was going to the trouble of introducing her to someone who could get her career started.

Tone recalled, "I thought it was a pickup from the start—she came with me so easily, but to her it wasn't anything of the kind." When they arrived, the "associate" wasn't there, and the apartment proved to be Tone's trysting place. Tone confirmed that he tried to kiss her a couple of times and lure her to the couch, but she resisted and scolded Tone for only having "that" in mind. He gave her a small amount of money, put her in a cab, and she was gone. Recalling the encounter to John Gilmore, author of *Severed: The True Story of the Black Dahlia Murder* (Amok Books, CA, 1998), Tone commented that he found the encounter to be a rather strange and unsettling experience. "There was something sad and pathetic about her," Tone said.

Without elaborating, Det. Harry Hansen commented that Elizabeth Short had been "a bum and a tease;" but being a bum and a tease was a gambit in her survival game, and she had her own rules. The cache of Elizabeth Short's love letters discovered by the *Examiner* revealed a romantic who dreamed of finding the right man— someone she could trust and give her heart to in an enduring relationship. While she could be a tease as a B-girl and in her attempts to advance her movie career, she apparently valued herself and chose not to have relationships with men she didn't find attractive. At the same time, she enjoyed the attention that her appearance inevitably aroused.

During her stay in Hollywood in 1944, Elizabeth frequented the Hollywood Canteen, where she danced with servicemen and met some of the movie star volunteers. Located near the corner of Sunset and Wilcox, the Canteen had many Hollywood celebrities on its staff, including Bette Davis, John Garfield, and Irene Dunne; and it was at the Canteen in September 1944 that she met actor Arthur Lake, who played Dagwood in the *Blondie* series at Columbia Studios. Elizabeth was able to get free meals at the Canteen by becoming a junior hostess like Georgette Bauerdorf, who was also acquainted with Arthur Lake. Georgette and Elizabeth were both attractive twenty-year-olds when they became Canteen volunteers in 1944, and they were both very popular with the visiting servicemen, who competed for an opportunity to cut in on the dance floor.

One night in mid-September, Elizabeth danced with Lt. Joseph Fickling, who at the time was a pilot stationed at the Army Air Base in Long Beach. Although it was against Canteen rules, they began dating, and Elizabeth found herself falling in love. But like many wartime love affairs, the romance was put on hold when Fickling received his orders and was sent to England. They corresponded, and their love affair became documented in Elizabeth's memory book and the packet of love letters found in her lost luggage.

It was shortly after Fickling's departure that Canteen hostess Georgette Bauerdorf was murdered on October 12, 1944. Georgette's body had been found floating in the bathtub in her West Hollywood apartment. She had been raped, beaten, and asphyxiated—a cloth had been stuffed in her throat. The cloth proved to be bandage material used at military hospitals, and the Sheriff's Department suspected she may have been murdered by a serviceman who had followed her home from the Hollywood Canteen. Several soldiers who had met Georgette at the Canteen became suspects and were brought in for questioning, but no arrests were made, and the murder of Georgette Bauerdorf remained unsolved.

Soon after the Bauerdorf murder, Elizabeth abruptly left Los Angeles and arrived in Medford in time for Thanksgiving with her mother and sisters. She then returned to Miami for the winter season of 1944–1945, and once again she stayed at the El Mar Hotel on Twenty-first Street. Though investigators found no record of her employment, she was often seen at a beachfront bar called The Grotto, operated by East Coast Syndicate boss Meyer Lansky. Police records indicate that she returned to Medford at the end of March 1945 and was employed as a waitress at St. Clair's restaurant in Cambridge. It was at St. Clair's that Elizabeth first met Marjorie Graham, who was a coworker. They would later encounter each other in Hollywood and become roommates at the notorious Hawthorne Hotel.

Following her seasonal travel pattern, Elizabeth returned to Miami in September 1945 and spent the winter at the Colonial Inn, an upscale hotel owned by Bugsy Siegel and Meyer Lansky, which was known by the FBI to be a hoodlum-run gambling establishment. Police investigators found no record of Elizabeth's employment during her stay at the Colonial Inn.

Briefly returning to Medford in the spring, Elizabeth shipped her luggage to Indianapolis on June 1, 1946. According to her mother, Lt. Joseph Fickling was returning from Europe to the United States, and Elizabeth was going to meet Fickling in Indianapolis, where he was scheduled to arrive in the first week of June. Police records indicate that she went on to Chicago and stayed at the Park Row Hotel from June 24 until July 9, before returning to Los Angeles for her third visit on July 12, 1946.

Six months later Elizabeth Short's mutilated and bisected body would be found among the weeds on Norton Avenue in Liemert Park.

During Elizabeth's five-month stay in Los Angeles between July 12 and December 6, 1946, police investigators established that she had resided in at least eleven different locations and had at least fifty different male acquaintances. Was the "person or persons unknown" among those acquaintances, or was the crime a random murder by a psychopath who had never known the victim? Det. Harry Hansen was convinced that the location of the sacred setting, the secret of the autopsy, and the manner in which the body was displayed spoke of a connective clue to someone among her acquaintances.

A number of detectives from Administrative Vice were assigned to the Hollywood area to trace Elizabeth Short's whereabouts and contacts prior to her sudden trip to San Diego on December 6. *Where did she live? Who did she know? Was she a B-girl or a prostitute? Was she involved in drug trafficking? Was she in some kind of trouble when she suddenly left the city?* But it was hard to get a fix on the Black Dahlia. According to former Administrative Vice Officer Vince Carter, "Elizabeth Short was always on the move, and she hadn't established any close relationships that we could pin down. Nobody seemed to really know her very well, but they all remembered what she looked like. She made a vivid impression, but was very secretive about her private life. She was a loner."

When Elizabeth arrived in Los Angeles on July 12, 1946, she checked into Room 21 of the Washington Hotel at 53 Linden Avenue in Long Beach. Similar to her situation in Miami, the Washington was near the oceanfront and a promenade populated by hotels, cafés, and cocktail lounges frequented by servicemen. A local Long Beach druggist, Arnold Landos, who remembered Elizabeth Short, told the *Examiner*, "She lived down the street at the Washington, which is now called the At-Water. She'd come into our drugstore frequently. She'd usually wear one of those two-piece beach costumes, which left her midriff bare. Or she'd wear black lacy things. Her hair was jet-black, and she liked to wear it high. She was popular with the men who came in here and they called her 'The Black Dahlia.'" The manager of the Washington Hotel, Fred Smelser, recalled that she was visited at the hotel by a number of servicemen, and there was "one army officer who saw her frequently." It was Lt. Joseph Fickling.

Hansen and Brown learned from Elizabeth's mother that her daughter had gone to Long Beach to meet Lt. Fickling, who was scheduled to be discharged at the Long Beach Army Air Base at the end of August. According to Phoebe, Elizabeth and Fickling had plans to marry. When Capt. Donahoe was informed about Fickling, the army pilot was quickly moved into the prime suspect hot seat only recently vacated by Red Manley. On finding that Fickling was no longer in the city, Hansen and Brown located him in Charlotte, North Carolina. The Charlotte police were requested to question him as to his whereabouts at the time of the murder.

Found living in his parents' home, Fickling denied that he had been in Los Angeles in January 1947. Fickling told the Charlotte police, "I met Betty in 1944 before I went overseas. We met again when I got back last year. We carried on a long correspondence, but there never was any talk of our marriage." Under questioning, Fickling acknowledged that he had rendezvoused with Elizabeth in Indianapolis when he returned to the States in June 1946. And he told the police that Elizabeth had taken a bus from Chicago to Long Beach where he was scheduled to be discharged. Fickling stated that he met her at the Long Beach bus terminal and took her to the Washington Hotel, where he often visited her when he was off-duty.

When Fickling received a week's leave in August prior to his discharge, he told police that he had stayed with Elizabeth at the Brevoort Hotel in Hollywood near Vine Street. Checking out the Brevoort, Hansen and Brown found a registration card signed by Fickling, indicating that he had registered there with his "wife" from August 20 to August 27, 1946. Fickling insisted that was the last time he had seen Elizabeth Short. Upon being discharged at the end of August, Fickling said he returned to his parents' home in Charlotte, and he obtained employment with 20th Century Charter Airlines, which ran flights between Charlotte and Chicago. Witnesses confirmed to the Charlotte police that Fickling had been on flight assignments to Chicago on the days when Elizabeth had disappeared and the murder took place.

Fickling insisted he had told Elizabeth that marriage for them was out of the question, and in the letter he had written to her in early December of 1946, he had stated, "Time and again I've suggested that you forget me, as I've believed it's the only thing for you to do to be happy."

Acknowledging that he had heard from Elizabeth while she was in San Diego, Fickling produced a letter he received from her dated December 13, 1946, in which she had written:

> *I do hope you find a nice young lady to kiss at midnight on New Years Eve. It would have been wonderful if we belonged to each other now. I'll never regret coming west to*

see you. You didn't take me in your arms and keep me
there. However, it was nice as long as it lasted.

In the same letter she had told him that she desperately needed money for something, and Fickling told the police he had wired her one hundred dollars while she was staying at the Frenches' home in San Diego.[12]

The last letter Fickling received from Elizabeth was from San Diego and postmarked January 8—the day before she vanished. She wrote: "Do not write to me here. I am planning to go to Chicago to work for Jack."

Fickling told police investigators that she had once told him that "Jack" operated a "modeling agency" in Chicago.

The devastating rejection by Lt. Joseph Fickling at the end of August, when he returned to Charlotte without her, was the beginning of her slide into the depths of the tinseltown trap.

It was on August 28, the day after "Mr. and Mrs. Joseph Fickling" checked out of the Brevoort, that Elizabeth Short checked into the notorious Hawthorne Hotel, owned by Nate Bass and operated by Syndicate minion, Glenn Wolfe, who also managed the Chancellor. And it was at the Hawthorne that a short, dark-complexioned mystery man, who drove an old 1936 or 1937 black Ford sedan, began paying Elizabeth's rent.

Four and a half months later, Elizabeth Short's mutilated and bi-sected body would be found in the weeds of Norton Avenue in Liemert Park.

---

12. In 1946 one hundred dollars was a considerable sum—equivalent to six hundred dollars today. The request for money was a pattern for Elizabeth. Following the death of Maj. Matt Gordon in 1945, his family was bewildered when she wrote to them asking for financial assistance.

Homicide Detective Harry Hansen (*left*) and Detective Finis Brown study the crime scene on Norton Avenue.
ANGELES TIMES PHOTO BY R. L. OLIVER

y Bersinger, the Leimert Park resident who first saw the body and called the police

In the left foreground Will Fowler studies the bisected remains of "Jane Doe #1." Next to him is Sergeant Harr Hansen. Behind Hansen is Finis Brown. The cement sack is in center foreground, and a crime lab technician is 1 the far right. The abdominal incision is visible in this photograph. DELMAR WATSON ARCHIVES

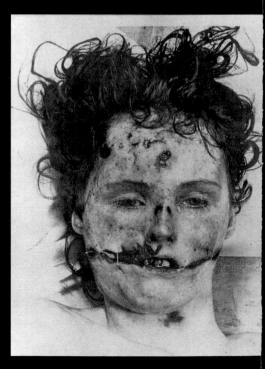

Although her mouth has been slashed open from ear to ear, Elizabeth Short's face has been sewn back together for identification purposes. Wounds to her face indicate she was repeatedly struck by a blunt metal object. The indentation marks could have been caused by the clip lock on the butt of a pistol. DELMAR WATSON ARCHIVES

A studio portrait of Elizabeth Short

A view of Salem Street as it crosses Medford Square, circa 1947
MEDFORD HISTORICAL SOCIETY

The Short sisters (*left to right*): Virginia, Dorothea, Eleanora, Elizabeth, and a neighborhood friend, circa 1934
UCLA DEPARTMENT OF SPECIAL COLLECTIONS/JOHN GILMORE COLLECTION

Dorothea, Elizabeth, Eleanora, and Murial, circa 193
UCLA DEPARTMENT OF SPECIAL COLLECTIONS/JOHN GILMORE COLLI

Elizabeth's father, Cleo
Short, photographed in
Harry Hansen's office
when he was brought in
for questioning

Detective Ray Geise
examines Elizabeth Short's
memory book found in her
lost luggage.

Former roommate, Lynn Martin, became a suspect in the Black Dahlia murder.
UCLA DEPARTMENT OF SPECIAL COLLECTIONS/*LOS ANGELES TIMES* COLLECTION

Gordon Fickling, the Army pilot Elizabeth hoped to marry w **she took the bus to Long Beach in July 1946**
UCLA DEPARTMENT OF SPECIAL COLLECTIONS/JOHN GILMORE COLLECTION

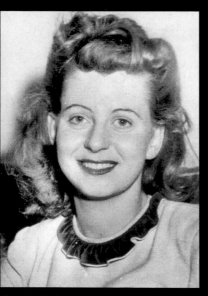

Marjorie Graham, who shared a room with Elizabeth at the Hawthorne
UCLA DEPARTMENT OF SPECIAL COLLECTIONS/ JOHN GILMORE COLLECTION

Major Matt Gordon and Elizabeth. Gordon was killed in a p **crash in India in November 1945.** UCLA DEPARTMENT OF SPECIAL COLLECTIONS/JOHN GILMORE COLLECTION

rime lab technician examines the note accompanying Elizabeth's belongings. The anonymous telegram sent to
from Washington D.C. is in the foreground, and to its left is the address book with Mark Hansen's name
bossed on the lower portion of the cover. ASSOCIATED PRESS

District Attorney William E. Simpson and Captain Jack Donahoe of Homicide (*standing*) examine an anonymous letter sent to the police department regarding the Black Dahlia.

Thelma Todd's Roadside Café on the Pacific Coast Highway. Her body was discovered in a garage in the hills to the rear of the building.

Thelma Todd as she appeared in the United Artists film *Corsair* in 1931

body of Thelma Todd as it was found on Monday, December 16, 1935

Standing behind actress Constance Bennett is the author's stepfather, Jeffrey Bernerd. To her left is Peter Lorrie, on the set at Gaumont-British in 1938. AUTHOR'S COLLECTION

In 1945 the author stands between his mother, Elizabeth Bernerd, and his brother, Robert, in front of their home on Roxbury Drive in Beverly Hills. AUTHOR'S COLLECTION

era French and her daughter, Dorothy, read about murder of their houseguest in the *Los Angeles nes.* UCLA DEPARTMENT OF SPECIAL COLLECTIONS/*LOS ANGELES ES* COLLECTION

Agness "Aggie" Underwood, the top Hearst crime reporte who was taken off both the Bauerdorf and Dahlia murder cases. LOS ANGELES PUBLIC LIBRARY, HISTORY DEPARTMENT PHOTO COLLECTION/*HERALD EXAMINER* COLLECTION

he *Examiner* city room Jim Richardson prepares next scoop. LOS ANGELES PUBLIC LIBRARY, HISTORY RTMENT PHOTO COLLECTION/*HERALD EXAMINER* COLLECTION

Ann Toth, Elizabeth's roommate at Mark Hansen's, is questioned by reporters. DELMAR WATSON ARCHIVES

Mark Hansen, proprietor of the popular Hollywood nightclub
LOS ANGELES DISTRICT ATTORNEY ARCHIVES

The showroom of the Florentine Gardens where Nils Thor Granlund (aka "NTG") staged his *All Girl Revue*
BRUCE TORRENCE HOLLYWOOD PHOTOGRAPH COLLECTION

The Florentine Gardens on Hollywood Boulevard as it appeared in 1947
LOS ANGELES PUBLIC LIBRARY, HISTORY DEPARTMENT PHOTO COLLECTION

bert "Red" Manley being booked at Hollenbeck on suspicion of murder by Detective Harry Hansen (*center*).
/ERSITY OF SOUTHERN CALIFORNIA/REGIONAL HISTORY CENTER

ective Finis Brown (*left*) and Ray Pinker examine
nley's lie detector test. UNIVERSITY OF SOUTHERN
FORNIA/REGIONAL HISTORY CENTER

Manley and his wife, Harriet, meet briefly at Hollenbeck
before his interrogation. UCLA DEPARTMENT OF SPECIAL
COLLECTIONS/*LOS ANGELES TIMES* COLLECTION

Preparing to retire, Harry Chandler opens the door to the Times Building for his son, Norman, who became the publisher of the *Los Angeles Times* in 1945. BRUCE HENSTELL COLLECTION

Norman Chandler, heir to the Chandler dynasty when his father died in 1944
DELMAR WATSON ARCHIVES

Mug shot of Bugsy Siegel taken in New York after his arrest on suspicion of murder in 1928

LOS ANGELES PUBLIC LIBRARY, HISTORY DEPARTMENT PHOTO COLLECTION/ *HERALD EXAMINER* COLLECTION

A Columbia Studio portrait of Bugsy Siegel's mistress, Virginia Hill

LOS ANGELES PUBLIC LIBRARY, HISTORY DEPARTMENT PHOTO COLLECTION/ *HERALD EXAMINER* COLLECTION

The Moorish mansion on Linden Drive where Bugsy Siegel was shot while sitting in the living room, which is to the lower right. LOS ANGELES PUBLIC LIBRARY, HISTORY DEPARTMENT PHOTO COLLECTION/*HERALD EXAMINER* COLLECTION

Bugsy's body on the sofa in the living room. The gunman stood outside the window in the background, which bordered the neighbor's driveway. The bloodstained complimentary copy of the *Los Angeles Times* is on the flo

DOA—June 20, 1947

THE HAWTHORNE HOTEL was just south of Hollywood Boulevard, behind the Roosevelt Hotel, and known to be a rendezvous for prostitutes who worked the Roosevelt and its popular Hollywood nightspot, the Cinegrill.

When questioned by reporters, Hawthorne desk clerk Jim McGrath recalled that Elizabeth Short had shared a room with two young women, Marjorie Graham and Lynn Martin. Miss Graham had known Elizabeth from Boston, where they had worked together as waitresses at St. Clair's in Cambridge. According to Graham, they had run across each other in a store on Hollywood Boulevard in August 1946. After Lt. Fickling had checked out of her life, Elizabeth had moved into the Hawthorne, where Marjorie had been sharing a room with Lynn Martin. Elizabeth had no money, and Marjorie and Lynn took her in. Two male residents of the Hawthorne, Harold Costa and Donald Leyes, told the police and reporters that they had been "boyfriends" of Elizabeth's roommates, who referred to her as "Beth."

"Whenever we took the girls out to dinner, they always asked us if they might bring Beth along," Costa told reporters. "They said the kid was broke and hungry."

After staying a month at the Hawthorne, Elizabeth checked out on September 28. The police tried to find her old roommates, but according to the desk clerk, Marjorie Graham and Lynn Martin had left the hotel shortly after Elizabeth's departure.

"Miss Short was always getting behind in her rent," the hotel clerk recalled. "Whenever she did, a short, dark-complexioned man—about thirty-five or forty—came in and paid her bill. He used to drive an old, black Ford sedan and park it in front. When Beth left the hotel last September, she piled her baggage in the short, dark-complexioned man's car and drove off."

Apparently the mystery man in the old dark Ford sedan drove Elizabeth to a residence at 6024 Carlos Avenue, which was just behind the Florentine Gardens nightclub. The house on Carlos was owned by the proprietor of the Florentine Gardens, Mark Hansen (no relation to Det. Harry Hansen). A multimillionaire, Mark Hansen owned a number of apartment buildings and rooming houses in the Hollywood area, as well as the Marcal Theatre on Hollywood Boulevard and the Roseland Ballroom in downtown Los Angeles. Some of the showgirls and B-girls who worked at the Florentine Gardens lived in Hansen's rooming houses, and some stayed as guests at his Carlos Avenue residence. Nils Thor Granlund, aka "NTG," who staged the nightclub floor shows and was considered a connoisseur of Hollywood beauties, frequently stayed at the Carlos residence, and he was known to cavort with the girls in his apartment above the garage.

In the ascendancy of Hollywood wannabes back in the 1940s, it was considered a step up the stairway to stardom to get in with the NTG/Hansen crowd. Betty Hutton, Yvone DeCarlo, Lilli St. Cyr, Jean Wallace, Gwen Verdon, and Marie "the Body" McDonald were among those who got their start in the Florentine Gardens floor show, which rivaled Earl Carroll's dinner theatre as one of the more popular Hollywood nightspots of the time. But despite the frequent booking of headliners, the Florentine Gardens could never escape its image as a hangout for Hollywood lowlife. The floor shows were only one pasty spangle above burlesque, and the B-girls and hookers were always there to make sure the booze flowed freely and the customers were satisfied. There was a secret card room above the foyer run by Bugsy Siegel's pal, Jimmy Utley, where moneyed customers were readily fleeced.

While the Florentine Gardens was ostensibly operated by Mark Hansen and Frank Bruni, it was commonly known by the cognoscenti of the Hollywood underworld that Hansen and Bruni were fronting for the Syndicate. Bugsy Siegel and Mickey Cohen had their own special table and bevy of chorines, which included Virginia Hill's rival for Bugsy's affections—Marie "the Body" McDonald. Because Bugsy controlled the Extras Guild, he could get the Florentine Gardens' chorines extra work in the movies at the drop of a G-string, and NTG, who staged the shows for Syndicate nightclubs across the country, could get the girls gainful employment in a number of venues.

Judy Walters, a former prostitute who once worked for Mark Hansen, recalled:

> I was supposed to have been another discovery like Betty Hutton or somebody. I was promised spots in NTG's shows at the Gardens instead of wet-nursing the customers. The drinks were watered, and the food wasn't fit for a dog, and we were supposed to see that the suckers left in good spirits and with empty pockets.
>
> Bugsy Siegel was around there once or twice—I don't know, maybe more than that, and I was looking for a way to get to Vegas, to work for Siegel and Moe Sedway, who was living at the Roosevelt Hotel then. I know they wanted NTG to head the Flamingo, so I stayed on, but whatever promises were made anyone at the Gardens it didn't ever happen. Instead of getting in the chorus and being a show

girl, I ended up dancing with winos and sex fiends at Hansen's Roseland Ballroom downtown.

According to Judy, an assistant manager of the Florentine Gardens was an "enforcer-cop" pal of Mark Hansen's. "The cops were on the take," Judy said, "and this undercover cop would keep his eye on what was going on just to make sure that the juice wasn't getting watered down. The real gangsters were the cops."

It was into this milieu that Elizabeth was moved to the Carlos residence on September 28 by the short, dark-complexioned man driving the old black Ford sedan. Elizabeth shared a room with pretty Hollywood starlet Ann Toth, who was one of Hansen's many girlfriends. Not long after Elizabeth moved in, she arranged for her friend Marjorie Graham to move into the home on Carlos, and she also became one of Mark Hansen's nonpaying guests.

Robert Slatzer, a young man from Columbus, Ohio, who had traveled to Hollywood to become a screenwriter, often went to the Florentine Gardens and dated Ann Toth several times before becoming the boyfriend of another Hollywood wannabe, Norma Jeane Dougherty. Norma Jeane had only recently signed as a starlet with 20th Century Fox, and the studio had changed her name to Marilyn Monroe. "Marilyn liked going to the Florentine Gardens and enjoyed Granny's [NTG's] shows and liked dancing in the Conga line," Slatzer recalled. "Though she was relatively unknown then, Mark Hansen knew who Marilyn was and occasionally he'd ask us over to his table where there'd always be three or four attractive women, and some questionable looking flashy characters."

Slatzer remembered that Elizabeth Short was at Hansen's table on several occasions, and she was attractive but seemed withdrawn and didn't have much to say. "Elizabeth Short and Marilyn spoke several times," Slatzer recalled, "and she would ask Marilyn what she should do to get a studio contract, but Elizabeth didn't have Marilyn's driving ambition. She dreamed of being a film star, but wasn't willing to make the effort. She seemed to have a defeated attitude, as I recall, and she hung around a bad crowd."

When questioned by reporters about Elizabeth Short, Ann Toth said, "We used to think the world of that kid. She was always well-behaved and sweet when I knew her. But Beth could not stand up to trouble, and she was always in hot water . . . she was skeptical of people, but despite that often stumbled into trash."

According to Ann Toth, Elizabeth had been promised extra work in the movies, and a role in NTG's next Florentine Gardens revue. It was inferred in the press that Elizabeth had become one of Mark Hansen's many girlfriends, but he adamantly denied to the police that he had ever been intimate with her. "She dated many different men while she was living here," Hansen said, "mostly hoodlums whom I wouldn't even let in my house."

Commenting on an occasional visitor of Elizabeth's, Ann Toth described him as a "short, dark complexioned man in his late thirties, five feet six inches tall, of medium build . . . a little fellow. He drove an older model black Ford sedan. Beth called him 'Maurice,' and he had promised to 'setup' Elizabeth in an apartment in Beverly Hills." Ann Toth had put a name to the mysterious "short, dark complexioned man" who used to park in front of the Hawthorne and pay Beth's rent—the mystery man who picked up Beth in his "old black Ford sedan" and helped her move to Mark Hansen's place on Carlos. Was it the same "1936 or 1937 black Ford sedan" seen by Robert Meyer and the newsboy, Bobby Jones, as it remained parked for several minutes at the site where Elizabeth Short's mutilated and bisected body was disposed of in the predawn hours of January 15, 1947? Apparently Det. Harry Hansen suspected that it was and that "Maurice" may have been the connecting link between Elizabeth's Hollywood acquaintances and the "sacred setting."

Witnesses at the Chancellor and the Florentine Gardens were uncomfortable talking about Maurice or mentioning the mystery man's name because he was a dangerous subject. Maurice was connected.

Maurice proved to be Maurice Clement, a minion of Bugsy Siegel and Mickey Cohen, who was a procurer for the Syndicate call-girl ring run by the notorious Hollywood Madam, Brenda Allen. Although Maurice was never publicly named by Capt. Donahoe or the press as a suspect, the Black Dahlia files recently found in the Los Angeles District Attorney's Office place him high on the suspect list.

```
    R301248              Lt. Frank B. Jemison           2-20-51


          Elizabeth Short                      Murder

The following are suspects in the murder of victim, Elizabeth Short:

    1. Carl Balsiger            12. Glenn Wolf
    2. C Welsh                  13. Michael Anthony Otero
    3. Sergeant "Chuck" name unknown  14. George Bacos
    4. John D. Wade             15. Francis Campbell
    5. Joe Scalis               16. Queer Woman Surgeon
    6. James Nimmo              17. Doctor Paul DeGaston
  → 7. Maurice Clement          18. Doctor A. E. Brix
    8. A Chicago police officer 19. Doctor M. M. Schwartz
    9. Salvador Torres Vera     20. Doctor Arthur McGinnis Faught
   10. Doctor George Hodel      21. Doctor Patrick S. O'Reilly
   11. Marvin Margolis          22. Mark Hansen
```

Maurice Clement is #7 on Jemison's suspect list, which includes six surgeons (#16 through #21) known to be abortionists with arrest records.

Former Columbia Studio employee Al Nolan recalled that Maurice Clement worked for the Talent Department at Columbia Studios. He setup the liaisons for Brenda's girls with the studio brass and their friends. According to Nolan, Elizabeth Short knew Maurice and was one of the girls he chauffeured around. At the time, it was common knowledge on the Columbia lot that a number of Brenda's girls maintained an apartment on North Gower Street, not far from the studio entrance.

Testimony recently found in the District Attorney's Black Dahlia files give further insight into Maurice Clement and Elizabeth's stay at Mark Hansen's. When questioned in 1949 by Finis Brown and Lt. Jemison for the Grand Jury, Ann Toth said that she knew Elizabeth was dating many different men, but knew little about them because Mark Hansen was extremely jealous, and Elizabeth had to be careful about bringing her boyfriends around the house on Carlos. "Beth had to be cautious," Ann Toth stated. "Everybody picked her up a block away, and everybody dumped her off a block away . . . because she wouldn't dare bring anybody to the house."

When Finis asked why, Toth said, "Well, Mark wouldn't like it. I mean he more or less possessed her from the time she came there, so naturally, she didn't even have anyone call for her there at the house ever. . . . If it hadn't been for Mark, I guess I would have found out lots of things because they would have called there, you know what I mean? I would have got acquainted with them, but he warned her not to bring anybody down there, not to go out with anybody else."

Ann Toth told the 1949 Grand Jury investigators that when Mark wasn't around Elizabeth would make secretive, outgoing calls on the house phone. Toth recalled that she often called somebody in Beverly Hills, and she often called Maurice:

Brown: Clement, was it?
Toth: Maurice Clement. Did you ever talk to him again?
Brown: Talked to him several times.
Toth: What is Clement?
Brown: Clement is a teacher . . .

Though Finis Brown acknowledged that the police had questioned Maurice Clement "several times," no transcript of Clement's LAPD interrogation has ever been made public, nor was it placed in the District Attorney's files. And when Ann Toth asked, "What is Clement?" Finis Brown deliberately misled her in saying, "Clement is a teacher." Finis was fully aware that Maurice Clement was an employee in the Talent Department at Columbia Studios, and he knew of Clement's contacts with Brenda Allen as a Syndicate procurer.

Toth: Clement . . . Little . . . on the dark side?

Brown: Little fellow.

Toth: Was he driving a Ford?

Brown: Two door sedan.

Toth: Yes.

[Finis quickly changes the subject]

Brown: Do you recall of her ever going to a doctor? Did you ever know of a time when she ever rode with you or anybody that you know of, and let her off on Hollywood Boulevard, at any doctor's place?

Toth: Mark [Hansen] might have driven her down. She was going to one on Hollywood Boulevard. I think maybe the teacher [Maurice] brought her down there once. It seems to me she said she was going to meet him one Sunday afternoon. But of course, he wouldn't be in his office on a Sunday afternoon.

Brown: Ever hear of Dr. Faught?

Toth: No.

Jemison: Or Dr. Paul de Gaston?

Toth: No.

Jemison: Did you ever hear her mention a Dr. Morris— C. J. Morris?

Toth: No, I don't remember the doctor's name she was supposed to be going to.

Jemison: Dr. Morris had been mentioned in connection with some abortions. He was a man that could perform an abortion in case a girl wanted it. Did she ever mention that?

Toth: No.

Jemison: You drove her downtown, in Los Angeles there near the Biltmore Hotel on one occasion, didn't you— near there?

Toth: Yes.

Jemison: About how long was that before she left for San Diego—do you have any idea?

Toth: About two weeks.

Jemison: Didn't she give you any reason whatsoever to be—to ask to be taken down there near the Biltmore Hotel? Didn't she tell you who she was going to meet?

Toth: I thought she was supposed to meet the school teacher there [Maurice].

Although California statutes require that Grand Jury testimony remain sealed unless there is an indictment, it was leaked to the press at the time that "a wealthy Hollywood man" had become the prime suspect in the Black Dahlia murder. The district attorney's Black Dahlia files reveal that the "wealthy Hollywood man" was Mark Hansen, proprietor of the Florentine Gardens. And on December 16, 1949, investigator Frank Jemison took Mark Hansen's testimony in the presence of Sgt. Ed Barret of the LAPD Homicide Division.[13]

Jemison: State your full name.

Hansen: Mark Hansen.

Jemison: Were you acquainted with Beth Short before her death?

Hansen: Yes, I knew her.

Jemison: Just how did you happen to meet her?

Hansen: Well, her and another girl had no place to stay and a fellow brought them over.

---

13. In *Black Dahlia Avenger*, author Steve Hodel claimed that the "wealthy Hollywood man" was his father, George Hodel. But the Grand Jury files confirm that George Hodel had been dismissed as a suspect. (See "The Hodel Hypothesis" in Appendix B.)

Jemison: Was that Marjorie Graham with Beth Short at that time?

Hansen: Yes. Yes.

Jemison: And can you remember the month and the year when this happened?

Hansen: I think it was in October, in 1946.

Jemison: Was she a pretty good-looking gal?

Hansen: Well I thought she was fair looking, average. If it wasn't for her teeth. She had bad teeth. Other than that she would have been beautiful.

Jemison: About how long did these two girls live there at that time in October?

Hansen: Perhaps a week or ten days; something like that.

Jemison: Did they leave at that time then?

Hansen: Well, I asked them to move because this Graham girl, she was inclined to be liquored up and I didn't like it at all, and this Short girl, she had always some undesirable looking character waiting for her outside and bringing her home.

Jemison: Did she have some boyfriends during the time she was there?

Hansen: There was one particular fellow that brought her home and came and got her. He didn't look very good. He had a coupé of some kind—I think it was about '38 or '39 Chevrolet or Ford; something like that.

Jemison: He didn't look so good to you?

Hansen: No. I saw him from the outside. I saw him standing—coming to the door picking her up.

Jemison: What did you tell Beth Short about this fellow that didn't look so good?

Hansen: I didn't tell her anything. I told her I wanted them to move—didn't want them—those damn girls liquored up. I asked them to move.

Jemison: You didn't have any bad feelings against Beth Short at that time, did you?

Hansen: No, I didn't have any hard feelings against her at all.

Jemison: With all your experience, didn't you kinda take an interest in her welfare and, you know, about these fellows she was going out with?

Hansen: I spoke to her about did she know the caliber of men they were. She said yes, she had been around; she knew what life was all about. That is what she said.

Jemison: Would you say she was a sexy-type girl?

Hansen: Well, I don't know if she was a sexy-type girl. She appeared to be a very nice girl.

Jemison: Well, as far as your knowledge of her is concerned would you say she was having intercourse with these various fellows, or more of the prostitute type or not?

Hansen: No, uh uh. Uh uh. She was—she appeared to be a more domestic type girl.

Jemison: Did she tell you that she was engaged to Gordon Fickling while she was there?

Hansen: Yes, she was engaged to some fellow—flyer or something. I think it was Gordon Fickling. He was in the east. She said she was engaged to be married.

Jemison: Did she indicate to you she was saving herself for him?

Hansen: Yes, more or less.

Jemison: Well then you say these two girls left your place about that time?

Hansen: Um hum.

Jemison: Where did they move to, do you remember?

Hansen: No, I don't. I think it was over to that apartment-hotel.

When Beth and Marjorie moved from Hansen's house on Carlos to "that apartment-hotel," they had moved into Room 726 of the Guardian Arms Hotel at 5217 Hollywood Boulevard, and they shared a room with two men they had met on the street—Bill Robinson and Marvin Margolis. Robinson told the police that the girls were broke, and he and Margolis had tried to find them a place to stay, but ultimately allowed them to share their apartment at the Guardian Arms, which consisted of a sitting room and a small bedroom.

"Beth slept on the sofa," Robinson said, and he "slept in the bedroom with Marge." According to Robinson, the girls moved in on October 10, and they both left on October 22. It was Robinson's understanding that both girls had become disenchanted with Hollywood and had decided to return to Massachusetts, but only Marjorie had enough money to make the trip. On October 22, Marjorie Graham took the Greyhound bus back to Boston.

Until Elizabeth could afford to buy a ticket home, she needed someplace to stay, and Marvin Margolis told the police that he had accompanied her back to Mark Hansen's residence on Carlos. Claiming to be Elizabeth's cousin, Margolis asked Hansen if Elizabeth could leave her luggage there overnight:

> **Jemison:** Well, isn't it a fact that she moved back over to the house there for a period of time prior to her going over to the Chancellor?
>
> **Hansen:** Yes. Here's what happened—she came back and visited, and Margolis was doing all the talking and he says she was going to move back home—and he carried the suitcase up and I says, "What's this?" He says, "Can she leave this here overnight? She's going away tomorrow and would like to leave these until tomorrow."
>
> **Jemison:** Who's doing the talking?
>
> **Hansen:** This cousin.
>
> **Jemison:** Margolis?

Hansen: Yes, and I said, "I guess that will be all right." That night I come home—Beth Short was there.

Jemison: Inside the house?

Hansen: I said, "I thought you were just going to leave your suitcases," and she said, "I didn't have no place to stay." Would I mind if she stayed. She kept staying and staying. Then she moved over to the Chancellor Apartment.

Jemison: Now on this second occasion when Beth Short left to go over to the Chancellor Apartments—

Hansen: Yes.

Jemison: How did she happen to be leaving your place on that occasion?

Hansen: Because I told her I didn't want her staying there. She said she would find a place and she did.

Jemison: What was your reason for asking Beth Short to leave?

Hansen: I didn't want her there. I didn't like the caliber of people she showed up with.

Jemison: Isn't it a fact that you felt sorry for her and she was a pretty nice girl—

Hansen: Yes, I told her to her face. She still went out and kicked around.

Jemison: You didn't like the idea of her kicking around?

Hansen: That's right. I didn't want that false business— cussing, drinking—I had no reason having her there.

Jemison: While she was living at the Chancellor Apartments, she came back to your house and got mail?

Hansen: I didn't see her but she was sitting there one night when I came home, with Ann about 5:30, 6:00 o'clock— sitting and crying and saying she had to get out of there. She was crying about being scared—one thing and another, I don't know. She said she was going to Oakland to a sister. She said she was scared.

Jemison: Did she have dinner with you that night?

Hansen: Yes, she did. She had dinner with Ann.

Jemison: Did you sympathize with her when she was crying?

Hansen: Yes, I did. I felt sorry for her.

Jemison: Did you take her home—up to the Chancellor Apartments?

Hansen: Yes.

Jemison: What did you talk about?

Hansen: She was talking about she was going to Oakland to visit her sister there and asked if she could come back to my house when she got back. I told her, "I don't think so. Better find another place."

Jemison: What did you tell her—it was on account of these boys?

Hansen: No, it was her whole makeup, because she picked up with bums. Not only them, but with bums.

Jemison: When you took her over to the Chancellor, did she ask you for any money that night?

Hansen: No.

Jemison: What was she doing for money?

Hansen: I don't know.

Jemison: When you took her over there that night did you take her up to her room?

Hansen: No, I left her off on the street.

Jemison: You believed she was going to Oakland?

Hansen: The next day—she says she was going the next day.

Jemison: She did leave the next day?

Hansen: I don't know.

Jemison: But you didn't see her again?

Hansen: I never saw her again.

Jemison: I am told by certain people who have known you that you have from time to time mentioned that you had some knowledge of the medical profession.

Hansen: No, I never have.

Jemison: Do you recall telling some people that?

Hansen: No, sir, I never have. I never had any knowledge of any medical profession whatsoever.

Jemison: Well now, will you try to remember—do you remember telling people you did have a connection with, for instance, abortions?

Hansen: Abortions? No, I never have. I never say no such thing. I never had any knowledge of such—

Jemison: Did you ever assist in connection with an abortion operation of some girl?

Hansen: No, no, never. I don't know anything about it.

Jemison: And then you never did attempt any abortion with instruments—surgical instruments?

Hansen: Oh, no. I don't know nothing about such—

Jemison: O.K. That is all I want, your answer.

On the night before she left for San Diego, Elizabeth had told Ann Toth and Mark Hansen she was scared; and on the following day, December 6, when she checked out of the Chancellor, she had told one of her roommates, Linda Rohr, that she was frightened. "She seemed worried or afraid," Linda recalled. What was it that had frightened Elizabeth in those last days at the Chancellor before she suddenly left the city? It may have had something to do with Maurice.

Another roommate, Sherryl Maylond, had stated that one of Elizabeth's frequent callers in her last days at the Chancellor had been Maurice, and on the night of January 15, shortly after the headlines about the "Werewolf Killer" hit the streets, a man by the name of "Clement" had entered the Hollywood bar where she worked and told the bartender that he wanted to "speak to Sherryl." It was Sherryl's night off, but the man returned the following evening and told Sherryl he had "to speak to her about Beth Short." Frightened, she refused to speak with him and avoided him until he finally left. Sherryl described Clement as a "slight, dapper, olive-skinned man."

Notations found within the 1949 Grand Jury files indicate that Det. Harry Hansen had questioned Maurice Clement about his relationship with the victim, and Clement had admitted that he had seen Elizabeth Short in the days just before she suddenly left the city. Clement had to admit he had seen her on at least six occasions in the first week of December because witnesses had seen them together.

> Also interviewed was Maurice Clement who stated he met her about December 1 in Brittingham's Restaurant on Sunset Blvd. At that time she was broke and he paid her dinner check. He stated he saw her possibly 3 or 4 times within that week.

(LADA ARCHIVES)

Witnesses said that Elizabeth frequented Brittingham's restaurant, which was just around the corner from Columbia Studios on Sunset and Gower. George Bacos, an usher at CBS across the street, stated to police that he had often seen her there, as had Nina Blanchard, who later became a famous modeling agency executive. At that time, Nina Blanchard was a waitress at Brittingham's, where many of the Columbia Studio executives and employees socialized. According to Blanchard, Elizabeth used to frequent Brittingham's and was also seen with studio executive Max Arnow, who was in charge of the Talent Department.

Max Arnow was notorious for supplying Harry Cohn and the Columbia brass with ladies of the night or day; and Maurice Clement, who was on the Columbia Talent Department payroll, was known to be Brenda Allen's procurer who chauffeured the ladies around to the big shots' trysting places for Arnow. A witness had seen Maurice and Elizabeth in conversation at Brittingham's on at least four occasions early in December 1946, shortly before she left the city.

Because there were witnesses, Maurice had to admit to Harry Hansen that the conversations at Brittingham's took place, but he lied to the police and stated that he had met Elizabeth for the first time that first week of December; however, the statements of Ann Toth and the desk clerk at the Hawthorne clearly establish that Maurice had met her at least as early as September, when he occasionally paid her rent at the Hawthorne and had offered to set her up in an apartment in Beverly Hills. In her testimony to the district attorney investigators, Toth had estimated that it was at least two weeks before she left the city—sometime in November—that she had dropped off Elizabeth near the Biltmore, where Toth believed she was meeting Maurice. And Toth thought it may have been Maurice who had driven her to a doctor's office on Hollywood Boulevard, shortly before Elizabeth suddenly left for San Diego.

Maurice Clement was high on the "Person or Persons Unknown" suspect list in the Black Dahlia files. And there was reason to believe that, when Elizabeth Short walked out of the Biltmore Hotel on January 9, 1947 and headed toward Sixth Street and into the night, Maurice Clement knew her destination.

One week later Elizabeth Short's mutilated and bisected body would be found among the weeds of Norton Avenue in Liemert Park.

Check Women Pals In Torture Murder

A Killer Lurks in the Shadows—

2 Women Sought in 'Dahlia' Slaying; New Clews Found

Mother Robs Banks; Held

Waitress Admits Midwest Holdups

DES MOINES, Jan. 22.—Mother of two daughters, a pretty 35-year-old woman confessed this afternoon she paid up a Des Moines bank today.

She also admitted holding up a St. Louis bank.

The woman was identified by Chief of Police Jack Brophy said the committed the hold up in St. Louis last as well as today

Last Companions of Girl Hunted

Two short, thin brunettes—frequenters of Hollywood hangouts—were sought by police yesterday as possibly the last companions of Elizabeth Short before she was slain January 15.

Search for these Hollywood women-about-town was geared into a larger hunt based on the ever-strengthening theory that "The Black Dahlia" may have been murdered by a woman.

Coupled with this theory was the growing belief that the 22-year-old girl was a prisoner in —ves of her life.

—dary theory—shoot,

Woman Sought as "Dahlia" Probe Takes New Turn

LOS ANGELES, Jan. 21 (UP)—Police made a complete about-face today in their efforts to find the torture-murderer of pretty Elizabeth Short, and began an intensive search for a woman, rather than a man, as the mutilator of the "Black Dahlia."

Former roommates of the strikingly beautiful 22-year-old girl were placed first on the list of those to be questioned. The decision to change all previous tactics of the

week-long search came after a meeting of the city's top-ranking police officials which began last night and lasted well into the morning.

One search in the new drive is for a girl roommate who disappeared Jan. 15, the day Miss Short's tortured and mutilated body, hacked in two, was found in a lovers' lane.

"Dahlia"
Continued on Page 3

WASHINGTON, has been asked to undertake a the American and British zones of occupied

This was disclosed today by a War Department official who asked that his name not be used. He said Mr. Hoover has not yet given his answer.

because of the recent agreement to unify them economically.

As a world authority on food problems since World War I

been a woman Angeles only two or three the murder.

Detectives have been groping for clues that would

"Letter to Follow"

BY THE TENTH day of banner headlines, the Black Dahlia murder had made a mountain of nickels for the Hearst newspapers, but after the inquest and exoneration of Red Manley, the Dahlia story began to wilt. Not that the public wasn't glued to every new facet of the case, but new clues and theories were becoming few and far between. When cornered by reporters at Central, Sgt. Harry Hansen was asked if he had any new suspects, and in one of his rare interviews with the press, he uttered his favorite one word response—"No."

But Donahoe, who could wheedle out the blarney at the pop of a flashbulb, told the press that there was a whole new turn in the Dahlia case. "We believe that the killer may have been a woman," Donahoe theorized to Aggie Underwood. "The murdered girl was known to have been in the city from January 9 to January 14 without her baggage and makeup kit. It seems logical that the Short girl may have been staying with a woman where she could get a change of clothes."

In support of his distaff murder theory, Donahoe advanced the possibility that the tortured girl's body was severed after death by a diminutive female butcher who was too weak to lift the entire 123-pound torso (but yet, according to Donahoe, was able to subdue her, tie her up, and place her in a bathtub—where Dr. Newbarr was convinced she was then bisected). Donahoe went on to recall to Aggie that three of the most infamous mutilation killers in Los Angeles crime annals were women—Winnie Ruth Judd, Clara Phillips, and Louise Peete.

Placing the focus on a woman as the killer intensified the search for Beth's old roommate at the Hawthorne, Lynn Martin, who had mysteriously vanished on the day that the murder story broke. She had been last seen by her former Hawthorne boyfriend, Harold Costa, at about 5:00 P.M. on January 15 as she got into a taxicab near the corner of La Cienega and Sunset Boulevards. Describing Lynn Martin as having a "bitter dislike for Miss Short," Donahoe considered her a hot suspect and disclosed to the press that "an intense search was underway for Miss Martin, who is still missing despite an ever expanding check on her whereabouts."

After receiving an anonymous tip, the police took Miss Martin into custody at a North Hollywood motel, at 10822 Ventura Boulevard, where she had gone into hiding following the murder. Subjected to a lengthy interrogation by Hansen and Brown at Central, it was learned that Lynn Martin's real name was Norma Lee Myer, a sixteen-year-old runaway from Long Beach. She was a wannabe nightclub singer/dancer who posed as a much older girl.

Like Elizabeth, Lynn had been a B-girl, but she had fallen into the tinseltown trap and became a prostitute at an early age. She had once lived at Glenn Wolfe's Chancellor Apartments on Cherokee, before moving to the Hawthorne, and sharing a room with Elizabeth and Marjorie.

Lynn told the police that she had only shared a room with Elizabeth for a week or two and didn't know her very well. Admitting there were times when they didn't get along, she said she had no particular feelings toward her. Police located the other roommate, Marjorie, who had left Hollywood on October 22 and returned to Cambridge, Massachusetts. Questioned about the "bitter dislike" Miss Martin may have had for Elizabeth, Majorie said she was unaware of a dispute and denied Capt. Donahoe's allegations that there was any animosity between the two. "I don't think so," Marjorie said. "At least it didn't appear so to me when I was still in Hollywood."

In the *Examiner* edition of Sunday, January 26, 1947, it stated:

> Figuring prominently in the inquiry is Lynn Martin, 16 year old dancer and former roommate of the slain girl.
>
> On the basis of facts related by Miss Martin, juvenile officers have been conducting a sweeping investigation of certain nightclubs and bars in the Hollywood area and the men who pickup girls in them.
>
> Miss Martin, whose real name is Lynn Myer, has provided lurid details of her associations with men who "picked her up" in various establishments in Hollywood.
>
> Among the men implicated by the girl are several prominent Hollywood personalities, authorities said.

Although Lynn Martin may have been good for several days of news copy and fitted into Donahoe's theory that the killer had been a woman, Hansen and Brown knew that the sixteen-year-old had nothing to do with the crime.

After discussions with Medical Examiner Dr. Frederic Newbarr, Hansen had concluded that the bisection of the body had been done with medical instruments by somebody with advanced medical knowledge. In his 1949 testimony to Grand Jury investigator Frank Jemison, Hansen stated, "I think a medical man was involved—a very fine surgeon. I base that conclusion on the way the body was bisected. . . . It was unusual in this sense, that the point at which the body was bisected is, according to eminent medical men, the easiest point in the spinal column to severe [between the second and third lumbar vertebrae] and he hit the spot exactly."

According to Hansen, Dr. Newbarr had concurred that the bisection of the body was done with medical instruments by a trained surgeon. "It was a fine piece of surgery," Newbarr told Hansen, remarking that the surgery was meticulous and "couldn't have been done in any 15 minutes, half hour or even an hour."

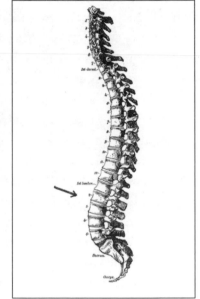

(GRAY'S ANATOMY)

The FBI concurred with Dr. Newbarr and Hansen's opinion. Having examined the autopsy photos, along with Dr. Newbarr's report, the FBI determined that the body had been bisected by someone with advanced medical knowledge: "The murderer had some training in dissection of bodies," the FBI report stated. "It is felt that the murder was committed indoors, where water, drainage facilities and perhaps medical equipment was available."[14]

However, the knowledge that the bisection of the body was "a fine piece of surgery" accomplished by a trained surgeon was never made known to the public. These observations were only recently discovered in FBI documents and the district attorney's Black Dahlia files. But while this vital information regarding the MO of the murder was never revealed to the public at the time, it was well-known by Homicide. Contrary to Donahoe's public state-

---

14. See page 341 of Appendix A.

ments, he knew that Lynn Martin, a runaway high-school dropout, did not have the medical knowledge or surgical experience to have committed the crime. Hansen suspected she may have known too much about Elizabeth's friends and connections and had vanished because she became frightened after seeing the headlines.

While being held in custody by juvenile authorities, Lynn Martin was interviewed by the *Herald Express* and made some insightful—and perhaps dangerous—observations. Culled from her sad life as a young girl on the streets of Hollywood, Lynn Martin stated to the reporter:

> There are a lot of girls in Hollywood who could end up like Beth Short . . . Hollywood draws them from all over the country.
>
> Hollywood is a lonely place when you come into it without home ties or friends and very little money. There are few places for a lonely girl to go except into a bar.
>
> Girls pick each other up in a store or a bar and start rooming together like old friends. It doesn't matter if they don't know anything about each other. It's somebody to talk to and share the rent with—like Beth and Marjorie and I. Sharing rent means more money for something to eat or a new pair of shoes.
>
> Even more important than food sometimes is having makeup and being able to keep your hair looking good, because if you look good, you can always get a man to buy you a big thick steak, some French-fried potatoes and a cup of coffee. Nothing ever tastes so good—at first. But the guys you pick up all insist you order steak or chops, and you get so sick of meat—meat all the time, and after a while you can hardly get it down.
>
> You don't drink at first, because you don't like liquor.

You don't like the taste. But you drink because when you're on a date in a bar you have to order something, and when you're out on a date the first thing is always a couple of drinks—and then a couple of drinks.

You're always lonely in Hollywood, even when you're out with people. They don't belong to you—those people. None of them really care what happens to you. Lots of times you can hardly stand the man you're with, but you can forget about that after a few drinks.

Lots of times the girls talk to each other about getting out of Hollywood and starting all over again. They're going back home, or they're going to get married to someone. Down in the heart of all of them is sort of a hazy dream about a husband and a house and a baby.

They talk about it, and they dream about it, but somehow they almost never do it. This life is like a drug. You can't give it up. It's not like having a nine to fiver. They can sleep late if they want—they're on their own time. And if they have family back home, they never want their families to know what kind of life they're leading—so if they write home, they make up stuff.

Most of the girls are pretty innocent and well meaning at first. The road downhill is gradual. They know their life isn't right, but after a while you take the easiest way.

Sooner or later they become pregnant, and many of them resort to an illegal operation—and sometimes some of them end up like Beth Short.

After the juvenile authorities returned Lynn Martin to her family in Long Beach, she once again disappeared and vanished for good. Perhaps she had painted too vivid a picture of the dead-end road Elizabeth had been traveling.

* * *

There had never been a murder in Los Angeles with an MO like the Black Dahlia case, but Aggie Underwood's memory morgue recalled an unsolved murder that had some similarities—the murder of Georgette Bauerdorf. Georgette, who had been a volunteer at the Hollywood Canteen along with Elizabeth Short in 1944, was the attractive young daughter of wealthy East Coast industrialist George Bauerdorf— a close friend of William Randolph Hearst. Her body had been discovered in the bathtub of her fashionable West Hollywood apartment on October 12, 1944, a little more than two years prior to Elizabeth's murder. Georgette had been assaulted, beaten, raped, and asphyxiated by a cloth forced into her throat. Her body had been placed in a bathtub, and the water had been turned on by the killer before he suddenly left the scene.

Aggie featured the Georgette Bauerdorf case in a front page article she wrote for the *Herald Express* edition of January 23, 1947. Under the subhead, WEREWOLVES LEAVE TRAIL OF WOMEN MURDER VICTIMS IN L.A., she included the Bauerdorf case along with seven other female victims of unsolved murders in recent Los Angeles history. The article raised the question of competency within the LAPD in making the streets of Los Angeles safe for young women.

There had been a growing concern among the citizens of Los Angeles about the number of unsolved murders on the police ledger, and Donahoe and the Sheriff's Department made every effort to convince the populace that an all-out effort was being made to solve the murder of Elizabeth Short. More than four hundred LAPD and Sheriff's officers were working the Black Dahlia case, knocking on doors, searching for witnesses, asking questions—and coming up empty handed.

Administrative Vice officer Vince Carter observed: "Miss Short's life in Hollywood seemed to follow a pattern. She didn't have any

Will 'Dahlia' Slaying Join Album of Unsolved Murders?

ELIZABETH SHORT   MRS ORA MURRAY   GEORGETTE BAUERDOF   GERTRUDE LANDON

The torture-slaying of Elizabeth Short, "The Black Dahlia," a week old today, may join the gory album of unsolved crimes against women in Los Angeles unless unexpected   clues turn up shortly. So far all clues have failed. Shown, above, are victims of some of most famous recent unsolved crimes in the city's history.

Hirohito
Emperor Sees the Dawn, Pens a Poem

By United Press
TOKIO, Jan. 23. A poem by Emperor Hirohito, based on his inspection of reconstruction activities at P bombed Mito City,

Werewolves Leave Trail of Women Murders in L. A.

In the gory album of unsolved murders, kidnapings and crimes against women in general, Los Angeles police may have to insert a new page—"The Mystery of the Sadistic Slaying of Elizabeth Short—the Black Dahlia." So far all

Comb Death Area

Aggie Underwood's front page story regarding the series of unsolved murders

visible signs of employment, she'd be broke, and then suddenly have some money. Her roommates, the bartenders, and the hotel clerks all came up with the same story. She was secretive—never one to confide. She never said what she was really doing, or who she was really going out with, or where she was really going.

"Several of Elizabeth's girlfriends at Carlos Avenue and the Chancellor said there were days when she would disappear," Carter recalled. "Each time she would be gone for a day or two after saying she was going to hitch a ride downtown to Sixth Street. Upon her return, she was always loaded with money and would pay all her bills. 'We never knew where she went, or where she got the money,' one of the girls said. 'She didn't have a job and didn't act as if she was looking for work. She would often borrow money from her friends, but always paid it back later.'

"I believe there were some acquaintances who knew her tragic story—like Lynn Martin, Ann Toth, Mark Hansen, and some of her roommates at the Chancellor," Carter said, "but they were afraid to talk about it because it involved some powerful and dangerous people. The Dahlia case was very complex. It went way beyond the Werewolf Killer story reported in the newspapers, and Sgt. Harry Hansen knew a lot more than he ever confided to anybody—including Big Jack Donahoe and Finis Brown."

After the first week of blazing headlines, the Black Dahlia case seemed to be stalled and was about to slip from the headlines to a spot beneath the fold, but a full moon rose over the city and Richardson providentially received a phone call from the "crazed Werewolf Killer."

Richardson recalled that, on the evening of Thursday, January 24, he was putting the next day's edition of the *Examiner* to bed, when he answered the phone and heard a voice he'd never forget:

"Is this the city editor?" the mysterious voice asked.

"Yes."

"What's your name, please?"

"Richardson."

"Well, Mr. Richardson, I must congratulate you on what the *Examiner* has done in the Black Dahlia case."

"Thank you," Richardson replied, wondering what the caller was getting at.

"You seem to have run out of material."

"That's right."

"Maybe I can be of some assistance," the caller said with a chuckle that sent a shiver up Richardson's spine.

"We need it," Richardson coolly commented.

"I'll tell you what I'll do," the caller said. "I'll send you some of the things she had with her when she, shall we say, disappeared?"

Richardson quickly scribbled, "Trace this call," on a piece of paper and flashed it in front of his secretary.

"What kind of things?" Richardson asked.

"Oh, say her address book and her birth certificate and a few other things she had in her handbag."

"When will I get them?"

"Oh, within the next day or so. See how far you can get with them. And now I must say good-bye."

"Wait a minute!" Richardson said, trying to keep the mysterious caller on the line.

"But aren't you trying to trace this call?" Richardson heard the caller say before the line went dead.

At the time, Richardson didn't know what to make of the call, but he had every reason to believe it was actually from the killer when an envelope postmarked January 24, 1947 was sent to the *Examiner* containing some of the contents known to be in Elizabeth's handbag when she vanished—including the claim stubs for her luggage checked at the Greyhound bus station on January 9.

Mailed at the main branch of the downtown Post Office and addressed to the "*Los Angeles Examiner* and other Los Angeles papers," the envelope was somehow intercepted by the postal inspectors and opened at Central in the presence of Capt. Donahoe, reporters, and homicide detectives. Addressed with words cut from Hearst newspapers, there was a paste-up note that read, "Here is Dahlia's belongings—letter to follow."

Included in the mysterious envelope along with the Greyhound claim stubs were Elizabeth's identification, her birth certificate, her Social Security card, her address book, the Matt Gordon obituary she always carried in her handbag, and business cards of several casual male acquaintances—including a man she had only recently met at the Hacienda Club in Mission Beach. Although the sender had soaked the envelope in gasoline to remove any residual fingerprints, the detectives found smudged prints, which were sent to the crime lab for examination but never publicly identified.[15]

It was assumed that only the killer could have possessed the contents of the handbag that Elizabeth was carrying when she was last seen alive, but Richardson may have wondered if the contents were still inside Elizabeth's handbag when somebody tossed it in the incinerator near Pico and Crenshaw. And he may have wondered if the contents were still inside the handbag when the police found it at the city dump. But if it all seemed a little too providential—the anonymous phone call, the phenomenal envelope, and the mysterious note—it was one of those big once-in-a-lifetime newsbreaks, and the red button in the cavernous press room was waiting to be pushed.

Among the contents of Elizabeth's purse that were found in the envelope was a brown address book in which she had written numerous names, addresses, and phone numbers. Upon examining the address book, Donahoe was quoted as saying, "This book is going to be dynamite!"

It was rumored that more than seventy-five names of prominent Angelenos and Hollywood personalities were listed on its pages. Donahoe refused to divulge the names for fear of "embarrassing persons not connected with the case," and the contents of Elizabeth's address book were never made public or allowed to be examined by reporters. Richardson learned that several names and addresses had been deliberately cut out of the book at some point prior to its being placed in the envelope, leading some to suspect that the excised names may have been a lead to the killer.

When it was discovered that the name of Mark Hansen, proprietor of the Florentine Gardens, was embossed in gold on the cover of the address book, Donahoe momentarily forgot his distaff theories and

---

15. Donahoe stated to the press that the prints had been forwarded to the FBI; however, Elizabeth Short's FBI file has no record of the FBI ever receiving these prints.

Elizabeth Short's address book and birth certificate, found among her belongings mailed to the *Examiner*

placed Mark Hansen high on his list of prime suspects. Upon being shown the address book by detectives, Mark Hansen identified it as one that had "once been sent to me from Denmark, my native country." He claimed it had been stolen from his desk about the time that Elizabeth moved out of his Carlos Street residence in October. "There were no entries in the book, no names of any individuals when I last saw it," Mark Hansen insisted. And police handwriting experts determined that all of the entries in the address book were written by Elizabeth Short.

The alleged killer's message to the *Examiner* and other Los Angeles newspapers, along with the contents of Elizabeth's handbag, had been a stroke of good fortune for Richardson, but lightning struck again on Monday, January 27, when a second message was received. This message was sent exclusively to the *Examiner* on a postcard and was also mailed at the main Post Office in downtown Los Angeles.

(LAPL PHOTO COLLECTION)

Here it is
Turning in Wed
Jan. 29 10 A.M.
Had my fun at Police
Black Dahlia Avenger

Capt. Donahoe told the press that he believed the postcard message was legitimate and constituted the "letter to follow" promised by the killer. "The fact that the postcard was written by hand, rather than lettered with words cut out of newspapers," Donahoe reasoned, "also supports the theory that the killer intends to turn himself in, and no longer needs to take pains to conceal his identity." In his statements to the press, Donahoe expressed optimism that the killer was, indeed, about to surrender. "In signing the postcard, 'Black Dahlia Avenger,'" Donahoe theorized, "he is indicating that he murdered Elizabeth Short for some avenged wrong, either real or imagined. So far we haven't seen any evidence of that, but we hope that the killer who is writing these notes keeps his promise to turn himself in on Wednesday."

The implication was that the killer was going to turn himself in to the *Examiner*; and as the days went by and Richardson and the city waited for the hour that the killer was to surrender, the Dahlia head-

lines and the public's fascination with the case reached a new high.

In a message that Donahoe publicly sent to the killer via a press release to the Los Angeles papers, he promised the killer, "If you want to surrender as indicated by the postcard now in our hands, I will meet you at any public location at any time or at the Homicide detail office at City Hall. Communicate immediately by telephone—MI 5217 Extension 2521 or by mail."

But if the killer had tried to call, he would have gotten a busy signal—the line was flooded with calls from crackpots and hoaxsters.

In his note to the *Examiner*, the "Black Dahlia Avenger" said he would surrender at 10:00 A.M. on January 29. By 9:00 A.M. that Wednesday morning, Donahoe had posted detectives at all the *Examiner* doors, waiting to nab the killer when he showed up. At the same time, reporters from other newspapers were sneaking into the Hearst building, hoping to beat the *Examiner* onto the street with the story. After chasing all the rival reporters out of the building, Richardson called Donahoe.

"Get your boys away from here," he told Donahoe. "Nobody's going to turn themselves in with them standing there all eagle-eyed. If he comes, I promise I'll call you!"

"All right," Donahoe said, playing the game. "But understand I'm taking him out of there at once. No deal this time. You can't hide out a murderer without getting yourself into real trouble. You know that, don't you?"

As the clock on the wall approached 10:00 A.M., Richardson took two of his little white pills and waited. "All that morning the city room was unusually quiet," Will Fowler remembered. "I don't think any of us really believed the killer would show, but there was always the outside chance that he would."

Noon rolled by and the Black Dahlia Avenger had not revealed himself. Richardson patiently waited by his phone in case he called. "All that day I had a king-size sweat," Richardson recalled. He "sweated" until midnight when the next day's edition had to be put to bed. The Black Dahlia Avenger never showed before they had to press the red button and roll the presses for the Thursday morning run. Richardson knew somebody had made a fool out of him, but he wasn't sure if it was the "Werewolf Killer," some crackpot, or "Big Jack" Donahoe.

Memory Morgue

WHILE JIM RICHARDSON held little admiration for Jack Donahoe and the upper echelons of the LAPD, he often played their game and ran with screaming headlines down dead-end avenues. However, there were other avenues of investigation that never received an assignment from Richardson, and Will Fowler disclosed an intriguing back-story regarding Richardson, City Hall, William Randolph Hearst, and the Black Dahlia case.

Richardson got his start in the newspaper business through his uncle, Friend Richardson, who had been a newspaper editor and protégé of William Randolph Hearst before becoming the Governor of California (1923–1927). It was Governor Friend Richardson who had appointed Fletcher Bowron to the judges' bench prior to Bowron's run for Mayor of Los Angeles in 1939; and the governor's nephew, Jim Richardson, had become a close friend of Bowron during the years when Jim Richardson had risen through the Hearst ranks to become the managing editor of the *Examiner*.

According to Will Fowler, Jim Richardson had once been a fiercely independent Hearst reporter and editor before succumbing to the chronic newspaperman's disease—alcoholism. In 1937 he had been fired by Hearst because of his drinking problem. After drying out, he worked for a period of time in the publicity department at Warner Bros., before his friend, Mayor Bowron, intervened with Hearst and persuaded him to rehire Richardson—with the proviso that he would never drink again. Richardson never drank again, nor was he ever the same fiercely independent newsman again. He was beholden to Mayor Bowron, and according to Will Fowler, there were avenues in the Black Dahlia case leading toward City Hall that Richardson knew would never be explored by the *Examiner*.

Up until the Dahlia case, Aggie Underwood at the *Herald Express* had also managed to maintain her independence and integrity. Aggie's article concerning the many unsolved murders of young women in the city may have ruffled some bristles at City Hall, but she felt that was her calling. It was during her research on all the open murder files on the police ledger that Aggie recalled the link between the murder of Elizabeth Short and the murder of Georgette Bauerdorf. And it wasn't until Aggie culled the correlation between the two murders from her memory morgue that she, too, was maneuvered into silence and a compromise of her journalistic integrity.

While Aggie's article about the city's numerous unsolved murders of young women was disturbing to many Angelenos, it was particularly upsetting to Sam Wolf, a close friend of my stepfather. Sam Wolf, who was Jeff's attorney, as well as the attorney for Monogram Pictures, was Georgette's uncle and guardian. At the time of her murder, he had been called upon by the coroner to identify the body. Sam and his wife were frequent visitors to our home, and I can recall several grim conversations about Georgette. Sam was deeply disturbed that the authorities never found the killer, and when Aggie's article appeared, it brought back all the pain regarding the unsolved murder of his niece.

Georgette Bauerdorf and Elizabeth Short were both born in 1924, but Georgette had been born into a wealthy New York family and had lived on Park Avenue before moving to Los Angeles. And while

Elizabeth had been waiting tables in Miami, Georgette had been a student at the Marlborough School and graduated from the exclusive Westlake School for Girls in Bel Air in June 1942.

Georgette's mother was Sam Wolf's sister, Connie, and according to Sam, Georgette had been sent to private schools on the West Coast because she wasn't getting along with her parents. She was extremely independent, very social, and somewhat of a "party girl." As her guardian, Sam paid her bills, supervised her education, and helped her find an apartment in the fashionable El Palacio at 8493 Fountain Avenue in West Hollywood, where her murder took place.

Through the years, the El Palacio, which stood on the corner of Fountain and La Cienega Boulevard, had been the transitory home of a number of film stars and celebrities, including Joan Crawford, John Garfield, Franchot Tone, and Evelyn Keyes. Mafioso Johnny Rosselli became an El Palacio resident after his release from prison in 1947, and his pal, actor John Carroll, was a tenant when he looked after Marilyn Monroe following the lapse of her initial contract at Fox. Because the apartment building was in West Hollywood and just outside the jurisdiction of the LAPD, the Bauerdorf murder investigation was handled by the Los Angeles County Sheriff's Department, which investigated West Hollywood homicides.

Georgette's body was discovered by Mr. and Mrs. Charles Atwood, who were the building managers and lived next to her apartment. The Atwoods told detectives they had been awakened sometime after midnight on Wednesday, October 11, 1944 by a "commotion" and what sounded like a crash of "something metallic." The next morning they found Georgette's door ajar and heard the sound of water running inside. Mrs. Atwood knocked on the door, and when no one answered, she entered with her husband and found the apartment flooded with water pouring from the bathtub faucet. To their horror, they discovered Georgette's body submerged in the bathtub.

When the detectives from the Sheriff's Department arrived, they determined that Georgette had been assaulted and raped in the bedroom and died from asphyxiation. Bloodstains were found on the floor near the bed, along with the cut and torn bottom half of her pajamas, which had been sliced by a knife. Apparently the killer had fled after placing the body in the bathtub and turning on the water. Because the water had been left running, detectives theorized that the killer may have been frightened off by someone approaching the building. Georgette's neighbor, prominent Hollywood drama coach Stella Adler, recalled that she had returned to her apartment sometime after midnight and noticed that Georgette's door was ajar.

At the inquest, it was determined by Medical Examiner Frank Webb that Georgette's murder had taken place close to midnight, and the cause of death was "obstruction of upper air passages by inserted cloth." Dr. Webb stated, "Abrasions on the knuckles of the girl's hands showed she had fought desperately against the attacker. Thumb and finger marks on her face, lips, abdomen, and thighs indicated the attacker was powerful with almost ape-like hands. . . . The victim had been asphyxiated prior to the time that the body had been placed in the bathtub."

Sheriff's detectives found Georgette's handbag on the floor near the bedroom door—its contents strewn nearby. The car keys were missing, and her green Oldsmobile coupé, which she normally kept in the Palacio garage, was gone. Three days later, Georgette's car was found parked at the curb in front of 7281½ East Twenty-fifth Street, not far from the corner of Twenty-fifth and San Pedro Street, south of downtown Los Angeles. The key had been left in the ignition, and sheriff investigators concluded that the car had been abandoned there by the killer. A neighborhood witness described seeing a tall man who walked with a limp get out of the car and head toward San Pedro Street.

Georgette was last seen alive by coworkers when she left the Hollywood Canteen near Sunset and Wilcox, at approximately 10:30 P.M., on the evening of Wednesday, October 11, 1944. Like Elizabeth Short, she served as a junior hostess and would socialize and dance with scrvicemen on leave in the Hollywood area. Her friend, June Ziegler, also a Canteen volunteer, told sheriff detectives that she recalled Georgette dancing with a number of different servicemen that evening, as she usually did, but during the previous week, she had danced with an army private whom Georgette had found to be annoying and quite bothersome. June described the private as having a limp and standing well over six feet tall.

Ziegler recalled a conversation she had with Georgette on the evening that the murder took place: "She was seated in her car near the Canteen when I arrived about six-thirty. She was knitting and appeared quite nervous. I climbed in the car, and we talked for about thirty minutes before we went inside. She told me she was nervous and asked if I would spend the night with her. At the time I did not pay much attention because I thought she was just nervous about a trip she had planned to visit her boyfriend, Jerry, in El Paso, which I knew she had kept a secret from everyone but myself."

Detectives found many fingerprints throughout the apartment as well as in Georgette's car. Prints were also found on a light bulb in a fixture above the entrance to Georgette's apartment. The bulb above the entryway had been unscrewed so that it could not be switched on, leaving the area outside the door in darkness. Investigators theorized the killer may have been recognizable to Georgette, so he unscrewed the bulb and stood in the dark to avoid recognition before forcing his entry once the door was opened.

The fixture was eight feet above the tiled entryway and could only have been reached by a person well over six feet tall. The prints of the killer, however, were never identified.[16]

---

16. That same light fixture still hangs outside the door of Georgette's old apartment at 8493 Fountain Avenue. In November 2003, I stood on the spot where the killer stood when he unscrewed the bulb. Though I stand 6'1" and have long arms, I was three inches short of reaching the light bulb. I estimated that the killer must have been at least 6'4" tall.

It was the body in the bathtub that compelled Aggie Underwood to pull the unsolved Bauerdorf case out of her memory morgue. She began to suspect that the Bauerdorf

Georgette Bauerdorf. (UCLA SPECIAL COLLECTIONS)

The entrance to Georgette's apartment was behind the gates and to the left. The light fixture is eight feet above the entry. (ANN WOLFE)

murder may have had a connection to the Black Dahlia case. Although the MO was quite different, there was that peculiar bathtub murder correlation. And Aggie had heard through her contacts in the Sheriff's Department that detectives had found and confiscated Georgette's diary, which documented that she had known Elizabeth Short when they both were working as volunteers at the Hollywood Canteen in September and October of 1944.

According to Aggie's source, both Georgette and Elizabeth had been familiar with a Hollywood celebrity they had met at the Can teen. The celebrity, a well-known actor at the time, became a suspect in both the Bauerdorf murder and the Black Dahlia case and was brought in for questioning. Although it was never mentioned by the Sheriff's Department, the LAPD, or the press, the actor was Arthur Lake, who was under contract to Columbia Pictures and played Dagwood Bumstead in the *Blondie* movies.

Hollywood Canteen records were checked by the Sheriff's Department, and a former hostess had recalled that Arthur Lake socialized with both of the murdered girls. When Lake met with detectives from the Sheriff's Homicide Division, he reluctantly told Det. Frank Esquival that he "may have talked to Elizabeth Short and Georgette Bauerdorf in the Canteen." Beyond that, he said he wouldn't be able to help the investigation.

"Dagwood looked us straight in the face from one to the other," Esquival recalled, "and said he wanted us to understand that his wife, Patricia, was the niece of Marion Davies, a close friend of William Randolph Hearst and George Bauerdorf, the murdered girl's father." Lake then said that any further questions would have to be handled through his attorney.

Sheriff's investigators believed that there was a link between the Bauerdorf murder and the Black Dahlia case and that Arthur Lake should be questioned further, but Det. Esquival told Aggie that the investigation into both cases had been blocked and that logical avenues of investigation were shut down.

After Aggie wrote her article about the unsolved crimes involving the murder of Georgette Bauerdorf, Elizabeth Short, and a number of other young women, which appeared in the *Herald Express* on January 27, 1947, she began working on a story about the similarities between the Bauerdorf murder and the Black Dahlia case and the Arthur Lake connection. But before the article was completed, she was told by managing editor Lou Young to kill the story, and she was told that she was being pulled off the Dahlia case.

"Why?" Aggie demanded to know. "Why don't you want me to do the Bauerdorf-Dahlia story?"

"Because the Boss said to kill it!" Lou Young explained.

"The Boss" was William Randolph Hearst, and Aggie suspected that Hearst may have killed the story connecting the Bauerdorf and Dahlia murders because of his friendship with the Bauerdorf girl's father, who abhorred notoriety. But why was Aggie pulled off the Dahlia case? Whatever the reason, she was angry and considered taking her talents to another newspaper when she was suddenly promoted from reporter to city editor.

"They kicked me up the ladder. . . . It made my head spin," Aggie recalled. "But did I want to be City Editor of the *Herald*, or did I want to be a reporter with my thumb on a doorbell?" No woman had ever been appointed city editor at a major metropolitan newspaper before, and Aggie found it a difficult promotion to resist.

"What about the Bauerdorf case?" she asked Lou Young.

"That is a word dat's verboten," Young replied. "We will not recognize that name anymore at the *Herald*."

"I decided that I wanted to be City Editor at the *Herald*," Aggie recalled, and she knew that acceptance of her promotion had to do with her silence. "That's all I'd ever say about the Bauerdorf or the Dahlia case," Aggie said. "But I'd lay awake many a night wondering if I did the right thing." Aggie strongly suspected there was a connection between Arthur Lake and the murder of Georgette Bauerdorf and Elizabeth Short, though it would be years before she discovered exactly what the connection was or precisely why "the Boss" had killed the Bauerdorf story and taken her off the Dahlia case.

When Elizabeth Short's killer failed to show up at the *Examiner* at 10:00 A.M. on Wednesday, January 29, the Black Dahlia case began running out of steam. Paste-up notes by the supposed killer continued to arrive at the Hearst papers, but Harry Hansen considered them to be hoaxes.

Dahlia "Slayer" Fails to Keep Appointment

After examining the first four notes, Ray Pinker's crime lab determined they were sent by the same person, and Donahoe dramatically stated, "We are dealing with a homicidal maniac who craves attention for his crime and may come forward in a bold and spectacular manner for his curtain call after he has wrung out the last drop of drama from his deed."

Esteemed questioned document examiner Clark Sellers was hired by Jim Richardson to analyze the one handwritten note among the first four notes, and in Sellers's report to the *Examiner* he stated, "It was evident the writer took great pains to disguise his or her personality by printing instead of writing the message and by endeavoring to appear illiterate. But the style and formation of the printed letters betrayed the writer as an educated person."

According to Will Fowler, Jim Richardson had privately concluded that the phone call from the killer, the first four paste-up notes, and the mailing of the contents of Elizabeth's purse had been contrived by Donahoe. "Richardson suspected that Donahue was covering up the murder, which was connected to the mob and some big-shot at City Hall," Fowler stated. "But it was an avenue Richardson didn't pursue."

It wasn't long before the press began receiving copycat paste-ups from various crackpots. More than a dozen notes were sent to the *Examiner* and the *Herald Express*—each more ludicrous than the last,

Note mailed to the LAPD on January 29, 1947, the day the killer was supposed to turn himself in (*above*).

Note mailed to the *Los Angeles Herald Express* on January 30, 1947 (*right*).

and it became difficult to discern between the first four notes and the spurious paste-ups that followed. In the meantime, the confessing Sams continued lining up, and Donahoe kept releasing his absurd headline-grabbing pronouncements. On February 1, 1947, Donahoe stated:

It appears impossible that the Short girl was murdered in the city. We are forced to this conclusion by the failure of any-one to report a possible place where she was killed within the city limits. If she was slain in a house or a room or motel in the city, it seems impossible that some trace has not been reported or found. This leads us to the conclusion that she was killed outside the city. The killer could not have emerged from the place in clothing worn when the murder was com-mitted and the body drained of blood. He could have been too easily detected and stains would have attracted attention.

Placing the murder outside the city got Donahoe and the LAPD somewhat off the hook for not solving the horrendous crime and ap-prehending the "homicidal maniac." Donahoe would suddenly disclose various sites outside the city as suspected murder locations—only to abruptly eliminate them.

A virtual fountain of babble, Donahoe kept floating out new theo-ries about the murder, which, he maintained, "may not have taken place in Los Angeles," "may have been committed by a woman with lesbian tendencies," "may have been committed by someone she knew," "may not have been committed by someone she knew." Finis Brown recalled that Harry Hansen didn't mind Donahoe babbling to the press, as long as it didn't effect his own investigation. But Hansen didn't trust Donahoe and felt he was deliberately manipulating the facts. Hansen suspected that the actual scene of the murder was somewhere near the site where Elizabeth Short's handbag and shoes had been discovered in the incinerator, near Pico and Crenshaw, but Donahoe seemed to go out of his way to dispel that notion.

Robert Manley had positively identified the purse and the shoes found in the incinerator as those Elizabeth was wearing on January 9, when he last saw her; however, several days after Manley's positive ID, Donahoe called in Elvera and Dorothy French from San Diego to identify the handbag and shoes. The Frenches said they weren't certain whether the items belonged to Elizabeth or not; and on January 28, 1947, Donahoe sent out a press release stating that the shoes and handbag recovered from the incinerator had not belonged to Miss Short after all and that Robert Manley must have been mistaken. Yet, the last time the Frenches had seen Elizabeth was on January 8, and they had not seen her or what she may have been wearing when Manley dropped her off at the Biltmore the following day.

Although Harry Hansen had little respect for Capt. Donahoe, there was a corrupt element within the LAPD that held him in high regard. According to Vince Carter, it was well known by a number of officers in Administrative Vice that the upper echelons of the LAPD were receiving payoffs from the Syndicate, and that the payoffs had been arranged by the Syndicate's operative at Central—Capt. Jack Donahoe:

> The old-line vice-payoff from the Mafia to corrupt police officials had tapered off after a new Syndicate territorial vice-map had been drawn up by Lucky Luciano and Meyer Lansky in the '30s. But when Captain Jack Donahoe came into power at Central in 1945, he seized the opportunity to reorganize and juice up the vice-take by key police officials, which included Chief Clemence B. Horrall, Assistant Chief Joseph Reed, and Captain William Burns of the Gangster Squad. As the vice-take enforcer, Donahoe did the dirty work and squeezed the juice that kept everybody happy, except the honest cops, who knew they'd never rise above the rank of Sergeant, and had to deal with the gangsters on the street, as well as those within the LAPD—like "Big Jack" Donahoe, as he was often called within the department.

According to Vince Carter, many officers in Administrative Vice knew that Donahoe was misleading the press and the public regarding the facts in the Black Dahlia case, but they were afraid to come forward because of Donahoe's underworld friends:

> Donahoe had a reputation as a killer, and he was a close friend of another killer—Jack Dragna, who was Lucky Luciano's West Coast representative. Somewhere along the way, Jack Dragna and Captain Jack Donahoe became friends. Dragna had control over the narcotics business, and Donahoe was an important contact. . . . It was Dragna who introduced Donahoe to Chickie Stein, Dragna's narcotics distributor in L.A., and she and Donahoe became quite close. Chickie was a beautiful Sicilian woman with dark brown eyes who was brought up in a New York whorehouse. Her mother had been one of Lucky Luciano's whorehouse madams. . . . Chickie was introduced to Dragna by Luciano when she was in her early twenties. Luciano trusted her completely, and when Luciano was arrested by Thomas Dewey, and Chickie's mother's prostitution business folded, Chickie came to Los Angeles as Luciano's West Coast heroin connection under Dragna's guidance. Donahoe and Chickie became close friends, and he presented her with a gold medallion with the Christ crucifixion on one side and the Star of David on the other. Chickie wore this around her neck on a fine gold chain. On one occasion she showed it to me, and Captain Jack Donahoe's name was engraved on one side of the medallion. Chickie was as proud of it as if it had been given to her by one of the mob bosses—which in my opinion was not too far off the mark.

Part of Donahoe's strategy in misleading the press and the public in the Black Dahlia case involved his references to Elizabeth Short as a suspected lesbian. Will Fowler and *Herald Express* reporter Bevo Means were told by a Donahoe underling and a deputy coroner that

Elizabeth couldn't have sex with men. "Something in the autopsy indicated lesbian pathology," they were told.

"It was a leak," Will Fowler recalled, "and Bevo jumped on it figuring if she couldn't have sex with guys, she was having sex with women." Following Donahoe's calculated plant of this sensational, misleading information, a number of stories appeared in the newspapers indicating that the autopsy report established that Elizabeth had infantile sex organs, and therefore, could not have normal relationships with men. This misinformation initiated by Donahoe has been promulgated by a number of journalists for more than fifty years.

However, in a letter to Mary Pacios, who knew Elizabeth and was the author of *Childhood Shadows: The Hidden Story of the Black Dahlia Murder*, Will Fowler finally acknowledged on February 25, 1988 that the disclosure of Elizabeth's inability to have sexual relationships with men was fiction. Fowler wrote: "Regarding my telling you Elizabeth Short had 'infantile sex organs,' *that is untrue*, and a ploy used to shock all of faint stomachs."[17] But beyond "shocking all of faint stomachs," this ploy also allayed suspicions that Elizabeth may have been pregnant when she was murdered—as did the lesbian stories propagated by the press. Hearst reporter Sid Hughes was told to canvass all the known lesbian bars in the city in an effort to establish that Elizabeth was an habitué who consorted with the lesbian clientele; and prestigious author and screenwriter Ben Hecht wrote a Dahlia article for the *Herald Express* in which he labeled Elizabeth a lesbian and maintained she was murdered by a lesbian acquaintance.

The Hecht article, which appeared in the *Herald Express* on February 1, 1947, was riddled with absurdity and relied largely on double-talk and pseudo-scientific mumbo-jumbo. Hecht writes: "The manner in which the 'Black Dahlia' was done to death, befouled and butchered after expiring under diverse torture, bespeaks

---

17. See Appendix A, page 340.

the looks, sex, height, weight, coloring, and even type of hair of the killer. It was a crime done by a lesbian—and not intended to be a crime. The killing itself may well have been part of the didoes to which the 'Black Dahlia' had submitted herself. She too, was an odd one, and because of her physical and glandular and psychic make-up given to humoring the fancies of women. . . ."

Bringing in spurious pseudo-science, Hecht goes on to say that the killer was a woman who was "a hyper

Ben Hecht, Author of 'Front Page,' Writes His Views on Dahlia Case

Ben Hecht, once an avid Chicago crime reporter, has graduated into writing and producing for pictures. He has come a long way from the days when he wrote "1001 Afternoons in Chicago," with a string of noteworthy novels and the great newspaper play, "The Front Page," the latter in collaboration with Charles MacArthur.

But Hecht has not forgotten newspaper days and when The Evening Herald and Express asked him to do a story on the "Black Dahlia" murder he made a typical Hechtian reply:

"Sure. I always was a newspaperman."

Here is Hecht's theory of the sensational crime, a theory based on the reasoning of a veteran reporter who has covered many big stories:

By BEN HECHT

The manner of a crime often presents a picture of the criminal. This is an axiom that came into police work with the advent of endocrinology—the study of our glands.

The manner in which the "Black Dahlia" was done to death, befouled and butchered after expiring under divers tortures, bespeaks the looks, sex, height, weight, coloring, and even type of hair of the killer.

Not only endocrinology but the history of similar crimes contribute a first look at our missing monster. In nearly all torture-crime cases and mutilation after death — homosexuality is the basic motive. It is the perverted sex type that usually, in the commission of a murder, explodes

beyond normality and elaborates its mischief with hack saws, axes and antic horrors.

It is for this reason that I believe the Black Dahlia's killer to have been a woman.

The sadism revealed in the butchery of the girl also indicates to me that there was no element of revenge in the killing. A man or woman seeking revenge may indulge with satisfaction in torture. (Continued on Page 2, Column 1)

thyroidic type of human, with an over developed thymus gland at work—driven into a thyroidal storm by some great shock."

Adding to his absurdities, Hecht proceeded to find faulty grammar as an indication that the killer was a female. Citing the handwritten note to the *Examiner* in which the killer proclaimed, "Had my fun at the Police," Hecht maintained that the killer's grammatical error in using "at" instead of "with" could only have been "a female malapropism, and an infantile one (an over developed thyroid bespeaks infantilism). Little girls often say, 'Give it *at* me!'"

Hecht then proceeded to provide a detailed description of the killer: "She is a woman of forty. She is 5 feet 6 inches tall. She weighs 115 pounds. She is thin, almost gaunt. She has a rudimentary bosom. Her face is long and narrow. She has a receding chin. Her teeth are slightly oversized. She has brown and very wavy hair. Her fingers are long. And she has large eyes—unusually large and arresting eyes. And she has a 'European' accent, as well."

Curiously, it was a perfect cross-gender description of Maurice Clement.

Though the Hecht article was a blatant con job, there was an odd postscript to its convoluted conclusion. After having had his fun *at* the reader, Hecht changed gambits and negated everything he had previously said about the Dahlia case by tersely stating that the killer wasn't a woman—it was a *man*, and that he knew the killer's name and the psychology behind the killing, but that he was unable to disclose "a second version of the crime and its perpetrator, which I am unable to offer this, or any other paper."

It was an odd conclusion to a very strange article. At that time, Hecht was one of the most highly paid writers in Hollywood, having written the screenplays for *Scarface* (1932), *Nothing Sacred* (1936), *Wuthering Heights* (1939), *Gone with the Wind*—not credited (1939), and *Notorious* (1946).

Hecht had not written a crime story for a newspaper since his days as a Hearst crime reporter in Chicago back in the twenties, and he may have done the article with the lesbian allegation as a favor. He was a pal of William Randolph Hearst, as well as Gene Fowler and his son, *Examiner* reporter William Randolph Fowler. He also palled around with Bugsy Siegel, Mickey Cohen, and the Brenda Allen Syndicate milieu. Hecht may have been telling the truth when he stated that he knew the name of the killer "and the psychology behind the killing."

By the end of the third week of intense investigations, Donahoe had to admit to the press that the police were stymied. They had no suspects, no leads, no clues, no witnesses—not even a murder site. The Black Dahlia case files were overflowing with false confessions, false leads, false suspects—but not one shred of real evidence. "No lead had any conclusions," Finis Brown stated. "Once we found

DAHLIA CASE 'IDIOTS' DELIGHT'; MORE 'CONFESSIONS' AND 'LETTERS'

HERALD ⚒ Express

Man, Two Women All Claim Torture Killing

Weird Jumble of Murder

something, it seemed to disappear in front of our eyes. Following any of those leads was like going down one-way streets with dead ends."

Harry Hansen believed that in order to identify the killer in the Black Dahlia case, it was essential to know the victim; but it was difficult to know Elizabeth Short. She was a very private person, who lived in her own dangerous dream world, and was constantly on the move to the next dream, the next guy, the next hotel, the next city. Nevertheless, Hansen was following his own leads and making progress with the case. "He was a brilliant detective, a smart, smart man; but a loner and an odd bird," Finis said. "He wasn't liked—not that he was disliked—he just wasn't liked. He was too removed and too above others in his own thinking and in his way of holding himself and his opinions about others and police work in general."

One of Hansen's problems was that he was an honest cop devoted to his calling. He always defended the Force, yet had to deal with the corruption that surrounded him. He had an intense dislike for his boss, "Big Jack" Donahoe, but kept his silence. The secret of the sealed autopsy established a motive in the pathological murder and provided avenues of investigation that Hansen believed Donahoe and the Gangster Squad were blocking. When Hansen discovered that Finis was reporting everything he was investigating to

Gangster Squad commander Willie Burns, he began to suspect that Finis was a Gangster Squad operative, and they had a falling out; Hansen stopped confiding in Finis and locked up his private Dahlia files.

"I was personally concerned that Harry kept saying he was going to yank the papers from the morgue," Finis recalled. "I said, 'Harry, you can't monkey with the coroner.' . . . He said I was a fine one to talk about ethics, and I was lucky I wasn't in jail, or off the Force . . . Then he laughed, but he was serious."

Former reporter Chuck Cheatham, who covered the Black Dahlia case for the *Long Beach Independent*, recalled, "Harry Hansen was well liked by some, and hated by others. I liked Harry. He wasn't on the take—not Hansen. Some people say they were all on the take, the police. They all had their circles of people they protected. But not Harry—straight as they come. His partner, Finis Brown, that's another story."

The district attorney's Black Dahlia files confirm that Harry Hansen's growing suspicion that Finis Brown was a secret operative of the Gangster Squad was correct. When Lt. Jemison called Gangster Squad officer Sgt. Conwell Keller to testify before the 1949 Grand Jury, Keller testified:

Jemison: Now, you were in the Record Division of Intelligence during part of this time?

Keller: In the Gangster Squad.

Jemison: Did you not as such have something to do with the use, delivery or filing of the records in connection with the investigation as to the death of Elizabeth Short?

Keller: Yes, I did.

Jemison: What did you do in that particular? To whom did you report and what did you do with your reports?

Keller: Well, in the office, we tried to keep the reports together—in other words to keep the complete file going all the time on that particular case.

Jemison: Was that while you were in the Gangster Squad?

Keller: That is correct.

Jemison: Gangster Squad—they had their own files?

Keller: We did at that time. Now, it is in Intelligence files.

Jemison: We understand. To your knowledge, was there also a file kept in Homicide?

Keller: I have never seen that file. I have heard of it.

Jemison: Did you cooperate with any members of Homicide in your investigations?

Keller: We—we had Sgt. Brown, who is assigned to—well, he was assigned to our detail, evidently worked with us. He was in our office during our investigation.

Although Hansen discovered that Finis and Donahoe were in league with the Gangster Squad in derailing the Black Dahlia case, he continued pursuing his own avenues of investigation, and he had begun deciphering the silent scream. Harry Hansen knew that a man with advanced medical knowledge had methodically bisected the body. He knew the approximate location of the murder site. He knew the dark secret of the autopsy. He knew there had been more than one person in attendance at the sacred setting. And he suspected that one of them was the short, dark-complexioned man who drove the old black Ford sedan—Brenda Allen's procurer, Maurice Clement.

BUNKO ARTISTS CALL it "cooling down the mark." After the con-man has played out his con and taken in the sucker, or the mark, he plays for time with diversions, false stories, and misinformation. With the passage of time and the dulling of wits, the mark often settles back in confusion and never solves the riddle of the con.

Cooling down the mark has often been the methodology of small-time con-artists, civic leaders, corporate executives, and government committees. In the Black Dahlia case, the general public proved to be the mark. New and diverting stories about the murder kept hitting the headlines until the public grew tired and confused. Each headline-grabbing diversion ultimately lacked substance but gave the impression that the police were doing their job. According to Capt. Donahoe, apprehension of the killer was always just around the corner—a corner that inevitably led to a dead-end on a cold trail.

By early February, the Black Dahlia case began dropping from the banner headlines to a spot beneath the fold. And in the ensuing weeks, Dahlia stories became sporadic and consigned to the back pages, as other murders and scandals made the headlines.

On February 10, 1947, the murder of aviatrix Jeanne French became the lead story. Her nude body was found in an isolated area of Culver City, seven miles west of Liemert Park. The victim had been "kicked and stomped to death," and the killer had written an obscenity and the letters "BD" or "PD" on her torso with red lipstick. Capt. Donahoe publicly stated that the Black Dahlia murder and the so-called "Red Lipstick Murder" of Jeanne French were related. But it was obvious to Harry Hansen and other investigators that there was no relationship between the two cases. The MO was totally different. The Jeanne French murder appeared to have been an act of pure rage. There were no knife wounds or surgical incisions, and the victim had been violently kicked to death at the site where her body was discovered; conversely, Elizabeth Short had been methodically mutilated and bisected by a person with advanced medical knowledge at a site other than where the body was found.

Donahoe's promulgated theory about the connection between the murder of Elizabeth Short and the murder of Jeanne French proved to be his last public pronouncement regarding the Black Dahlia case. On February 19, he was summarily removed from his position as commander of the Homicide Division and transferred by Chief of Detectives William Bradley to robbery detail. According to Vince Carter, Donahoe's problems began when Hansen learned that Donahoe had arranged for two officers from the Gangster Squad to conduct advance interviews with some of the personalities found in Elizabeth Short's address book. When Hansen arranged to question these personalities, he found in many cases that they had already been questioned by Gangster Squad officers Archie Case and James Ahern.

"Captain Donahoe was afraid that when Hansen questioned the people whose names were left in the address book, they would come up with evidence connecting them to the names that had been removed," Carter recalled. "That was the reason he sent the two Gangster Squad detectives out ahead to interview the people whose names were in the book." It was a violation of procedure, and Hansen became furious with Donahoe and complained to Chief of Detectives, William Bradley. Hansen had discovered that Case and Ahern had been assigned by Assistant Chief Joe Reed and Donahoe to find out how much certain people in the address book may have known about the connection between the Black Dahlia and an important public figure on the police commission. One of those interviewed by Case and Ahern was Columbia contract player, Arthur Lake, who was a close friend of the Chandler family heir—Norman Chandler, publisher of the *Los Angeles Times* and head of the police commission.

"After that, things were never the same between Hansen and Donahoe," Vince Carter recalled. "Hansen never did like Donahoe, or the way he handled the Black Dahlia case, and their relationship became more and more strained. Finis Brown became the go-between until Donahoe was finally transferred to robbery detail."

Following the Red Lipstick Murder, there were a number of gang land shootings, earthquakes, and Hollywood scandals that captured the headlines. On February 22, 1947, a mysterious shooting made the news. It was reported that Brenda Allen's friend and partner, Sgt. Evan V. Jackson of the Vice Squad, killed a robber with his service revolver. According to the newspaper coverage, Sgt. Jackson was sitting in a car with a lady acquaintance by the name of Marie Blanque when a hoodlum approached the car with a gun. Sgt. Jackson managed to shoot the robber, who died instantly, but an accomplice escaped in a getaway car.

Although the headline stories of the shooting quickly faded to the back pages, it did not escape the attention of Sgt. Charles Stoker, who noted that the shooting took place near the Ambassador Hotel in front of Brenda Allen's apartment at the corner of Ninth Street and Fedora Avenue. Deciding to attend the inquest, Stoker noted that Brenda Allen was in attendance, and he soon learned that she was the "Marie Blanque" who was said to be in the car at the time of the shooting. The inquest established that the dead man was Roy "Pee-Wee" Lewis, a Mafia gunman from Chicago, and that the weapon he was carrying was a machinegun. His intention wasn't robbery; it was to kill the driver of the car—Brenda Allen.

Disturbed that Homicide and Administrative Vice were anxious to keep the name of Hollywood's vice-queen out of the papers, Stoker assumed it was because of the police pay-offs and her association with Sgt. Jackson, which could have ignited a newsflash firestorm. The fact that Brenda Allen was the intended victim of the shooting—which took place less than five weeks after the murder of Elizabeth Short—was never disclosed by the press or the police.

There was talk within Administrative Vice that the attempted murder of Brenda Allen had been contracted by Jack Dragna, and it had something to do with Brenda's knowledge about the murder of Elizabeth Short and the site where the murder took place. Brenda Allen's apartment at Ninth Street and Fedora Avenue and the girls' bungalow court on Catalina were approximately thirty blocks from Thirty-ninth Street and Norton and fifteen blocks from the incinerator on

Crenshaw where the purse and shoes were found. Shortly after the shooting incident, Brenda moved out of the Fedora apartment and went into hiding. Several months later, Stoker learned she was operating out of a house she had rented above the Sunset Strip on Cory Avenue—well within Bugsy Siegel's vice-map territory.

According to Robert Slatzer, there were rumors in Hollywood that the Black Dahlia killing was connected to Brenda Allen and the mob, and he recalled that Marilyn Monroe had been very disturbed by Elizabeth Short's murder. "Marilyn was convinced that she had 'gotten herself in trouble' and was murdered by some of the underworld figures that hung around the Florentine Gardens," Slatzer recalled. "Marilyn became frightened by what had occurred and never went back there."

It was five months after the Black Dahlia murder and four months after the attempted murder of Brenda Allen that Bugsy Siegel's murder hit the headlines—June 20, 1947. On the Friday night that Bugsy was shot, I had gone to the movies with some school friends and didn't return home until close to midnight. When I entered the house, everyone was up, and the household seemed unusually tense. My mother was upset with Uncle Vern about something, and Jeff was trying to calm my mother down—only to be interrupted by the phone, which was constantly ringing. My brother, Robert, filled me in on Bugsy's murder, which had taken place just across the alleyway earlier in the evening. My first instinct was to run over there and check out the scene, but Linden Drive and the alleyway had been blocked off by the police.

The next morning I was up by sunrise and hurried around the corner before the spectator parade began. I found Bugsy's house had been sealed and several Beverly Hills police officers were guarding the entry. But by walking up the neighbor's driveway, I could look through the lattice fence behind which the gunman had stood at about 10:45 P.M. and fired the shots that killed Bugsy as he sat on his sofa reading the newspaper. The police had put a chalked "X" on the spot in the fence where the gun had rested. The drapes of the window through which the killer had fired were still open, and I could see the bloody spot where Bugsy had been sitting when the shots smashed through his head—an easy shot—scarcely fifteen feet from where I stood.

Several days later, I learned about "Bugsy's trunk," which Uncle Vern had stashed in our garage sometime that Friday. Vern was unusually sober and circumspect for a number of days after Bugsy's murder, and it wasn't long before he moved out of the chauffeur's quarters in the garage. I gathered that my mother had been upset when she learned that Vern had been at Bugsy's to retrieve the trunk on the day of the murder. At my mother's insistence, Vern was never allowed to enter the house again, though I knew he often visited Little Tah when my mother wasn't home. Toward the end of that year, my grandmother moved out as well, and it was around Christmas that I noticed for the first time that "Bugsy's trunk" was gone. I never saw Little Tah or Vern again, and they became a subject that my brother and I sensed was not to be discussed. Little Tah died in 1954, and Vern was eventually disbarred and moved to Las Vegas, where he died of alcoholism in 1959.

It would be a number of years before I fully understood Vern's connection with Bugsy Siegel and the Syndicate and his role as a bagman for the mob. But I knew at the time that he was connected with the underworld and some shady people at City Hall. I never knew exactly who Vern was speaking to when he used our taproom phone, but from things I overheard, I knew that the murder of Elizabeth Short had something to do with Bugsy Siegel.

Although the Black Dahlia case would reemerge in the news from time to time, by the end of 1947, one of the most notorious murders of the twentieth century left Homicide without a suspect or a clue, and the LAPD file on the Black Dahlia case was stamped "Open and Unsolved."

The 1940s was a period of time in my life that I tried to forget and put behind me—my parents' divorce, Uncle Vern and my drunken grandmother, Bugsy's trunk, the L. A. smog, and the Black Dahlia headlines. As the years passed, those melancholy memories and all the painful associations seemed to recede, but as I grew older, the inexorable Black Dahlia mystery kept reemerging like a bad dream that wouldn't go away.

PART II:

...Inside an Enigma

PERHAPS BECAUSE MY older brother was handsome and aristocratic, he was always Robert—never Bob; whereas, I was always Don—never Donald. But having an older brother who was handsome and aristocratic had its advantages. Robert became the chosen escort of many girls in the fashionable Hollywood teenage set of the 1940s and frequented their homes and parties. He dated Shirley Temple, June Haver, and Peggy Ann Garner, and escorted Darryl F. Zanuck's daughter, Darrylin, and Walt Disney's daughter, Diane, to Hollywood events. As a tag-along, I got to mingle with the stars at the Zanuck beach house, attend private studio screenings, and wander through Hollywood sound stages and studio backlots.

I especially liked to tag along with my brother to Walt Disney's home in Holmby Hills. Uncle Walt and I shared an enthusiasm for old-time trains. While my miniature railway was in the miniscule HO gage, Mr. Disney had a real steam train that stood about two-and-a-half feet tall. There were at least a hundred yards of track in his backyard that ran through miniature mountains, over bridges, through dark forests, and past scenic streams and waterfalls.

On weekends, Mr. Disney was usually by the station in his back-yard wearing his engineer's outfit, which included a bandana and an oilcan. He eagerly waited for passengers and took great joy in giving visitors rides. Sometimes I'd be his only customer. Mr. Disney would sit behind the coal car, and I'd ride on top of a gondola car, and we'd go round and round until I was train sick. I think Mr. Disney sensed that I was a dreamer and somewhat melancholic, and he'd tell me stories of his difficult boyhood in Topeka, Kansas, and how he used to sell newspapers on a steam train that ran between Topeka and Abilene. He said he used to dream that one day he wouldn't have to get off the train at Abilene and could just keep on going.

I believe that was the beginning of Disneyland. The dream started out in his childhood and further developed in his backyard where he enjoyed giving adventure rides to young kids and old kids alike. The rides eventually extended to Anaheim, and soon the whole world could jump on board.

Two of my brother's friends at Beverly High were Bob Dozier and "Buzz" Kirkeby. Dozier was the son of film star Joan Fontaine and RKO studio executive William Dozier; Kirkeby was the son of Arnold Kirkeby, president of the Kirkeby hotel chain, which included the Beverly-Wilshire Hotel and the Sunset Towers. I used to enjoy go-ing to the Kirkeby mansion in Bel Air because there was a giant swimming pool, which was more like an exotic tropical lake, with a picturesque waterfall. The mansion was a reproduction of a French chateau and was used in the 1960s as the home of the Clampetts in *The Beverly Hillbillies* television series.

On several occasions, I was aware that Bugsy Siegel and Virginia Hill were guests at the Kirkeby mansion. I recognized Bugsy because we went to the same barber—Harry Drucker. Drucker's barbershop was above Jerry Rothschild's fashionable clothing store on North Beverly Drive, and I'd go there for my haircuts with my stepfather. It was an exclusive barbershop for the Hollywood crowd; to gain entry, you had to be buzzed in by a receptionist downstairs. It wasn't long before I realized that Drucker's was a bookie joint, and a lot of Hollywood big shots went there to have their wallets trimmed. Drucker had a special glassed-in barber chair booth with a private telephone in which Bugsy could have a haircut and manicure while talking on the phone and not be overheard. Decades later, I learned from Drucker that Bugsy used this phone for his private business matters because he suspected that his own phones were tapped.[18]

I had also seen Bugsy Siegel and Virginia Hill at the Del Mar Turf Club. During the racing season, Jeff and my mother kept a box at the Del Mar Race Track, which was north of La Jolla, and in the summer of 1946, Bugsy and Virginia Hill shared a box not far from ours. The King Brothers and their entourage had the box next to us. There were four fat King Brothers and Momma King, who was the fattest of all and ran the Syndicate family of erstwhile film producers with a heavy hand. Hymie King, the youngest and dumbest of the lot, used to take me to the morning workouts and taught me how they fixed the races. As I understood it, the Syndicate only fixed about one in a hundred races to avoid suspicion, but one was enough. It was an arrangement made with the jockeys, who shared in the payoffs. Those who didn't cooperate had grievous problems. Bets on the fix were made at the track—seldom with the Syndicate bookies.

As soon as Bugsy knew the race was fixed, he'd tip off a few Turf Club pals and big shots. They would place their bets just before post-time and make a killing. When J. Edgar Hoover and FBI agent Clyde Tolson vacationed at Del Mar in the summer of 1946, their box was not far from Bugsy's, and I've often wondered if they didn't have an investigative ear peeled for Bugsy's latest tip.

***

18. Benjamin "Bugsy" Siegel's FBI file confirms that his suspicions were correct. During 1946 and the early months of 1947, J. Edgar Hoover had placed Siegel's Los Angeles and Las Vegas phones under electronic surveillance.

When Bugsy Siegel first arrived in movieland, not many people in Hollywood knew that he was a ruthless killer and one of the founders of Murder, Inc. Born on February 28, 1905, in the Williamsburg district of Brooklyn, Benjamin "Bugsy" Siegel (née Siegelbaum) was the son of Russian-Jewish immigrants. In the early years of the twentieth century, Williamsburg was a teeming district of crowded tenements, pushcart peddlers, and street thugs. Although he didn't finish high school, Bugsy was well schooled in survival on the streets of Williamsburg and quick to learn that violence was a means to the things that became important to him—power, money, and influence. As a Williamsburg street urchin, he set up a protection racket for the local street vendors. Any vendors who felt they didn't need a gang of kids for protection soon had their vending carts doused with kerosene and set aflame.

Two of the early members of Bugsy's Williamsburg street gang were George Raft (née Ranft) and Meyer Lansky (née Mair Suchowljansky). While Raft grew up to play gangsters on the screen, Bugsy and Meyer Lansky grew up to be the real thing. By the time they were in their teens, Bugsy and Meyer had moved to the more profitable streets of Manhattan's lower East Side and formed the notorious Bugs and Meyer Mob, a murder-for-hire gang involved in bootlegging and armed robbery on the side. By the time he had turned twenty-one and graduated from the streets of the lower East Side, Bugsy's crime syllabus included hijacking, white slavery, robbery, rape, extortion, narcotics running, bootlegging, and murder.

In many ways, Bugsy and Meyer were opposites. While Meyer was calculating and had a cool head for devious business methods, Bugsy was a hothead known for his paroxysms of brutal violence. Some likened his murderous episodes to seizures in which a pathological explosion of energy would transform him into a deadly and efficient homicidal monster. Early on, his homicidal rages had earned him the nicknames "Bugs" and "Bugsy," but nobody dared use these nicknames to his face because he was known to pistol whip and—upon occasion—kill those who did.

Recalling their days as street thugs in New York, Meyer Lansky said, "When we were in a fight, Benny would never hesitate. He was even quicker to take action than those hot-blooded Sicilians, the first to start punching, shooting, or stabbing. Nobody reacted faster than Benny."

Not one to assign a murder for hire to another, Bugsy enjoyed the kill and found delight in shooting or knifing his victims. When he set out to murder his old pal Bo Weinberg in 1934 as a favor for Dutch Schultz, he called Bo and suggested they go out to dinner. They then drove around until they stopped on a dark deserted street where Bugsy pistol-whipped Bo repeatedly. Bugsy then pulled out a knife and slashed him across the face and throat. The bodies of his victims were seldom discovered. Borrowing from Sicilian tradition, which perfected the art of the rub out, Bugsy would personally disembowel his victims so that intestinal gases would not raise their bodies from a watery grave in the East River. In his lengthy FBI file, the Bureau conservatively attributed more than thirty brutal murders to Benjamin "Bugsy" Siegel before his move to Southern California. Some of his victims, such as Salvatore Maranzano, were both stabbed and shot.

Unlike his brother, Maurice Siegel, who became a respectable Beverly Hills physician, Bugsy had a split personality. There was Bugsy, the heroin-addicted homicidal monster, and there was Benny, the handsome young man with movie star looks who could be charming, affable, and quite generous. But it was Bugsy who used Benny as a front.

In the spring of 1928, at the age of twenty-three, Benny married his childhood sweetheart, Esta Krakower. Meyer Lansky was his best man. Initially, Esta had no idea that Benny was a gangster. She knew him as a devoted husband, who operated a truck-for-hire business with Meyer Lansky on Cannon Street down on the lower East Side.

The truck rental business appeared to be quite lucrative, as Bugsy kept a suite at the Waldorf and purchased a fashionable home in Scarsdale. The trucking business, however, proved to be a front for bootlegging and hijacking enterprises of the Bugs and Meyer Mob.

Although the Bugs and Meyer Mob had their own booze shipments unloaded off boats on the shores of New Jersey, New York City was quite thirsty in the Roaring Twenties, and Siegel often hijacked Mafia booze shipments to increase his inventory. The hijackings put the Sicilian gangsters at odds with the Jewish gangsters and led to inter-gangland warfare. It was the cooler-headed Meyer Lansky and Mafioso Lucky Luciano who recognized that joining forces could lead to bigger profits; it was Lansky and Luciano who put together the Syndicate, which was essentially an amalgamation of the Sicilian Mafia and the Bugs and Meyer Mob—or as columnist Walter Winchell later put it, the merging of "the Cosa Nostra with the Kosher Nostra."

While there were ethnic traditionalists within the Mafia, such as Luciano's Capo, Giuseppe "Joe the Boss" Masseria, and his Sotto Capo, Salvatore Maranzano, who refused to join forces with the Jewish gangsters, they were quickly and efficiently eliminated in what became know as the "Sicilian Vespers"—the murderous modernization of the Mafia. On April 15, 1931, Lucky Luciano invited "Joe the Boss" Masseria to dine with him and discuss Mafia matters at the Nuovo Villa Tammaro restaurant in Coney Island. Near the end of the meal, Luciano excused himself to go the men's room. Bugsy Siegel and two armed henchmen then entered the restaurant, and Bugsy blasted Masseria into the eternal land of the Godfathers. As a result of Bugsy's efficiency, Lucky Luciano became the ultimate Godfather, and the Syndicate soon became the overlords of the underworld.

For a period of time, the Syndicate proved to be a cooperative underworld venture that became highly profitable. Literally millions of dollars were rolling into their coffers monthly. By the time Prohibition was repealed in 1933, the Syndicate's cash flow was overflowing. Although bootlegging days had come to an end, Meyer Lansky and Lucky Luciano agreed that millions more could still be made in gambling, narcotics, prostitution, and the race-wire.

There are historians of the annals of criminology who maintain that Bugsy Siegel first left the East Coast and moved to Los Angeles in 1936 or 1937, when he was assigned by Luciano and Lansky to take over the Syndicate interests in Southern California; however, Bugsy's forays into the land of sunshine and shadow began in the early 1930s. His brother Maurice, along with his sister, Bessie, had moved to Los Angeles in 1933, and Bugsy became a frequent visitor. After the end of Prohibition, it was Bugsy who first envisioned the new underworld opportunities dawning on the West Coast. In 1934 he rented an apartment at the Piazza Del Sol, next to the Clover Club on the Sunset Strip, and his lavish lifestyle became increasingly bicoastal. He found that he had a natural affinity for the movieland dream factory, and his dream was to infiltrate the film colony with gambling establishments, call-girl rings, race-wire connections, and narcotic depots.

In his testimony before the Kefauver Committee in 1950, Johnny Rosselli recalled that Bugsy Siegel began making more frequent trips to the West Coast in 1934. The Kefauver Committee's Chief Counsel, Rudolph Halley, asked Rosselli:

Q. Did you know Bugsy Siegel?
A. Yes, sir.
Q. How long did you know him?
A. Oh, I don't remember, but I know it was a number of years. He used to come out to California all the time.
Q. You would see him when he came?
A. Yes, sir, I think he has lived there since maybe '34, '35, '36; somewhere along there.
Q. What business was he in?

A. To tell you the truth, I never did know what his business was at the time. He seemed to get along alright. He had plenty of money. He went around with the best people.

Q. Who are the best people?

A. In that circle, the motion picture industry, you would always see him with very nice people.

Q. Who, for instance?

A. Oh, Countess di Frasso.

Q. I can just see the wheels working in there, Mr. Rosselli, trying to think, "Who can I mention that I won't hurt?"

A. Not at all.

Bugsy's circle of Hollywood friends had included Cary Grant, Mary Pickford, George Raft, Gary Cooper, Jean Harlow, Jack L. Warner, Clark Gable, the Countess di Frasso—and for a brief period of time, Thelma "The Ice Cream Blonde" Todd.

After Bugsy's thwarted attempts to operate a casino in Thelma Todd's Sidewalk Café, and her untimely death in December 1935, Bugsy returned to the East Coast and laid low in the Waldorf Towers for several months. It was a difficult time for the mob in New York. No amount of cold cash could bribe District Attorney Thomas E. Dewey, and he was turning up the heat. Dewey was after organized crime and intent on putting Lucky Luciano in jail. On December 10, 1935, Luciano was indicted for racketeering, and on June 7, 1936, he was found guilty of compulsory prostitution by the Manhattan Supreme Court.

It was shortly after Luciano's conviction that Bugsy decided to make a permanent move to Los Angeles, where District Attorney Buron Fitts and the City Hall were still for sale. Returning to Los Angeles in the summer of 1936 with his wife Esta and their two daughters, Millicent and Barbara, Bugsy rented a home on McCarty Drive in Beverly Hills from opera star Lawrence Tibbett. With his matinee-

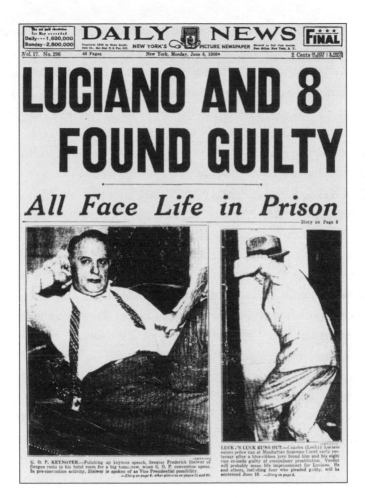

DAILY NEWS **FINAL**

NEW YORK'S PICTURE NEWSPAPER

Vol. 17. No. 298   48 Pages   New York, Monday, June 8, 1936   2 Cents

LUCIANO AND 8 FOUND GUILTY

All Face Life in Prison

Story on Page 3

G. O. P. KEYNOTER.—Polishing up keynote speech, Senator Frederick Steiwer of Oregon rests in his hotel room for a big tomorrow, when G. O. P. convention opens. In pre-convention activity, Steiwer is spoken of as Vice Presidential possibility.
—*Story on page 2; other pictures on pages 24 and 25.*

LUCK'S LUCK RUNS OUT.—Charles (Lucky) Luciano enters police van at Manhattan Supreme Court early yesterday after a blue-ribbon jury found him and his eight vice co-lords guilty of compulsory prostitution. Verdict will probably mean life imprisonment for Luciano. He and others, including four who pleaded guilty, will be sentenced June 18. —*Story on page 2.*

idol good looks and affable charm, Bugsy had been well cast as the mob's leading man in movieland. Introduced to the Hollywood crowd by MGM star Jean Harlow, George Raft, and producer Mark Hellinger, Bugsy was accepted by film-land society as a colorful, and rather mysterious, figure.

While establishing a network of Syndicate bookie joints, brothels, and clandestine casinos in Hollywood and the western section of the city, Bugsy hobnobbed with film stars and studio brass. Joining the exclusive Hillcrest Country Club, he was often seen at the Santa Anita Turf Club and the fashionable Hollywood nightclubs on the Sunset Strip. As a partner in the legendary Clover Club, Bugsy controlled its private upstairs gambling room, and for many years, he was a partner with Charlie Morrison in the Mocambo nightclub on the Sunset Strip. FBI reports confirm that Billy Wilkerson, a former bootlegger pal of Bugsy's and founder of the *Hollywood Reporter*, operated the Trocadero nightclub, Ciro's, and La Rues on the Strip as a front for Bugsy and the Syndicate. According to the California Crime Commission, the Syndicate operated more than thirty bars, at least seventy-five bookie joints, nineteen brothels, seventeen casinos, and fourteen nightclubs in the Hollywood area—including the Florentine Gardens, fronted by Mark Hansen and Frank Bruni.

When Siegel first arrived on the West Coast, Jack Dragna (née Anthony Rizzotti) was the Mafia Capo of Los Angeles, and Johnny Rosselli was Dragna's Sotto Capo. Both Dragna and Rosselli were Sicilians and had risen to power during the bootleg wars of the Prohibition era. Although they, too, had an ethnic aversion to cooperating with Bugsy Siegel and his associates, Lucky Luciano demanded their cooperation—and according to Mafia code, refusal to obey the Godfather meant death. At the instruction of Lansky and Luciano, a vice-map was drawn up that divided the city into territories controlled by Siegel and areas controlled by Dragna. Siegel inherited the western portion of the city, which included Hollywood and Beverly Hills, while Dragna controlled the central city, the valley suburbs, and Long Beach, which was the Port of Los Angeles.

Born in Corleone, Sicily, in 1891, Dragna was a short, barrel-shaped man who broke English out of the side of his mouth. Immigrating to the United States in 1914, he became associated with the Capone Gang in Chicago before becoming the Mafia boss of Southern California during Prohibition. Ruthless in his rise to power over the Southern California underworld, Dragna's methodology included murderous persuasion and generous payoffs to City Hall. He lived with his wife, Frances, in an unpretentious home in Los Angeles at 3927 Hubert Street and maintained a winery and a more lavish ranch house in Cucamonga, where the Cosa Nostra rites were held and blood oaths of Omerta were exchanged. In the Los Angeles Directory of 1937, Dragna listed his profession as "rancher"—and, indeed, from the productive fields of the Los Angeles basin, the FBI estimated that he reaped several million dollars annually from his various rackets.

```
Dragna Benardo mach r1904 Workman
  "  Bessie A slswn r647 W 18th
  "  Chas driver F-ABCo r Burbank
  "  Edw (Anna) driver h344 W 65th ⓞ
  "  Henry whsmn r2703 N Main
→ "  Jack I (Frances) rancher h3927 Hubert av
  "  Jos (Kath) slsmn h3526 Lowell av ⓞ
  "  Louis T r702 W 46th
  "  Lucille J bottler r2703 N Main
  "  Mary slswn r647 W 18th
  "  Morris M slsmn GSCo r Inglwd
  "  Thos (Rachael) liquors 1327 W 7th h5003
        9th av
  "  Thos jr (Jacqueline) clk r5003 9th av
  "  Thos F (Julia) rancher h702 W 46th ⓞ
Drago John (Kath) lab h2106½ S LaBrea av
  "  Margie r2106½ S LaBrea av
  "  Vincent 631 Clover ⓞ
```

Although Dragna lacked the sophistication and polish of Bugsy Siegel, by the end of Prohibition he had ruthlessly built an extensive gangland empire in Southern California, and he had shot himself to the top of the underworld and controlled the gambling, prostitution, and narcotics trade. Along with Mafioso Tony Cornero, Dragna ran gambling ships three miles off the coast that were popular with Angelenos and the movie colony.

Dragna's Sotto Capo, Johnny Rosselli, had the silky smoothness that Dragna lacked, and Rosselli was the Mafia's man in Hollywood when Bugsy arrived. Rosselli, who was close to Joe Schenck at Fox and Harry Cohn at Columbia, had gained control of the International Alliance of Theatrical and Stage Employees (IATSE), which supplied craftsmen and technicians to the studios. With their domination over the labor force, Rosselli and union boss Willie Bioff were extorting money from the studios to ward off threatened wildcat strikes. Warned by Dragna not to muscle in on Rosselli's turf at IATSE, Bugsy soon took over the Extras Guild and had a two-toned shoe in the door of the Screen Actors Guild, along with his pal George Raft. The enmity between Dragna and Bugsy grew when Bugsy muscled in on the gambling ship enterprise, and along with Tony Cornero, launched the S.S. *Rex*, which operated off the shores of Santa Monica. Only Lucky Luciano's insistence on cooperation prevented Dragna from resorting to open warfare over Bugsy's encroachment.

In 1938 Bugsy moved with his wife and children into an elegant Mediterranean-style thirty-five-room mansion at 250 Delfern Drive in Holmby Hills. He also kept a suite of rooms at the Sunset Towers on the Sunset Strip,[19] which became his rendezvous with Syndicate cash courier Virginia Hill and a bevy of Hollywood beauties culled from the ranks of studio starlets and the chorus lines of Slapsie Maxie's and the Florentine Gardens.

It was Jean Harlow's ex-boyfriend Longy Zwillman who introduced Bugsy to the Countess di Frasso (née Dottie Taylor). The Countess Dorothy Dendice Taylor di Frasso was a vivacious millionairess from Watertown, New York, who had married the impoverished Italian Count Carlo di Frasso before heading for Hollywood

---

19. The Sunset Towers was owned by Arnold Kirkeby. According to Siegel's FBI file, Kirkeby was a front-man for the Syndicate, which used laundered mob money for real estate ventures. These ventures included the Beverly Wilshire Hotel, the Sunset Towers, the Blackstone Hotel in Chicago, and the Warwick in New York City.

and the entitled high life. The height of Hollywood's social season was Marion Davies's annual birthday party for William Randolph Hearst, at which, in 1938, the Countess di Frasso was escorted by Mr. Benjamin Siegel. The attractive twosome were also seen in the receiving line at a formal reception for the visiting Duke and Duchess of Windsor, held at Pickfair, the legendary estate of Mary Pickford and Douglas Fairbanks in the heights of Beverly Hills—a million miles from the streets of Williamsburg.

The countess provided Bugsy with an air of respectability that went along with his slick manner, slick hair, and slick attire; gossip columnists referred to Mr. Benjamin Siegel as a "sportsman" and "bon vivant." Few in movieland suspected that he was one of the founders of Murder, Inc. or that he was calling the shots in the underworld murders that occasionally plagued the city. Hollywood society flocked to the lavish parties that Bugsy threw at his Holmby Hills mansion, and it wasn't until Bugsy was arrested for the murder of Harry "Big Greenie" Greenberg in September 1940 that film-land realized they had a notorious gangster in their midst.

A former goon for Murder, Inc., Harry "Big Greenie" Greenberg had been in hiding from the law. In need of money, he made the mistake of contacting his former boss, Louis "Lepke" Buchalter, and demanding some cash—or he was going to sing to the cops. Big Greenie knew too much, and a contract went out. When he was found to be hiding out in a Hollywood rooming house at 1804 Vista Del Mar Avenue, the contract went to Bugsy, who had the rooming house staked out by his brother-in-law, Whitey Krakower. Whitey found that Big Greenie was in the habit of driving off each night at about 8:00 P.M. to get a *Daily Racing Form*. On the night of November 22, 1939, Bugsy and another Murder, Inc. alumnus, Abe "Kid Twist" Reles, drove to Hollywood in a stolen Buick and met Allie "Tick" Tannenbaum and Frankie Carbo, who were waiting two blocks away from Big Greenie's in a stolen Mercury. When they got to Big Greenie's

place, Abe Reles recalled that Bugsy said, "We'll turn both cars around—that's a dead-end street, and we don't want to get bottled up. You take the Buick, and you'll be the crash car. If anybody comes after us when we hit Greenie, you know what to do."[20]

Parked across from Big Greenie's rooming house on the west side of the street, they didn't have to wait long before his Ford convertible coupé with yellow wire wheels pulled up and parked parallel to the curb. Abe Reles recalled that Bugsy quickly stepped out of his car, walked up to Big Greenie, and pistol whipped him before four pistol shots were fired into his fractured skull. Big Greenie's lifeless body

---

20. The "crash car" was often used in major robberies and assassinations to block pursuing vehicles.

slumped over the wheel as Bugsy got back into the stolen Mercury. The only witness was a pedestrian who saw the Mercury drive away into the night with its lights off. The "crash car" proved to be unnecessary.

Big Greenie's murder remained unsolved for months, and Mr. Benjamin Siegel would have remained a mysterious Hollywood sportsman and bon vivant, but when Abe Reles was later arrested in New York for racketeering, he became a stool pigeon and began to sing. Reles had been involved in dozens of contract murders, and his gift of total recall filled twenty-five D.A. steno-books with horror stories of mob murders and violence. One of the killers named in Reles's aria was Bugsy Siegel, who he named as one of the founders of Murder, Inc. and the mob boss who was involved in the recent Hollywood rub out of Big Greenie Greenberg.

Booked on September 14, 1940, for suspicion of murder, Bugsy was incarcerated in the old county jail building in downtown L.A., where money was known to talk, as well as sing—in high C-notes. While under indictment for murder, Bugsy was housed in a special jail apartment, had his meals catered by Lindy's in Beverly Hills, and was frequently chauffeured to Hollywood nightclubs in the evening.

Ironically, it was *Examiner* editor, Jim Richardson, who exposed the special prisoner privileges granted to Bugsy Siegel. One afternoon Richardson received an anonymous call, and a man's voice said, "There's something phony going on in this town!"

"There always is," Richardson said.

"I ain't kidding. I seen Bugsy Siegel on the Strip last night."

"You're seeing things, pal." Richardson said, "Bugsy's in the can for murder."

"Not last night! Just ask around—check it out." Deciding it was worth investigating, Richardson assigned reporters Sid Hughes and Howard Hertel to "check it out." Keeping vigil at the county jail, the reporters spotted Bugsy exiting the side door with Deputy Sheriff Jimmy Pascoe. Bugsy was smartly dressed in one of his tailored Jerry

Rothschild suits and fancy silk ties as he drove off in the backseat of the deputy's unmarked official car. Following them to Beverly Hills, the reporters spotted Bugsy picking up actress Wendy Barrie at Lindy's restaurant and going out for a night on the town. When Bugsy and the actress emerged from Slapsie Maxie's nightclub close to midnight, they were met with a blinding flash as Hertel's camera clicked and captured "something phony going on in this town." Bugsy cursed and ran to Deputy Pascoe's car and sped off, but it was too late. The next day, Richardson splashed the photo of Bugsy and Wendy Barrie on the *Examiner* front page, and Angelenos read all about the indicted murderer, Bugsy Siegel, being out on the town during eighteen days of his first month of incarceration.

Wine, Women, Trips Bring Jail Probe of Bugsy Siegel

Many Trips From Cell Reported Made by Suspect

Wine, women and 19 trips "outside" have made imprisonment in the county jail one long, lush vacation for Benjamin (Bugsy) Siegel, millionaire mobster accused of a ruthless, gangland murder, the *Examiner* learned last night.

A double-barreled investigation, directed by Sheriff Eugene W. Biscailuz and Superior Judge Frank G. Swain, is under way into the amazing special privileges assertedly accorded Siegel, who is alleged to have superintended the slaying last November

of Harry (Big Greeny) Greenberg.

Objects of the inquiry are the following alleged episodes:

Numerous visits made by Siegel to the offices of a dentist, Dr. Allan Black, 415 North Camden drive, Beverly Hills.

Visits by Siegel, said to have (Continued on Page 3, Cols. 1-6)

Richardson discovered that the jail's physician, Dr. Benjamin Blank, had received more than $32,000 in payments from Siegel and arranged for Siegel to stay in the doctor's private county jail apartment, where a trustee was assigned to be his butler and serve him specially prepared gourmet meals—including roast pheasant and caviar.

In addition to the eighteen trips outside the jail during his first month of incarceration, Siegel was allowed female visitors who were entertained in his private quarters and served lemonade spiked with whiskey.

The *Examiner* reported, "Siegel not only is permitted to keep an extensive wardrobe of costly 'mufti' for his trips outside of jail, but while in the jail wears a tailor-made uniform with notched lapels, razor-edged creases, and made of cloth far superior in quality to the usual jail denim. . . . Siegel's shoes are shined each morning for him by his 'valet,' a trustee who keeps Bugsy's raiment in apple-pie order."

There were investigations and reprimands, but the story soon faded from the news, and the murder charges against Bugsy were eventually dropped when Bugsy donated $30,000 to the Los Angeles district attorney's election campaign, and Abe "Kid Twist" Reles was tossed out of his sixth floor hotel window, bringing an abrupt end to his singing career. With the death of Reles, the prosecution was left without a witness; however, Reles had disclosed that Bugsy's brother-in-law, Whitey Krakower, was also involved in Big Greenie's murder. But shortly after Krakower was brought in for questioning by the New York district attorney, he was shot down on the streets of Manhattan. The murder of Esta Siegel's brother proved to be the coup-de-grâce to the Siegel marriage. Esta filed for divorce and moved back to New York City with the children.

Although Bugsy threatened Jim Richardson and said, "he would take care of him" if he didn't keep his name out of the paper, the damage had been done, and Bugsy was henceforth shunned by Hollywood high society. In 1941, Bugsy sold his Holmby Hills mansion and moved to Florida, where he and Virginia Hill purchased the Hearst estate on Palm Island in Miami and operated the Colonial Inn, The Grotto, and several other lucrative enterprises with Bugsy's partner, Meyer Lansky.

When Siegel moved to Miami, Jack Dragna may have thought he

was rid of his nemesis, but Bugsy's heart was in tinseltown. It wasn't long before he returned to Hollywood, set up headquarters above the Formosa Café, and began expanding his gambling, narcotics, and prostitution empire—which included Brenda Allen's pricey call-girl ring. During the war, Bugsy and Virginia could often be seen at the Sunset Strip nightclubs. Virginia was known to drop thousands of dollars on lavish parties at Ciro's, the Trocadero, and the Mocambo. Often referred to in the gossip columns as a "Southern oil heiress," Virginia Hill's elegant parties were popular with Hollywood's café society. Few realized she was the cash courier for "Joey Ep" of the Syndicate and received a percentage of the large amounts of cash she delivered and distributed.

Hollywood columnist Florabel Muir was in Perc Westmore's beauty salon having her hair done when she overheard Virginia Hill tell her manicurist that someone had sent her ten one-thousand-dollar bills. "She pulled the bills out of a package," Florabel recalled, "and she asked Perc Westmore to change one of the bills into smaller denominations and handed out fifty-dollar tips all around." When Virginia departed, she left the empty package behind, and when Florabel examined it, she noted that it had been airmailed from Chicago by "J. Epstein." Virginia played several walk-on bit parts in films at Universal before Bugsy persuaded Harry Cohn to give her a contract at Columbia Studios, where she briefly attended acting classes with a long-suffering drama coach and did several more walk-ons before walking out on her movie career.

Recruiting former boxer Mickey Cohen as his strong-arm man, Bugsy became intent on infiltrating the race-wire system that crisscrossed the nation. The race-wire was an intricate and tricky operation. It involved spotters at the track who were able to quickly transmit odds and results to a communication post near the track. They would then send it out on the Continental Wire Service, which was controlled by James Ragen and the Mafia in Chicago. After the end of Prohibition, the race-wire and the Syndicate network of bookie joints had become the cornerstone of the mob's empire. The combined take from the nation's bookies ran into the billions. Chicago newsman Len O'Connor stated, "The race-wire was the bookmakers' only available source of instantaneous information concerning *all* the betting opportunities currently existing at *all* the tracks, and indeed, the cash flow of the bookie joints was significantly greater than that of the tracks." Therefore, whoever controlled the race-wire was the nation's bookie czar, and according to mobster Mickey Cohen, Bugsy had imperial ambitions. Mickey recalled:

> Benny Siegel began pushing another wire, the Trans-America Service, because he didn't have any cut with Continental. Jack Dragna and Johnny Rosselli—the guys Benny was pushing out of action—did. Russell Brophy was Ragen's son-in-law and in charge out here [Los Angeles]. So Benny tried politely to talk to Ragen and Brophy and bring the matter about without any hassle. When he couldn't get no cooperation with Brophy, Benny just said, "Well, we're going to break the whole thing up." So he gave orders to knock the service out.

Assembling his usual gang of goons, Mickey Cohen charged into the Continental Wire Service in downtown L.A., which was secretly located on the ninth floor of the Newmark Building at Seventh Street and Hill Street. Mickey recalled:

> We tore that fucking office apart. In fact, we busted Brophy's head open pretty good because he got out of line a little bit. But actually, the instructions were to knock him in pretty good anyway.
>
> With the Continental joint out of commission, Benny figured that he would be able to get with Ragen in Chicago, but Ragen didn't see the light, so a truck went by

and shot him down. When he didn't die fast enough from the hit and went to the hospital—he was poisoned.

Benny Siegel's knocking over Ragen and Continental was kind of a slap in the face to Dragna, who thought he was running the West Coast. Dragna was really from the old moustache-Pete days. The worst thing you can do to an old-time Italian mahoff is to harm his prestige in anyway, and that's what took place when Benny came out here.

Adding to the conflict between Dragna and the Siegel/Cohen faction was Bugsy's takeover of the Brenda Allen call-girl ring. Brenda had been operating within Dragna's vice-map territory behind the Ambassador, but Bugsy and Mickey Cohen had enlarged her business to the moneyed Hollywood crowd and muscled in on her lucrative vice operation. Although Brenda was operating over one hundred pricey call girls from her Hollywood telephone exchange, her communication center was in Dragna territory at Ninth Street and Fedora Avenue—yet, the Syndicate cut was going to Bugsy.

While the growing animosity between Bugsy Siegel and Jack Dragna simmered for years, it wasn't until Bugsy began abandoning his Los Angeles Syndicate empire for the sunny sands of Las Vegas that the feud between Bugsy and Dragna broke into open warfare. When he was in Vegas developing his Flamingo Hotel project, Bugsy appointed his henchman, Mickey Cohen, to handle the day-to-day Los Angeles Syndicate operations, but Cohen lacked Bugsy's discretion and began aggressively moving in on Dragna's bookmaking operations.

When Dragna could no longer bite the bullet, he began spitting them out, and the shooting war broke out in May 1946. It started with the gangland killing of Paulie Gibbons, a forty-five-year-old Syndicate bookmaker from the East Coast who worked with Mickey Cohen. Gibbons was brought down in a hail of bullets in front of his Beverly Hills home on May 2, 1946. Then on October 3, two other

Siegel and Cohen associates, Benny "The Meatball" Gamson and George Levinson got theirs when gunmen entered their West Hollywood apartment and shot them to death.

The gangland killings and attempted assassinations made headlines for days but remained unsolved. Although neither Homicide nor the press seemed to have a clue about who was responsible, the average cop on the beat and the below-average man on the street knew it was the Mafia Capo of Los Angeles, Jack Dragna.

Elizabeth Short returned to Los Angeles in July 1946, just as the underworld war was heating up, and with her dream of becoming a movie star, she had little comprehension of the dark side of the movieland maze, where the studios, the nightclubs, the unions, and many of the major talent agencies had been infiltrated by the mob.

Ann Toth stated that Elizabeth Short had questionable associations, and though she was skeptical of people, she "often stumbled into trash." And Mark Hansen commented, "She dated many different men . . . mostly hoodlums." With her ambition of becoming a movie star, she may have perceived Maurice Clement, who chauffeured Brenda Allen call girls around for Max Arnow at Columbia Studios, as merely an entrée to the Hollywood studio world. But if Maurice had offered "to set her up in an apartment in Beverly Hills," as Toth stated, Maurice certainly had something else in mind. Elizabeth had little concept of the dangers of these associations or that she could end up one day as a subsidiary casualty in the underworld war being waged in the City of the Angels. When Elizabeth returned to Los Angeles, she dreamed of becoming another Deanna Durbin, but six months later, she would end up another Jane Doe.

When her bisected body was found on Norton Avenue in Leimert Park, it wasn't mentioned by Capt. Donahoe or the press that her remains were found in the weeds approximately 250 yards from the backyard of Jack Dragna's home at 3927 Hubert Street, near the corner of Thirty-ninth and Norton. Nor was it ever mentioned that the letter "D" had been carved by a knife into the pubic area of the victim's flesh. The D is clearly visible in police photographs held today in the Black Dahlia files of the Los Angeles District Attorney's Office. Did the D stand for Dahlia—or could the D have stood for Dragna? Whatever the meaning of the psychopath's message, the silent scream from the sacred setting was certainly heard at the nearby home of Mafia Capo, Jack Dragna—and La Famiglia.

M E M O R A N D U M

TO: H. L. Stanley, Chief of the Bureau of Investigation
ATTENTION: Arthur L. Veitch, Deputy District Attorney
IN RE: Elizabeth Short Murder - Los Angeles Police Department
                   Records, Reports, Statements, Correspondence, Evidence
                   and Information.
FROM: Frank B. Jemison, Lieutenant - Bureau of Investigation

SOME PEOPLE BELIEVED that the "D" cut in the shaved pubic region of Elizabeth Short is of the same type as found on the body of the French woman.

Facts reveal that the pubic region of Elizabeth Short's body was not shaved.

Experts in handwriting have stated that it would be impossible to determine any type of handwriting from the so-called "D" cut into the pubic region of Elizabeth Short's body.

The "D" memorandum (LADA ARCHIVES)

FIVE MONTHS AFTER the murder of Elizabeth Short, Bugsy Siegel flew from Las Vegas to Los Angeles and was shot to death in the living room of his Moorish Beverly Hills mansion on Friday evening, June 20, 1947.

Although he was spending most of his time in Vegas, Siegel frequently visited L.A. to raise cash for his Flamingo Hotel project, which had gone several million dollars over budget. Bugsy had viewed Nevada as an oasis within the United States judicial system, where race-wires, prostitution, and gambling operations were legal; and he dreamed of moving his Syndicate empire to Vegas and making untold millions within the borders of legitimacy.

The Flamingo dream had been hijacked from his old Syndicate associate, Billy Wilkerson, who had initiated the Vegas venture in 1945 when he purchased the land and commissioned the architectural concept. Siegel had been brought in as a partner when Wilkerson needed additional financing, but Bugsy became obsessive about the Flamingo project and aced Wilkerson out—threatening to kill him if he didn't back out quietly. Wilkerson fled to Paris and remained in hiding until the news of Bugsy's assassination.

One of his Flamingo associates, Moe Sedway, recalled Siegel exclaiming, "Moe, we're going to take this land, and we're going to build the godamnnest biggest hotel and casino you ever saw. I can see it now: 'Ben Siegel's Flamingo'—that's what I'm going to call it. I'm going to have a garden and a big pool and a first-class hotel. We're going to make Reno look like a whistle-stop!" But from the beginning, things started coming up snake eyes.

In 1946 there were still wartime shortages of construction material. Siegel was paying a premium to obtain what he needed, and thieves were stealing the precious building supplies at night. In September, rains pounded down for days, flooding and reflooding the building site, and construction snafus were driving Bugsy up the wall. Deciding that the aisles in the hotel's kitchen pantry were too narrow, he had them reconstructed at a cost of $30,000—the equivalent of $200,000 by today's standards. Walls that were found to block views were torn down and rebuilt with massive windows. When a heavy beam in the private penthouse, which was to be Bugsy's and Virginia Hill's love nest, was found to be only five-feet-ten-inches above the floor, Bugsy Siegel had one of his paroxysms. After pistol-whipping the foreman, Bugsy literally "raised the roof" at an additional cost of $22,500.

Importing the finest marble from Italy and insisting on the choicest hard woods and gilded accessories, Bugsy's obsession to build the most luxurious hotel and casino in Las Vegas led to giant overruns in cost. The construction budget was originally $1.5 million, but by the end of September 1946, the project had cost more than $3.5 million—and costs were still skyrocketing. After he raised additional cash from Meyer Lansky and Lucky Luciano, the Syndicate bosses became increasingly skeptical about the venture. When Lansky visited the project in the fall of 1946, he began to realize that Bugsy was building a gilded marble palace out in the sagebrush.

As construction costs continued to soar, Siegel's bank account began to tumble and checks began to bounce. A check for $150,000 to contractor Del E. Webb was returned with the stamp "insufficient funds." Desperate for cash, in October 1946, Bugsy sold his interest in the Florentine Gardens for $100,000 to Barney Vandersteen, a friend of Mark Hansen. And in an effort to raise additional cash, he instigated a series of jewel robberies orchestrated by his Syndicate henchman, Albert Louis Greenberg, and the McCadden Gang.

Al Greenberg ran narcotics traffic out of his Hollywood bar, Al Green's Nightspot, at 1735 N. McCadden, and had once been a bootlegger for the Bugs and Meyer Mob before relocating to Hollywood when Siegel moved west. Al had met Elizabeth Short in 1944 when she was learning the B-girl trade with Lucille Varela. And in 1946, Elizabeth frequented Al Green's Nightspot, which became the center of operations for the jewelry thefts instigated by Siegel to raise cash for his Las Vegas gamble. The McCadden Gang included Louis and Marty Abrams, two alumni of the Bugs and Meyer Mob, and Al Greenberg's friend, Jack Anderson Wilson, a giant, six foot, four inch strong-arm thug who walked with a limp.

The theft of more than $150,000 in jewels from a residence at 1220 Sunset Plaza Drive was pulled off by Greenberg on November 11, 1946. The jewels were fenced through Bugsy's cohort, Maurice Reingold, owner of a fashionable jewelry store next to Drucker's barbershop on Beverly Drive. Selling real estate holdings and borrowing additional funds from his friend George Raft, Bugsy promised Meyer Lansky and Lucky Luciano that the Flamingo would open by Christmas, 1946. He missed by one day.

Although the hotel wasn't ready to open, the showroom, restaurant, and casino opened on Tuesday, December 26, with Jimmy Durante, singer Rose Marie, and Xavier Cugat's orchestra headlining the showroom. A number of Hollywood stars were scheduled to attend the grand opening. Two Lockheed Constellations had been chartered to fly in the celebrity guests, who were to include Clark Gable, Lana Turner, Cary Grant, Joan Crawford, and Caesar Romero. But heavy rains in Los Angeles grounded the flights. Only Sonny Tufts showed up, having driven across the desert in his car.

Recalling the opening night, Rose Marie said, "The show was spectacular, everything was great, but nobody came. The local cowboys weren't interested. We worked to nine or ten people a night for the rest of the two-week engagement." During those two weeks, the casino at the Flamingo had more dealers than customers, and Bugsy became increasingly paranoid and violent. Accusing a dealer of cheating, Bugsy had to be restrained by his own bodyguards from killing him. Furious at a press agent for bad publicity and for referring to him as "Bugsy," he chased him around the Flamingo pool like a crazy man before striking him in the head repeatedly with the butt of his pistol. Westbrook Pegler had made some derogatory comments about Siegel in his syndicated column; when Bugsy spotted the columnist in the Flamingo Casino, he threatened to kill Pegler, and once again, his bodyguards had to restrain him.

With a $300,000 loss in the first ten days and a growing cash crisis, Bugsy temporarily closed the Flamingo in the first week of January, and FBI files indicate that he flew to Los Angeles on Monday, January 6, 1947. When he arrived in L.A., Bugsy was acting irrationally, according to Bernard Ruditsky, a private detective, who worked for Siegel as a debt collector and managed Sherry's nightclub on the Sunset Strip. Compounding his financial problems, on January 5, Governor Warren announced there was to be no more offshore gambling in California, and the S. S. *Rex* was impounded and all its gambling equipment dumped into the sea. At a meeting held at the Linden Drive mansion attended by Ruditsky and Siegel's friend, Allen Smiley, there was a discussion about collecting various debts owed to Siegel. Ruditsky recalled that Bugsy started screaming obscenities, throwing art objects against the wall, and stamping out lit cigarettes into the carpet as he threatened to rub out all of his debtors.

Ruditsky concluded that Siegel was in way over his head with the Flamingo project and decided to stay away from him because he was acting a little crazy. Ruditsky also concluded that Virginia Hill was a nut case, and he observed that they were both going off the deep end—especially when they were on drugs, which was becoming an increasing habit. He testified before the Kefauver Committee:

Mr. Ruditsky: I think she, too, is psychopathic.

Senator Wiley: Who is psychopathic?

Mr. Ruditsky: Virginia Hill. She called me one night, and she said, "You better get over here right away; I have trouble at the house." I went over there. There were three or four people in there that I didn't know. She was sitting there. Al Smiley was there. There was a fellow by the name of Swifty Morgan there. They were having dinner. She was there in a bathing suit and had a gun in her hand. She said, "I am going to kill everybody in the house, the maid, and the Chinese butler, and everybody." She said, "They have been stealing and robbing me." Well. Looking at the woman, when you see her, you know she is a definite—definitely a mental case. That was my opinion of her.

When Siegel returned to Los Angeles on Monday, January 6, 1947, he was on a desperate cash foray, and at 10:30 A.M., Al Greenberg's McCadden Gang robbed the Mocambo nightclub on the Sunset Strip, escaping with a small fortune in jewelry and more than $6,000 in weekend receipts. The jewelry had been put on display at the Mocambo by Siegel's friend Maurice Reingold, who had a history of frequent thefts of his heavily insured jewelry. The accountant, Isabelle Koch, described the leader of the trio that robbed the Mocambo as a forty-five-year-old man with a felt hat who held the employees at gunpoint saying, "Let's nobody be no heroes now," while a younger man, who walked with a limp and was described as at least six feet, four inches tall, swept the jewels out of the safe into a satchel. The leader in the felt hat was later identified as Al Greenberg.

According to the FBI files, Siegel planned to stay in Los Angeles for several days and had purchased a TWA ticket for a flight to New York on January 14, 1947, for a week's visit with Esta and his two children, who were living in an apartment at 88 Central Park West. But on the morning of January 14, the FBI learned that Siegel had suddenly canceled his trip.

It was on January 9, 1947, three days after the Mocambo robbery, that Elizabeth Short returned to Los Angeles from San Diego and was dropped off by Red Manley at the Biltmore Hotel before walking out of the Olive Street exit and vanishing that evening; it was on the morning of Tuesday, January 14, that Bugsy cancelled his flight to New York. Sometime that night, Elizabeth Short was killed by being repeatedly struck on the head by a blunt metal instrument and having her face slashed open with a knife.

On January 15, the day Elizabeth's mutilated and bisected body was discovered on Norton Avenue, Bugsy made reservations at the Colonial House in Palm Springs, which was known to be a Syndicate retreat. FBI reports establish that Siegel planned to stay in Palm Springs for ten days before returning to Las Vegas.[21]

On January 16, the day after Elizabeth Short's body was discovered, an article in the *Los Angeles Times* disclosed that four suspects had been arrested on the evening of January 15 in connection with the Mocambo robbery. The *Times* article stated, "Shuttled into a show-up on the ninth floor of the Hall of Justice were Al Greenberg, 42, operator of a cafe at 1735 N. McCadden Place, and Louis Abrams, 47, both ex-Sing-Sing convicts, along with Marty Abrams, 50, the latter's brother, and Harry Burnow, 31. Another younger thief, described by the Mocambo accountant as six feet, four inches tall, was not apprehended."

While Al Greenberg was identified in a lineup as the Mocambo thief who held the accountant at gunpoint, he was inexplicably released from custody for "lack of evidence." Greenberg was subsequently

---

21. See FBI Report in Appendix A, page 343.

involved in another jewel robbery connected with Maurice Reingold on April 2, 1947, when he broke into the Beverly Hills apartment of Mrs. Samual Genis at the Grosvenor Apartments at Charleville and Rodeo Drive. Held at gunpoint, Mrs. Genis was beaten by Greenberg and forced to disclose the location of her valuable jewels (which had been sold to her by Maurice Reingold). She was robbed of more than $150,000 in fine diamond and emerald jewelry. When Mrs. Genis identified Al Greenberg's mug shot as the gunman who robbed her, the Beverly Hills Police discovered that Greenberg had suddenly left town.

By the time Bugsy Siegel returned to Las Vegas on January 27, he had secured another bundle of cash and supervised the completion of the two-hundred-room luxury Flamingo Hotel, which reopened on March 1. Once the hotel was opened along with the casino and showroom, the ledgers slowly began to improve, but every day proved to be another desperate cash crunch. Many of the people who worked for Siegel at the time recalled that he was increasingly violent and out of control. When Siegel heard that Ray Kronsen, the desk clerk at the El Rancho Vegas, had referred to the Flamingo as "a place run by gangsters," Bugsy exploded and pistol-whipped the clerk into an unconscious, bloody pulp.

Paul Price, Siegel's publicist, recalled, "No one could tell which way Benny was going to flip, and you had to be very careful what you said." Price observed that Bugsy and Virginia Hill were having violent arguments over the attention he was giving to Marie "The Body" McDonald. On May 17, Virginia was heard screaming that Bugsy was "a rotten murderer," and he beat her severely. Suffering from a broken nose and numerous contusions, Virginia attempted suicide before being hospitalized. She subsequently flew to New York, where she had restorative surgery before flying to Paris on June 10, for what was termed "an extended holiday."

Learning that Siegel's henchman, Al Greenberg, was in New York

City, Beverly Hills Police Chief Clinton Anderson flew to New York and arrested Greenberg on June 18, 1947, for the April 2 robbery of Mrs. Genis at the Grosvenor. Denying that he was involved in the jewel theft, Greenberg insisted he was staying at Siegel's Flamingo Hotel in Las Vegas from March 30 to April 5. "Benny Siegel will vouch for me," Greenberg stated. But two days later, Bugsy Siegel was dead. Both Maurice Reingold and Al Greenberg were indicted for the theft; however, once again Greenberg was inexplicably released.

When Bugsy Siegel flew to Los Angeles on that fatal Friday, June 20, 1947, for what would prove to be his last cash-raising venture, he was met at Mines Field by Al Smiley. According to Siegel's FBI file, Smiley drove Bugsy in his powder-blue Cadillac to the Linden Drive mansion, where they arrived at approximately 12:30 P.M. In the mid-afternoon, Smiley drove him to Drucker's barbershop at 222 N. Beverly Drive. After a haircut and manicure, Siegel walked to the nearby office of attorney Joe Ross on South Beverly Drive, where, according to Ross, they discussed financial matters relating to the Flamingo. Ross said that Siegel was to meet somebody that night at a restaurant in Ocean Park to iron out new financial arrangements.

Returning from the attorney's office to the Linden Drive mansion at about 6:30 P.M., Smiley and Siegel remained there for approximately one hour before driving to Ocean Park, where they dined at Jack's at the Beach, a mob-connected hideaway restaurant, popular with the film colony. Managed by Sonny Meyers, Jack's at the Beach was owned by Barney Vandersteen, Mark Hansen's friend who had purchased Siegel's interest in the Florentine Gardens. Vandersteen, who was also an investor in the El Rancho Vegas, owned the Pig n' Whistle restaurant chain in Los Angeles and controlled several Syndicate gambling establishments in Redondo Beach.

Witnesses who had been dining at Jack's at the Beach recalled that at one point Siegel left his table and joined a group at a booth in the rear corner where he was engaged in what appeared to be a business conversation with Barney Vandersteen. Smiley and Bugsy then departed the restaurant at approximately 9:45 P.M. and drove to the Beverly Wilshire Hotel drugstore before returning to 810 Linden Drive at approximately 10:30 P.M.

It was a policy of Jack's at the Beach to offer departing dinner guests a complimentary copy of the *Los Angeles Times*, with the inserted note, "Good night. Sleep well!—with the compliments of Jack's." After returning to the house, Bugsy perused his complimentary newspaper as he sat on the living room sofa and conversed with Smiley. Although the front drapes were always drawn when Bugsy was home, it was a sultry summer night, and somebody had opened the windows and the drapes on the south side of the living room, which bordered the driveway of the neighboring home of Mr. and Mrs. Belousoff at 808 N. Linden Drive.

Engaged in conversation, neither Smiley nor Bugsy heard the car that pulled up in front of the neighbor's house; nor did they hear the gunman as he stepped out of the car and casually walked up the Belousoffs' driveway to the wooden trellis bordering Bugsy's open living room windows. Quietly placing his 30-30 rapid-fire carbine on a notch of the wooden trellis, the gunman was a mere fifteen feet from his target when he squeezed the trigger and rapidly fired off the entire clip.

The first bullet smashed into the side of Bugsy's head and out his left eye, which was plastered fourteen feet away onto a doorjamb. As his mangled head was thrown back against the sofa, the second shot hit his face and exited through the neck. Altogether, nine shots were fired, four hit Bugsy, and one ripped through Smiley's coat as he dove to the floor. Bugsy Siegel's slick hair and attire became soaked with the blood that was gushing from his head and dripping onto the complimentary copy of the *Los Angeles Times*, which had fallen to the floor—along with the note, "Good night. Sleep well!—with the compliments of Jack's."

The following Saturday, and for weeks to come, Hollywood was abuzz with whodunit rumors about Bugsy Siegel's murder—and

Drucker's barbershop was besieged with customers who were anxious to be brushed up on all the latest lowdown. I remember going to Drucker's with Jeff shortly after the murder and hearing all the in-the-know theories about who killed Bugsy Siegel and why: "Meyer Lansky ordered the rub out because Benny was skimming off the Flamingo tables;" "Mickey Cohen killed him so he could take over Bugsy's territory;" "Dragna killed Siegel because he hated him for muscling in on his operations;" and "Frank Costello had him assassinated because the Flamingo had gone too far over budget."

Drucker's customers and the barbers would repeat all the stories ad-nauseam, but Harry Drucker didn't say a word; he'd just smile his knowing smile. Drucker was discreet. It would be years before I learned the origins of Drucker's discretion. Harry's brother Jack had once been a member of the Bugs and Meyer Mob, and Harry Drucker had once been Bugsy's barber at the Waldorf Astoria, where he had also been Lucky Luciano's and Frank Costello's barber. Harry Drucker could be trusted—he kept the secrets. When Siegel moved to California, he took Drucker with him and set up his bookie/clip joint on Beverly Drive, where Bugsy had his special, private barber chair. Through the years, Harry Drucker overheard a lot of private conversations in that glassed-in booth where Bugsy had his last haircut and manicure. But Drucker's secrets were like the bubbles in the LaBrea Tar Pits—they took decades to surface.

By the 1980s, Drucker had moved his barbershop, along with Bugsy's booth, to a new location behind a Wilshire Boulevard men's shop in Beverly Hills, where many celebrities and "important" people unknowingly had their hair cut in Bugsy's booth—including Elvis Presley, Chief Justice Earl Warren, and President Ronald Reagan.

I had never spoken to Drucker about Bugsy Siegel because it seemed unpropitious, but one Saturday in the mid-1980s, after about one thousand haircuts and my hair turning gray, I managed to turn the chitchat to the demise of Bugsy Siegel. In the course of our conversation, one of Drucker's Siegel-secrets bubbled to the surface from the dark depths of L.A.'s mob chronicles.

"Why did they kill Benny Siegel?" I politely inquired.

"Because he was crazy," Drucker replied.

"But wasn't he always crazy?"

"Not like those last months," Drucker said.

"Then it wasn't that he was skimming off the top and all those other stories?"

"No—no—no," Drucker insisted. "He became a certified nut case—a danger to everyone. So they had to kill him."

"You mean Lansky and Luciano okayed it?"

"No, the police," Drucker stated.

"The police?"

"They let Dragna kill him," Drucker said, as he reverted to his knowing smile. "Do you want me to trim your eyebrows?"

In the brief investigation into the murder of Bugsy Siegel, the police never mentioned Jack Dragna as a possible suspect, though he was known to have the means and the motive. Like the murder of Elizabeth Short, the Benjamin "Bugsy" Siegel case was stamped "Open and Unsolved."

But in 1973, while being interviewed by Martin Gosch for *The Last Testament of Lucky Luciano*, Luciano revealed that Siegel had been murdered by Jack Dragna; and in 1987, Eddie Cannizzaro, Jack Dragna's former driver and bodyguard, made a deathbed confession to federal agents that he had been the gunman who shot Bugsy Siegel for his boss—the Mafia Capo of Los Angeles. Beverly Hills homicide detective Les Zoeller, who inherited the Siegel case in 1980, investigated Eddie Cannizzaro's claims and verified that, indeed, Cannizzaro had been Dragna's driver and bodyguard, and the details in Cannizzaro's confession were correct. "Jack Dragna orchestrated it," stated Det. Zoeller, who believed Dragna had the motive as well as the connections to murder Bugsy Siegel and get away with it. Increasingly psychopathic, Bugsy had become an alarming liability to the Syndicate—as well as to the friends of the underworld at City Hall.

Knowing he would never be named as a suspect or brought in for questioning, it was Jack Dragna who had Bugsy Siegel murdered five months after the Black Dahlia's body had been discovered in the weeds near Dragna's home.

Was Bugsy Siegel the demented killer who had slashed open Elizabeth Short's face from ear to ear, pistol-whipped her, carved the letter D into her flesh, and had the bisected remains displayed in the proximity of Dragna's backyard? The FBI reports, which refer to Bugsy as "insane," indicate that he was a pathological killer capable

Benjamin Siegel D.O.A 6/20/47

of committing such an act, and he also had the opportunity. But what was the motive? Why would Elizabeth Short have become a grim casualty of the mob warfare being waged on the streets of Los Angeles?

In 1952 a *Los Angeles Times* reporter asked Det. Harry Hansen what he thought had happened to the psychopath who had murdered the Black Dahlia and why he had never struck again. Hansen's one-word response was—"Dead."

PERHAPS IT WAS only appropriate that the Wicked Witch of the West, actress Margaret Hamilton, handed out diplomas to the graduating class of Beverly Hills High School in 1949. Following graduation, some of my affluent classmates fell under a dark spell. Many who survived the Korean War were confounded by bad luck, bad health, bad marriages, bad attitudes, or bad drugs. Perhaps the worst spell of all was cast on my friend Manny Robinson, Edward G. Robinson's son, who succumbed to all of the above at an early age.

It was through Manny that I met Arthur James at the Holiday House in Malibu. Owned by prominent artist Gerald Murphy and his wife Sara, the Holiday House stood on the cliffs overlooking the Pacific Ocean and became a hideaway for Hollywood celebrities who didn't want to be seen in public with the wrong woman—or the wrong man. Lana Turner and Johnny Stompanato used to stay there, as did Marilyn Monroe, upon occasion, with a young congressman from Boston named Jack Kennedy.

One evening in the early fifties, at a Murphy Holiday House party, Manny Robinson, Arthur James, and I were discussing ephemeral

Hollywood lore, when James casually mentioned that he had known Elizabeth Short. What James had to say brought back flash-frames of "Werewolf Killer" headlines, Uncle Vern, and Bugsy's trunk.

James said he first met Elizabeth Short in Hollywood in the summer of 1944. He spotted her in a bar he frequented off Hollywood Boulevard, and she had an inner quality that he found intriguing. After he had drawn several sketches of her, they soon became friends. At that time, James was a struggling artist and managed several Hollywood rooming houses owned by Mark Hansen—the same Mark Hansen of Florentine Gardens fame. James recalled arranging for Elizabeth to stay at one of Hansen's rooming houses near Hollywood Boulevard and Van Ness, where James painted several oil portraits of her. Recalling that Elizabeth had suddenly left town toward the end of 1944, James said that he totally lost track of her until the summer of 1946, when she returned to Hollywood and stayed at Hansen's place on Carlos. Describing Hansen as some kind of avaricious control freak, James said that during the war the city was flooded with servicemen on leave looking for dates, and Hansen would recruit pretty girls to work the Florentine Gardens and several of his downtown dancehalls, making sure the boys in uniform had a good time and spent all their furlough dough.

According to James, Hansen would allow the girls he perceived as having "special qualities" to stay at his place on Carlos, and Hansen reserved them for special customers in the Hollywood crowd. James said some "big shot" had taken a fancy to Elizabeth and gotten her pregnant, and Hansen had tried to set her up with an abortionist. Instead, she fled to San Diego. The last time James said he saw her was several days before she left the city, and he had heard that the "big shot" was Norman Chandler, heir to the Chandler dynasty. James recalled that he hadn't heard from Elizabeth again or known what had happened to her until he recognized her picture in the paper and read the gruesome stories.

I initially passed off what James said as booze blather. However, in thinking about it later, what James had said fit together with several pieces of the Black Dahlia puzzle. And if Elizabeth was pregnant at the time she was murdered, it changed the whole concept of the crime—the motive, the MO, the suspects. Could the heir to the Chandler dynasty have been the "big shot" who took a fancy to the Black Dahlia and gotten her pregnant?

After reconsidering what Arthur James had told me, I was determined to speak with him further about Elizabeth Short. But the next time I saw Arthur James, he was quite sober, and when I brought up the Black Dahlia topic, he was coldly evasive and obviously did not want to talk about it. Years later I learned why sobriety may have brought about discretion—James had a rap sheet and a "white slavery" arrest record relating to Elizabeth Short.[22]

According to Administrative Vice officer Vince Carter, it was common knowledge within the upper echelons of the LAPD that Norman Chandler was a womanizer, who carefully guarded his private life from public scrutiny. As publisher of the *Los Angeles Times*, one of the things Norman Chandler insisted on was that the Chandler name and Chandler activities be kept out of the paper. Vince Carter stated, "A lot of what was *not* printed about Chandler was common knowledge in Administrative Vice and the upper echelons of the Los Angeles Police Department—a department of the city government in which Chandler always had an intense and close, if usually covert, working relationship."

Although Norman Chandler wielded great power and controlled

---

22. In John Gilmore's book, *Severed: The True Story of the Black Dahlia Murder* (Amok Books, CA, 1998), Gilmore discusses Arthur James's relationship with Elizabeth Short and his trip to Phoenix, Arizona, with her in November 1944, where he was arrested for transporting a minor across the border and spent time in jail. Elizabeth avoided arrest and briefly returned to Hollywood before heading back to Medford in mid-November.

much of the political, business, and social strata of the city, he was a very private person. He was always the gracious and debonair gentleman in his public life; yet, there were barriers that he placed around himself that were seldom crossed by associates, personal friends, or even members of his own family. He was secretive. Norman's polite and polished demeanor often concealed a privatized man of invincible self-will. In the 1960s, noted sculptor Jacques Lipchitz was commissioned to do a bronze bust of Norman Chandler that was to stand in the foyer of the *Times* building alongside the busts of his father and grandfather. Chandler traveled to Rome for the sitting, but Lipchitz had a difficult time depicting his subject. He struggled for days and weeks to capture Norman's inner quality. Searching his face and engaging him in conversation in an effort to discover the essence of the man, Lipchitz became more and more frustrated and repeatedly complained, "I cannot find Norman! I cannot find Norman!"

Increasingly annoyed and impatient with the sittings, Norman became restless, and his mind wandered to his own private thoughts, and without realizing it, his face began to reveal the inner man. Shouting "I've found him! I've found him!" Lipchitz quickly completed the sculpture that stands today in the foyer of the *Times* Building. When the bronze bust was unveiled, Norman's friends and family found it disturbing. It was too harsh, too cold—almost sinister. They felt it didn't properly reflect the urbane and sophisticated qualities of the heir to the Chandler dynasty.

After Norman Chandler died in October 1973, his wife Dorothy "Buff" Chandler remarked to a friend that, in all the years of their marriage, she had never really reached him. She stated, "Everyone loved him, and no one knew him." But according to Vince Carter, the intelligence units within the LAPD knew Norman Chandler quite well and made it their business to discover everything they could about the mogul who was the heir to the Chandler dynasty and wielded so much power in the city.

"Contrary to popular opinion, there's no honor among thieves," Vince Carter observed, "and the upper echelons of the LAPD made a deliberate effort to know a great deal about Norman's private life, and they knew more than he was ever aware of." Police criminologist Ray Pinker was ahead of his time in the art of electronic surveillance and was indicted in 1942, along with Chief Horrall, for having the Gangster Squad place electronic surveillance in many of the key offices of City Hall—including the mayor's. Private Det. Fred Otash, at one time an LAPD officer on Ray Pinker's staff of surveillance experts, confided that Norman Chandler was among many of the city's leaders that Pinker had put under surveillance. "Chief Horrall wanted to know everything that was going on with Norman Chandler," Otash stated. "Chief Horrall and Assistant Chief Joe Reed were fully aware of Norman's womanizing and playboy lifestyle."

Norman's marriage to Dorothy had been arranged by his father, Harry Chandler. The daughter of a wealthy and socially prominent Long Beach family, Dorothy was known to be an ambitious and strong-willed woman, but her father-in-law always believed a woman's place was in the home. It wasn't until Harry Chandler died in November 1944 that Dorothy's political and social ambitions were emancipated. Becoming active in the *Los Angeles Times* and its editorial policies, she built her own apartment on the top floor of the *Times* building at First Street and Broadway, where it was widely rumored that she was having an affair with an employee on the *Times* staff.

Although the Chandlers had their own estate in Los Feliz, Dorothy spent most of her time at the *Times* building penthouse, and Norman spent most of his time at his suite at the California Club. Harry Chandler had been among the founders of the California Club, which was exclusive to the more powerful businessmen in the city. Located in downtown Los Angeles on Sixth and Flower Streets, it had a convenient private rear entrance on Hope Street—just behind the Biltmore Hotel.

Before retiring from the LAPD and becoming an illustrious private investigator, Fred Otash had been ensconced at the California Club, where he kept the distinguished residents and power brokers of the city under surveillance for Ray Pinker and the Gangster Squad. According to Otash, it was at his California Club suite that Norman Chandler rendezvoused with women who were often brought there by his playboy friend, actor Arthur Lake, who was on Brenda Allen's "A" list. Although Dorothy Chandler did not care for Lake because of his licentious lifestyle, Lake was one of the few people Norman was close to. They had been friends for many years, and Norman had been best man at Arthur Lake's wedding to Patricia Davies Van Clive, who was said to be the niece of actress Marion Davies.

Arthur Lake had first met Elizabeth Short in 1944 at the Hollywood Canteen. Both of their names had been found in the Bauerdorf diary, and Lake admitted that he knew Elizabeth when he was brought in by the Sheriff's Department for questioning.

If Arthur James was correct—that Elizabeth Short had been pregnant when she was murdered, and the father of the unborn child was Norman Chandler—it would explain the extraordinary efforts by the Chandler faction at City Hall to cover up the secret circumstances of the horrendous crime.

Having also fallen under the spell of the Wicked Witch of the West, I became mesmerized by the shallow history of Hollywood and, after graduating from high school, enrolled as a cinema major at USC, where I led a rather celluloid life before falling under the spell of British author, philosopher, and raconteur G. K. Chesterton. I found Chesterton to be an inspiration—an erudite voice in the wilderness of Hollywood and Vine. I devoured *The Man Who Was Thursday* and all of Chesterton's Father Brown detective stories in which the investigation goes beyond the crime and solves the confounding riddle of good and evil. Perhaps it was because of Chesterton that I changed my major to journalism and enrolled at Loyola University in Los Angeles. My stepfather had known Chesterton and proved to be a trove of Chesterton lore. Before the war, Jeff had known many people I admired, including Winston Churchill, Lowell Thomas, and Charles Chaplin. Jeff had a remarkable, if bombastic wit, and I looked up to him as an endless fountain of Anglo-anecdotes and knowledge. He was too cultured for Monogram, but kept making films there until he died in August 1950.

One of my mother's social friends had been journalist Ben Williamson, who worked for Henry Luce and was in charge of the *Time-Life* office in Beverly Hills. Having worked for Luce since 1937, Ben seemed to know everybody. He could pick up the phone and talk to Louis B. Mayer, Eleanor Roosevelt, Mickey Cohen, or William Randolph Hearst—even Howard Hughes. One night Howard Hughes called Ben about a *Time* magazine cover story Ben was writing about Hughes and his flying boat, the "Spruce Goose." Hughes asked Ben to meet him at his bungalow at the Beverly Hills Hotel, and it proved to be Hughes's last public interview.

Ben was a poker player and would get into some of the big games up at Ben Hecht's Angelo Drive castle, where Jack Warner, Sam Goldwyn, Joe Schenck, Harry Cohn, and Mark Hellinger would sometimes vie for the pot. Ben recalled that Ben Hecht had always been chummy with the mob—going back to the days when he was a crime reporter in Chicago and long before he wrote the screenplay for the classic gangster film, *Underworld*. During his Hollywood years, Hecht socialized with Bugsy Siegel, Alan Smiley, and Mickey Cohen, and in 1950, Hecht and Cohen staged a gala charity event at Slapsie Maxie's to raise money for the Jews in Palestine. Hecht gave an impassioned speech to the crowd of bookies and Hollywood dignitaries, and more than $200,000 was raised that evening for the cause—but somehow the money never arrived in Palestine. Mickey Cohen explained that the boat carrying the cash was torpedoed and sunk, but Ben Williamson and Hecht always suspected that the money went down in one of the big game pots up at Hecht's Angelo Drive castle.

My mother and Ben Williamson were married in 1953, and perhaps suspecting I had more ink in my veins than celluloid, Ben would give me occasional *Time-Life* research assignments relating to the film industry and L.A. history. When he learned I was interested in the Black Dahlia case, he suggested that I speak to Aggie Underwood at the *Herald*, who Ben felt knew more about the case than anybody. Calling Aggie to set up an appointment, he also arranged for me to cull through the *Herald Express* newspaper morgue, so I'd arrive at my appointment well-informed. It took me two afternoons to cull through all the *Herald*'s Black Dahlia stories that had appeared back in 1947.

The crime had a haunting effect on me when I first read the newspaper coverage as a teenager, and rereading the Dahlia articles seven years later was disquieting—as well as fascinating. Reading the coverage of the crime in total within a condensed period of time was very different from reading the sensationalized coverage day by day as it occurred. I was able to get a more focused and objective viewpoint, and "Big Jack" Donahoe's con game on the press and the public became quite evident.

I found that Arthur James had been interviewed by the *Herald* on January 22, 1947 and had discussed his friendship with Elizabeth Short, but there was nary a word that she might have been pregnant. Only the story about her roommate, Lynn Martin, inferred that possibility.

Ben Hecht's article about Elizabeth Short's alleged lesbianism proved to be a ludicrous hoax, and in reading through the statements of people who were in touch with Elizabeth in those last days before she left the city, it became more and more apparent that she was afraid of something or someone.

I came across a significant interview with a resident of Liemert Park that had escaped me back in 1947. It was headlined: POLICE SEEK MYSTERIOUS "THIN MAN" IN BLACK DAHLIA CASE. The article was dated January 24, 1947 and concerned the police's house-to-house search and interrogation of the neighborhood around Norton Avenue. The questioning of neighborhood residents took place over a period of days, and police investigators knocked on doors in an ever-widening circle from the site where the body was found.

Nothing of significance was discovered until Lt. W. C. Wagoner and Officer R. T. Asdel knocked on the door of Mr. W. A. Johnson, who lived at 3815 Welland Street, six blocks east of Norton. Johnson told the investigators that on Tuesday, January 14, the day before the body was discovered, he had been cutting shrubs in his yard and had later driven over to the vacant lot on Norton to dump a bundle of cuttings at about 9:00 P.M. in the evening. As he slowed his car to a stop, Johnson said he noticed "a 1936 model sedan parked on the west side of Norton directly opposite the fireplug near where Miss Short's body was discovered on the following day."[23]

Johnson noticed that the right door of the sedan was open. Standing near the car was a man gazing at the vacant lot. Johnson described him as "approximately forty-five years of age, no more than five feet eight inches tall, thin build, wearing a tan top coat and a dark hat pulled low."

As Johnson stopped on the empty street and pulled to the curb, he said the man seemed startled and acted strangely. When Johnson took his bundle of cuttings out of his car and dumped them in the lot, the short, thin man crossed the street and walked slowly past Johnson's car, hands in pockets, as he scrutinized Johnson and then craned a look into his car. Noticing that the man was acting suspiciously and fearing that he may be a bandit, Mr. Johnson got into his car and drove away, then circled the block and returned to see what the man was doing. As he turned back down Norton, Johnson could spot the sedan in the beam of his headlights, and he noticed that the man had closed the open door and was sitting behind the wheel. When the man saw Johnson approaching, "He sped away with grinding gears and burning tires," Johnson recalled.

---

23. The top of the fireplug can be seen in the lower left of the photo on page 13.

Was it the same "1936 or 1937" dark Ford sedan spotted on the following morning before dawn when the body was dumped in the lot at the same spot where the "thin man" had been gazing? If so, the location where the body was discovered had been calculated before the murder.

While Jack Dragna's house was three short blocks east of Norton, Mr. Johnson's house was six blocks east. When Donahoe's investigators were knocking on doors in an ever-widening circle from the site on Norton, what did the Mafia boss of L.A. have to say when the police knocked on the Capo di Capo's door? In the entirety of the newspapers, there was not a word about the proximity of Jack Dragna's home to the location where the body was found.

While continuing my search through the history of the Black Dahlia case in the *Herald Express* newspaper morgue, I came upon coverage of the Bugsy Siegel murder, and I noted that in all the articles relating to Bugsy's murder, there was not one mention of the most obvious suspect—Jack Dragna.

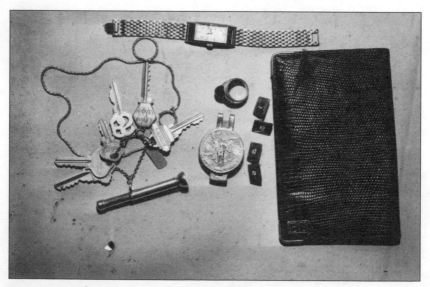

Possessions found on Bugsy Siegel's body

One of the *Herald* stories included a photo of items found on Bugsy's body, which included a gold key chain. Linked to the key chain was a solid gold hypodermic needle, which had been a gift from Virginia Hill, and a gold key to the house on Linden with Bugsy's initials on it.

A separate article that appeared on July 2, 1947, revealed that, several days following Bugsy's murder, a gold key with Bugsy's initials on it was found on the sidewalk on Temple Street, close to the entrance to City Hall—and it matched the one on Bugsy's key chain. The honest citizen who found it, Herbert Michel of 346 North Vermont Avenue, turned the key over to the police department, who could not explain how it got there. I wondered if Uncle Vern had accidentally dropped it on a mission to City Hall.

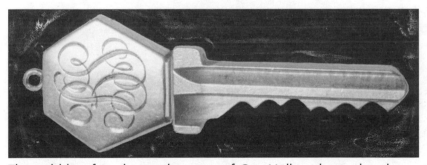

The gold key found near the steps of City Hall is identical to the one on Bugsy Siegel's key chain. (LAPL PHOTO COLLECTION)

After absorbing all that had been put to ink on the Black Dahlia case and stored in the *Herald Express* newspaper morgue, I felt I was ready for my meeting with Aggie, who—I had been forewarned—was quite formidable. But the scheduled meeting was cancelled and rescheduled and again cancelled and rescheduled a number of times, until I realized that she either: 1) was just too busy, 2) didn't really want to discuss the Dahlia case, or 3) needed time to review it prior to our discussion. I figured it was 2.

Back in those days, *Life* magazine's weekly edition was locked down and put to bed by 4:00 P.M. on Sunday afternoon. My mother frequently gave lock-down soirées for Ben's staff and literary friends, which sometimes included Adelle Rogers St. John, Robert Benchley, Dorothy Parker, and Nunnally Johnson. Ben Hecht would occasionally show up, and I made a point of being there one Sunday when I heard he was going to attend.

Being innately withdrawn is a big handicap for a would-be investigative journalist. Asking personal and interrogatory questions has always been very difficult for me, and only an excruciating desire for the facts can get me to stick my quivering nose into somebody else's business. On those occasions, I find I have to invent a person who isn't me. I can sustain the invention and become a pale version of Joe Friday for about twenty minutes before lapsing into a stuttering Inspector Clouseau.

Ben Hecht was a real challenge. He had a cold, penetrating gaze that I found unnerving. Joe Friday lasted about thirty seconds.

"I found your piece in the *Herald* on the Black Dahlia quite interesting."

"Did you?"

"Bu—But I found it strange—you said she was murdered by a lesbian, then at the end—"

"I didn't write it."

"Oh . . ."

"Fowler wrote it."

"Oh . . ."

"I wrote the end."

"Who was the man?"

"The man?"

"The man who killed her? You said at the end that it was a man who killed her—a man you could identify."

"You don't want to know."

At the time, I assumed Hecht was referring to Gene Fowler, Will

Fowler's father, as the writer of the article. Both Hecht and Gene Fowler had worked for Hearst in the old days, and I knew they were close friends; and in rereading the Hecht piece years later, it became apparent that the article was, indeed, written in Gene Fowler's pseudo-Barrymoresque satirical style—except for the end, which was pure Hecht.

Both Hecht and Fowler had become prominent, wealthy, and successful writers since their Hearst newspaper days and had no motive in writing a misleading junk piece for the *Herald*—unless it was a favor for old man Hearst. But why would Hearst want them to write such a convoluted, misleading story? This piece of the Black Dahlia puzzle didn't seem to fit with anything, until years later when the piece fell into place in the mid-Atlantic—where I finally had my interview with Aggie Underwood.

By 1962, Ben Williamson had become the national news editor for *Time* magazine, and he and my mother moved to New York City. I had been working at Samuel Goldwyn Studios on the *Loretta Young Television Show*, and during the show's hiatus, I was on my way to Europe for a holiday. I had a ticket for a bunk in Tourist Class on the *Queen Mary*, and Ben and my mother were putting me up at their Fifth Avenue apartment until the sailing date.

My Black Dahlia puzzle box had been stored away for years, until my mother gave one of her parties during my stay—and Aggie Underwood was one of the guests. I didn't remind Aggie of the appointments she had failed to keep almost a decade earlier, but I discovered that she, too, was sailing on the *Queen Mary* on her way to a holiday in Europe and the Greek Islands. When the boat sailed, I spotted Aggie on the passenger list, but decided I wasn't going to bother her—besides, she was in Cabin Class, and I was down in the bowels of the ship in Tourist. However, in mid-Atlantic, I felt Joe Friday coming on, and I snuck into Cabin Class and found Aggie in the Mermaid Bar. While engaging her in holiday chitchat, I slowly steered the conversation into the Dahlia latitudes. Perhaps it was because Hearst had died and she was safely in the mid-Atlantic that Aggie felt free to talk about the Black Dahlia case.

Aggie said that she had always believed there was a connection between the murder of Georgette Bauerdorf and Elizabeth Short, and she had been totally mystified when "the Boss" ordered her off both the Bauerdorf and the Dahlia case. She said she sat at her desk in the city room and did her knitting for several days, neither answering the phone nor speaking to anyone, in a silent protest. She said she had intended to leave the *Herald* when she was suddenly bumped upstairs to the city editor's desk.

Later she learned that it had to do with the Arthur Lake connection. Aggie recalled that she had heard from contacts in the Sheriff's Department that both Arthur Lake and Elizabeth Short had been mentioned in the Bauerdorf girl's diary, and Lake had been brought in for questioning. After the Black Dahlia murder and the mailing of the contents of Elizabeth Short's purse to the *Examiner*, she learned that Arthur Lake's phone number had been found in Elizabeth's address book. Aggie said that she knew that Arthur Lake had married the niece of Hearst's mistress, actress Marion Davies, but she didn't know until some years later that Lake's wife, Patricia Davies Van Clive, wasn't Marion Davies's niece—Patricia was the illegitimate daughter of William Randolph Hearst and his long-time paramour, Marion Davies. Hearst wanted no Draculan shadows of sensationalism cast across his children or his children's children—"the Boss" determined there were to be no scandals involving Arthur Lake.

Aggie said that though she couldn't write about the Bauerdorf/Dahlia connection, she had followed the Dahlia investigation through the years and concluded that the case had been controlled and covered up by City Hall.

"Did you ever hear that Elizabeth Short was pregnant?" Joe Friday asked.

"That was something I heard from the beginning down in the squad room," Aggie said.

"Was that the control question?"

"It could have been. I knew Harry Hansen pretty well, but he wouldn't talk about it. That was a 'Yes' as far as I was concerned."

Aggie recalled that another officer involved in the case told her there was a crazy underworld abortionist involved, and Hansen brought him in for questioning several times and was pressing for an indictment, but Chief Horrall wanted to squash it. According to Aggie, the doctor died suddenly at his home in Pasadena.

"His death was said to be a suicide," Aggie recalled.

"Do you think the cops killed him?" Joe Friday asked.

"I'm going to stick to my knitting on that one," Aggie replied.

THE SPANGLER CASE was another "OPEN and UNSOLVED" file in the LAPD Homicide Division. There were several significant parallels to the Black Dahlia case, with one major exception—they never found the body.

Jean Spangler was a statuesque twenty-seven-year-old brunette, who had also been one of Mark Hansen's girls at the Florentine Gardens, where she worked as a dancer in 1947. Like Elizabeth and so many other wannabes, Jean made every effort to meet the right people and be seen in all the right places. Becoming a girlfriend of Bugsy Siegel's henchman, Mickey Cohen, she was escorted by Cohen to a number of Hollywood nightspots—Slapsie Maxie's, La Rues, Ciros, the Mocambo—and she soon became a member of the Extras Guild and started getting bit parts in movies.

While waiting for that big break, both Elizabeth and Jean seemed to have traveled through the same circuitous corridors on their road to infamous fame. Jean, too, hung around Brittingham's restaurant next to Columbia Studios. Hoping to become a Columbia starlet, Jean was promised a screen test by Maurice Clement's boss, Max Arnow, who had introduced her to the head of the studio, Harry Cohn.

VOL. XLVI—NO. 305

Glamour Girl Body Hunted; Parallel to 'Dahlia' Case Seen

Big Park Search Organized

Fearful that they have another "Black Dahlia" horror on their hands, 100 policemen and an army of jail trusties today will search Griffith Park's Fern Dell for the body of Jean Spangler.

Her purse—ripped and pawed over—was found there at dawn Sunday. That was some 36 hours after the blue-eyed screen and television beauty had stepped, laughing gaily, from her sister-in-law's home, and into mystery.

PARALLELS SEEN—

And last night, organizing today's search, police were more than half convinced that if they do find the girl's body, it too may be mutilated—as was the body of Elizabeth Short, "the Black Dahlia," when it was found tossed into the weeds on a vacant lot in January, 1947.

Sinister parallels have developed between the case of the Black Dahlia, and the case of Jean Spangler.

Like Elizabeth Short, Jean Spangler loved the gay life.

Like Elizabeth, Jean haunted night spots and the company of men.

Like the Black Dahlia, the lost T-V glamour girl was always willing, perhaps too willing, to make a sudden, impulsive date with a stranger, regardless of danger.

OFFER CLEWS—Terry Taylor (right), proprietor of restaurant on Sunset boulevard, and Al Lazaar (left), "table interviewer" at restaurant, said they saw the missing Jean Spangler last Saturday morning. She reportedly was with a strange man.
—Los Angeles Examiner photo.

"Fear New Dahlia Death"

Several weeks before she vanished, film star Robert Cummings, who was working at Columbia on *The Petty Girl*, had spotted Jean on the set, where she was working as a bit player. They became casual acquaintances, and Cummings told police that he was sitting on his dressing room steps when he saw her walk by, happily whistling a tune.

"You sound happy," he recalled saying to her.

"I am," she replied. "I have a new romance."

"Is it serious?" Cummings inquired.

"Not really, but I'm having the time of my life," Jean responded.

Robert Cummings said he didn't know the identity of the new boyfriend, but it was rumored to be film star Kirk Douglas, who Jean had met while working as a bit player on *Young Man with a Horn*.

Like Elizabeth Short, Jean Spangler suddenly became famous and made the headlines—but not in the way she had dreamed. On Wednesday, October 7, 1949, Jean Spangler vanished and was never seen again.

Jean Spangler
(LAPL PHOTO COLLECTION)

On that Wednesday evening, she had told her sister-in-law, Sophie, she was going to be out late because she was working on a movie that was shooting at night. When Jean had not returned to her Park LaBrea apartment at 6216 Colgate Avenue by late the next day, Sophie filed a missing persons report at the Wilshire Division of the LAPD. Believing that the missing girl would probably show up, the Wilshire police did not bother to send a missing persons report out on the teletype. But on Friday, October 9, a groundskeeper at Griffith Park, Hugh Anger, found Jean Spangler's purse near the park's entrance on Fern Dell Road.

Seeing that one end of the double-straps had been ripped from the purse, police suspected that a struggle had occurred. The contents of the purse seemed to have been undisturbed, however, and among the items found inside was a note in Jean's handwriting:

(LAPL PHOTO COLLECTION)

Kirk,
  Can't wait any longer. Going to see Dr. Scott. It will
work best this way while Mother is away . . .

Jean's mother, Mrs. Florence Spangler, who was visiting relatives in
Kentucky when her daughter vanished, told the police that she
thought her daughter had been murdered. On October 12, 1949, the
Daily News ran a story headlined:

MOTHER SURE FILM PLAYER MURDERED

The mother of film actress Jean Spangler, who mysteriously
disappeared five days ago, said today she is convinced her
daughter has been murdered, and gave Police the name of

the man she thought responsible for the girl's death. "I am sure this man hired somebody to do away with my daughter," said Mrs. Florence Spangler, who arrived here today from a vacation in Kentucky. Police refused to reveal the name of the man named by Mrs. Spangler but said they had already questioned him at some length.

The man was said to be Kirk Douglas. Douglas had been questioned at length by Finis Brown's brother, Det. Thad Brown, who had reason to suspect that the "Kirk" in Jean's note was the Hollywood actor. Douglas and his attorney denied that he knew Jean Spangler or had ever dated her; however, Jean's mother adamantly insisted that Douglas had picked Jean up at their apartment on at least two separate occasions. Moreover, one of Jean's friends told the police that Kirk Douglas had dated Jean often, and others stated they had recently seen them together at a party. Under further questioning, Douglas admitted that he had forgotten he may have met her on the set of *Young Man with a Horn*, and he had forgotten that he may have asked her out on a date or two.

Although Jean had told her sister-in-law, Sophie, that she was working on a movie the night she left her apartment and never returned, police investigators found no record of a film that was shooting on the night of October 7.

When questioned by detectives, several of Jean's friends confirmed that she was three months pregnant at the time she vanished, and they suspected she was headed for a rendezvous with the Hollywood abortionist, Dr. Scott, while her mother was out of town. Some believed that Dr. Scott had botched the operation, and when the victim died, her body was disposed of—perhaps buried in Griffith Park. But that didn't explain how her purse ended up on the street or why the straps had been torn as if she had been in a struggle. "Death by violence is indicated in her disappearance," Det. Thad Brown tersely observed.

In the week before she vanished, a witness stated that Jean had been in Palm Springs—where Kirk Douglas had been vacationing. She was seen at the resort in the company of David "Little Davy" Ogul, a Mickey Cohen henchman. By coincidence, Little Davy Ogul also vanished forever—two days after Jean's mysterious disappearance. When Little Davy's abandoned Cadillac was later found in West Los Angeles, Mickey Cohen made the comment, "I'm afraid that guy ain't living. He was swallowed up."

Police investigators learned that Jean had met with somebody on the evening of Tuesday, October 6. Friends had seen her in front of the Town and Country Market near her apartment, and they told the police that she got into a sedan that had driven into the market parking lot.

On Wednesday evening, the night that she disappeared, she was seen at The Cheese Box restaurant at 8033 Sunset Boulevard by Al "The Sheik" Lazaar, a Hollywood radio personality who knew Jean and did a nightly live radio broadcast from The Cheese Box. Lazaar said he saw her sitting at a booth with two men he didn't recognize at about midnight. Upon approaching their table to interview Jean, he noted that she "appeared to be arguing with the two men," and one of the men abruptly waved him away, indicating they did not want to be interrupted. Lazaar said he "veered away and didn't attempt to conduct the interview" because of the argument that was going on. Terry Taylor, the proprietor of The Cheese Box, confirmed Lazaar's recollection of Jean being there with two unidentified men and said they had left together about midnight. It was the last time Jean Spangler was seen alive—or dead.

Shortly after the disappearance of Jean Spangler, Kirk Douglas arrived at the entry of Columbia Studios to meet with his new flame, actress Evelyn Keyes. Assuming that the studio guard would know who he was, Douglas proceeded to walk into the studio entry; however, the guard stopped him.

"Sorry, you're not allowed to go in," the guard said.

"What do you mean I'm not allowed to go in? I'm Kirk Douglas.

I have an invitation from Evelyn Keyes. There must be some mistake."

"Sorry, but those are my orders."

"Who gave you those orders?" Douglas demanded to know.

"Harry Cohn."

Douglas said he was flabbergasted and had no idea why Cohn had barred him from the lot. But an associate of Max Arnow later related, "Cohn had been furious over the death of his starlet, Jean Spangler, and blamed it all on Douglas."

Two rumors have persisted through the years as to what happened to Jean Spangler:

1. Kirk Douglas had a romance with Jean, and she became pregnant. Three months into her pregnancy she contacted Dr. Scott, a known Hollywood abortionist. Scott accidentally botched the illegal abortion, Jean died, and the remains were hidden.

2. When Mickey Cohen heard that Jean was pregnant, he got greedy and sent one of his boys, Little Davy Ogul, to shake down Kirk in Palm Springs. When Kirk's agent, Charlie Feldman, heard about the shakedown of his rising star, he told Harry Cohn's pal, Johnny Rosselli. Rosselli talked it over with Jack Dragna, and the problem was quickly solved—nobody was ever bothered again by Jean Spangler, or Mickey's goon, Little Davy.

Det. Thad Brown might have checked 2—"Death by violence is indicated in her disappearance," he had observed.

The disappearance of Jean Spangler and her mother's insistence that she had been murdered came at an awkward time for Police Chief Horrall and the upper echelons of the LAPD. Solving the Spangler case was not expedient for the powers that be at City Hall. Her disappearance came right in the middle of the 1949 Grand Jury investigation into unsolved crimes in Los Angeles and contingent payoffs by the underworld to police officials. Some of the payoffs had allegedly been from a Syndicate abortion ring involving a "Dr. Scott."

The Los Angeles Grand Jury investigation of 1949 evolved from the growing concern of the average citizen over rampant crime and corruption within the city. The motto of the LAPD was "To Protect and to Serve," but the public began demanding to know who exactly the police were protecting and serving? In a speech to law enforcement officers, J. Edgar Hoover had stated, "When big city rackets and criminal elements are allowed to operate with impunity, you can be sure that city officials are receiving payoffs."

The unsolved murder of Bugsy Siegel had not ended the Sunset Strip wars. They had continued with numerous gangland killings and attempts to assassinate Siegel's successor, Mickey Cohen. Cohen seemed to have a charmed life. Bombs were set off under his Brentwood home, his black Cadillac was riddled with machinegun bullets, shotguns blasted at him on the Sunset Strip—but a guardian devil seemed to be looking over the padded shoulders of his numerous pastel, silk suits.

In 1948, Mickey Cohen took over a three-story building on the Sunset Strip and called it Michael's Exclusive Haberdashery. Located at 8092 Holloway Drive, the haberdashery was Mickey's fortress headquarters for his bookmaking activities. On the night of August 19, 1948, Mickey was sitting in the haberdashery office having a discussion with three of his henchmen, Jimmy Rist, Albert "Slick" Snyder, and Harry "Hooky" Rothman. When the conversation concluded at about 10:30 P.M., Hooky walked to the front door to leave, and Cohen, who was a compulsive hand-washer, walked to the washroom. As Hooky opened the front door on Sunset Boulevard, two gunmen lunged toward him—one with a shotgun, the other with a revolver. Without saying a word, the man with the shotgun aimed it at

Hookey's head and pulled the trigger, blasting away his face and killing him instantly.

Albert Snyder was still sitting at Cohen's desk in the inner office talking to Jimmy Rist when he heard the gunfire. The man with the revolver ran into the office shouting, "Where is that S.O.B.?"—and without waiting for an answer shot Snyder in the chest.

Jimmy Rist told reporters, "When the guy with the pistol shot 'Slick' I was already up and in the air. I made a grab for him. I got my right hand on the barrel and my left hand on the butt of the gun, and we went to the floor. I was still twisting the pistol when the fellow with the shotgun fired at me. I could see this big thing coming. . . . It looked like a cannonball. That's when he shot off my ear and everything went bleary."

In the meantime, the "S.O.B." was in the washroom, compulsively washing his hands. "When the shooting started, it sounded like a war broke out," Cohen recalled. "I laid myself down on the washroom floor so my foot was holding the door shut, and my body was against the tile so I'd have some protection. After it quieted down and I looked out, Slick was laying by the desk screaming 'get me a doctor! Get me an ambulance!' Then I went out to the front door and saw Hooky was laying there—I seen he was dead."

The shooting on the Sunset Strip led to further public outcry and a demand in the editorials of the *Los Angeles Daily News* for a Grand Jury investigation into the gang wars, racketeering, and series of unsolved murders that plagued the city. While the *Los Angeles Times* editorialized that there was no need for a Grand Jury investigation, the *Los Angeles Daily News* stated in an editorial titled "In the Jungles of L.A.:"

> The Mickey Cohen gangland shootings affair is another indication that the jungle is creeping up on Greater Los Angeles. There have been other signs over the past several years: The employers of violence, the vice promoters, the shake-

down artists and gambling tycoons have moved into the Los Angeles area and made it a profitable stand for graft and robbery. What needs to be known is the relative responsibility of various local law-enforcement agencies for the Los Angeles area's unenviable reputation as a mobster's paradise.

Adding to the crisis looming ahead for law enforcement was Sgt. Stoker's arrest of Brenda Allen. Although he had been warned by Gangster Squad officers Archie Case and James Ahern to cease his Brenda Allen investigation, Stoker proved to be more than an honest cop; he became a crusader. When Stoker received death threats and vows of brutal retaliation if he did not remain silent and close down his investigation, he realized that the vice-queen's empire extended into the towers of City Hall. He defied superiors and, on September 11, 1948, brought *Daily News* reporters with him on an arrest raid at Brenda's Hollywood Hills hideaway.

Placed under arrest by Sgt. Stoker, Brenda Allen shields her face
from the camera as she is escorted from a house in the Hollywood
Hills, along with one of the call girls. (BRUCE HENSTELL COLLECTION)

With mayoral elections coming up in November 1949, Chandler's
man, Mayor Fletcher Bowron, and the *Los Angeles Times* tried to
block the growing demand for an investigation into civic corruption,
but public outrage led to the instigation of the Grand Jury process.
Among the subjects proposed to be investigated by the 1949 Grand
Jury were the Sunset Strip wars, the Brenda Allen prostitution ring
scandal, the Syndicate abortion ring, and the numerous unsolved
murders of young women—including the infamous Black Dahlia case.

Alarmed by the looming Grand Jury investigation, Chief Horrall,
Assistant Chief Joe Reed, and Gangster Squad Capt. Willy Burns
made a Herculean effort to derail the impending investigation into the
murder of Elizabeth Short. Soon after the 1949 Grand Jury was impaneled, and it was revealed that the Black Dahlia case would be

among the unsolved crimes being investigated, Los Angeles Police Chief Clemence B. Horrall tried to take it off the jury agenda by making the dramatic announcement that the LAPD had finally apprehended the psychopathic killer of Elizabeth Short.

VOL. XLVI—NO. 31   LOS ANGELES, TUESDAY, JANUARY 11, 1949

Suspect in Dahlia Case Reveals New Secrets of Killing

Knows Too Much

Bellhop, 27, Said to Know More About Slaying Than Police

Leslie Dillon, a 27-year-old Santa Monica hotel bellhop who knew far too much about the fearsome things a killer did to "the Black Dahlia," last night was held on suspicion of being that killer.

"He is the best suspect we have ever had," said Police Chief C. B. Horrall, who has seen three score suspects eliminated in the manhunt which began January 15, 1947.

On that morning, the body of 22-year-old Elizabeth Short was found in the weeds of a vacant Los Angeles lot. Her body had been cut in half, s c r u b b e d clean, and thrown in the lot. It bore marks of incredible sadistic tortures—before death.

Since then, the police have kept secret a set of "key questions" which only the killer could answer, they believed.

Worked in Many Hotels

"Dillon had all the answers," said Chief Horrall yesterday, as Dillon, who also calls himself Jack Sands, was booked. "More, he knew things even we didn't know about the murder."

Dillon, an Oklahoma boy who worked in many hotels, including San Francisco as well as Santa Monica, was arrested at the end of a fiction-like six-weeks trap-setting by Police Psychiatrist Dr. J. Paul De River.

De River first contacted the man after he had received a letter, signed "Jack Sands." The writer said he had read in a magazine of De River's work in the Black

GRILLED—Leslie Duane Dillon, alias Jack Sands, called by Police Chief C. B. Horrall "the best suspect we have ever had" in the Black Dahlia slaying, is shown during quiz y e s t e r d a y.
—Los Angeles Examiner photo.

Crash Bodies Brought Out | 130,000 Slain, Reds Report

"Suspected Black Dahlia Killer Arrested"

On January 10, 1949, twenty-eight-year-old Leslie Dillon, a hotel bellhop, was arrested on suspicion of murdering Elizabeth Short, and Chief Horrall stated, "There's no doubt in my mind that Dillon is the hottest suspect there has ever been in this case." Police staff psychiatrist Dr. Paul De River proclaimed that Dillon was a psychopath who "knew more about the Dahlia murder than the police did, and more about abnormal sex psychopathia than most psychiatrists."

After being booked and paraded before reporters and photographers at a chaotic press conference in which Dillon pleaded hysterically for help, the suspect was quickly led away in handcuffs by five armed guards. A district attorney spokesman announced, "We're not going to let anybody talk to him—except ourselves, until we've got a closed case." But the case against Dillon never closed, and the Dillon episode became one of the more bizarre chapters in the Black Dahlia twilight zone.

The case against Dillon was orchestrated by Dr. Paul De River, one of the most unusual figures within the Los Angeles Police Department. Allegedly a psychiatrist, De River was a friend of Chief Horrall, who had appointed De River as a psychiatric consultant to the LAPD. As chief of the so-called "Sex Offense Bureau," De River was in charge of assembling files on sex crimes and keeping cross-references on every known sex offender. Although he was a civil servant and not a police officer, as a close friend of Chief Horrall, he became an enforcer within the department and was instrumental in bringing about the false charges against Leslie Dillon in what became known as the "Dillon Catastrophe."

According to Dillon, the charges brought against him started when he wrote a letter to Dr. De River in October 1946 expressing his interest in the Black Dahlia case. At the time, Dillon was an aspiring mystery writer living with his wife and baby in Florida. While working as a bellhop in a Miami hotel, he had read an article in a detective magazine that quoted De River in his analysis of the pathological nature of the Black Dahlia case.

In his letter to De River about the murder, Dillon mentioned that he had closely followed the case because he was living in Los Angeles at the time. Expressing his own convictions about the pathological nature of the crime, Dillon stated that a friend of his, Jeff Connors, had once met Elizabeth Short at a Hollywood bar, and might be helpful to the police. After reading the bellhop's letter, De River telephoned Dillon, who was surprised to hear that the police psychiatrist found his analysis of the crime to be of value. De River told Dillon he was interested in talking to him further.

Former Homicide detective, Sgt. Stephan Bailey, who was working the Dahlia case, recalled that Dillon had written De River at about the time the 1949 Grand Jury was considering looking into the Black Dahlia murder. Bailey recalled that there was a lot of pressure within the department to deflect the Grand Jury investigation. Only an arrest of a viable suspect could conceivably stop the Grand Jury from placing the Black Dahlia case on its calendar. "At the time De River was first contacted by Dillon, and then personally talked to him, we were getting more and more flak about the unsolved killing," Sgt. Bailey said. "It was the cause and effect of circumstances . . . some showing had to be put on to get us out of the red. . . ."

The "showing" proved to be an attempt by the Los Angeles Police Department to frame Leslie Dillon for the murder of Elizabeth Short. When De River informed Chief Horrall of the letter from Dillon and his subsequent telephone conversation, Horrall, along with Assistant Chief Joe Reed and Willie Burns of the Gangster Squad, hatched a scheme to arrest Dillon. Unable to extradite Dillon from Florida without evidence, they decided to lure Dillon to California, where they would arrest him for the Black Dahlia murder and forcibly coerce him into signing a confession.

Initiating several telephone conversations with Dillon, De River spoke in depth to him about the nature of the crime, the site on Norton where the body was discovered, the findings within the autopsy report, and the depraved mindset of the killer. De River then proceeded to disclose to Dillon aspects of the murder that only the killer would know. Stating that he was impressed with Dillon's knowledge of the crime and its pathology, De River told Dillon he would be interested in hiring him as an assistant in his Sex Offense Bureau at the LAPD, and perhaps they could work together on a book about the Dahlia case. He then offered to meet Dillon in Las Vegas and said he would send him plane tickets and arrange his accommodations.

"I flew to Las Vegas where he was waiting at the airport," Dillon recalled. De River then offered to drive Dillon to Los Angeles in his chauffeured unmarked police limousine. The "chauffeur" was Lt. Willie Burns of the Gangster Squad, who was recording Dillon's conversations.

On the way to Los Angeles, Dillon recalled that they spoke once again in depth about the Dahlia murder and went over Dillon's informed theories and insight into the pathology involved. De River asked how Dillon's friend Jeff Connors happened to meet Elizabeth Short at a Hollywood bar and suggested that when Dillon was talking about Connors, he may have actually been talking about himself. The conversation then took an abrupt turn to the possibility that Dillon could be mentally unstable and that his underlying subconscious pathology may have led him into talking to the police about such a bizarre case.

"The conversation right away became more and more psychological on his part," Dillon remembered, "and when we got to the town of Banning and stopped in a motel, the doctor told me out of a clear sky that he believed I had murdered Elizabeth Short." The "chauffeur" then snapped handcuffs on Dillon, marking the beginning of an incredible journey through the smoggy twilight zone of Los Angeles jurisprudence. Dillon recalled the following:

> They kept me in the motel room until three or four other men arrived, and then they began to question me. In the middle of it, De River insisted I was "too knowledgeable," and "too intelligent" to conceal the truth from myself.
>
> I said I didn't know what I'd be concealing from myself, and he said "facts too painful to remember." Then he be-

gan to ask me intimate details about the mutilations and the things that had been done to the Dahlia. But the only things I knew about them was what I'd read in the papers and from the detective magazine and what De River had told me. But De River would ask me a question and then put the answer right in my mouth.

Unable to locate "Jeff Connors," Dillon's supposed friend, who had once met Elizabeth Short, De River maintained that Connors was an aberration—a schizoid extension of Dillon's self.

Transported from Banning to The Strand Hotel in Los Angeles by Archie Case and James Ahern of the Gangster Squad, Dillon's grilling went on for a week. "I couldn't talk to anyone," Dillon recalled. "I couldn't make a call to my wife or try to find a lawyer or anyone to help me. . . . They just kept questioning me. They wouldn't stop. They made me take off all my clothes and took photographs of me stripped naked. While they had me handcuffed to a radiator, they kept on with the questioning. . . . They really got nasty."

Trying to force Dillon to confess, Case and Ahern told Dillon they'd been tracking him for two years and could blast away all his alibis. De River told Dillon that he *must* confess—that he had done something so horrible that he had driven awareness of the murder into his subconscious and that confession was the only way he could avoid going totally mad. Dillon was told if he confessed and faced what he had done, he would not be treated as a criminal, but as somebody who was mentally ill.

"He [De River] wanted me to confess that I'd killed the Dahlia, and I couldn't confess to it," Dillon recalled. "But they had me just about convinced I was crazy or something, and that maybe I *did* kill the Dahlia, and then just forgot about it."

In a moment of desperation, Dillon managed to write a note on a postcard about his plight and drop it from the hotel window to the street below.

(LAPL PHOTO COLLECTION)

The note was addressed to Los Angeles attorney Jerry Geisler and read:

> *I am being held in room 219 & 21 Strand Hotel . . . in connection with the Black Dahlia murder, by Dr. J. P. de River, as far as I can tell. I would like legal counsel—*
> Leslie Dillon

The next day, Dillon was taken to Central and ushered into the office of Chief Horrall by Burns, Ahern, and De River. Horrall informed Dillon that he was being booked for the murder of Elizabeth Short. He was then led away for further interrogation and inducements to confess.

"It went on for about ten hours," Dillon said. "I was losing track of what was happening. I kept insisting I hadn't killed her, but the Doctor tried again and again to convince me that I was blocking out the truth, and that it was necessary for me to *confess* the truth and be free of the troubles I was feeling . . . it was like a nightmare."

The day after Dillon was booked and paraded before the press, somebody had found the postcard Dillon had dropped from The Strand Hotel window, and it was forwarded on to Jerry Geisler's office. One of Geisler's attorneys contacted Dillon's mother who subsequently retained Geisler to file a writ of habeas corpus. Shortly after Dillon's arrest, the case against Dillon began falling apart. Witnesses placed Dillon in San Francisco at the time of the Black Dahlia murder, and employment records confirmed he was working at a San Francisco hotel as a bellhop on the days in question. Geisler's investigators established that Dillon and his wife had not moved to Los Angeles until January 24, 1947, and his friend, Jeff Connors, proved not to be an aberration, but was found to be living in the Bay area. Connors verified to Geisler and the police that Dillon's story about him having once met Elizabeth Short at a Hollywood bar was correct.

Hearing that Geisler's habeas corpus motion was on its way and knowing they had no evidence to answer it, the D.A.'s office quietly issued a statement that the police had insufficient evidence to hold their "hot suspect." Avoiding reporters and further statements about the matter, Horrall and De River tried to lay low until the Dillon Catastrophe drifted off into the smog.

Accusing Horrall of "high-handed bungling and illegal methods in the reopened Black Dahlia investigation," City Councilman Ernest Debs called for an inquiry into Dillon's false arrest and accused De River of being a con artist. It was discovered that De River was neither a doctor nor a trained psychiatrist, and the institution in which he claimed to have studied had no record of him as a student. Subsequently, De River was indicted for forging narcotic prescriptions and resigned from the LAPD.

On January 22, 1949, Leslie Dillon walked out of Central into the streets of Los Angeles, where he was a shaken, but free man. With the release of Dillon, the Black Dahlia case was reconfirmed on the Grand Jury's agenda. It was scheduled to be the last investigation of the 1949 Grand Jury's term—when the mayoral election would be safely concluded. Harry Lawson, an independent man of integrity, was appointed Grand Jury Foreman, and Frank B. Jemison, a highly respected district attorney investigator, was assigned to reinvestigate the murder of Elizabeth Short. But the Black Dahlia case was rapidly growing cold, and the forest of disinformation planted in 1947 had grown quite thick. The path that Jemison and the impaneled jury would have to take through the Byzantine maze of civic corruption was dark and tangled—far deeper and far darker than the few good men chosen to serve on the jury could ever suspect.

TO THE AVERAGE citizen, the Grand Jury is a sequestered legal procedure within the sacrosanct precincts of jurisprudence, and few know the mechanics of the process and its pitfalls. In a system designed to avoid bias and collusion, each of the seventy-five Los Angeles Supreme Court judges selects two prospective veniremen (jurors) known to be community stalwarts of trust and integrity. The list of 150 is then culled down to thirty names, which are placed in a selection box. Nineteen of the names are then randomly drawn, and these selected veniremen serve for one year on the Grand Jury, which reviews pressing criminal matters for possible indictment. The presiding judge of the Supreme Court selects the Grand Jury foreman, and the jury then works with the District Attorney's Office and the Police and Sheriff's Department in reviewing the scheduled cases and calling on witnesses to testify. All sessions are closed, and the records sealed, unless an investigation results in an indictment.

While the selection system ensures the integrity of the jury, the Grand Jury also depends on the integrity of the law enforcement agencies that render testimony and submit evidence on the scheduled cases. The jury's decisions are weighed upon the evidence and testimony brought before it; however, if the district attorney, the investigators, or the police department are corrupt or dishonest, it gravely impedes the jury's just decision-making process.

In 1949, the Los Angeles district attorney, William Simpson, and the upper echelons of the law enforcement agencies were in league with the power brokers at City Hall, and while the Grand Jury Foreman, Harry Lawson, and the district attorney investigator, Frank Jemison, were honest men, they soon found themselves lost in the dark and tangled jungles of power and influence that had overtaken the city.

Assigned to the case in October 1949, Jemison was assured by Chief Horrall and Assistant Chief Joe Reed that he would have their total cooperation in supplying the Grand Jury with whatever information they might need from within the police files. Chief Horrall went so far as to assign Finis Brown to assist Jemison in his investigation of the Black Dahlia case. Few people knew at the time that Finis Brown was a Gangster Squad operative, and his loyalties were to the corrupt LAPD inner circle. Finis found himself in a delicate situation. His brother Thad Brown, who had become chief of the Detective Division, was a protégé of Norman Chandler and was known to be Chandler's choice for the next police chief. In his Gangster Squad assignments, Finis had to be cautious and avoid casting shadows on his brother's good name. Early on, Harry Hansen had discovered that Finis was a member of the Gangster Squad and concluded that Chief Horrall, "Big Jack" Donahoe, and the Gangster Squad were deliberately misdirecting the Black Dahlia investigation, and when he learned that Horrall had assigned Finis as the liaison to Jemison, Hansen wanted little to do with the predictable Grand Jury inquiry.

In the early weeks of his investigation, Jemison, along with his assistant, Walter Morgan, prepared a history of the Black Dahlia case and a lengthy list of suspects. Prior to hearing the Dahlia case, the 1949 Grand Jury was scheduled to conduct a number of other inquiries into criminal matters involving racketeering within the city. During their investigation into the Sunset Strip wars, the numerous attempts to assassinate Mickey Cohen, and the murder of six of his henchmen, a secret conference was held with Cohen and his attorney, Sam Rummel; it was attended by Simpson, Lawson, and Jemison.

In the course of the meeting, Cohen and his attorney agreed to appear before the Grand Jury and "tell all" regarding the rackets in L.A., payoffs to police and the Sheriff's Department, and Jack Dragna's personal vendetta against him. His testimony was to include disclosure that the L.A. Police had tried to shake him down for a series of $20,000 payments to avoid raids on his betting parlors and prostitution rings. Part of the deal that Sam Rummel made with the Grand Jury was immunity from prosecution, as well as the assignment of a bodyguard by the California attorney general to protect Cohen from Dragna and the Gangster Squad enforcers within the LAPD, who followed and harassed Cohen wherever he went. Rummel had informed the state's attorney general, Fred Howser, that he believed "certain officers within the LAPD" were motivated to assassinate his client.

At Howser's request, the LAPD and the Sheriff's Department agreed to withdraw their officers, who had been keeping Cohen under constant surveillance, and the Attorney General assigned Special Agent Harry Cooper to protect Cohen until his Grand Jury testimony scheduled for July 28, 1949. But on the night of Wednesday, July 20, Cohen was exiting Sherry's nightclub on the Sunset Strip with his girlfriend Dee David, henchman Neddie Herbert, and Cooper when gunmen opened rapid fire from behind a billboard across the street. In his testimony before the Kefauver Committee, Bernard Ruditsky, manager of Sherry's, described what occurred:

> **Mr. Ruditsky:** Every night that Mickey came in, for the protection of my customers, I sort of watched the place

and walked around outside and inside. When he would come out I would walk out and tell the parking lot boys to have the cars ready for him . . . and when Mickey come out he come out with Neddie and this girl, Dee David, and Harry Cooper, the Attorney General's man who had been with him every night. I used to talk to Harry every night. He was a likable sort of a fellow. This night when they come out I walked toward them at the steps. I was there talking to Harry Cooper when Mickey's two cars pulled up. I was facing out. Cooper had his head turned to the side and Dee David had her back facing south. Mickey was facing south when these shots come. They sounded like firecrackers to me. I saw the people falling on the sidewalk. I realized then that it was shots from across the street. I had no pistol or anything with me, so I ran back to my car where I kept one in the glove compartment and I started to cross the street. Florabel Muir, of the *Mirror* and the *Daily News* in New York, she came over with me. I had a big light and we started searching around. We found the shotgun slugs there. I walked down the stone embankment, the steps there, and the car had been on a dead-end street and by that time they backed out and got away. I came back and there was a lot of excitement and confusion. We tried to get ambulances and we aided the injured. I stood out there in the street thinking it was a real professional job.

Senator Tobey: Where was Mickey all this time?

Mr. Ruditsky: He was hit in the shoulder.

Senator Tobey: Was he down?

Mr. Ruditsky: This fellow, Frank Niccoli, put him in his car. He took Harry Cooper and Mickey and drove them to the hospital immediately. The others were on the street.

Neddie Herbert and the girl, Dee David—they were lying
on the sidewalk and we moved them in as far as we could
and got them out of the way in case of any further trouble.
They fired, I think, seven blasts. I think it was a 12-gauge
shotgun and they plugged them pretty good.

Senator Tobey: There were no clues?

Mr. Ruditsky: As far as I know, no.

The fusillade wounded Cohen in the shoulder; Dee David was seri-
ously wounded in the back; three slugs shattered Neddie Herbert's
spine; bodyguard Harry Cooper was hit twice in the abdomen; and
Florabel Muir was slightly wounded in the buttocks by a ricochet.
Neddie Herbert died several hours later at the Queen of Angels Hospital, and Harry Cooper was given only a slim chance of survival.

When the shooting was reported in the L.A. newspapers, Angelenos were mystified over why the California attorney general had assigned Officer Cooper to protect a notorious gangster. Cooper lived—
but refused to talk about it. However, to those few who knew the inside story, it was obvious that someone had leaked information regarding Cohen's forthcoming testimony before the Grand Jury about
payoffs to the LAPD and the Sheriff's Department. And whoever was
behind the latest rub out attempt was willing to open fire on a busy
boulevard while Cohen was standing with a group of people and a
state officer. It spoke of desperation.

As the only press witness to the shooting, columnist Florabel Muir
scooped her rivals—and was one of the few to note that Gangster
Squad officer Sgt. Darryl Murray happened to be a patron of Sherry's
that night. Murray was there with his wife, an attractive blonde who
was seen getting up from their table and exiting the nightclub just as
Mickey Cohen's party was getting ready to leave.

Lawrence Vaale, a witness who lived across the Street on Sunset
Boulevard in an apartment at 971 North Hammond, told the *Examiner*

that he was awake when he heard the gunfire, which was followed by voices and the sound of running feet. Looking out his window, he saw a pretty blonde running to a gray Buick two-door sedan parked on the street outside his window. One man was at the wheel, another was already in the back seat, and a third man and the blonde were hurriedly getting into the car.

"C'mon, Chuckie, let's get out of here!" the woman said as she jumped into the Buick, which roared off into the night and headed west on Sunset.

The witness was quoted by the *Examiner* as stating that he "believed the blonde was inside Sherry's watching Cohen and came out just ahead of him as a signal to the two gunmen waiting across the street, while the third man waited at the wheel of the car." He described the woman as "about thirty-five, 120 pounds, shapely, with blonde hair combed straight back. She was wearing a dark suit and no hat." It was a close description of the wife of Sgt. Darryl Murray.

To those who knew of Cohen's scheduled appearance before the Grand Jury and his pending testimony, it was clear who would be highly motivated to have him silenced. When State Attorney General Fred Howser was asked by the *Examiner* why he had assigned Harry Cooper as Cohen's bodyguard, he tersely replied that it was because Cohen's attorney, Sam Rummel, suspected certain officers in the LAPD had reason to assassinate his client.

While recovering in the hospital, Cohen decided it was healthier not to testify before the Grand Jury. And as a postscript to the vice-capades of 1949, Sam Rummel was assassinated by a shotgun blast as he entered his Laurel Canyon home several weeks later. Police were unable to round up a suspect.

Although there was a concerted effort within the corridors of power at City Hall to keep the lid on the inquiry into civic corruption until after the November mayoral elections, the lid popped off when the Grand Jury began looking into the Brenda Allen prostitution ring scandal. Sgt. Charles Stoker, the honest Vice Squad officer who had arrested Brenda Allen, testified before the Grand Jury that he had discovered that the Syndicate Madam was allowed to operate her exclusive Hollywood call-girl ring because she had been paying off top officials in Administrative Vice, including Sgt. Stoker's superior, Sgt. Elmer Jackson, and the officer in charge of Administrative Vice, Lt. Rudy Wellpott. Stoker also disclosed that it was Brenda Allen who had been in the car with Sgt. Jackson when Roy "Peewee" Lewis had been shot by Jackson on February 21, 1947, in front of her former residence at Ninth Street and Fedora Avenue.

The *Daily News* leaked Stoker's testimony and brought forth the fact that there were wire recordings—made by Stoker and his electronic surveillance expert, Jim Vaus—of payoff meetings between Hollywood's leading madam and top police officials, as well as of intimate associations involving Brenda's girls and some of the top brass at City Hall. It was rumored that one of the recordings concerned a conversation relating to the murder of Elizabeth Short. The *Daily News* charged that these recordings were well known to Chief Horrall, but he had suppressed them and taken no action concerning the criminal activities of his officers. As a result, Horrall was called before the Grand Jury, along with Sgt. Elmer Jackson, Lt. Rudy Wellpott, and Assistant Chief Joseph Reed. They denied the accusations under oath and claimed that Sgt. Stoker had perjured himself.

But, as Stoker had observed, Brenda Allen was "as shrewd as they come." After Stoker arrested her in the presence of *Daily News* photographers, the notorious Brenda Allen call-girl ring became public knowledge, and the District Attorney's Office had no choice but to bring pandering charges and place her in jail. But Brenda knew too much. She knew all about the Syndicate influence at City Hall and the payoffs to LAPD officials. She knew too much about the private life of public dignitaries. And she knew too much about the murder of Elizabeth Short. She had it all on tape, and she knew she had City Hall by the testimonies. She held all the cards, if she played them right. Brenda publicly came forward and confirmed that Stoker had been telling the truth, and she had obtained copies of the surveillance recordings from Jim Vaus and kept them in a safe deposit box in a bank vault in downtown Los Angeles.

When Brenda was escorted by the Grand Jury foreman to her bank on Broadway to retrieve the incriminating tapes, vast crowds of Angelenos showed up to witness the event. Sure enough, there were the tape recordings, along with a number of other documents and items that Brenda had secreted to insure her well-being—should the need arise. Among the items was a mysterious photograph of some lilies that had been sent to her apartment shortly after the murder of Elizabeth Short. The photograph of the lilies was printed in the *Examiner*, and when asked about it, Brenda explained that the lilies had been sent to her in 1947 by Sgt. Jackson along with a revealing note; but neither Brenda nor the District Attorney's Office would divulge the note's contents.

Vice Squad officer, E. V. Jackson, sent the vase of lilies to Brenda Allen with a card that was rumored to have referred to the Black Dahlia. (USC REGIONAL HISTORY CENTER)

After the Grand Jury listened to Brenda's tapes, Chief Clemence Horrall, Assistant Chief Joe Reed, Sgt. Elmer Jackson, and Lt. Rudy Wellpott were indicted for perjury and bribery on August 16, 1949. Horrall resigned from the police department, but when the wire recordings and documents vanished from the district attorney's safe and Brenda Allen decided not to testify, Horrall, Reed, Jackson, and Wellpott were acquitted for lack of evidence. Soon freed from jail, Brenda resumed plying her trade.

JUST A LINE TO SAY HELLO
AFTER A BRIEF VACATION

THANK YOU FOR YOUR COURTESY
IN THE PAST.

SINCERELY,
BRENDA ALLEN
HOLLYWOOD 2555

Ironically, the only officer to be publicly punished as a result of the 1949 Grand Jury investigation was Sgt. Charles Stoker—the honest cop. Reduced in rank and placed on the street as a traffic cop, Stoker was subsequently framed by the LAPD on burglary charges and found guilty of "insubordination and conduct unbecoming an officer." Publicly reviled and ridiculed in the *Los Angeles Times* and the Hearst newspapers, Stoker, a devout Catholic, spent the next twenty-five years of his life working as a brakeman in the Southern Pacific Railway yards of Los Angeles, where he died a forgotten man on March 10, 1975.[24]

---

24. A similar fate befell Sgt. Jack Clemmons, the first officer on the scene following the death of Marilyn Monroe. Clemmons insisted that Marilyn Monroe had been murdered, and LAPD officers in the Intelligence Division (the former Gangster Squad) had covered up the crime. Two of the officers named in the cover-up were Archie Case and James Ahern. As a result, false charges were drummed up against Clemmons, and he too was dismissed for "insubordination and conduct unbecoming an officer" and was publicly reviled in the press.

Among the revelations testified to by Stoker before the 1949 Grand Jury was the existence in Los Angeles of a Syndicate abortion ring, protected by Lt. Willie Burns and members of the Gangster Squad. Operated by a group of MD's who were paying protection money, Stoker told the Grand Jury that the leader of the abortion ring was Dr. Leslie C. Audrain, whose office was in Room 417 at 1052 West Sixth Street in Los Angeles. Stoker found that Audrain had a criminal record as an abortionist and worked under a number of aliases—including Dr. C. J. Morris and Dr. Scott. The designated LAPD unit responsible for apprehending and arresting abortionists was the Gangster Squad, but Stoker had discovered that they only arrested abortionists *outside* Audrain's abortion ring who were not paying protection money.

In Stoker's book about his bitter experience within the LAPD, *Thicker 'n Thieves* (Sutter & Co., Santa Monica, CA. 1951), he refers to two Gangster Squad detectives as enforcers of the abortion ring payoff racket. When the detectives discovered that Stoker was conducting an investigation into Dr. Audrain, they threatened Stoker and told him to shut down his investigation. The two detectives once again proved to be officers Archie Case and James Ahern, who also worked the Black Dahlia case for "Big Jack" Donahoe and were involved in the arrest and grilling of Leslie Dillon for Dr. De River.

Stoker's revelations about Dr. Leslie Audrain and police payoffs came at the same time that Det. Harry Hansen was pushing for the arrest of Dr. Audrain in connection with the murder of Elizabeth Short. Aggie Underwood had stated that there was an abortionist whom Harry Hansen suspected of being involved in the murder of Elizabeth Short, but Chief Horrall had blocked the arrest. And in an interview that appeared in the Pasadena *Star News* in 1987—forty years after the crime—Finis Brown finally hinted at the truth. The article stated:

> Brown has an idea of who the Dahlia murderer was, a theory he has never made public. "I didn't want the newspapers

to get any of it," he explains. Now after 40 years he has decided to reveal it. He believes that Elizabeth Short was killed by a man who ran a Hollywood abortion clinic. "The girls were going to this doctor," he says. "We couldn't prove he was the killer, but some of the things I found out he was doing to some of the girls made me think he was the one."

The doctor committed suicide two years after the murder, just as Hansen and Brown found him and were about to start asking questions.

Dr. Leslie C. Audrain allegedly committed suicide at his home in Pasadena on May 19, 1949.

As an operative of the Gangster Squad who was positioned in the Homicide Division, Finis Brown knew far more about the Black Dahlia case than he ever revealed. In examining the Grand Jury notes and testimony recently discovered in the Black Dahlia files at the Los Angeles District Attorney's Office, it becomes clear that Brown had been strategically placed as a liaison to the Grand Jury by Horrall and Reed to mislead the Grand Jury's investigation.

In the process of narrowing Jemison's list of suspects in the Dahlia case to the "prime suspects" to be investigated by the Grand Jury, Brown led Jemison to believe that the prime suspects to be investigated were Leslie Dillon, Mark Hansen, Cleo Short, and a relatively new suspect, Henry Huber Hoffman. And the Black Dahlia files clarify that, during the term of the 1949 Grand Jury, the hearings centered on those four prime suspects.

At the opening of each Grand Jury hearing in the Black Dahlia case, it was formally stated:

> This Jury at this time is engaged in a review of the records and information of the Los Angeles Police Department regarding suspects in the murder of Elizabeth Short, with par-

ticular attention to such evidence as has been procured and gathered or might be obtained, concerning the following persons: one, **Leslie Dillon**; two, and/or **Mark Hansen**; three, and/or **Henry Huber Hoffman**; and four, and/or **Cleo Short**, who is the father of Elizabeth Short. Now we are paying attention to the material in hand as to whether or not any of those persons should be charged with that crime.

Yet, Brown knew from the beginning that all four prime suspects had alibis, lacked advanced medical training, and could not possibly have committed the crime.

Although Mark Hansen had been cited as one of the suspects, logic dictated that if he had murdered Elizabeth Short, he would hardly have mailed the belongings from her purse to the *Examiner*, which included her address book with his name embossed on the cover. And Jemison and the jury soon learned from Det. Harry Hansen's testimony that only someone with "advanced medical knowledge" could have bisected the body.

In addition, on the night of January 14, 1947, a number of witnesses had placed Mark Hansen at the opening of a movie theater in Long Beach and at a party that followed at the Long Beach Hilton. Barney Vandersteen, Mark Hansen's associate who had purchased Bugsy Siegel's share in the Florentine Gardens, testified to the Grand Jury that after the party on the night in question, Hansen had been a guest at his home in Redondo Beach until well after 3:00 A.M. on the morning of January 15:

> **Jemison:** As of this date would you say that you had seen Mark Hansen in the city of Long Beach?
>
> **Vandersteen:** Yes. I would like to refer to the records of an opening of a theater, and a party given by Charlie Skouras—
>
> **Jemison:** In other words, Mr. Vandersteen, we may be able

to establish no doubt the date of this particular occasion when the theatre was opened?

Vandersteen: There is no question about that.

Jemison: On that occasion did you see Mark Hansen?

Vandersteen: Yes.

Jemison: Did you spend some time looking at a moving picture, as you remember?

Vandersteen: Yes.

Jemison: Thereafter what did you do?

Vandersteen: After that we went—we drove to the Hilton Hotel in which there was a party arranged for the guests who attended the opening.

Jemison: Would you say you saw Mark over at the Hilton?

Vandersteen: Yes, I sat down with him; had dinner at his table.

Jemison: Did that last till some time late in the morning—about what time did it let out—did you leave?

Vandersteen: I would say it was after two o'clock—well after two.

Jemison: After you left the Hilton where did you go from there?

Vandersteen: We went from the Hilton Hotel to my home.

Jemison: Did Mark Hansen go with you to your home?

Vandersteen: Yes, he followed me in the car.

Jemison: Did it take some time to get to your home in Redondo Beach?

Vandersteen: Yes, it took a long time because the weather was bad.

Although Mark Hansen had been promulgated by Brown as one of the four prime suspects, it soon became clear to Lt. Jemison that

Hansen had a solid alibi, and the police investigators had known from the beginning where he had been on the night in question.

Despite the Dillon Catastrophe, Brown also pushed Leslie Dillon as a prime suspect. But after journeying to San Francisco to investigate Dillon's whereabouts on the date of the Black Dahlia murder, Jemison discovered that Dillon, too, had an alibi that had already been established in the course of the police investigation. And in his brief testimony before the Grand Jury, Det. Harry Hansen confirmed the alibis of both Mark Hansen and Leslie Dillon. He also acknowledged that in 1947, he and Brown had checked out the whereabouts of Cleo Short on the night of January 14 and determined that he could not have committed the crime. When questioned by Jemison, Det. Harry Hansen said he knew nothing about the fourth prime suspect, Henry Huber Hoffman.

Henry Hubert Hoffman was introduced as a suspect shortly after the Dillon Catastrophe in January 1949. The police were desperate to present another plausible Black Dahlia suspect before the Grand Jury, and Hoffman proved to be a windfall patsy for Gangster Squad detectives Case and Ahern. An ex-convict, once jailed for mail fraud, Hoffman had been the manager of the Astor Motel at 2101 South Flower Street. His ex-wife, Clara, who divorced him in 1948, informed the police that she believed he had been involved in the murder of the Black Dahlia. She said she had found a bundle of bloodied women's clothing in Unit 9 of the motel, along with a considerable amount of blood on the floor and mattress at about the time of the Black Dahlia murder. Gangster Squad Chief Willie Burns assigned operatives Case and Ahern to check out her story. The two detectives spent months trying to build a case against Hoffman for the murder of Elizabeth Short, and to establish that the murder had taken place in Unit 9 of the Astor Motel.

Subsequently, it was leaked to the press—just prior to the commencement of the Grand Jury inquiry into the Black Dahlia case—

that the LAPD had discovered the murder site. On September 13, 1949, the *Herald Express* article headlined "Black Dahlia Murder Site Found" stated: "It was reported that the room where the murder took place was less than a 15-minute drive and in a bee-line from the vacant lot where the nude and bisected body of the girl was discovered . . . and the room was on one of Los Angeles's busiest streets."[25]

Although Finis Brown managed to have Henry Huber Hoffman listed as a prime suspect by the Grand Jury, the suspicions once again proved to be without evidence or plausibility. Clara Hoffman's accusations against her ex-husband kept changing, along with the supposed location where she found the bloodied mattress and clothing. Hoffman submitted to a lie detector test that was conducted under Jemison's supervision, and he passed with flying colors.

After thousands of man-hours spent running down false trails in the Grand Jury investigation, all four prime suspects put forward by Brown and presented by the district attorney and the LAPD to the Grand Jury in the Black Dahlia case proved to be patently innocent of the crime, and it was apparent that Brown had known of their innocence from the outset.

The testimony of Sgt. Conwell Keller of the Gangster Squad that Brown had secretly been a liaison of Willie Burns aroused suspicions that the Grand Jury had been misled; and in the midst of the Grand Jury hearings, an unsettling event occurred involving Brown that confirmed the suspicions of jury foreman Lawson and investigator Jemison.

On the morning of July 14, 1949, Lola Titus, a former dancer at the Florentine Gardens, entered Mark Hansen's home behind the nightclub and shot Hansen twice while he was shaving in his bath-

---

25. In *Black Dahlia Avenger*, Steve Hodel claims that the location of the murder site mentioned by the *Herald* was his father's house in Los Feliz, which Hodel states was only fifteen minutes from Thirty-ninth and Norton; however, the Black Dahlia Grand Jury files clarify that the location leaked to the press was the Astor Motel on South Flower Street. (See "The Hodel Hypothesis," Appendix B.)

room. Wounded in the abdomen and arm, Hansen was rushed to the hospital. Remaining conscious en route, Hansen kept screaming, "Get me Brown! Get me Finis Brown! I've got to speak to Brown!"

While being transported from the ambulance into the emergency room of the Hollywood Receiving Hospital, a reporter for the *Hollywood Citizen News* noted that Hansen was hysterically calling for Finis. Perplexed by Hansen's plea, the reporter did some investigating and learned that Brown had often been seen at the Florentine Gardens. It had been rumored by several former employees that one of the assistant managers at the Gardens was an undercover cop on the take. It proved to be Finis Brown.

Lola Titus had once been a girlfriend of Mark Hansen, and when Hansen rejected her, she tried to blackmail him over shady Syndicate operations under his purveyance. Shortly after Hansen confided in Brown about his problem, Titus was arrested for narcotics trafficking and posing for lewd photographs. Suspecting she had been setup by Mark Hansen, she shot him in revenge.

Although the LAPD tried to squelch Brown's connection to Mark Hansen, rumors about his "undercover work" at the Florentine Gardens began circulating at the District Attorney's Office. Mystified by Brown's involvement in the shooting, Lawson asked Brown about the incident; however, Brown carefully skirted around the nature of his association with Mark Hansen:

Lawson: What was your involvement in this Lola Titus shooting?

Brown: Lola Titus, a short time before this shooting—I think around March or April of this year—was called to my attention by informants. I was told that she was involved in lewd pictures, lewd photography as a model, and also possibly connected up with some narcotics. I secured a picture of her in the nude and checked our records and found that she had been a dancehall girl.

Lawson: The point of my questioning was, when you learned Lola Titus was the one that shot Hansen, why weren't you surprised you got a call?

Brown: I wasn't surprised because as far as Hansen knew I was the only one who knew Lola Titus was—

Lawson: You had discussed Lola Titus with him?

Brown: I had, yes. He had given me some information on her.

Lawson: Were you one of the officers that had some part— had frequented his nightclub, ostensibly cooperating with him with respect to bad characters, persons of ill-repute, that he knew?

Brown: That's right.

Lawson: And that took place in what period of time?

Brown: 1947, first of '48, through '48 to the present time.

Lawson: Did you know when Hansen was taken to the hospital, that he said, "Get Brown for me. Get in touch with Brown."

Brown: That is what I understand.

Lawson: How did you get that information, sir?

Brown: Well, that was through—when I came in the next day, the newspaper reporters told me that.

Lawson: I see. Did you talk to Mark Hansen about the matter then?

Brown: I did that night—around eight o'clock, seven-thirty or eight o'clock. I went to his room in the hospital and talked to him. He told me that—it was Lola Titus who did it.

Lawson: Well, I have always been curious to know why Mark Hansen wanted to see you and was shot on account of this Titus thing—

Unsolved L.A. Crimes Ripped By Grand Jury

Above is a recent photo of Elizabeth Short, 22, victim of the "werewolf" murder, known as "The Black Dahlia" because of her dark beauty and her penchant for sheer black dresses.

Pointing a grave finger of condemnation at law enforcement officials for their failure to solve many mysterious murders and disappearances of women, the 1949 Los Angeles County Grand Jury in its final report today painted a black picture of:

1. Crime, corruption and gangsterism which included charges that evidence indicated that law enforcement officers many times accepted bribery pay-offs to cover up law violations.

2. That Los Angeles women and children are continually in danger because of the failure of the authorities to apprehend criminals who commit sex crimes and murders.

3. That dope peddlers, abortionists, bookmakers and gamblers carry on a nefarious and extensive traffic and "the criminals, in many cases, have gone unpunished."

4. That "attempts have been made by some public servants and private citizens to discredit the acts of the 1949 Grand

(HEARST NEWSPAPERS)

Although jury members felt that they'd been misled and police officials had withheld information, the Black Dahlia case had been scheduled at the end of their term, and there was no time to reexamine witnesses and redirect their questions to other suspects before their adjournment on December 29. The Grand Jury did, however, issue a seething rebuke of the LAPD for deliberately covering up details of the crime and protecting underworld elements who were involved in murders, crimes, and racketeering within the city. The Grand Jury Final Report stated:

> This jury has observed indications of payoffs in connection with protection of vice and crime, and gross misconduct on the part of some law enforcement officers.
>
> Testimony given by certain investigation officers working this [Black Dahlia] case was clear and well defined, while other officers showed apparent evasiveness. There was not sufficient time left to the jury to complete this investigation, and this Grand Jury recommends that the 1950 Grand Jury continue the probe into the Black Dahlia case.

An article that appeared in the *Herald Express* on January 12, 1950 quoted the Grand Jury's final report, enumerating the jurors' findings that some LAPD officers were receiving payoffs from gangsters, bookmakers, and abortionists, and there had been a "cover-up" in the Black Dahlia investigation.

Although Grand Jury foreman Harry Lawson called for a continuation of the investigation into the Black Dahlia case by the next impaneled jury of 1950, it did not happen. The jury's files, the transcripts of testimony, and Lt. Frank Jemison's notes were all eventually carted off to the cavernous LAPD warehouse in East L.A., where the truth hidden in Jemison's investigation papers would gather dust and remain in the dark for more than half a century.

AS A RULE of law, unless there is an indictment that stems from a Grand Jury investigation, the files are sealed and never made public; however, in the Black Dahlia case, some of the Grand Jury investigation material inadvertently became accessible in 2003 when the Los Angeles District Attorney's Office established its archives and opened up to researchers some of its files on notable twentieth century criminal cases. Among these files was a portion of Grand Jury investigator Frank B. Jemison's file on the murder of Elizabeth Short. This unintentional disclosure of Grand Jury proceedings and testimony proved to be a windfall of new information that had been hidden from the public for more than half a century.

In speaking to a former file clerk who handled the assembly of the files for the archive, I learned there had originally been sixty-five file boxes of accumulated Black Dahlia investigative material, which included the files of the LAPD, the Sheriff's Department, and the District Attorney's Office. The file clerk recalled that the sixty-five boxes were culled through in the early months of 2002 and reduced to thirty-five boxes, which remain in the LAPD warehouse. But two file boxes involving Jemison's 1949 Grand Jury investigation into the Black Dahlia case were among those placed in the archives of historical criminal cases at the D.A.'s office.

Included in Jemison's files are transcripts of testimony before the Grand Jury, as well as Jemison's extensive notes on his investigation, which contain many missing pieces of the Black Dahlia puzzle.

In examining Jemison's notes, it becomes evident how Finis Brown and the Los Angeles Police Department manipulated the Grand Jury and maneuvered them down dead-end paths. Having requested the LAPD to supply him with a list of key officers involved in the original Black Dahlia investigation, Jemison discovered that most of the officers were members of the Gangster Squad rather than Homicide, indicating that the case was clandestine and far more complex than presented to the public.

```
      5.   The following members of the Department worked on
the case:

           Sgt. Ahern (g)
           Waggoner (g)
           J. J. O'mara (g)
           Jones (g)
           Case (g)
           Williams (g)
           Sgt. C. Keeler (g)
           Harry Hansen
           Greeley
           Cannaud (g)
           Hedrick (g)
           Jaccapuzzi (g)
           Meyers (g)
           Barnes (g)
           Wm. Burns
           Capt. Kearney
           Inspector Collins
           Chief Horrall.

(g)  On Gangster Detail at time.

- - - - - - - - - - - - - - - - - - - -
```

On the list of officers that worked the Dahlia case, only Harry Hansen and Officer Greeley were with Homicide. Finis Brown proved to be a Gangster Squad operative, but his name was omitted from the list. (LADA ARCHIVES)

The fact that the Black Dahlia case had been handled by the enforcers of the city's vice-ridden underworld was a confidential matter hidden from the public for more than fifty years; however, when William Worton became the interim police chief after the resignation of Chief Horrall, he made the terse announcement that the office of "Assistant Police Chief" was being dispensed with. Reed was forced into retirement, and Burns was transferred.

In the closing weeks of the 1949 Grand Jury's tenure, Jemison realized he had been misled by Brown into investigating suspects who had already been found by Homicide to be innocent; and Jemison's notes indicate that he began a reinvestigation into other possible suspects, in the expectation that the Black Dahlia case would be placed on the 1950 Grand Jury agenda.

OFFICE MEMORANDUM

TO: LIEUTENANT FRANK B. JEMISON
IN RE: NOTES TAKEN ON BLACK DAHLIA MURDER
FROM: INVESTIGATOR WALTER MORGAN

1-5-50, case #30-1268
(1) Elderado Scott, M. D., 7266 Sunset;
(2) Mascott, Vet., 7131 Santa Monica Boulevard;
(3) Doc Scott hangs out at bars on strip; 30 years, 6 ft., 165 pounds, sandy hair, blue eyes, light complexion, Southern drawl, 1948 Olds convertible, '98 series;
(4) Walter Scott, Abortionist, 5947 Hollywood Boulevard, Olympia 2802;
(5) Dr. Morrell, 2618 Castle Heights Place.

1-6-50, case #30-1268, Wood, Dr. J. P. or J. S. rented 417. 1945 deposit slips in California Bank changed to Morris, C. J., May, 1946 -- Biochemical Laboratory -- C. J. Morris left October 31, 1948. Wood lived in Long Beach; had office in downtown area; J. P. Story Building. Janitor and elevator operators were here in 1946 and 1947. Morris had a girl working for them. Mr. Morris paid rent -- late 30's, five feet six inches, nice dresser, dark hair, gentile -- Morris was being investigated by Medical Board. Morris connected with some sanitarium in Pasadena -- abortion ring (?), change of names on door -- lots of girls going in

---

Room 417 at 3122 West Sixth Street was the office that Sgt. Stoker discovered to be the center of the abortion ring run by Dr. Leslie C. Audrain. Dr. C. J. Morris was the name on the door, but that name proved to be the alias used by several abortion ring doctors. (LADA ARCHIVES)

The extensive memos and notations of Jemison and his assistant, Walter Morgan, suggest they had accepted the opinion of Det. Harry Hansen, the medical examiner, and the FBI that an individual with advanced knowledge of surgical technique was involved in the bisection of the body. In the early months of 1950, Jemison began an investigation into Dr. Audrain's Syndicate abortion ring and abortionists who may have been connected to the murder and mutilation of Elizabeth Short.

Ann Toth had testified that, in the days before Elizabeth left the city, either Mark Hansen or perhaps Maurice Clement had driven Elizabeth to a doctor's office on Hollywood Boulevard. One of the names Jemison found in Elizabeth's address book was Dr. Arthur M. Faught, a known Hollywood abortionist with offices in the Cherokee Building at 6636 Hollywood Boulevard. Jemison learned that Dr. Faught had succumbed to a sudden heart attack in September 1949—just as the Black Dahlia inquiry began. However, on February 1, 1950, Jemison questioned Dr. Melvin M. Schwartz, who had shared Suite 215 in the Cherokee Building with Dr. Faught. Schwartz recalled an incident when Elizabeth Short had visited the office in search of Dr. Faught, just before she suddenly left the city for San Diego:

Jemison: What type of a doctor was Dr. Faught?

Schwartz: Dr. Faught was a medical doctor, a M.D., physician and surgeon.

Jemison: Well, in the fall of 1946 were you located in a suite with Dr. Faught?

Schwartz: Yes sir.

Jemison: Sometime in the fall of 1946 did Beth Short come into your office?

Schwartz: It was approximately 12, 14 days before Christmas. There was a young lady, stepped in the suite of offices looking for Dr. Faught, who later appeared to be the same one that we have seen in pictures . . . Beth Short.

Jemison: Did you discuss her identity with Dr. Faught along about that time—just after the murder?

Schwartz: He called me in and asked me if I recognized the picture, and I said I didn't. He said, "Haven't you seen her up here?" And I said, "My God, that face does look familiar."

Jemison: Well, go ahead and tell about your conversation and experience with Beth Short.

Schwartz: She walked in the office, asking for Dr. Faught, I told her the doctor left his office and he wouldn't be back until 9 o'clock the following morning. I questioned her as to what her trouble was. She seemed to be rather reluctant to talk, this was in the reception room, there were other patients waiting. We stepped into Dr. Faught's office, and she pulled an address book out, and she wanted to call somebody. She did call somebody from that office. It was a type of conversation you couldn't tell who she was talking to or what it was all about, but it was on the shady side, I do recall that.

Jemison: Do you know whether she called a man or a woman?

Schwartz: It appeared to be a man the way she talked.

Jemison: What did she say—anything about that call?

Schwartz: I have big ears, inasmuch as it was a peculiar setup. I tried to determine what type of a conversation it was, but . . . you couldn't tell being at one end of it . . .

Jemison: You have now seen a photograph of Beth Short, would you say that was the girl that was in there that afternoon?

Schwartz: I would say it resembles her very, very closely.

Jemison: And you're quite positive that you never saw her after that?

Schwartz: I'm positive. Incidentally, I asked Dr. Faught the following day whether or not the patient had returned to see him, and he said no.

Jemison's notations included abortionists who worked out of the Sixth Street office of Dr. Leslie C. Audrain. Under the heading "Suspects," Jemison lists several known Syndicate abortionists, including Dr. A. E. Brix, and he indicates that the doctor's name and address were found in Elizabeth Short's address book. On the bottom of the list is the name of Dr. C. J. Morris, aka Dr. Leslie Audrain, who was identified by Sgt. Stoker as the ringleader of the Syndicate abortion ring. After his name and address, Jemison makes the notation "was written by Beth Short in her address book."

Among the list of Jemison's suspects were a number of abortionists. The names of Dr. A. E. Brix and Dr. C. J. Morris were found in Elizabeth Short's address book. (LADA ARCHIVES)

Sgt. Stoker had first become aware of Dr. Audrain and the Syndicate abortion ring when he was alerted by an inspector of the California State Medical Board. The inspector had learned of the ring through an informant and requested that Stoker conduct a secret investigation because it had been discovered that the Gangster Squad was receiving payoffs and protecting Audrain's activities.

Stoker enlisted the help of policewoman Audrey Davis, who posed as a "girl in trouble," and visited Audrain's office in Room 417 at 1052 West Sixth Street. An arrangement was made for an abortion at a fee of $200. An appointment was made for the following week, when Stoker hoped to make an arrest. But the day prior to the scheduled appointment, Stoker was told by the medical board inspector that Audrain had been informed of the investigation. When Officer Davis showed up for the scheduled appointment, Audrain's office was locked and remained closed for more than a week. Audrain had been tipped off. Subsequently, Stoker was warned by Gangster Squad officers Case and Ahern to drop his investigation.

Jemison learned that Dr. Audrain had died suddenly at his home in Pasadena in May 1949—just as the Grand Jury Black Dahlia investigation was about to get underway. His death was said to be a suicide. Although Jemison was unable to interview the suspect, according to Aggie Underwood and Finis Brown, Det. Harry Hansen *had* interviewed the abortionist several times and was pushing for his indictment as an accomplice in the murder of Elizabeth Short. However, Hansen's interviews with Dr. Audrain remain in the LAPD warehouse and were not included in the Black Dahlia files recently found at the DA's office; nor is there any indication that they were ever brought to the attention of Jemison or the Grand Jury.

Jemison's notations also indicate that he had reexamined Elizabeth Short's address book in an effort to find leads to prime suspects among people she had known. One scrap of paper found among his notes, which seems inscrutable upon initial examination, proves to be an important lead in the Black Dahlia case and takes the Byzantine trail back to the short, swarthy man who was the driver of the "1936 or 1937" black Ford sedan—Maurice Clement.

Notations found on the invitation to the District Attorney's Office Christmas party. (LADA ARCHIVES)

On District Attorney William Simpson's invitation to the DA's 1949 Christmas party, Jemison had written the names and addresses of several suspects he found in Elizabeth's address book. At the top is "Red Morris (Bob)" with an address in Huntington Park, which proved to be "Red" Manley—whose middle name was Morris. His name is followed by several aliases used by Dr. Leslie Audrain that are associated with his office on West Sixth Street—"Dr. Morris," "Dr. Stott," and "Dr. Scott." The name and address of Dr. A. E. Brix, another known abortionist who lived in the Silver Lake district, was also found in Elizabeth's address book. On the bottom of the invita-

Far from their days as street toughs in Brooklyn, Bugsy Siegel and George Raft remained close friends in Hollywood. DELMAR WATSON ARCHIVES

Jack Dragna, the Mafia boss of Los Angeles from 19 until his death in 1956
UNIVERSITY OF SOUTHERN CALIFORNIA, REGIONAL HISTORY CENTER

Bugsy Siegel's Flamingo Hotel, shortly after its completion in March 1947. Bugsy and Virginia Hill stayed in the fourth-floor penthouse. CORBIS/BETTMAN

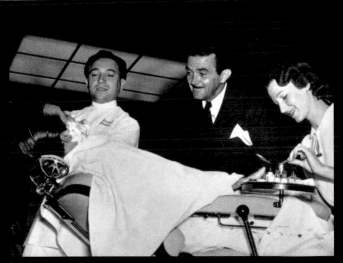

ugsy Siegel wearing his denim
il uniform, tailored by Jerry
othschild's of Beverly Hills
LMAR WATSON ARCHIVES

Harry Drucker gives Bugsy Siegel a haircut while Billy Wilkerson looks on.
W. R. WILKERSON III COLLECTION

he Clover Club, with its popular gambling casino, stood on Sunset Boulevard near La Cienega. The Piazza Del
ol, where Bugsy Siegel lived in 1935, is the building just beyond the Clover Club sign. DELMAR WATSON ARCHIVES

The El Palacio Apartments in West Hollywood. Georgette Bauerdorf's apartment was to the left of the center entry. Her bedroom was on the second floor, behind the window to the upper left. ANN WOLFE

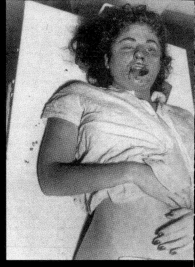

A morgue photo of Georgette. Her mouth h[ ] been torn when the killer stuffed a cloth ba[ ] dage into her throat. UCLA DEPARTMENT OF SPECI[ ] COLLECTIONS/JOHN GILMORE COLLECTION

Georgette's body as it had been found in the tub
UCLA DEPARTMENT OF SPECIAL COLLECTIONS/JOHN GILMORE COLLECTION

ickey Cohen inspects the damage caused by a bomb placed nder his Brentwood home. DELMAR WATSON ARCHIVES

Following the attempt to assassinate Cohen at his Sunset Strip Haberdashery, Mickey stares at the spot where one of his henchmen had been shot and killed. LOS ANGELES PUBLIC LIBRARY, HISTORY DEPARTMENT PHOTO COLLECTION/*HERALD EXAMINER* COLLECTION

llowing the shooting, Cohen and his associates were brought into the West Hollywood Sheriff's Station for estioning. Sitting beneath a cemetery calendar: (*left to right*) Mike Howard, Mickey Cohen, Sol Davis, and mes Rist, who was wounded. LOS ANGELES PUBLIC LIBRARY, HISTORY DEPARTMENT PHOTO COLLECTION/*HERALD EXAMINER* COLLECTION

After arresting Brenda Allen at her Hollywood home in 1948, Sergeant Charles Stoker examines her client card file, which included the names of some prominent personalities and dignitaries.
UCLA DEPARTMENT OF SPECIAL COLLECTIONS/*DAILY NEWS* COLLECTION

Brenda Allen looks over the shoulder of her attorney, Max Solomon (*right*), while the deputy city attorney, Lindsey Dickey, thumbs through Brenda's client file. The names were never divulged. UNIVERSITY OF SOUTHERN CALIFORNIA, REGIONAL HISTORY CENTER

ickey Cohen and electronic surveillance specialist
mes Arthur Vaus, with one of his devices that
corded Brenda Allen's telephone conversations
ith Administrative Vice Officer E. V. Jackson. The
cordings later vanished from District Attorney
mpson's safe. UNIVERSITY OF SOUTHERN CALIFORNIA,
GIONAL HISTORY CENTER

Brenda Allen takes the stand before the 1949 grand jury.
UCLA DEPARTMENT OF SPECIAL COLLECTIONS/*DAILY NEWS* COLLECTION

eutenant Frank B. Jemison
S ANGELES DISTRICT ATTORNEY ARCHIVES

Vice Squad Officer Sergeant E. V. Jackson (*left*) and his
superior, Lieutenant Rudy Wellpott, on trial for perjury
during the 1949 vice scandals. UCLA DEPARTMENT OF SPECIAL
COLLECTIONS/*DAILY NEWS* COLLECTION

Gunmen were concealed behind the billboard on the south side of Sunset Boulevard when they fired at Mickey Cohen's party in front of Sherry's. LOS ANGELES PUBLIC LIBRARY, HISTORY DEPARTMENT PHOTO COLLECTION/ *HERALD EXAMINER* COLLECTION

The scene in front of Sherry's on the Sunset Strip after the attempted assassination of Mickey Cohen. Mortally wounded, Cohen's henchman, Neddie Herbert, lies on the sidewalk. The shooting took place shortly before Cohen's scheduled grand jury appearance.
DELMAR WATSON ARCHIVES

Shortly after the shooting at Sherry's, Sam Rummel was shot and killed by an unknown assailant in front of his Hollywood home. DELMAR WATSON ARCHIVES

Following the arrest of Brenda Allen and his testimony before the grand jury, Sergeant Charles Stoker was removed from administrative vice and demoted to traffic, before being railroaded out of the police department on false charges. UCLA DEPARTMENT OF SPECIAL COLLECTIONS/*DAILY NEWS* COLLECTION

rman Chandler's friend, actor Arthur Lake, with his
fe, Patricia. Patricia was the daughter of William
ndolph Hearst and his mistress, actress Marion
vies. UNIVERSITY OF SOUTHERN CALIFORNIA/REGIONAL HISTORY
ITER

Harry Chandler (*left*) and William Randolph Hearst.
LOS ANGELES PUBLIC LIBRARY/HISTORY DEPARTMENT PHOTO COLLECTIO

hur and Patricia Lake sit to the left of William Randolph Hearst at a party held in Marion Davies's Santa Monica
ch home. Hollywood columnist, Louella Parsons, stands behind Hearst. LOS ANGELES PUBLIC LIBRARY/HISTORY DEPARTMENT
TO COLLECTION

Captain Jack Donahoe, photographed in his office at Central on the occasion of his promotion to inspector in 1956, shortly before his forced retirement for drug dealing

UNIVERSITY OF SOUTHERN CALIFORNIA/
REGIONAL HISTORY CENTER

Framed Black Dahlia murder suspect, Leslie Dillon (*center, weari* *overcoat*), is flanked by (*left to right*) Dr. J. Paul De River, Lieuten Willie Burns, Chief C. B. Horrall, and Captain Francis Kearney.

UNIVERSITY OF SOUTHERN CALIFORNIA/REGIONAL HISTORY CENTER

Police Chief C. B. Horrall (*left*) and Assistant Chief Joe Reed prepare to testify before the 1949 grand jury during the vice-squad scandals. Both Horrall and Reed ultimately resigned.

UCLA DEPARTMENT OF SPECIAL
COLLECTIONS/*DAILY NEWS* COLLECTION

John Gilmore in his office at the historic Bradbury Building in downtown Los Angeles
JOHN GILMORE ARCHIVES, PHOTO BY JAMES DAVIDSON

Administrative Vice Officer Vince Carter is shown with famous New York photographer, Arthur "Weegee" Felig, during a visit to Los Angeles in

VINCE CARTER

Vince Carter and the author (*right*) at Carter's home in Victorville, California in 2004
ANN WOLFE

The bungalow court on Catalina Street behind the Ambassador Hotel, where Brenda Allen's girls stayed. The murder of Elizabeth Short is believed to have taken place in the rear bungalow. ANN WOLFE

Arrested in New York and brought back to Beverly Hills by B.H. Police Chief Clinton Anderson, Al Greenberg, leader of the McCadden Gang, shields himself from photographers. UNIVERSITY OF SOUTHERN CALIFORNIA/ REGIONAL HISTORY CENTER

A mug shot of Al Greenberg
ASSOCIATED PRESS

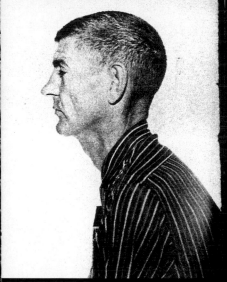

The fourth man—Jack Anderson Wilson

AUDRAIN, Leslie C.   '27
General   Rush Med. Col. '07
Born '76   Calif. Lic. '22
1052 W. 6th St.
Los Angeles 14   MA. 4502

Dr. Leslie C. Audrain, leader of the Syndicate abortion ring in Los Angeles. His address and room number were found in Elizabeth Short's address book.

Maurice Clement, Brenda Allen's procurer,
who worked in the Talent Department at
Columbia Studios

In 1950, Detective Harry Hansen exhibits a picture of Elizabeth Short retained in the voluminous Black Dahlia files. UNIVERSITY OF SOUTHERN CALIFORNIA/REGIONAL HISTORY CENTER

tion is a question mark followed by "Apt. 107—1616 No. Normandie Ave., Hollywood 27."

Opposite the names of Dr. Morris, Dr. Stott, and Dr. Scott, Jemison had put another question mark next to the number of the address on West Sixth Street—Room 417, indicating that it may have been difficult to decipher, but 1052 West Sixth Street—Room 417 proved to be the address of Dr. Leslie C. Audrain. The address after the question mark on the bottom of the Christmas party invitation—"Apt. 107—1616 No. Normandie Ave., Hollywood 27"—was discovered to be that of Brenda Allen's procurer, Maurice Clement. The question mark may have indicated that Jemison had difficulty reading Elizabeth's handwriting or that she had not written down the name connected with the address, but his subsequent note regarding Apt. 107 clearly establishes that he found the address to be Maurice Clement's, and Clement worked at Columbia Studios.[26]

(LADA ARCHIVES)

26. Though a number of names and addresses had been cut from the address book, Maurice Clement's and Dr. Audrain's addresses may have escaped elimination because Clement's name was illegible or missing, and only Audrain's aliases appeared in the book. Although names had been cut from the pages, modern forensic technology could allow the detection of the missing names by fluorescing the pen or pencil indentations on the pages that follow. This missing evidence could still be ascertained today in Elizabeth Short's address book, which remains sealed within the LAPD Black Dahlia files.

> 7. Maurice Clement, Apartment 107, at 1616 North Normandy was working
> at Columbia Studios at the time of the murder. His name appeared in
> this victim's address book. He knew Short socially and is a likely
> type of character but has been partially eliminated by Los Angeles
> Police Department. See their reports.

(LADA ARCHIVES)

Another notation with the two names "(1) Michael Anthony Otero" and "(2) Maurice Clement" indicates that Clement "Saw her . . . about 6 times," and one of the occasions was on December 1, 1946—in the week before she left the city.

Michael Otero, a teacher at Santa Monica High School was an acquaintance of Maurice Clement. Both admitted seeing Elizabeth Short about six times each in the week before she left for San Diego.
(LADA ARCHIVES)

Although Maurice Clement was never publicly named as a suspect, there was reason to believe he was among the "Person or Persons Unknown:"

- Maurice Clement was known to drive a car matching the description of the one seen at the site where the body was found.
- He was identified by the clerk at the Hawthorne as a frequent visitor who often paid Elizabeth Short's rent.
- He was identified as the person who transported Elizabeth to Mark Hansen's residence on Carlos Street.
- Ann Toth stated he was a frequent caller at the Carlos Street residence and offered to set Elizabeth up in a Beverly Hills apartment.
- He was identified by Elizabeth's roommate at the Chancellor as someone who frequently called her.
- He was identified as someone who was seen with her at Brittingham's on at least four separate occasions in the days before she suddenly left Los Angeles.
- He lied to the police in stating he had only met Elizabeth in early December 1946.
- Ann Toth said she had driven Elizabeth down to the vicinity of the Biltmore Hotel in mid-November, where she thought Elizabeth was meeting Maurice Clement.

However, there were those in officialdom who went out of their way to avoid mentioning Maurice Clement or bringing him in as a suspect because he was the link to the true nature of the crime and the perpetrators. As the procurer who often drove around the Brenda Allen call girls for the Columbia Studio brass, Clement was connected to one of the major Syndicate prostitution rings within the vice-map of the city controlled by Bugsy Siegel—a vice-ring known to pay generously for police protection. As with Dr. Audrain, investigative scrutiny of Clement was a peril to the upper echelons of the LAPD, who were receiving lucrative payoffs and had been successful in covering up the motive and nature of the crime—and its connective link to the Syndicate. Jemison had placed Clement as number seven on his suspect list, and he may have arrived at the conclusion that Clement was a prime suspect along with Dr. Leslie Audrain (aka Dr. Morris, Dr. Stott, or Dr. Scott), but the 1950 Grand Jury was deflected by District Attorney William Simpson from continuing the Black Dahlia investigations, and it was taken off the 1950 Grand Jury calendar. While Jemison's notes and the Grand Jury transcripts were buried in the dark of the LAPD warehouse for more than fifty years, a review of the files recently unearthed in the District Attorney's Office supply a number of crucial pieces to the Black Dahlia murder puzzle—enough to translate the "silent scream" of the "sacred setting."

Elizabeth Short's friend, Arthur James, said he had learned of Elizabeth's pregnancy shortly before she left for San Diego. And *Examiner* reporter Will Fowler, the first reporter on the scene at Norton Avenue, observed that there was an incision on the victim's abdomen that appeared to be from a hysterectomy, and the uterus had been removed. Surgeons and medical experts who examined photos of the body that were found in the Black Dahlia files have also confirmed Fowler's observations. Upon examining the photos, eminent professor and surgeon Dr. Michael Keller stated, "There appeared to be a willful attempt to perform or simulate the performance of a hysterectomy which at that time would have been done though a lower vertical midline as the photos appear to show. That was a medical decision." The addresses of at least four different abortionists were found in Elizabeth Short's address book, and the Grand Jury transcripts indicate that in the last days before she suddenly left the city, Elizabeth had tried to visit Dr. Faught, a known abortionist with offices on Hollywood Boulevard.

These new discoveries give voice to the "silent scream":

- Elizabeth Short was pregnant.
- There was an abortionist involved in the crime.
- It was a double murder.

That was the dark secret of the autopsy report—withheld from the public to this day. That was the control question.

But this was hardly the accidental murder of a woman and her unborn child in the process of an illegal abortion. Because there was no ecchymosis in the surgical procedures, and Elizabeth Short had died from the bludgeoning and knife cuts to the face prior to the abdominal incision, we know, therefore, that the uterus, along with the fetus, were removed after Elizabeth's death. The abortion was post-mortem.

That Elizabeth Short was pregnant and the fetus was removed after her death paints an entirely different picture of the crime, and it provides the most important element in solving a homicide. It establishes motive. As mad and depraved as the murder was, it explains the motivation behind the madness, and it begins to give substance to the shadowy figures who were in attendance at the "sacred setting."

Harry Hansen was correct in believing that Elizabeth Short's murder was connected to one of her acquaintances. The connection was with the man who had fathered the child—someone whose name may have been cut from her address book. According to Fred Otash, it was Norman Chandler, heir to the Chandler dynasty, and the most powerful man in the city of Los Angeles—the man who literally designated the mayor, appointed the police chief, controlled the LAPD, ran the city council, and published the *Los Angeles Times*.

Was the most powerful and influential man in the city of Los Angeles the father of Elizabeth's unborn child? Arthur James, who had spoken to Elizabeth in the days before she fled the city, recalled that she spoke of her pregnancy and named Norman Chandler as the father. Former Administrative Vice officers Vince Carter and Ron Hardman believed Norman Chandler was the connection to the Black

Dahlia murder; and Fred Otash, the former LAPD officer who had placed Norman Chandler under surveillance for Ray Pinker, knew that Elizabeth Short was among the young women Norman Chandler and his friend Arthur Lake entertained at Chandler's California Club penthouse, located just behind the Biltmore Hotel.

If Brenda Allen's procurer, Maurice Clement, had arranged a liaison for Elizabeth Short with Norman Chandler, and she had become pregnant with his child, it would explain many mysteries in the Black Dahlia case. It was understood that Brenda Allen girls didn't get pregnant, and if they did, they'd go to a Syndicate abortionist. Those who didn't cooperate had serious problems—especially if someone as powerful as the heir to the Chandler dynasty was involved. Indeed, if Elizabeth didn't proceed with the abortion, as Maurice Clement must have warned her, she would indeed have had reason to be afraid of somebody or something.

The night before she left Hollywood for San Diego on December 6, 1946, Mark Hansen and Ann Toth found Elizabeth in tears and saying she was "scared". Her Chancellor roommate Sherryl Maylond said there had been a number of calls from Maurice, and Elizabeth had become afraid and said that she "had to get out of there!" Her landlady also observed that she seemed to be worried about something and was anxious to leave the city. Elizabeth may have been warned that she must submit to an abortion or else find herself in great peril. Apparently, she was frightened to the degree that she didn't want anyone to know where she was going. She told her roommates, as well as Mark Hansen and Ann Toth, that she was going to Oakland over the holidays to visit her sister Ginnie. But Ginnie said she had not heard from Elizabeth for some time and that there were no plans for a visit.

Instead, Elizabeth headed south to San Diego where she knew no one.

While staying at the home of Elvera and Dorothy French in Pacific

Beach, they observed that Elizabeth appeared to be anxious about something—biting her fingernails "down to the quick." They sensed she was "hiding out." According to Jemison's notations, on or about January 4, she made the mistake of calling Mark Hansen and asking for money, and she told him where to send it in San Diego. Two days later, "three strangers" appeared at the Frenches' door looking for Elizabeth. Once more she became frightened. After she turned to Red Manley for help, he arrived in San Diego on January 8 and assisted her in moving from the Frenches' home. On the following day, Thursday, January 9, he drove her to Los Angeles. On the drive north, Manley described Elizabeth as being worried or anxious and recalled that she was frequently looking at the occupants of cars behind them, as though she was concerned that she was being followed.

Evidently, Elizabeth had no intention of returning to Los Angeles to stay. She had written Gordon Fickling on January 7, stating she was planning to go on to Chicago, where she'd be modeling for "Jack."

But there was someone she wanted to see before she went on to Chicago—someone she called from a payphone in Laguna Beach. Robert Manley said she had called somebody in Los Angeles.

For a person who struggled to get by, as young women like Lynn Martin and Marjorie Graham did from day to day, the implication that she was pregnant with the child of the richest and most powerful man in the city wouldn't have escaped Elizabeth. Money had always been important to her—she had tried to eke it out of her father, who had left the family broke. She had tried to obtain money from "Chuck," the sergeant at Camp Cooke who had abused her, from the parents of Matt Gordon after he died, from Mark Hansen, and from Gordon Fickling.

It would have been a temptation to try to get some help from Norman Chandler. After all, he wasn't like the others. He was distinguished, cultured, a gentleman from a respectable family. Surely he would help her. She would leave town, go to Chicago—never bother him again.

Elizabeth may have tried to call Chandler from the payphone in Laguna Beach—perhaps left a message that she needed to see him. His private apartment, she knew, was just behind the Biltmore.

If Norman Chandler felt threatened, he may have stalled for time and called Assistant Chief Joe Reed, who traditionally did the trouble shooting for the Chandlers. A subsequent call from Reed or "Big Jack" Donahoe to Dragna could solve the problem. As in the Jean Spangler case, the problem might simply vanish. But the Brenda Allen call-girl ring was within Bugsy Siegel's vice-map. Brenda's business was a Bugsy Siegel/Mickey Cohen operation.

It was an awkward situation. Bugsy was spending most of his time in Vegas, and the cops and Dragna didn't get along with Mickey. Although Dragna couldn't talk to Mickey, he could talk to Bugsy, even if they loathed each other. Bugsy happened to be in town that week. He had arrived on January 6—the day of the Mocambo job—and one of *his* girls was causing the trouble. He had stolen Brenda from Dragna's territory, and it was Bugsy's responsibility—not Dragna's. Solving an embarrassing problem for the mogul who ran the city would be a major marker for the mob.

When Elizabeth and Red Manley arrived in Los Angeles, she checked her baggage at the Greyhound Bus Station and said she was going to meet her sister Ginnie at the Biltmore Hotel. But after driving her to the hotel, Manley was unable to locate Elizabeth's sister before he had to say good-bye. He left Elizabeth in the lobby at approximately 6:30 P.M. We know from Ginnie's statements that she had no plans of visiting Elizabeth in Los Angeles, and we can only conclude that whoever it was that Elizabeth was planning to meet at the Biltmore, or in its proximity, was somebody whose identity she did not want to disclose—perhaps one of the people whose name and phone number had been cut from her address book.

The bell captain at the Biltmore said that Elizabeth had used the lobby payphone to make several calls after Manley left, and she was seen in the ladies room applying candle wax to her teeth. The bell captain saw her waiting in the lobby until approximately 10:00 P.M. She then left the hotel alone. Because there was a time lapse of approximately three and a half hours between Manley's departure at 6:30 P.M. and the time Elizabeth left the hotel at 10:00 P.M., one could safely conclude that either the person she had hoped to meet in the lobby never showed up, or she had been waiting in the lobby until the appointed time she was to meet that person at a nearby location—someplace within walking distance of the hotel. The last time Elizabeth Short was seen alive was when she walked out of the lobby of the Biltmore Hotel and headed south on Olive toward Sixth Street on the evening of January 9, 1947.

It was just a short walk from the Biltmore to the rear entrance of the California Club, which was on a dead-end street that led to the main downtown library. The library closed at 9:00 P.M., and the street was deserted and dark. There was just the one street light on the corner, and initially, Elizabeth may not have recognized her abductors. Among them was someone who knew her—someone who could readily recognize the girl with the distinctive walk who was causing all the problems—even though she had tried to change her appearance.

Newspapers reported various sightings of Elizabeth Short between January 9 and January 14, the night of the murder. But these sightings were investigated and discounted because the witnesses invariably described the victim as having jet-black hair, and detectives knew that she had dyed her hair red before leaving San Diego.

Reason dictates that if Elizabeth had voluntarily changed her mind and decided to stay on in the city, she would have returned to the Greyhound Bus Terminal and picked up the luggage containing her clothing and her all-important makeup kit.

Reason dictates that, at some point during that week, she would have contacted some of her acquaintances—Ann Toth, Mark Hansen, Marvin Margolis, Bill Robinson, or her former roommates at the

Chancellor. Or that she would have written to her mother, who said that she received a letter from Elizabeth at least once a week.

And reason dictates that she was abducted at some point shortly after she walked out of the Biltmore and was then held captive during the interim week at a location that Harry Hansen believed to be not far from Pico and Crenshaw—where her shoes and handbag had been found in the incinerator.

On the morning of January 14, Bugsy Siegel cancelled his scheduled trip to New York. That evening, Mr. Johnson, a Liemert Park resident, spotted a suspicious thin, little man standing on Norton Avenue near an older dark sedan and staring at the spot where the body was to be discovered the next day. That night, Elizabeth Short was brutally murdered—her face slashed open from ear to ear with a knife, her head repeatedly bludgeoned by a blunt metal instrument, her uterus and fetus removed, the identifying tattoo sliced from her leg, strange cut marks made on her body, and the letter D carved into the pubic area of her flesh. The bisected corpse was then transported to the vacant lot on Norton Avenue, where it was displayed not far from Jack Dragna's home, before being discovered on the morning of January 15 by Mrs. Bersinger.

A 390 W—415—down in an empty lot on Norton one block east of Crenshaw—between Thirty-ninth and Coliseum Streets . . . Proceed to investigate . . . Code Two . . .

Rogue Cops

FOLLOWING THE GRAND Jury's exposure of underworld pay-offs to LAPD officers, Governor Earl Warren appointed the California Crime Commission to investigate the infiltration of criminal elements in Southern California, and the winds of change began whistling through the mean streets of Los Angeles.

After the resignation of Chief Horrall in August of 1949, Mayor Bowron temporarily appointed William Worton as interim chief until the police commission selected Horrall's replacement. Thad Brown was Norman Chandler's choice, and it was assumed that Thad would be named as the next chief. However, Norman Chandler lacked the Machiavellian antennae of his father and failed to detect the back-room skullduggery going on in City Hall. To the surprise of many, it was William Parker who received the appointment by the commission. And for the first time in more than half a century, a non-Chandler choice became the Los Angeles police chief, and Parker wore the chief's badge for the next sixteen years.

A dedicated politico, Parker was an ambitious man who had an obsession for promotion and had set his eyes on the chief's swivel chair early on in his career. Having served as lieutenant in the office of

Chief James "Two Gun" Davis during the 1937 corruption scandals, he knew his way around the smoky backrooms of City Hall.

Corruption became more sophisticated under Parker's regime. His juice was political favor, and he envisioned J. Edgar Hoover's desk in D.C. as the big payoff. Cooperating with Gov. Warren's Crime Commission, Parker declared war on the criminal elements in the city, and under Parker's regime, it became increasingly difficult for underworld enforcers to operate within the department. When it was discovered that Capt. Jack Donahoe had become a major dealer in a Mafia drug ring, Parker accepted Donahoe's early retirement, rather than make an arrest and have the ugly story appear in the press.

Donahoe died on June 18, 1966, and the *Los Angeles Times* gave him a glowing eulogy. The obit stated: "One of the most noted detectives in the country, Capt. Jack Arthur Donahoe died yesterday at his Hollywood home after a lengthy illness. He was found dead in his living room chair by his wife." It was never mentioned in the press that Donahoe had died of a bullet through the heart or that the coroner's report indicated that he died of "Self-inflicted gunshot wound to the chest . . . Cause of Death—Suicide."

Vince Carter recalled that during Parker's regime many of Chief Horrall's former underworld enforcers were transferred or went into forced retirement, but Archie Case and James Ahern became Parker's golden boys and received special assignments.

It was while researching *The Last Days of Marilyn Monroe* in 1992 that I first met former Administrative Vice officer Vince Carter. At the time, Vince was writing his book on the shady history of the Los Angeles Police Department, *LAPD's Rogue Cops* (Desert View Books, 1993), and after a number of conversations, I found that he knew a great deal about the Black Dahlia case, as well as the murder of Marilyn Monroe. Vince, I discovered, had been an acquaintance of Case and Ahern, and it was through Vince that I learned that Case and Ahern had played an intricate role in the murky history of the

LAPD and were instrumental in the police commission's appointment of Parker as the new chief.[27]

During World War II, Parker served in Army Intelligence, and when he returned to the LAPD, he was promoted to deputy chief. He soon saw his opportunity to be named chief when Horrall resigned. One of Parker's confidants was Lt. James E. Hamilton, a drinking buddy who had worked with him in Army Intelligence. After the war, Hamilton had become the chief investigator for the police commission and was close to Joe Reed and Norman Chandler, who wanted to know everything that was going on in the backrooms of Central. But Hamilton was an opportunist whose loyalties bent with the changing breeze.

While Hamilton's job was essentially to conduct investigations *for* the police commission, according to Vince Carter, he was privately conducting investigations *of* the commission to detect which way the breeze was blowing for his pal Parker. Although it was assumed that the majority of the commission would vote for Thad Brown, Hamilton had observed that Norman Chandler and a member of the police commission, Mrs. Curtis Albro, were often in each other's company, and Hamilton had them put under surveillance by two trusted members of the Gangster Squad—Case and Ahern. They tailed Chandler and Mrs. Albro to Arthur Lake's beach house in Santa Monica and staked out the hideaway until Chandler and Mrs. Albro left the next morning.

Having technician Fred Otash install cameras and bugs in the beach house, as he had at the California Club, Hamilton monitored and observed Chandler at every opportunity. Vince Carter revealed, "Hamilton continued his surveillance until he had accumulated

---

27. While Stoker refers to Case and Ahern in *Thicker 'n Thieves* as "Joe Small and William Ball," in *LAPD's Rogue Cops*, Vince Carter refers to them as "Frank Bain and Jerry McGhee." Carter said he used pseudonyms for Case and Ahern to protect Ahern, who was still living at the time. Archie Case died in 1978, and James Ahern died in 1999.

enough evidence of lovemaking between Chandler and Mrs. Albro to blow Chandler out of the water."

Oblivious of his predicament, Chandler ran a story in the *Times* indicating that Thad Brown would be appointed the next Los Angeles Police Chief. The *Times* story stated that three of the five commissioners had given their support to Thad Brown, including Mrs. Albro, and it was only a matter of a formal vote to make the appointment official. Shortly before the official vote, however, Norman Chandler was informed of the enormous scandal waiting for him in Parker's closet should Thad Brown be appointed. Mrs. Albro suddenly died on July 29, 1950, and four days later the vote swung to Hamilton's friend, William H. Parker, who would become the Los Angeles Police Chief for the next sixteen years.

Lt. James E. Hamilton's weather vane proved to be pointing in the right direction. Parker promoted him to captain and appointed him as Chief of the Gangster Squad, which became known as the notorious Intelligence Division under Hamilton's watch. Case and Ahern became Hamilton's favored officers within the Intelligence Division, and during the next decade, Parker's closet became a warehouse of intelligence gathering on politicians, film stars, studio moguls, and the private lives of power brokers from L.A. to Washington D.C.

I learned from Vince Carter that one of the cushy assignments that Hamilton gave to Case and Ahern was their appointment as security officers to the Kennedy family during their visits to Los Angeles. When Robert Kennedy was a member of the Kefauver Committee, he operated out of Capt. Hamilton's office when he was on the West Coast, and Case and Ahern became Robert Kennedy's drivers and security guards. When Sen. John Kennedy visited the city and stayed at Peter Lawford's beach house, Case and Ahern kept a watchful eye on him, as they did at the 1960 Los Angeles Democratic Convention and on the occasions of numerous visits to Los Angeles during his presidency.

In the course of researching my Marilyn Monroe biography, I

learned from Vince Carter and other confirming sources that Case and Ahern had accompanied Robert Kennedy to Marilyn Monroe's house on the night she died, and it was Capt. James Hamilton of the LAPD Intelligence Division who arrived on the scene after the film star's death and orchestrated the "locked bedroom" suicide scenario. And I discovered that the rise of Case's and Ahern's careers—from the depths of intrigue and blackmail within the LAPD to the heights of murder and cover-up—began one night back in January 1947, when they became inadvertently involved in the Black Dahlia case.

After the end of World War II, Case and Ahern were two young detectives working out of the Wilshire Station on Pico Boulevard. Occasionally they would work with Vince Carter and Sgt. Ron Hardman on stakeouts of suspected narcotics dealers. As they whiled away the hours during the stakeout of a suspect, Case and Ahern revealed to Carter and Hardman that, on the night of January 14, 1947, they were staking out Lucey's Bar and Grill on Melrose Avenue, which was located near RKO and Paramount Studios, when an incident occurred that changed their lives. Owned by Syndicate front man, Nathan Sherry, Lucey's was popular with the late night film crowd and known for its rush hour traffic in drugs. Failing to spot the drug dealer they were looking for, Case and Ahern recalled that they left Lucey's at closing time and drove their unmarked police car south on Western Avenue as they headed back to Pico and the Wilshire Station. When they crossed Wilshire and were approaching Eighth Street and Crenshaw, they spotted a dark sedan run a red light as it traveled east with its lights off. Ahern, who was at the wheel, doused his lights, did a u-turn, and gave silent chase. He saw the sedan's brake lights flash as it turned south off Eighth onto Catalina near the Ambassador Hotel. As Ahern turned the corner in pursuit, Case spotted the car pulling to the curb.

"They're stopping up the block," Case said. "They're parking."

The two detectives pulled into a parking spot a half block down the street. Turning off their motor, they watched as three men got out of the dark sedan and walked toward a bungalow court at 836 Catalina Street. The detectives quietly bailed out of their car and quickly walked toward the bungalows, as a fourth man—the driver— got out of the sedan, locked the door, and walked around the car to the sidewalk. Case and Ahern followed him toward a rear bungalow and intercepted him as he opened the front door. Shoving his badge in the man's face, Ahern barked, "Police!"

Taken by surprise, the driver panicked and fled through the door into the bungalow. Charging through the door in pursuit, the two detectives pulled their guns and ordered the driver and his three companions to raise their hands. After being searched for weapons, the four men were told to produce identification. The man who seemed to be the leader of the group pulled out his wallet, took out a card, and handed it to Ahern. It was a police courtesy card.

"Go ahead, turn it over," the man said. Turning over the card, Ahern saw that on the backside was a handwritten notation: "The bearer is a friend of mine. Any courtesy you can show him will be appreciated." The card was signed by Capt. Jack Donahoe. Donahoe's home phone number was below the signature.

"Call him. Go ahead," the man said, motioning toward the phone. Capt. Donahoe had been the detectives' boss when they were working Robbery, and as Ahern walked toward the phone in the bungalow hallway, he anticipated that Donahoe wasn't going to be happy about a predawn phone call. As the detective picked up the phone, he noticed a smear of blood on the wall. Glancing down the hallway, he saw more bloodstains. While Case held the four men at gunpoint, Ahern followed the blood trail to the bathroom, where he found blood spattered all over the walls, the floor, even the ceiling. The sides of the tub and the washbowl were covered in blood. Bloody towels were on the floor and in the hallway.

"God almighty," Ahern yelled to Case, "this place looks like a slaughter house!"

When questioned about the blood, the men refused to talk to anyone but Capt. Donahoe. Getting the uneasy feeling that they may have gotten into something over their heads, the detectives called the number on the card. Unhappy, indeed, about being awakened, Donahoe demanded an explanation. Ahern detailed what had occurred, described the bloody bungalow, and identified the man who held the courtesy card.

"Hold everything," Donahoe said. "I'll be there in twenty minutes."

In 1947 Dohahoe was living at 7811 Harvard Boulevard in Inglewood, approximately four miles from Catalina Street and the Ambassador Hotel. When Donahoe arrived and viewed the scene, he took the man who had produced the courtesy card into the kitchen. After about ten minutes, Donahoe returned to the living room and informed Case and Ahern that the men had been in a wild poker party. There had been a lot of drinking and a bloody fight had broken out, which accounted for all the blood. Ahern noted, however, that there was no upset furniture or signs of a struggle, and the four men had bloodstains on their clothes, but no signs of injuries. Donahoe went on to explain that the injured participants had been taken home.

Case and Ahern were told to leave, and Donahoe told them he would take responsibility for everything. Leaving the four men in the bungalow, Donahoe walked with the two detectives out to the sidewalk and told them to forget about the incident and what they had seen. "You don't know what you're dealing with," Donahoe warned. "This guy could put all three of us in hell with one phone call."

After returning to the Wilshire Division, it was dawn by the time Case and Ahern went off duty and departed for their respective homes. They hoped to sleep in late, but Ahern slept fitfully and was fully awake by noon. Going into the kitchen to get something to eat, he turned on the radio. After the latest smog alert, a newscaster reported the discovery of a young woman's body in a vacant lot on Norton Avenue in Leimert Park. The woman's nude body had been mutilated and severed.

Grabbing the phone, Ahern called his partner. They shared the gut feeling that the woman's body was connected with what they had seen at the bungalow court on Catalina Street. Deciding to take a ride over to Norton Avenue where the body was discovered, they found the area swarming with police, the press, and the curious. Learning that the coroner had not yet removed the body, they made their way to the grisly scene. It was evident to Ahern that the murder had not occurred where the body was discovered because little blood was found at the site, and the remains were virtually drained of blood.

Capt. Donahoe had ordered more than fifty police officers to search the area surrounding the lot where the body was found, and he announced to the press that an exhaustive investigation would take place—"Every lead would be followed up by Homicide's best investigators."

But Case and Ahern knew there would never be a search warrant for the bungalow court at 836 Catalina Street behind the Ambassador Hotel, and the four occupants of the dark sedan would never be questioned. It was understood by Case and Ahern that the incident at the bloody bungalow wasn't to be reported or discussed. According to James Ahern, the man who had produced Donahoe's courtesy card— the man who "could put all three of us in hell with one phone call"— was Benjamin "Bugsy" Siegel.

Brenda Allen's bungalow court on Catalina, where the Ambassador call girls stayed, would have been a logical location to detain Elizabeth Short after abducting her in the vicinity of the Biltmore Hotel, and it would have been in convenient proximity to the offices of the Syndicate abortion ringleader, Dr. Leslie Audrain, at 1052 West Sixth Street—less than five blocks away. The incinerator where Elizabeth Short's shoes and handbag were found was at a mid-point between the bungalow on Catalina and Thirty-ninth and Norton.

If the abortionist who bisected the body was Dr. Leslie Audrain, as Harry Hansen suspected, Audrain had already left the bloody bungalow by the time Case and Ahern arrived. But who were the three henchmen in the bungalow with Bugsy Siegel? Although Case and

Ahern did not reveal their identities, it's likely that the driver was the swarthy little man who worked for Brenda Allen, the procurer who was known to drive Elizabeth around in his old black Ford sedan— Maurice Clement. Clement matched the description given by Mr. Johnson, the Leimert Park resident who had spotted a man staring at the spot where the body would be discovered fourteen hours later. And there's reason to believe that one of the other two men was Al Greenberg, owner of Al Green's Nightlife Bar and boss of the McCadden Gang. Greenberg, who had worked with Bugsy back in the days of the Bugs and Meyer Mob, had been involved in a number of jewel robberies for Bugsy at the time of the murder, and he also knew Elizabeth Short, who had once worked for him as a B-girl.

Although neither the police nor the press had ever publicly connected Bugsy or the Syndicate with the Black Dahlia murder, in 1999, the FBI's legendary mind-hunter, John Douglas, author of *The Cases That Haunt Us* (Scribner's, NY, 2000), did an in-depth analysis of the Black Dahlia case. As an FBI specialist in behavioral analysis and criminal profiling, Douglas was instrumental in analyzing the Son of Sam case; identifying Seattle's Green River Killer; arresting San Francisco's Trailside Killer, David Carpenter; and finding the Tylenol Poisoner.

In profiling the Black Dahlia case, Douglas examined the inquest documents, studied the FBI reports, and the published case histories, but was denied access to the sealed (or lost) autopsy report; and he made his observations in 1999, prior to the availability of the Black Dahlia files at the Los Angeles District Attorney's Office.

Unaware that Elizabeth Short was pregnant at the time of the murder, Douglas observed that the photos of the body exhibited an incision in the abdomen compatible with that of a hysterectomy. "A vertical incision that looked like a hysterectomy incision was between her pubic area and navel," Douglas noted.

Although only limited information was available to him at the time, Douglas made many perceptive observations. Questioning whether or not the murder was a pathological "lust crime," which normally involves a lone killer, Douglas found contradictions to the "lust crime" patterns. Lust crime killers are seldom methodical and often repeat their crime using a similar MO. Douglas noted that there were no similar case histories, either before or after the Black Dahlia case:

> To do what he did to his victim, both ante mortem and postmortem, he also had to have a house or an apartment. It could be small and run-down as long as it was some place private, with access to running water, where he knew he would not be interrupted. So now we know the UNSUB [unknown subject] can't have been poor—at least not compared to his victim. He had to have some money for rent as well as car expenses.
>
> And this is not the type of crime we'd expect a jealous boyfriend to commit in the heat of passion. Nor is it, to shoot down another theory suggested by some, the actions of a frustrated suitor, who in a drunken frenzy, went nuts when he learned that this girl was the ultimate tease— didn't even have the proper equipment to have sex with him. These scenarios—and/or one involving a female offender—do not match the profile of this UNSUB as evidenced by the crime.
>
> Lust crime killers have disorganized personalities, yet this UNSUB was able to imagine, plan, and carry out this time-consuming, complicated crime. For this reason we'd expect him to have some criminal history before his encounter with Beth Short. . . . You don't jump into this kind of thing without some criminal evolution and development.

Limited to the information available to him at the time and based on the presumption that there was only one UNSUB involved in the crime, Douglas executed a cogent profile of the principal person involved in the murder of Elizabeth Short:

THE UNSUB:

He was a white man, no younger than his late 20's and possibly older, with a high school education.

He lived alone, made his living working with his hands rather than his brains, was adept with a knife, and was comfortable wallowing in blood. The killer was familiar with prostitutes.

He was rigid, patient, compulsive, and deliberate.

He drank alcohol, possibly took drugs, and probably had a police record for either threatening or assaulting someone with a knife.

The killer was under great personal or financial stress. . . . He and Short spent several days together. Maybe he had a physical handicap or stuttered, and Short made fun of it. . . . The mixture of personal stress, alcohol or drugs, and anger exploded into a murderous rage.

BUGSY SIEGEL:

Bugsy Siegel was forty when the murder took place. He dropped out of high school in his sophomore year.

Bugsy Siegel was divorced in August 1946, and was having violent arguments with Virginia Hill. He was a hands-on killer, adept with a knife, and was comfortable wallowing in blood. He was familiar with prostitutes.

Bugsy Siegel was rigid, patient, compulsive, and deliberate.

Bugsy Siegel drank alcohol, took drugs, and was known to threaten, assault, and murder people with both a knife and a gun.

Bugsy Siegel was under great personal and financial stress. Bugsy Siegel had a mental handicap and was prone to murderous rages. He may have exploded into a paroxysm of violence—pistol-whipping his victim before slashing open her mouth from ear to ear.

Douglas believed that the mutilation reflected both rage and a meticulous attempt to avoid identification of the victim. "The washing is to eliminate forensic clues," Douglas stated, "and the severing of the body is for easier and less apparent transport." The higher risk of transporting the body without being observed may have occurred at the site of the actual murder, rather than at the vacant lot where the body was disposed, Douglas noted.

Unaware of the proximity of Jack Dragna's home, Douglas questioned why the remains were put on display in the weeds of Norton Avenue, but he observed that whatever the reason, the display of the remains in the vacant lot on Norton was a deliberate and calculated choice. "There must have been some connection to the neighborhood," Douglas observed.

The proximity of the remains to Jack Dragna's home would indicate that Dragna was not directly involved with the crime—the lot on Norton would have been the last place he would have disposed of the body. The slashing open of the mouth from ear to ear, with its Sicilian implication and the display of Elizabeth Short's bisected and mutilated body in that location was a deliberate and calculated choice made by Bugsy Siegel. Addressed to "D," the remains carried a special pathological message.

Five months later, Dragna sent his response.

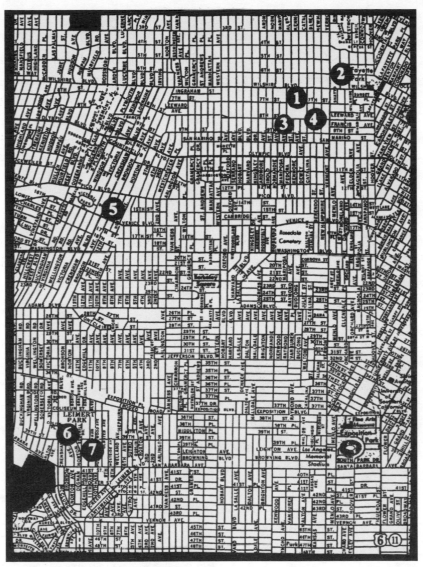

1. The Ambassador Hotel
2. The Office of Dr. Leslie Audrain
3. Brenda Allen's apartment and Communication Center
4. The bungalow on Catalina Street
5. Café where the victim's shoes and handbag were found in the incinerator
6. Site where body of Elizabeth Short was discovered
7. Home of Mafia boss Jack Dragna

(CALIFORNIA STATE LIBRARY)

IF THREE OF the men that Case and Ahern had encountered at the scene of the murder were Bugsy Siegel, Al Greenberg, and Maurice Clement—who was the fourth man? Transcribed statements in the files of the LAPD would indicate that the fourth man was Jack Anderson Wilson (aka Arnold Smith), a member of Al Greenberg's McCadden Gang, who was six feet, four inches tall, and walked with a limp.

In *Severed*, the most respected of the nonfiction investigative books on the Black Dahlia case, author John Gilmore claims that Jack Anderson Wilson was the sole perpetrator of the Black Dahlia murder. Gilmore's conclusion was based on numerous interviews he had with Wilson over a period of years and discussions with LAPD Det. John St. John, who had inherited the Dahlia case in 1968.

The Wilson interviews, which are filed at the Los Angeles Sheriff's Department, as well as the Homicide Division of the LAPD, leave little doubt that Wilson was involved in the murder of Elizabeth Short. He knew too much about the details of the crime—things that only someone who was at the scene could have known. However, Wilson was hardly the type of person that the top echelons of the LAPD would go out of their way to protect. He was merely an obscure thief with a long rap sheet of burglary and assault offenses who hung around Al Green's Nightlife Bar back in the forties.

At the time he encountered Jack Anderson Wilson, Gilmore had been working on *Severed* for several years, but was without a clue to the identity of the "person or persons unknown." Having researched and written *Severed* prior to the opening of the District Attorney's files in 2003, Gilmore was thrown off by the planted rumors regarding Elizabeth Short's inability to have sexual relations and was unaware that someone with advanced medical knowledge was involved in the murder. Lacking knowledge of her pregnancy and the motive behind the crime, Gilmore was convinced that the killer was a lone psychopath—as had been promulgated by Donahoe and the press.

There were a number of people in the Hollywood/Babylon milieu who were aware of Gilmore's ongoing research into the case, and while working out of his office at the Bradbury Building in downtown Los Angeles, he was contacted in October 1981 by a man who referred to himself as "Eddie." Eddie said he was in touch with a "Mr. Smith" who had knowledge about the Black Dahlia murder. An arrangement was made for Gilmore to casually meet Mr. Smith at Eddie's home in the Silver Lake district, which Gilmore described as an obvious center of a small-time burglary ring: "The garage was filled with stuff that probably came from burglaries, and there were too many electronic things around the house—stereos, hi-fi equipment, golf clubs, and a lot of silverware."

Gilmore recalled that Eddie introduced him to two friends staying at the house: an Indian, who Gilmore later learned was involved with Eddie in the burglary of Hollywood homes, and a tall wiry man, who was introduced as "Arnold Smith." Gilmore guessed that Smith was at least six feet, four inches tall, and he noticed that he walked with a limp.

After a few drinks and some idle talk about Hollywood, Eddie turned the conversation toward unsolved Hollywood murders and confided that Arnold Smith had known the Black Dahlia and even had a photograph of himself with Elizabeth Short. Smith told Gilmore that he had met her at Al Greenberg's café on McCadden through his friend Henry Hassau, who had also been a member of the McCadden Gang. Gilmore recalled, "Smith told me there had been a number of robberies that involved several men that hung around Greenberg's café, including Henry Hassau, and a man named Bobby Savarino." According to Smith, they and Al Greenberg had been involved in a robbery of a nightclub on the Sunset Strip about

Mocambo holdup confessed by 'bigshot,' 3 others held

NIGHTCLUB ROBBERY SUSPECTS
William Hassau, left, and Robert Savarino

Robert Savarino, 28, confessed today to the Mocambo Club holdup on Jan. 6, police said, but he refused to implicate any of the three other suspects held with him in the Beverly Hills jail.

the time of the Black Dahlia murder, and Hassau and Savarino had been arrested. Smith told Gilmore that he had been afraid that he, too, would be apprehended.

Initially, Gilmore didn't realize Smith was talking about the jewel robbery at the Mocambo, which had been carried out by Al Greenberg's McCadden Gang for Bugsy Siegel back on January 6, 1947. Arnold Smith was the "tall, six-foot-four younger man with the limp," identified by the accountant as the thief

who "scraped the jewelry from the tray removed from the safe." Although Arnold Smith escaped arrest for the Mocambo robbery,

Henry Hassau and Robert Savarino were arrested by sheriff's deputies on the afternoon of January 14, the day Elizabeth Short was murdered. Al Greenberg was arrested several days later.

Following the meeting at Eddie's house in Silver Lake, there were several other meetings in the fall of 1981 that followed a pattern: Gilmore would receive a call from Smith at his Bradbury Building office, and a time and meeting place would be arranged; Smith would not reveal his real name, where he lived, or how Gilmore could get in touch with him; as Smith was an obvious alcoholic, they would inevitably meet in a downtown Los Angeles bar, where his information about the murder of the Black Dahlia was dribbled out while Gilmore provided rounds of drinks, and an occasional C note. They usually met at the 555 Club on Main Street's skid row, where Gilmore would often gain little more than a hefty bar bill.

In reviewing the transcripts of their conversations, it becomes obvious that Smith was teasing Gilmore with tidbits of information in exchange for drinks and cash. Because of his alcoholism, "Smith" was often rambling, evasive, and incoherent in recalling events that had taken place well over three decades prior to their meetings; yet, there are moments of vivid truth that left Gilmore hooked on these disjointed recollections.

At one of their meetings, Smith showed Gilmore the photograph he had of Elizabeth Short. Gilmore said that Smith kept it in an old See's Candy box wrapped with rubber bands. The photograph had been taken at a nightclub in 1946, and Elizabeth Short could be seen sitting at a table next to a much younger Mr. Smith and another couple.

Robert Slatzer, author of *The Life and Curious Death of Marilyn Monroe* (Pinnacle, 1974), had also seen this photo of Smith and Elizabeth Short together. In an interview that Slatzer recorded for Gilmore in 1982, he recalled that in 1974 he had an office in the Taft Building at Hollywood and Vine and was working on a book about a notorious Hollywood jewel thief, Duke Monteverde, who was known as "The Duke of Thieves." The Duke would occasionally drop by Slatzer's office, and one day brought along a tall, lanky associate who said he had known Slatzer in the old days when Slatzer was dating Marilyn. Slatzer didn't recognize him, but on another visit Smith showed Slatzer an old photograph of Smith when he was much younger. Slatzer noted that the picture was taken at the Florentine Gardens, and Smith was sitting next to Elizabeth Short. More than twenty-five years had passed and Smith looked quite different—time and alcohol had taken their toll—but Slatzer recognized him as someone he had once met back in 1946.

Slatzer said, "He was one of those slick underworld people who used to hang around the Florentine Gardens and could often be seen sitting at Mark Hansen's table flashing hundred dollar bills. I don't remember what he called himself then, but it wasn't 'Smith.' " Slatzer had always believed that Elizabeth Short had been murdered by some of the mobsters who hung around the Florentine Gardens, and in the course of his taped 1982 interview with Gilmore, Slatzer said he had been told by a prominent underworld figure and a friend of Johnny Rosselli's, that "Bugsy Siegel was connected to the murder of Elizabeth Short."

During one of John Gilmore's interviews with Smith, he told Gilmore that the person responsible for Elizabeth Short's murder was "Al Morrison." Gilmore patiently tried to get an ID on Al Morrison but found Smith to be cagey and deliberately evasive. He referred to Al Morrison as a "hot shot who lived in Nevada."

Smith repeatedly placed Al Morrison at the scene of the murder, along with Al Greenberg. At one of Gilmore and Smith's meetings, after several drinks, Smith began talking about the killing:

> **Gilmore:** Tell me about Al Greenberg, and when he came and told you about it—about the Black Dahlia killing.

Smith: So many killings going on and you know that the other guy, the writer—or so he called himself. His name's Henry [Hassau]. He was the one that was gonna fucking shoot Mickey Cohen. Just a crazy sonovabitch. He figured he had things smooth, but he didn't know shit from Shinola.

Gilmore: This is the guy that stuck up the Mocambo?

Smith: Well, yeah. They were all afraid of getting arrested right then.

Gilmore: Including Greenberg?

Smith: They all were taken in except Al.

Gilmore: You said he came over to the hotel on Sunset?

Smith: He came over with the newspapers—the ones that had the picture of *her*.

Gilmore: He brought you the papers?

Smith: He wanted me to know in so many words that I keep my trap shut.

Gilmore: About the Black Dahlia?

Smith: He had a way of having things in his mind, you see, and he could direct this in a way that you got the point.

Gilmore: When was it that he told you what he'd done?

Smith: It was later. He got to drinking. He drank a bottle of Fleishman, and he said something about it being time we talk about it . . . And then he looked at me and said, "Somebody that does this doesn't have to be crazy. Somebody that can do this has reasons for doing it that isn't understood on a normal level." And it took me a long time to find out what he was after.

[In the transcript, Gilmore makes the notation: "I order drinks at this point because I see that he is getting abstract again and I want to pin down some details before he gets into a stupor."]

Initially, Smith maintained the pretense that he had not attended the crime and had been told details of the murder by Al Greenberg but as the meetings continued, it became apparent that Smith had been at the scene of the murder and was involved with the disposal of the body.

Gilmore: This is the room where she was, right? This is what Al is thinking and telling you. . . .

Smith: They had done a few other things to the body and I figured she'd still been alive, from what I'm being told when they did it. . . .

Gilmore: What was done—these other things you say you have information on?

Smith: She was naked only they'd tied her hands and these were up overhead like this, and they had stabbed her with a knife a lot, not deep, not enough that would kill you but jabbing and sticking her a lot and then slitting around one tit, and then they'd cut her face across it. Across the mouth. . . . There was this idea that she was not dead because her eyes were open and they had a look in them that she was not dead. But, oh yeah, she was dead.

Gilmore: This is not in the bathroom?

Smith: No, this is not in the bathroom. But in the bathroom these boards are put across the tub, straight across it and . . . she was brought into the bathroom at first, if I recall exactly what the information is I have. I think dragged the rest of the way.

Gilmore: Dragged in?

Smith: Well, by the legs dragged in that way. She had to be laid across the tub, on top of the boards, and then. . . . He ties the arms and tied her hands to the faucet handles and thing for the shower, the pipe. She was laying across one board just underneath the back part, and the other one was underneath the hips here, under the ass—see a rope around each leg and pulled them downwards, pulling them so that you then tied these ropes around the bottom of the can—the toilet bowl.

Gilmore: You said on the phone . . .

Smith: The idea was first cutting off the legs at the top of her legs, but then this would have to be done twice, so the decision was to separate—to cut her in half—that way to move the two parts easily, and get her . . . you know, this was the way to transport . . .

Gilmore: You said that the corpse was cut in half for disposal purposes . . . I want to get back to the situation with the boards. The body was on the planks over the bathtub.

Smith: Her middle was over the tub and the boards were width-wise so she was open, at the waist and back, and so the cut was across the middle, pulled tight like she was so it could go clean through and have her body opened.

Gilmore: So the body was being cut at this time.

Smith: Yes. But blood did come out and on to the boards and some even jumped out of her, came out and upwards in such a way as like this, see, but it was clean through and then I think there was some trouble going through her backbone—of the bone's part there.

Gilmore: You said the draining of this . . .

Smith: When the one board was removed from underneath this rear part, that low section went down into the tub, but hanging at an angle, and drained in this manner. The same with the top half, which hung down into the tub and there were marks made on the body's back, the upper part where it was against the faucets. Both sections of the body drained in this manner as leaning, you could say laying down at the incline into the bathtub, but the bottom section, the hips and these parts of the legs was leaning against the slope of that part of the tub, but the upper part was straight down. That is how I understand it.

Gilmore: So you were saying about the boards, then.

Smith: She stayed in the tub and the boards were taken down and out back, and the boards and stuff were put into the incinerator.

Gilmore: How long was the body in the bathtub?

Smith: The body was in the bathtub that night. The tub had been filled with the water.

Gilmore: So the body was untied and it was still in the tub, in the water?

Smith: It was in the water but this was drained and it was filled again and the body was in the water at this time.

Gilmore: Was it submerged?

Smith: The body tended to stay higher, I believe, with the surface as it came up. You see, there was movement in the bathtub with the body when the tub was filled with water. And whatever skin contact there was, this was removed when there was the draining.

Gilmore: How do you mean removed?

Smith: It was removed by cleaning it off.

Gilmore: But about the cleaning up. The blood on the floor must have presented a problem.

Smith: The mop and the rags were used, like I said and then these things and the boards went down and these were put into the incinerator and lighted on fire. And there was the thought about the bag.

Gilmore: What is the bag?

Smith: The cement bag that was outside. The water hadn't gotten to the bag.

Gilmore: Then you said there was getting rid of the body.

Smith: There was this oilskin tablecloth off the kitchen table. But this wasn't enough, so there were these curtains and the shower curtain from the hall there, by the pipe. She was wrapped over in the curtains, both parts in the two curtains, I think it was the shower curtain to take the sections to the car. The bag was on the floor of the trunk.

Gilmore: This is the cement sack?

Smith: Yes, and she was put into the trunk of the car, and then drove until the place was reached there that he could put the . . . put her out of the car.

Gilmore: How did he take her out of the car?

Smith: Took her out of the car?

Gilmore: I mean how did he take both sections out of the car?

Smith: The top section was carried by the arms held up like this and put down on the ground, and the bottom section was on the bag and put down that way.

Gilmore: Did he turn the body over?

Smith: The body was put down in this manner—the bottom section was moved by one leg this way [demonstrating] more away from the sidewalk, and then the top part was picked up again and put in order.

Gilmore: What happened to the cement sack?

Smith: Left it there where it was when he took hold of the foot or the ankle and put that away from the sidewalk.

Gilmore: What about the shower curtain and the table cloth?

Smith: This was in the trunk of the car.

Gilmore: It was left in the trunk of the car?

Smith: It was put into a storm drain.

Gilmore: In this same area?

Smith: No.

Gilmore: And he didn't leave anything at the scene?

Smith: (laughs) The body was left at the scene.

Gilmore: But her clothes, and purse, and her shoes—

Smith: No, no, the clothes . . . there was nothing of the clothes that was not cut and burned—except the shoes and her purse. The pocketbook was on the floor in the car on the floorboard. It was put in the incinerator.

Gilmore: This is the incinerator that is at this café?

Smith: That's the café. It is just around the corner and not far if you go around the corner and up Crenshaw.

Gilmore: And the storm drain?

Smith: You mean with the shower curtain and that stuff? That was on Melrose. You think I should go to the gas chamber?

Gilmore: For what?

Smith: For compounding a murder, a homicide in the City of Los Angeles. Conspiracy.

Gilmore: Yeah, conspiracy.

Smith: But, I didn't conspire.

Gilmore: No, I understand that.

Smith: What if I said I was doing the same thing as we're talking about?

Gilmore: I think it's in all of us to some degree. Just the turn of events that sets the moment right.

Smith: It was right all right.

Gilmore: What do you mean?

Smith: Killing her—the events you're talking about. The

things you're talking about. That it is according to Al
Morrison over in Nevada, and being Mister Hot-shot. According to him, it's okay to kill somebody, you just do it
in whatever way you do, and it's personal in its use, if you
understand what I'm saying.

The full eighty-one-page text of the "Arnold Smith"/John
Gilmore transcripts were reviewed and studied by eminent criminologist Larry Moncrief, a former police officer and instructor at the
Police Academy in Modesto, California. Moncrief, who has frequently served as an expert witness in criminal cases, concluded that
"Smith's statements had the ring of truth, though he was often intoxicated during the interviews. . . . He had too much knowledge
and seemed to know the innermost thoughts of the killers. He understood how and why certain things occurred and expected Gilmore to
understand."

Moncrief also pointed out that Smith knew many details consistent
with facts in the Coroner's inquest transcript, and he recalled these
details after the passage of more than thirty years: "Smith just had
too much knowledge. The way the body was cut up, marks on the
body—the way the body was disposed of."

Although in *Severed* John Gilmore concluded that Smith was the
only person involved in the murder, and he had made up the involvement of Al Morrison and Al Greenberg to protect himself, Moncrief
believed that Al Greenberg and Al Morrison—the big shot from
Nevada—were involved in the murder, and there may have been
others.

In analyzing the Gilmore transcripts of his conversations with
Arnold Smith, it becomes evident that Smith was the fourth man en-
countered by Case and Ahern at the bungalow court on Catalina
Street. Those in attendance at the "sacred setting" were:

Benjamin "Bugsy" Siegel   Albert Louis Greenberg   Jack Anderson Wilson

Maurice Clement   Dr. Leslie C. Audrain

- **Benjamin "Bugsy" Siegel,** the pathological killer who slashed Elizabeth Short's face with a knife and struck her repeatedly on the head with a blunt metal instrument.
- **Albert Louis Greenberg,** Bugsy's henchman and the boss of the McCadden Gang.
- **Jack Anderson Wilson** (aka Arnold Smith), member of the McCadden Gang.
- **Maurice Clement,** Syndicate procurer for Brenda Allen and driver of the car.
- **Dr. Leslie C. Audrain,** the abortionist who had bisected the body and left the bungalow prior to Case and Ahern's arrival.

The Silent Scream

THE SILENT SCREAM of Elizabeth Short still echoes in the corridors of criminology, and from time to time the infamous murder case reemerges from the unsolved homicide files of the twentieth century. Many people have speculated about the identity of the killer or killers and questioned the motivation for the crime; but there's reason to believe that Det. Harry Hansen had deciphered the silent scream and solved the case long ago.

Hansen knew the secret of the autopsy—that the victim was pregnant at the time she was murdered, and a postmortem hysterectomy had been performed. In his testimony before the Grand Jury, Hansen acknowledged that the bisection of the body was performed by someone with advanced surgical skills. He also knew that the address of Dr. Leslie Audrain, leader of the Syndicate abortion ring, was in Elizabeth Short's address book. According to Aggie Underwood and Finis Brown, Hansen believed an abortionist was involved in the crime and had been pushing for an indictment, which was blocked by Chief Horrall.

On several occasions, Hansen had also questioned Brenda Allen's procurer, Maurice Clement, and the Grand Jury files indicate that

Clement had been placed high on the suspect list. Along with Sgt. Stoker, Hansen also would have been aware that Brenda Allen was the Syndicate madam working within Bugsy Siegel's vice-map; and Hansen would have recognized the significance of the body being displayed in the proximity of Jack Dragna's home on Hubert Street. But the psychotic killer, Bugsy Siegel, had been assassinated in the months following the Black Dahlia murder, and Dr. Audrain had suddenly died just as the Grand Jury was beginning its investigation. By the time Hansen was brought before the Grand Jury in November 1949, he undoubtedly had the answers to many questions that were never asked by the investigators. Although Hansen was an honest cop, he was not a crusader like Sgt. Stoker. There is reason to believe that Det. Harry Hansen took the secret of the silent scream to his grave.

After Hansen retired in 1968, the unsolved Black Dahlia case was inherited by Det. John St. John, who was popularly referred to as "Jigsaw John" because of his legendary investigative talents. While he carried Badge #1, bestowed upon him by Chief William Parker, few understood the origins of St. John's legendary reputation, which was largely the result of Parker's PR savvy. Although St. John had indeed worked Homicide and Robbery, his genius lay in the gift of the gab, and he was primarily an LAPD public relations figure devoted to restoring the LAPD's tarnished image after the 1949 vice-capades. From his office at Warner Bros. Studios, he was involved in the creation of Jack Webb's *Dragnet* television series, for which he served as technical director, and his reputation as the invincible Homicide investigator was enhanced by the TV series *Jigsaw John*, which was based on his mythological exploits that once again eulogized Parker and the LAPD.

By the time St. John inherited the Black Dahlia murder in 1968, it had become a cold case in the LAPD deep-freeze, more a matter of public relations than investigation. And while St. John readily dismissed the occasional investigative journalist's newly postulated suspects—

including the father of Janice Knowlton, author of *Daddy Was the Black Dahlia Killer*—he had to polish Badge #1 and do his homework when John Gilmore presented Arnold Smith as a viable suspect.

Following several meetings with Gilmore and reading the Arnold Smith transcripts, St. John found Arnold Smith to be a credible suspect. After reexamining the LAPD Black Dahlia case files and conferring with Finis Brown, the crime-lab, and several detectives who had worked the case, St. John concluded that Smith may have been present at the murder site and involved with the transportation of Elizabeth Short's body to the lot on Norton Avenue; however, St. John maintained that Smith was using Al Greenberg and "this Al Morrison character as a smoke screen." St. John said, "His reference to the others are in the form of this other guy supposedly telling Smith these things, which Smith is telling you. It's the old story of 'Let me tell you about what happened to this pal of mine,' when it's actually yourself you're talking about." He persuaded Gilmore that Smith was "throwing Morrison out as a decoy. What Smith is doing," St. John said, "is airing what he possibly knows of the murder firsthand, while putting it in someone else's mouth—an as-told-to story, if you get my drift."

Although St. John was quick to dismiss the possibility that Smith had related the truth regarding Al Greenberg and Al Morrison, he must have known that Al Greenberg had been the boss of the McCadden Gang, had known Elizabeth Short, and been a henchman of that "hot shot from Nevada," Bugsy Siegel. Faced with Gilmore's transcripts, however, St. John had to concede that Smith was a viable suspect; he told Gilmore he'd like to locate Smith and bring him in for questioning: "He may be the one we've been looking for all these years!"

Smith had been careful about not revealing his true identity or where he lived, and it was decided that when he called again, Gilmore would meet him and bring along a "friend," who would be an undercover officer. The officer would buy the drinks and attempt to engage Smith in recorded conversation. Gilmore warned St. John that the meeting would have to be on short notice because he never knew when Smith would call. It was only when he was thirsty and short of money that Gilmore would hear from him.

The call came in late December 1981, and a meeting was arranged at the 555 Club on Main Street. After several rounds of drinks, the undercover officer, Louise Sheffield, began asking Smith about Al Greenberg, the Mocambo robbery, and the McCadden Gang's connection to Bugsy Siegel and Mickey Cohen. But according to Sheffield, "Smith seemed nervous and uncomfortable, and seemed to have a negative response towards me. . . . He spoke only briefly about 'Al Morrison.'"

Meanwhile, St. John had made a positive ID on Arnold Smith. Mug shots were obtained from an arrest in Oregon, along with a long rap sheet for robberies, assaults, and petty crimes. Smith proved to be Jack Anderson Wilson, aka Grover Loving, Jr., aka Hanns Anderson Von Cannon aka Arnold Smith. Following the meeting with Gilmore and Officer Sheffield at the 555 Club, police surveillance established that Arnold Smith was staying in Room 202 at the Holland Hotel, on Seventh Street in downtown Los Angeles.

After reviewing eighty-one pages of Gilmore's transcripts and listening to tapes of the Smith interviews, John St. John concluded that Gilmore was correct—Jack Anderson Wilson, aka Arnold Smith, was involved in the murder of Elizabeth Short. But shortly after St. John acknowledged that Smith was a viable suspect, Gilmore made the mistake of going to the newly merged *Herald-Examiner* with the Smith transcripts and the story of his discovery. On January 17, 1982, the newspaper ran a front-page story that mentioned Arnold Smith and Al Morrison, the big shot from Nevada, as "hot new suspects" in the Black Dahlia murder.

Angry with Gilmore for leaking the story to the press, St. John told him, "I'm concerned. I want to keep a lid on this!" He then asked Gilmore to get more on tape before they brought Smith in for questioning. "What we're going to have to do is have you try to pin him down," St. John said. "I want to bust this guy so bad it's killing me!"

Another meeting was set up at the 555 Club in late January 1982, but before the meeting could take place, the case against Jack Anderson Wilson went up in flames. Wilson was lying on his bed in Room 202 at the Holland Hotel when the room was enveloped in a raging fire. Firemen broke into the room to fight the blaze and discovered his burning body. Although Room 202 was the only room in the hotel that was consumed by the fire, it was a raging inferno that took the firemen thirty-five minutes to extinguish.

The fire captain recalled that Wilson's charred body was lying on the left side of the bed, which had burned and collapsed onto the floor, and the fire had been extraordinarily intense. "The plaster-like wall surfaces and the underlying support structures had burned away, exposing the frames of the walls and ceiling," the captain said. The bureau, the bed, and all the furniture in the room were totally burned. Although there was no evidence how the fire started, arson was suspected because of the intensity of the blaze. Arson investigators said that the death of Jack Anderson Wilson was "possibly other than accidental." The "fourth man" may have been murdered.

There is an interesting postscript to the Arnold Smith/Jack Anderson Wilson transcripts. While reading Wilson's rambling interviews with Gilmore, I noted that Wilson had described two different murders. One was the murder of Elizabeth Short, but the MO of the other murder was quite different—and I realized that Wilson was describing the murder of Georgette Bauerdorf.

A tall man with a limp was described as bothering Georgette at the Hollywood Canteen in the days before her murder. The rap sheet of Jack Anderson Wilson gave his height as 6'4". He had been in the army in 1943 and discharged in 1944, following a leg injury. The Bauerdorf murder took place in October 1944. The hotel where Wilson occasionally stayed in 1944 was located at Sunset and Wilcox, opposite the Hollywood Canteen. Aggie Underwood stated that a witness had described "a tall man with a limp" getting out of Georgette's car when it was abandoned at Twenty-fifth and San Pedro

Streets, which proved to be six blocks from Wilson's mother's house at Thirty-first and San Pedro. And Jack Anderson Wilson was tall enough to reach the light bulb above Georgette's front door.

Describing the murder that matched the Bauerdorf MO, Jack Anderson Wilson (aka Smith) said:

Wilson: He wanted to do it ever since he saw her.

Gilmore: He told you that?

Wilson: Oh, he said as much, you know you see someone and you feel a certain way, and with her, it was the idea to do that to her.

Gilmore: To actually kill her? So then it's premeditated isn't it?

Wilson: If it was or if it wasn't, it was the only reason he continued to see her.

Gilmore: So it wasn't a crime of passion?

Wilson: Oh, it was, but it was something that had to happen sooner or later.

Gilmore: Why is that?

Wilson: Because it was something she wanted to happen to her. It was the road she was on and that was the road's reaching at the end of it.

Gilmore: So it was willed.

Wilson: In a matter of speaking. Everyone is entitled to go nuts. You said that yourself.

[Gilmore notes that Smith seems to go off into a trance-like state.]

Wilson: She didn't say anything, and he went to her and grabbed her by the arm like this and pulls her back but she hauled off and let him have it with the purse. Just swung it out and caught him across the side of the face.

He slugged her once and her knees got weak. He pulls her back into the room and he leans her against the wall while he locks the door with the key. He said he then grabbed her and pushed her and she fell down like it was against or on to the couch and then off that and is on the floor with her dress up on her body. He said he stood over her and said something about he was going to screw her ass. She started to yell so he bent down and slugged her again. He said he put his hand on her neck and held her head still while he hit her a couple of times. She didn't move. Now he didn't know what he was going to do, except he went out of the room, through the door he had locked and went downstairs to the rear on the first floor to the kitchen. There was a large knife, like a long butcher knife that was two inches, the height of the blade near the wooden handle. He said he didn't know what he was going to do with the knife, except to scare her or keep her back up in the room. He went upstairs and she hadn't gotten up off the floor, but upon an elbow or an arm and was looking around.

Gilmore: She was just on the floor like that? She hadn't tried to get out?

Wilson: No, and she was on the edge of the couch, I think maybe he had her arm—up here at this part of her arm, but this wasn't a couch like you think, it was a studio bed. She was scared of the knife and got up and was moving but he ran to her and hit her again, but it didn't put her out and didn't seem to stop it. So it was necessary at that point to indicate that he was going to hurt her with the knife.

Gilmore: What happened then?

Wilson: He tore at the clothes, not tearing but cutting at the clothing. . . . He said something and I can remember him being scared. He put rags in her mouth, and he knocked her out a few times. He had to do that when the spirit overtook him. But I told you this, and some of the rest of it I don't know. It was so long ago. It's only by chance that we're talking now. You understand the trouble I could get into because of what he did . . . if he could somehow make it seem that he didn't do it.

What Jack Anderson Wilson had described in this instance was not the murder of Elizabeth Short, but the lust-murder of Georgette Bauerdorf at her El Palacio apartment on October 12, 1944. It was two years later that Wilson became involved in the McCadden Gang robberies and the murder of Elizabeth Short.

The Black Dahlia murder is a cold, cold case. What survives today is the *best-evidence*—all that can be factually brought together to establish the perpetrators of what is considered to be one of the most notorious murders of the twentieth century; however, enough tangible evidence has evolved through the decades to name the person or persons unknown, name the motive, name the location of the crime, name the reason why the body was transported to Norton Avenue, and name those responsible for the cover-up.

Although there's no statute of limitations on murder, it's doubtful that the Los Angeles Police Department or the District Attorney's Office will ever reopen the Black Dahlia case—it's not in their interests to do so. Yet, justice has been ill served, and the people's right to know the truth has been denied. Because civic leaders and law enforcement officials long ago abdicated their responsibilities in the Black Dahlia case, the *best-evidence* must be placed before the court of public jurisprudence. You are the jury. God remains the Judge.

*   *   *

More than half a century has gone by since the murder of Elizabeth Short, but there are times when it seems like it was only yesterday that the screaming headlines about the Black Dahlia case landed on our doorstep. I can still vividly remember when I first heard about the crime and began to realize that there was a dark side to money, power, and influence, and that the truth and what was printed in the newspapers were not necessarily the same.

The weather had turned warmer during the day, and there was no fruit frost warning that night on the ten o'clock news. Because of a Boy Scout meeting that Wednesday, I had not seen the newspapers and first heard about the bizarre murder of Jane Doe #1 and some of the gruesome details on my bedside radio, where a jovial, smiling figure of Charlie McCarthy sat on the rim of the speaker, wearing his monocle, boutonnière, and funny top hat. . . .

ACKNOWLEDGMENTS

I'm indebted to many people for making this book possible:

Retired LAPD officer, Vince Carter, directed me through the mean streets and back alleys of Los Angeles. I would have made many wrong turns if it weren't for Vince. Thank you!

John Gilmore's *Severed* was the nonfiction forerunner of investigative books into the murder of Elizabeth Short and proved to be the Baedeker to Dahlia-land. Thanks, John, for all your help.

I'm grateful to Mary Pacios, who was always there with her unique insight and advice. Mary often pointed me in the right direction and has always remained a true friend of "Snow White."

Fellow Beverly Hills High School alumnus, Will Fowler, was of invaluable assistance over the years. I'm deeply indebted to Will, who passed away before this book was completed.

The staff of the Medford Historical Society, especially Mike Howard and Ryan Hayward, were extremely helpful to me, and I thank them for their guidance. And I'd like to thank Faye Adams of Medford High School for all her assistance.

I would also like to thank Dace Taub and her staff at the Regional

History Center at the University of Southern California; Carolyn Cole of the Los Angeles Public Library History Department Photo Collection; Jeffrey Rankin and the staff of the UCLA Special Collections Department, for all their help and invaluable expertise. And a very special thanks goes to Sandi Gibbons who guided me through the archives of the Los Angeles District Attorney's Office.

I'm deeply indebted to George Irish of Hearst Newspapers for his special assistance, and to the Hearst Corporation for their kind cooperation.

Thank you, Dave Pascoe, for lending your computer genius along with your exceptional knowledge to this project, and for keeping the pixels in place and warding off the glitches. Both Dave, along with Kelly Wilson, went far out of their way to be of assistance. And thank you Don May for your photo expertise.

Graphic artist, Jay Pelletier, was of invaluable aid in organizing the photos and graphics. Thank you, Jay!

And to Alan and Cathy Buster, I owe a special debt of gratitude for their excellent research, advice, and friendship.

Sadly, Robert Slatzer, who was both a friend and contributor to this book passed away in March 2005. I'll always be grateful to Bob and his wife, Debbie, for all their help and support.

Once again, the gold-medal winner of the paper chase is my agent, Alan Nevins, of The Firm. Alan believed in the book from day one, and saw it through all its travails.

I am indeed grateful to Judith Regan of ReganBooks and would like to express my gratitude to my editors, Cal Morgan and Anna Bliss, for their support and excellent advice and assistance. And my gratitude to production editor Vivian Gomez.

A very special thanks to my wife, Ann, who often saved me from the swamps of hyperbole, and frequently rescued me from noir ghosts of other times and other places.

APPENDIX A

LAPD Summary of the Crime Scene

SUMMARY OF THE ●IZABETH (BETH) SHORT MURD● INVESTIGATION

At 11:05AM, January 15, 1947, a call was received by the Complaint Board from a woman who did not identify herself that there was a woman down in a vacant lot on Norton Avenue between 39th Street and Coliseum in the middle of the block, west side.

At 11:07AM, a radio car was dispatched to the scene, officers F. S. Perkins, #4057, and W. E. Fitzgerald, #3940, who found the body and called the University Detective Division. Officers S. J. Lambert, #2359, and J. W. Haskins, #892, responded to the call.

Capt. Jack Donahoe, Homicide Division, was notified. The call car was out on a natural dead body on Westmoreland Avenue so officer Marty J. Wynn, Homicide Division, was dispatched to the scene. Capt. Donahoe then telephoned the address where the call car, operated by Sgt. F. A. Brown, #248, and Harry L. Hansen, #859, of Homicide Division, was located. They responded to the call, arriving at the scene at 11:30AM. Upon the arrival of Sgts. Brown and Hansen who were assigned to the case, they found present officers Perkins and Fitzgerald, Lt. Paul Freestone, Det. Lt. Jack Haskins, Sgts. Wynn and Vaughn, Forensic Chemist Ray Pinker, photographer Laursen from Sci. Investigation Division, and representatives and photographers from the newspapers. Pictures had been taken by the newspapers of the body. They were later joined by Lt. Leland V. Jones of the Scientific Investigation Division.

The body was that of a white, female, American, approximately 20 years of age, 5'6" tall, weighing 115#, brown-reddish hair recently hennaed, green eyes, fingernails bitten down to the quick. The body was nude; there was no jewelry on the body. There were no women's clothes found in the vicinity. The post mortem condition of the body revealed no indication of rigor mortis. The body was lying on its back, head to the north and feet to the south, on the west side of Norton Avenue, approximately 2' west of the sidewalk. The body was just south of a paved driveway approach to this lot which is the first driveway north of the center block fire plug. The body had been cleanly severed at the middle line and the lower half was lying about 1' to the south of the upper half, the upper half being slightly off line to the west of the lower half. Both parts of the body were lying absolutely flat with pretruded entrails of the lower half lying under the buttock.

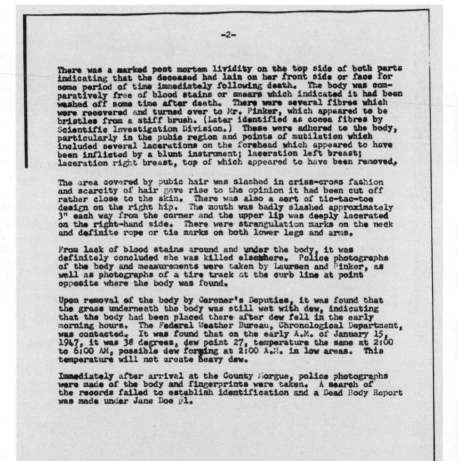

-2-

There was a marked post mortem lividity on the top side of both parts indicating that the deceased had lain on her front side or face for some period of time immediately following death. The body was comparatively free of blood stains or smears which indicated it had been washed off some time after death. There were several fibres which were recovered and turned over to Mr. Pinker, which appeared to be bristles from a stiff brush. (Later identified as cocoa fibres by Scientific Investigation Division.) These were adhered to the body, particularly in the pubic region and points of mutilation which included several lacerations on the forehead which appeared to have been inflicted by a blunt instrument; laceration left breast; laceration right breast, top of which appeared to have been removed.

The area covered by pubic hair was slashed in criss-cross fashion and scarcity of hair gave rise to the opinion it had been cut off rather close to the skin. There was also a sort of tic-tac-toe design on the right hip. The mouth was badly slashed approximately 3" each way from the corner and the upper lip was deeply lacerated on the right-hand side. There were strangulation marks on the neck and definite rope or tie marks on both lower legs and arms.

From lack of blood stains around and under the body, it was definitely concluded she was killed elsewhere. Police photographs of the body and measurements were taken by Laursen and Pinker, as well as photographs of a tire track at the curb line at point opposite where the body was found.

Upon removal of the body by Coroner's Deputies, it was found that the grass underneath the body was still wet with dew, indicating that the body had been placed there after dew fell in the early morning hours. The Federal Weather Bureau, Chronological Department, was contacted. It was found that on the early A.M. of January 15, 1947, it was 38 degrees, dew point 27, temperature the same at 2:00 to 6:00 AM, possible dew forming at 2:00 A.M. in low areas. This temperature will not create heavy dew.

Immediately after arrival at the County Morgue, police photographs were made of the body and fingerprints were taken. A search of the records failed to establish identification and a Dead Body Report was made under Jane Doe #1.

INQUEST HELD ON THE BODY OF ELIZABETH SHORT,
AT THE HALL OF JUSTICE, LOS ANGELES, CALIFORNIA,
ON JANUARY 22, 1947, AT 10:30 A.M.

--*-*-*-*

PHOEBE MAE SHORT, being first duly
sworn, testified as follows:

Q   BY THE CORONER: Please state your name.

A   Phoebe Mae Short.

Q   Where do you reside?

A   115 Salem Street, Medford, Massachusetts.

Q   Have you viewed the body of a deceased person in the mortuary here?

A   I have.

Q   Was that someone you knew in life?

A   It was.

Q   What was her name?

A   Elizabeth Short.

Q   Did she have a middle name?

A   No middle name.

Q   Was she related to you?

A   My daughter.

Q   Do you know her address?

A   The address was in San Diego at the time.

Q   That is the last address you had for her?

A   That's right.

Q   Do you recall what that was?

A   2750 Camino Padera Drive, Pacific Beach.

- 1 -

1	Q	Did she have an occupation as far as you knew?
2	A	As far as I know she was a waitress.
3	Q	Where was she born?
4	A	Hyde Park, Massachusetts.
5	Q	What was her age?
6	A	Twenty-two.
7	Q	At the time of her death was she single, married, wid-
8		owed, or divorced?
9	A	Single.
10	Q	And had never been married as far as you know?
11	A	As far as I know she was not.
12	Q	What is your information as to the date of her death?
13	A	I was notified January 15.
14	Q	That she died on January 15.
15	A	Yes.
16	Q	Do you know where she died?
17	A	She was murdered here in Los Angeles.
18	Q	Is it your information that her body was found on a
19		street out here in some part of Los Angeles?
20	A	That's right.
21	Q	Were you here at the time?
22	A	No, I was not.
23	Q	You were in Massachusetts?
24	A	That's right.
25	Q	How long since you had seen your daughter?
26	A	In April, 1946.
27	Q	Where did you see her then?
28	A	At my own home in Massachusetts.
29	Q	Did she remain with you for some time then, was she
30		living there or just on a visit?
31	A	She had come home from Florida in February and left in
32		April the same year.

-2-

1   Q   While she was at home did she tell you of any trouble
2 or anyone that she feared or had any trouble with anyone or any
3 enemies?

4   A   No, she did not.

5   Q   Or tell you of any love affairs?

6   A   Yes, she was in love with Gordon Fickling at that time.

7   Q   Have you since corresponded with her?

8   A   I have.

9   Q   And what address did you use for correspondence?

10   A   Well, that one in Hollywood and this last one in San
11 Diego.

12   Q   Do you have the address in Hollywood?

13   A   It is in my bag. That was the Chancelor Apartment in
14 Hollywood.

15   Q   Did you have a later address in San Diego?

16   A   The one that I mentioned.

17   Q   Has she corresponded or been in communication with any
18 of your other relatives?

19   A   No, she just regularly wrote me once a week.

20   Q   And those were the last addresses you had for her?

21   A   That's right.

22   Q   Are you giving to the officers every assistance you can
23 towards determining who the perpetrator of this crime was?

24   A   I am.

25

26

27   JESSE W. HASKINS, being first
28 duly sworn, testified as follows:

29   Q   BY THE CORONER: Please state your name.

30   A   Jesse W. Haskins.

31   Q   What is your occupation?

32   A   Detective Lieutenant, Police Department, Los Angeles,

1   attached to University Detective Bureau.

2   Q   Mr. Haskins, were you called to the scene of the find-

3   ing of the body of the deceased person, Elizabeth Short, over

4   whom we are holding this inquest?

5   A   I was.

6   Q   When did you receive that call?

7   A   Approximately 11:05 the morning of the 15th of January.

8   Q   And what time did you arrive at the scene?

9   A   At 11:18.

10   Q   And where did you go in response to the call?

11   A   Went on Norton Street between Coliseum and 39 Street.

12   Q   Where did you find the body of the victim in this case?

13   A   Found the body on the west side of Norton. From Coliseum

14   to 39 on the property line it is 1200 feet, it's all vacant pro-

15   perty. There is a fire plug in the center of that which would be

16   600 feet from Coliseum or 600 feet from 39 the other way. The

17   body was 54 feet north of the fire plug toward Coliseum.

18   Q   What is in that block, any houses or buildings?

19   A   The nearest houses face on Claybourne and there is a

20   back wall that comes up to the property line of Norton.

21   Q   On the east side of Norton?

22   A   Yes, and they are clear across the property lines of

23   the houses that face east on Norton.

24   Q   How wide is Norton Street?

25   A   Sixty feet wide, and 120 feet east of the property line

26   to the walls of the houses that face on Claybourne.

27   Q   The body was found on the west side of Norton?

28   A   Yes, and from that point it is 585 feet to Crenshaw, all

29   vacant property.

30   Q   Is that grown up with weeds?

31   A   Weeds and grass and rose clippings and such.

32   Q   Tell the Jury more definitely where you found the body,

- 4 -

1 please?

2   A   The location of the body when we arrived there was as

3 I said, 54 feet north of this fire plug which was directly in the

4 center of this 1200 foot space. The sidewalk is in on this street

5 and the curbs in and also the indentations for the driveways are

6 in and paved. The driveway measures five foot from the curb in

7 the sidewalk. The sidewalk is five foot wide. The body was lying

8 with the head towards the north, the feet towards the south, the

9 left leg was five inches west of the sidewalk. The legs were

10 spread out and the body was severed in two. The body was lying

11 face up and the severed part was jogged over about 10 inches, the

12 upper half of the body from the lower half.

13   Q   Were there weeds at this location or grass?

14   A   Just grass at this location.

15   Q   High enough to hide the body?

16   A   The body would not be hidden at all from the street on

17 Norton. It could have been hidden from the other direction, Cren-

18 shaw, because there are some tall weeds between there and where

19 the body was found.

20   Q   Is this a sidewalk or is it a much traveled location?

21   A   It is possible there is a great deal of travel on the

22 street for cutting across to the two streets otherwise there is

23 no reason for anybody to walk across there.

24   Q   Did the body appear to have been dead for some time?

25   A   From my observation it looked fresh.

26   Q   Would you say death had occurred after midnight of the

27 15th or prior to midnight or would you be able to form any opinion?

28   A   My opinion would be that it would be since midnight of

29 the 15th.

30   Q   Did you find any blood or tracks or anything of that

31 nature at the scene?

32   A   We did. Down this driveway which leads from where the

- 5 -

PASD 73 D-45
4-4406

1   body was found to the street there was a tire track right up
2   against the curbing and there was what appeared to be a possible
3   bloody heel mark in this tire mark; and on the curbing which is
4   very low there was one spot of blood; and there was an empty paper
5   cement sack lying in the driveway and it also had a spot of blood
6   on it.
7   Q   Any other container or sack or cloth that the body might
8   have been transported in?
9   A   There was not.
10   Q   From your examination of the body would you be able to
11 form any opinion as to whether the crime had been committed at this
12 scene or brought there from some other location?
13   A   It had been brought there from some other location.
14   Q   Was there any clot of blood on the body or did it appear
15 to have been washed?
16   A   The body was clean and appeared to have been washed.
17   Q   Do you know who reported the finding of the body?
18   A   All I know is how our Communication Division was noti-
19 fied of it and we were unable to locate the party. It was a
20 woman's voice which called the Communication Division at approxi-
21 mately 10 minutes before we received the call from them; and their
22 statement at this time was that there was a nude body on the west
23 side of Norton about half way from Coliseum to 39th and the flies
24 were bothering it and it needed attention and the call necessarily
25 was put over the air as a 390 down.
26   Q   Is there anything else you can tell the Jury with regard
27 to the facts surrounding the finding of the body or what you found
28 at the location?
29   A   No, I don't recall of anything else that would help the
30 Jury.
31   Q   Do you have the name of any witnesses who have been

- 6 -

```
 1   cently?
 2        A    I do not.  Only from investigation of other officers.
 3        Q    Did you have the name of one, Robert Manley?
 4        A    I have.
 5        Q    Is he here this morning?
 6        A    He is.
 7        Q    I'll call him later that's all then, thank you.
 8
 9
10                                ROBERT MANLEY, being first duly
11   sworn, testified as follows:
12        Q    BY THE CORONER:  Please state your name.
13        A    Robert Manley.
14        Q    Where do you live?
15        A    8010 Mountain View.
16        Q    Your occupation?
17        A    Salesman.
18        Q    That is Mountain View in South Gate?
19        A    That's right, sir.
20        Q    Were you acquainted with the deceased in this case,
21   Elizabeth Short?
22        A    Yes, sir.
23        Q    How long had you known her, approximately how long?
24        A    Approximately, a month.
25        Q    When did you see her, meet her the last time?
26        A    I saw Miss Short January 9th, which was the last time.
27        Q    Where was that?
28        A    I left Miss Short at the Biltmore Hotel at 6:30 P. M.,
29   January 9, 1947.
30        Q    Where had you picked her up from?
31        A    I had driven her to Los Angeles from San Diego.
32        Q    Had you met her in San Diego and brought her to Los
```

-7-

1 Angeles?

2   A   Yes, sir.

3   Q   Had she asked you to bring her to Los Angeles?

4   A   Yes.

5   Q   Did she say why she wanted to come to Los Angeles?

6   A   She said she didn't like San Diego.

7   Q   Did she say what she was going to do when she got here

8 or where she was going?

9   A   She said she was going to meet her sister in Los Angeles

10 and was going to spend a couple of days up in Berkeley with her

11 sister and then go on to Boston which was her home.

12   Q   And you left her at the Biltmore Hotel?

13   A   That's correct.

14   Q   Did she give you any address where she expected to stay

15 here?

16   A   No, sir.

17   Q   And that was the last time you saw her?

18   A   That was the last time.

19   Q   And that was January 9th?

20   A   Yes, sir.

21   Q   At what time?

22   A   6:30.

23   Q   And you haven't seen or heard from her since?

24   A   No, sir.

25   Q   Is there anything else you can tell the Jury for the

26 benefit of the officers that might aid in determining the perpe-

27 trator of this crime?

28   A   No, sir.

29   Q   You have given them every assistance you can, have you?

30   A   Yes, sir.

31

32

-8-

- 8 -

1   H. L. HANSEN, being first duly

2   sworn, testified as follows:

3   Q   BY THE CORONER: Please state your name.

4   A   H. L. Hansen.

5   Q   And your occupation?

6   A   Police Officer, City of Los Angeles, attached to the

7   Homicide Division.

8   Q   Mr. Hansen, have you made a follow-up investigation of

9   the death of the deceased, Elizabeth Short?

10   A   Yes, we have.

11   Q   Have you been able to determine as to any possible iden-

12   tification of the person who may have committed this crime?

13   A   As to now, we have no definite information as to who

14   perpetrated it.

15   Q   And you are following all clues you receive?

16   A   Every effort to locate the criminal is being made.

17   Q   Is there anything else that you can say that might assist

18   the Jury in arriving at a verdict?

19   A   I think it has been pretty well covered.

20

21

22   FREDERICK D. NEWBARR, being first

23   duly sworn, testified as follows:

24   Q   BY THE CORONER: Please state your name.

25   A   Frederick D. Newbarr.

26   Q   What is your occupation?

27   A   Physician and Surgeon.

28   Q   And you are the autopsy surgeon for the coroner?

29   A   Yes, sir, chief autopsy surgeon, Los Angeles County.

30   Q   Did you perform an autopsy on the body of Elizabeth

31   Short over whom we are holding the present inquest?

32   A   Yes, sir.

- 9 -

```
PASO 78 8-5
67-4030
```

1   Q   When did you perform the autopsy?

2   A   January 16, 1947 at 10:30 A. M.

3   Q   From your examination of the body would you be able to
4 form any opinion as to the date of the death as to whether it was
5 on the 15th or prior to the 15th?

6   A   It was my opinion that the appearance of the body was
7 such that the death occurred not more than 24 hours previous to
8 the 15th, probably less.

9   Q   So that the death would have occurred either on the 14th
10 or 15th?

11   A   Yes, sir.

12   Q   Will you please state to the Jury either briefly or in
13 full as you like, the result of your autopsy findings, please?

14   A   The immediate cause of the death was hemorrhage and
15 shock due to concussion of the brain and lacerations of the face.
16 The body is that of a female about 15 to 20 years of age, measur-
17 ing 5'5" in height and weighing 115 pounds. There are multiple
18 lacerations in the midforehead, in the right forehead, and at the
19 top of the head in the midline. There are multiple tiny abrasions,
20 linear in shape on the right face and forehead. There are two
21 small lacerations, ¼" each in length, on each side of the nose
22 near the bridge. There is a deep laceration in the face 3" long
23 which extends laterally from the right corner of the mouth. The
24 surrounding tissues are ecchymotic and bluish purple in color.
25 There is a deep laceration 2½" long extending laterally from the
26 left corner of the mouth. The surrounding tissues are bluish
27 purple in color. There are five linear lacerations in the right
28 upper lip which extend into the soft tissues for a distance of 1/8".
29 The teeth are in a state of advanced decay. The two upper central
30 incisors are loose and one lower incisor is loose. The rest of
31 the teeth

~ 10 ~

areas of subarachnoid hemorrhage on the right side and small hemorrhagic areas in the corpus callosum. No fracture of the skull is visible. There is a depressed ridge on both sides and in the anterior portion of the neck. It is light brown in color. There is an abrasion irregular in outline in the skin of the neck in the anterior midline. There are two linear abrasions in the left anterior neck. There are two depressed ridges in the posterior neck, pale brown in color. The lower ridge has an abrasion in the skin at each extremity. The pharynx, larynx are intact. There is no evidence of trauma to the hyoid bone, thyroid or cricoid cartilages or tracheal rings. There is a small area of ecchymosis in the soft tissues of the right neck at the level of the upper tracheal rings. There is no obstruction in the laryngotracheal passage. There is an irregular laceration with superficial loss in the skin of the right breast. The tissue loss is more or less square in outline and measures 3 &¼" transversely and 2½" longitudinally ; Extending toward the midline from this irregular laceration are several superficial lacerations in the skin. There is an elliptical opening in the skin located 3/4" to the left of the left nipple. The opening measures 2 & 3/4" in a transverse direction and 1 & 1/4" in a longitudinal direction in its midportion. The margins of these wounds show no appreciable discoloration.

    Q   Doctor, I don't believe it will be necessary for you to read all of this. It is rather long and I don't think we need to read all of it here. The essential findings with regard to the cause of death have already been expressed; and that is the concussion of the brain and the lacerations of the face. The portion of your findings with regard to the chest, would you read that on the second page where, the organs of the chest, were they in a norma...

1 left lung is pink in color and well aerated. The right lung is
2 somewhat adherant due to fairly firm pleural adhesions. The
3 lung is pink in color and well aerated. There is calcified
4 thickening of the 9th rib on the right side in the scapular line.
5 The heart shows no gross pathology.

6 Q Then the next paragraph with regard to the severing
7 of the body?

8 A The trunk is completely severed by an incision which
9 is almost straight through the abdomen severing the intestine at
10 the duodenum and through the soft tissues of the abdomen passing
11 through the intervertebral disk between the 2nd and 3rd lumbar
12 vertebra. There is very little ecchymosis along the tract of the
13 incision. There is a gaping laceration 4½" which extends longi-
14 tudinally from the umbilicus to the suprapubic aera. On both sides
15 of this laceration there are multiple superficial lacerations.
16 There are multiple criss cross lacerations in the suprapubic aera
17 which extend through the skin and soft tissues. No ecchymosis is
18 seen.

19 Q Was there any evidence of any sexual assault? You might
20 read the last paragraph, and I believe that covers it, on the next
21 page.

22 A The stomach was filled with greenish brown granular
23 material, mostly feces and other particles which could not be
24 identified. All smears for spermatazoa are negative.

25 Q Is there anything else which would contribute to the
26 medical cause of death?

27 A No, sir, I don't think so.

28 Q Your finding is that the real cause of death was hemor-
29 rhage and shock due to blows on the head?

30 A Blows on the head and face.

31

32

- 12 -

338

VERDICT OF CORONER'S JURY

STATE OF CALIFORNIA,
County of Los Angeles } ss.

In the Matter of the Inquisition upon the Body of

_____ ELIZABETH SHORT _____, Deceased,

Before BEN H. BROWN, Coroner.

We, the Jurors summoned to appear before the Coroner of Los Angeles County at

Room 102, Hall of Justice, Los Angeles, California,

on the __22nd__ day of __January__ A. D. 1947, to inquire into

the cause of the death of __Elizabeth Short__

having been duly sworn according to law, and having made such inquisition and hearing the

testimony adduced, upon our oaths, each and all do say that we find that the deceased was named

__Elizabeth Short__

a __female__, married single, widowed unknown native of __Mass.__

aged about __22__ years, and that __She__ came to h__er__ death __found on the__ __15th__ day of

__January__ , 19__47__, at __Norton St., Between 39th and__

__Coliseum Drive, Los Angeles,__

Los Angeles County, California, and that this death was caused by __Hemorrhage and shock__

__due to concussion of the brain and lacerations of face; and from__

__the testimony introduced we find said injuries to have been in-__

__flicted on the deceased by some person or persons unknown at this__

__time to this jury and at some location unknown to this jury; and__

__we find this to be a homicide and recommend that every effort be__

__made to apprehend the perpetrator or perpetrators responsible__

__therefor.__

all of which we duly certify by this inquisition in writing, by us signed this __22nd__

day of __January__ , 19__47__

Choteau W. Paul _____, Foreman.

Paul L. Todd	H. W. Rose
Robert Kessler	Fred Waller
H. W. LaChat	H. E. Brier
C. R. Moore	W. D. Tucker

Will Fowler's letter to Mary Pacios [Humphrey]

Will Fowler
4626 Natick Av.
Sherman Oaks, CA 91403
Feb. 25, 1988

Mary Humphrey
Studio Two
2898 Glascock St.
Oakland, CA 94601

Dear Mary:

Regarding my telling you Elizabeth Short had "infantile sex organs:" <u>That is untrue</u>, and a ploy I use to shock all of faint stomaches, and phony would-be biographers and article writers.

I hope this helps you in some small way.

Best wishes, and good luck,

Will Fowler

FBI documents indicating that the victim's body had been bisected by a trained surgeon.

APPENDIX A

Federal Bureau of Investigation
United States Department of Justice

Los Angeles, California
February 25, 1947

Director, FBI   ATTENTION: IDENTIFICATION DIVISION

RE: ELIZABETH SHORT
     "BLACK DAHLIA" MURDER IN LOS ANGELES
     INFORMATION CONCERNING

Dear Sir:

The manner in which ELIZABETH SHORT's body was dissected has indicated the possibility that the murderer was a person somewhat experienced in medical work. The Los Angeles Police Department has undertaken to develop suspects among the medical and dental schools in the area, as well as among other students who have anything to do with human anatomy.

The University of Southern California Medical School was reluctant to turn over a list of their students to the police department without being assured that the names would not be indexed into police or FBI records as suspects in the case. This assurance has been given them.

I feel that we can be of much assistance to the Los Angeles Police Department in this case and the Bureau's expeditious attention to this project will be sincerely appreciated by the RECORDED 62-8262?-40

At the completion of the Bureau's search, it is requested that the list be destroyed or returned to the Los Angeles Office.

Very truly yours,

R. B. HOOD, SAC.

342

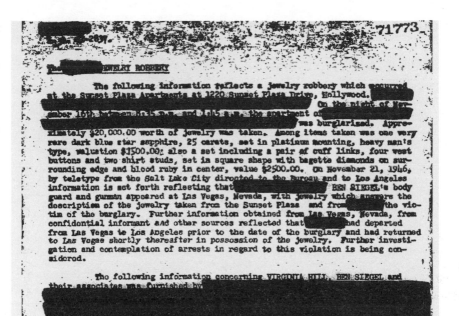

71773

JEWELRY ROBBERY

The following information reflects a jewelry robbery which occurred at the Sunset Plaza Apartments at 1220 Sunset Plaza Drive, Hollywood. On the night of November 16th, between 11:15 p.m. and 1:15 a.m. the apartment of ▮▮▮▮▮▮▮▮ was burglarized. Approximately $20,000.00 worth of jewelry was taken. Among items taken was one very rare dark blue star sapphire, 25 carats, set in platinum mounting, heavy man's type, valuation $3500.00; also a set including a pair of cuff links, four vest buttons and two shirt studs, set in square shape with bagette diamonds on surrounding edge and blood ruby in center, value $2500.00. On November 21, 1946, by teletype from the Salt Lake City directed to the Bureau and to Los Angeles information is set forth reflecting that ▮▮▮▮▮▮▮▮ BEN SIEGEL's body guard and gunman appeared at Las Vegas, Nevada, with jewelry which answers the description of the jewelry taken from the Sunset Plaza and from ▮▮▮▮▮ the victim of the burglary. Further information obtained from Las Vegas, Nevada, from confidential informant and other sources reflected that ▮▮▮▮ had departed from Las Vegas to Los Angeles prior to the date of the burglary and had returned to Las Vegas shortly thereafter in possession of the jewelry. Further investigation and contemplation of arrests in regard to this violation is being considered.

The following information concerning VIRGINIA HILL, BEN SIEGEL and their associates was furnished by ▮▮▮▮▮▮▮▮▮▮▮▮▮▮▮

L.A. 62-2821

Director, FBI

July 22, 1946

Re: REACTIVATION OF THE CAPONE GANG
     MISCELLANEOUS INFORMATION - CRIME SURVEY

SIEGEL is referred to by underworld informants of this office as the man in control of the Western States and he is referred to as a person who can put his friends in touch with the underworld boss of any city in the United States. He acquired his title of BUGSY because many of the associates in the old days considered him as "going bugs" when he got excited in that he acted in an irrational manner. There seems to be no doubt in the fact that he seems to be generally respected and feared by underworld characters because he is supposed to personally have killed at least thirty different individuals.

FBI SALT LAKE CITY 1-15-47   1-15 AM XX PM MST MMH

SAC LOS ANGELES

             URGENT

BANJAMIN "BUGS" SIEGEL, MISCELLANEOUS INFORMATION CONCERNING.

DEPARTURE PLANS NOT YET DEFINITELY KNOWN. SIEGEL HAS RESERVATIONS AT

COLONIAL HOUSE, PALM SPRINGS, BUT IS ATTEMPTING TO OBTAIN BUNGALOW AT

SOME OTHER UNDISCLOSED PLACE IN PALM SPRINGS FOR TEN-DAY PERIOD.

                              NEWMAN

END

9½ FBIM LA RCLV

                         JAN 15 1947

Siegel's FBI files confirm that he traveled from Las Vegas to Los Angeles on
January 6, the day of the Mocambo robbery. The dispatch above indicates
Siegel made reservations in Palm Springs on January 15, the day Elizabeth
Short's body was discovered.

APPENDIX B

The Hodel Hypothesis

In the investigative nonfiction books published about the Black Dahlia case, two authors accuse their fathers of being the pathological killer. In *Daddy Was the Black Dahlia Killer* (Pocket Books, 1995), Janice Knowlton offers no concrete evidence of her father's guilt and relies on flashbacks of repressed childhood memories. Knowlton insists that, while undergoing therapy, she recalled witnessing the murder of Elizabeth Short by her father when she was a child, and she vividly recalls for the reader every minute detail—including her father's inner thoughts. She also distinctly remembered that her father, who lacked medical training and/or surgical instruments, sawed the body in half with a Skil power saw.

Seven years later, in *Black Dahlia Avenger* (Arcade Publishing, 2003), author Steve Hodel claimed that it was *his* father, George Hodel, who killed the Black Dahlia—not Knowlton's. The author maintains that his father murdered not only Elizabeth Short, but at least thirty-one other women as well. Once again, however, the evidence is demonstrably unsubstantiated.

Hodel's Evidence

Exhibit #1: Pictures of Elizabeth Short found among his father's possessions

Steve Hodel claims that two photos found in his father's album in 1993 are pictures of Elizabeth Short. Exhibiting them in chapter 4 of *Black Dahlia Avenger*, he states, "Here were two photographs, both of a vividly beautiful dark-haired woman . . . I felt I did know her and had seen her somewhere in the past. Where?"[1]

Hodel came to the conclusion that the woman in the pictures was the Black Dahlia, and he based the premise of his book on this discovery. To anyone of visual discernment, however, the pictures in George Hodel's photo album look nothing like Elizabeth Short. Members of her family have come forward with a public statement that the Hodel photos "are not Betty—not even close."[2] And Mary Pacios, the author of *Childhood Shadows* who knew Elizabeth Short, has confirmed, "It's definitely not her."[3]

In November of 2004, CBS aired a segment on *48 Hours* about Hodel's claim that his father was the Black Dahlia killer. CBS hired Sunni Chapman, a professional photo identification expert for the New York City Police Department, to examine the photos. Using the E-Fit Recognition computer system for facial identification, Chapman examined the two questioned photos and compared them with known photos of Elizabeth Short. She concluded that they were not the same person. Chapman states she was "85 percent certain that these two photographs are not of the same woman."[4]

Hodel was scarcely five years old when his mother and father separated in 1944, and many readers have observed that the photos of the woman Hodel recalled having seen "somewhere in the past" resemble photos of Hodel's mother, Dorothy Hodel, when she was a young woman (see photos of both women in *Black Dahlia Avenger*).[5]

The two photos found in George Hodel's album that Steve Hodel maintains are pictures of Elizabeth Short.

Elizabeth Short, 1946

Exhibit #2: The George Hodel telegram to Elizabeth Short

Among the items found in Elizabeth Short's memory book was an unsigned telegram sent by an admirer in Washington D.C. to Elizabeth's address in Miami. Although there is no substantiating evidence, Hodel maintains that the unsigned telegram was sent by his father in October or November 1945, when he was studying the Chinese language in Washington D.C.[6] Upon close examination, however, it's evident that the date of the telegram is July 1944, when his father was residing in Los Angeles.

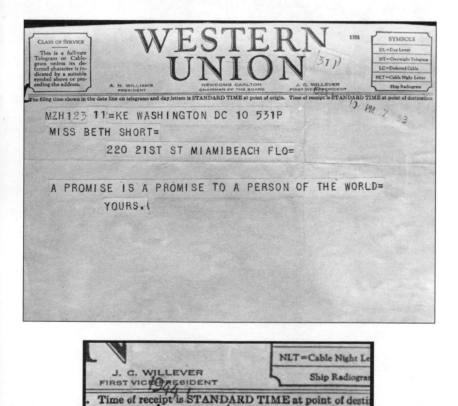

Exhibit #3: The incriminating Man Ray Thought Print

Hodel claims that a Man Ray photo proves that his father murdered the Black Dahlia. His father was a friend of Man Ray when the Surrealist lived in Hollywood during the war, and Dr. Hodel apparently admired his artistry.[7] According to Steve Hodel, the position of the mutilated body of the victim found on Norton Avenue, with her arms bent above her head, duplicated the pose of Man Ray's *The Minotaur*, a surreal photo of a nude woman with her arms bent above her head like the horns of the mythological bull. Hodel claims that this is a "Thought Print" that proves his father was the killer. Hodel states, "Much as I wanted to deny it to myself or to look for other possible explanations, I now realized that the facts were undeniable: George Hodel, through the homage he consciously paid to Man Ray, was provocatively revealing himself to be the murderer of Elizabeth Short. Her body and the way she was posed was George Hodel's signature—on his own surreal masterpiece . . . in a 'still death' tribute to his master."[8] However, it is more likely that Elizabeth Short's arms were bent back above her head because her wrists had been tied to the bathtub shower pipes when she was bisected.

Exhibit #4: It was Dr. George Hodel who sent the paste-up notes to the *Examiner* and other newspapers.

Steve Hodel employed handwriting expert Hannah McFarland to examine nine of the notes sent to the *Examiner* and other Los Angeles newspapers. She was asked to compare the handwriting to nine examples of his father's handwriting. The notes with the handwriting of the alleged killer were labeled "Questioned Documents Q-1 thru Q-9;" and Dr. Hodel's handwriting samples were labeled "Known Documents K-1 thru K-9." According to Hodel, McFarland verified that the handwriting on the paste-up notes sent to the newspapers originated with his father, therefore confirming that George Hodel was the Black Dahlia Killer.[9]

Upon evaluating McFarland's report, however, it becomes clear that the results were inconclusive. Ordway Hilton, author of *Scientific Examination of Questioned Documents* and the accepted authority among forensic societies and document examiners, maintained that Known Documents and Questioned

Documents used for comparison must be from the same approximate time-frame. "Writing habits change gradually," Hilton stated, "therefore, only material written two or three years before or after the disputed writing serves as satisfactory standards."[10] But only two of the nine samples of George Hodel's handwriting were near the 1947 date of the Questioned Documents: K-6 was written in 1943, and K-9 was written in 1949; others were written in 1924 and 1998—decades before and after the Questioned Documents.[11]

In addition, reliable document examination should utilize originals. Ms. McFarland only had second and third generation photocopies of the Questioned Documents to work with.

Contrary to Hodel's claim that McFarland reported that the handwriting on the paste-up notes originated with his father, the report merely states that after comparative analysis of the Known and Questioned documents that "it is highly probable that the printer of Q-2, Q-4, Q-7, and Q-9 printed K-1 through K-8."[12]

However, only the package sent to the *Examiner* containing items from Elizabeth Short's purse was accepted by authorities as originating from the killer. That package had no handwriting on it, nor was it examined by Ms. McFarland. Therefore, it is a false assumption to conclude that the nine notes examined by Ms. McFarland were necessarily mailed by the killer.

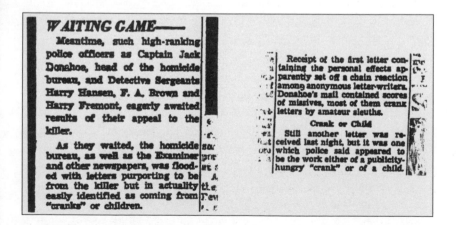

WAITING GAME——

Meantime, such high-ranking police officers as Captain Jack Donahoe, head of the homicide bureau, and Detective Sergeants Harry Hansen, F. A. Brown and Harry Fremont, eagerly awaited results of their appeal to the killer.

As they waited, the homicide bureau, as well as the Examiner and other newspapers, was flooded with letters purporting to be from the killer but in actuality easily identified as coming from "cranks" or children.

Receipt of the first letter containing the personal effects apparently set off a chain reaction among anonymous letter-writers. Donahoe's mail contained scores of missives, most of them crank letters by amateur sleuths.

Crank or Child

Still another letter was received last night, but it was one which police said appeared to be the work either of a publicity-hungry "crank" or of a child.

An expert hired by the *Examiner* at the time claimed that the first four notes were sent by the same person. Homicide believed that all the notes that followed may have been hoax notes sent by various hoaxsters.[13] Of those first four notes, only one was examined by Ms. McFarland: Q-5. To designate notes Q-1 through Q-9 as notes sent by the killer is a fallacy. Only the second note, Q-5, which was mailed to the *Examiner,* could possibly be considered to be written by the killer. And in her report, McFarland states, "My opinion of Q-5 is inconclusive due to lack of identifying characteristics in these samples."[14] Therefore, if one accepts that the second note (Q-5) was actually sent by the killer, the results of McFarland's report are, at best, "inconclusive."

The *48 Hours* producers at CBS hired two forensic experts to compare the handwriting of George Hodel with the notes allegedly sent to the newspapers by the killer. Both experts concluded there was no evidence that the notes were written by the same person. John Osborn, one of the most respected document examiners in the field, stated, "There is simply not enough evidence to prove one way or another whether his father was the writer or not the writer."[15]

Exhibit #5: Between 1947 and 1949, Dr. Hodel brutally murdered Elizabeth Short and thirty-one other women.

Dr. Hodel suddenly returned from China in September of 1946 because he had suffered a serious heart attack, and he was hospitalized in Los Angeles during September and October of 1946. It is not plausible that he would then get out of his hospital bed and proceed to violently murder Elizabeth Short and thirty-one other women.

Exhibit #6: The murder took place at the home of Dr. George Hodel on Franklin Avenue in the Los Feliz district of Hollywood.

Based on information leaked from the 1949 Grand Jury investigation, the *Herald Express* ran a story on September 13, 1949 stating that the murder of the Black Dahlia took place in a room that was less than a fifteen-minute drive from the spot where the bisected body was found, and the room was on one of Los Angeles's busiest streets.

Steve Hodel claims that the "room" was at his father's house in the Los Feliz district of Hollywood.[16] But the district attorney's Black Dahlia files clearly establish that the "room" suspected of being the scene of the murder was at the Astor Motel, managed by suspect Henry Hubert Hoffman on South Flower Street[17]. This was also confirmed by the *Herald Express* on September 14, 1949, in an article that identified the suspected murder site as "a South Flower Street motel room." The drive from the Hodel house on Franklin Street takes twenty-five to thirty minutes. Albeit, both Dr. George Hodel and Henry Hubert Hoffman were eliminated as suspects by the Grand Jury investigators, and neither location was involved in the murder of Elizabeth Short.

Exhibit #7: It was George Hodel who accompanied Elizabeth Short when she checked into Mr. & Mrs. Johnson's hotel on January 12, 1947.

Without offering any evidence, Hodel insists that it was his father, Dr. George Hodel, who was identified by Mr. and Mrs. William Johnson as the man who checked into the Washington Boulevard hotel with the victim during the "missing week" prior to the murder. The Johnsons had told the police that Elizabeth Short and a man claiming to be her husband had registered as "Mr. and Mrs. Barnes" on Sunday, January 12, 1947—only two days before the murder. Hodel states, "After the detectives showed the Johnsons separate photographs retrieved from Elizabeth Short's luggage, the Johnsons positively identified both the victim and the man who had checked in." And Hodel claims that the man in the photo identified by the Johnsons was his father—Dr. George Hodel.[18] However, a photograph of the Johnsons examining the photo that detectives used to identify Elizabeth and her companion appeared in the *Examiner* on January 22, 1947, and the man in the photograph is clearly not George Hodel.[19]

In addition, the police had discredited the hotel managers' story when the Johnsons described the woman they believed to be Elizabeth Short as having jet-black hair. The detectives knew her hair had been hennaed, and the Johnsons subsequently admitted they had made a mistake. The district attorney's Black Dahlia files clearly state that in follow-up investigations all the supposed sightings of Elizabeth Short during the missing week had been disproved and discredited. The report concludes, "No one reported seen from January 9, at approximately 10:00 P.M., until the body was found by Mrs. Bersinger at 10:30 A.M., January 15, has been definitely identified as Elizabeth Short."[20]

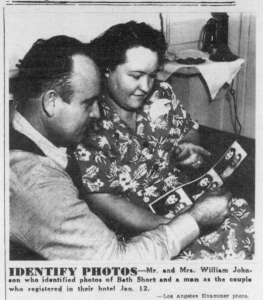

IDENTIFY PHOTOS—Mr. and Mrs. William Johnson who identified photos of Beth Short and a man as the couple who registered in their hotel Jan. 12.

—Los Angeles Examiner photo.

The Johnsons are seen examining an arcade photo strip from Elizabeth Short's memory book. It was used in the identification of the couple that had checked into their hotel.

The man with Elizabeth in the photos is not George Hodel.

George Hodel, 1949

Exhibit #8: The black sedan seen at the crime scene on Norton Avenue belonged to Hodel's father.

Hodel claims that the car spotted leaving the crime scene on Norton Avenue belonged to his father, who was known by the police to drive a post-war, black Packard sedan in 1949. Referring to the Packard, Hodel states, "This vehicle, registered to George Hodel, matched the car leaving the Elizabeth Short crime scene the morning of January 15, 1947."[21] However, the car identified by witnesses at the crime scene was described as a 1936 or 1937 black Ford sedan, and on page 153 of the *Black Dahlia Avenger*, Hodel describes the car seen at the crime scene by witness Bob Meyer as "a 1936 or 1937 Ford sedan, black in color."

> Meanwhile, search was being made for a 1936 black Ford sedan seen at the Norton avenue site early yesterday by Bob Meyer, 3900 South Bronson avenue.
>
> "I saw a car drive up and park about 6:30 a. m.," Meyer told police. "It stayed about three or four minutes, then drove off."
>
> He explained tall weeds obscured his view and that he had seen nothing to arouse his suspicions at the time.
>
> But police studied stains on the curbing and tire tracks in the street, both of which strengthened the belief the slayer had used the black sedan.
>
> Identity of a man said to have paid the girl's room rent at a Hollywood hotel also was being sought by police. He was reported to own a black sedan about 10 years old.
>
> An auto of similar description was seen near the spot where Betty's body was found early Wednesday morning.

Exhibit #9: Dr. George Hodel was a prime suspect in the Black Dahlia murder.

Dr. George Hodel became a suspect in the Black Dahlia case when he was arrested on a morals charge in October 1949. At the time of Hodel's arrest, Tamar Hodel, the doctor's fifteen-year-old daughter, told the police that she had been involved in an incestuous relationship with her father, and he had murdered the Black Dahlia. This occurred just as the Black Dahlia case was about to go before the 1949 Grand Jury, and the LAPD hoped Dr. Hodel might rescue them from the "Dillon Catastrophe." Dr. Hodel was placed under close surveillance by the LAPD, and his house was bugged. But after many man-hours of investigation and the interrogation of many witnesses who knew George Hodel, it became evident that he was not linked to the crime.

At Hodel's trial for incest and immoral behavior, family members testified that his daughter, Tamar, was a pathological liar. Dr. Hodel was acquitted in December 1949, and it was recommended that Tamar receive psychiatric care.

Although Steve Hodel claims that the LAPD knew his father had murdered Elizabeth Short, Grand Jury investigator Frank Jemison's notes, clearly establish that after an extensive investigation, Dr. Hodel was eliminated as a suspect.[22]

10. Doctor George Hodel, M.D., 5121 Fountain Avenue, at the time of this murder had a clinic at East First Street near Alameda....Two microphones were placed in this suspect's home (see the logs and recordings made over approximately three weeks' time which tend to prove his innocence. See statement of Dorothy Hodel, former wife.)... See supplemental reports, long sheets and hear recordings, all of which tend to eliminate this suspect.

Exhibit #10: Dr. George Hodel was a surgeon, and Homicide believed a surgeon was involved in the murder of Elizabeth Short.

Although Steve Hodel claims his father was a surgeon, his medical records indicate he was a general practitioner who specialized in the treatment of venereal diseases. When his ex-wife, Dorothy Hodel, who had known him since the 1920s, was asked by the Grand Jury investigators if her husband had practiced surgery, her response was that he was not a surgeon.

```
13    Q. You understand that a very serious crime has been
      committed here and the District Attorney would not like it
14    if you were to withhold any information in connection
      with a murder of this type and we would like to have you
15    give us any and all information you may have in connection
      with this murder on this suspect George Hodel. If there is
16    anything you have to tell us, tell us.

17    A. I have nothing to tell you that would bear out any idea
      you may have that he did this. All I know is that he is not
18    the sort of man that would psychologically be the kind to do
      it. He has a fine record as a doctor and is a dedicated man.
19    He has never had a fashionable practice. He could have had.
      He is a man that really cares about medicine, not of earning
20    money, but it is incredible to me that he should be in
      any way connected with it.

21    Q. You know that Dr. Hodel has had practice with surgical
      tools?
23    A. I know he has never practiced surgery. His branch of
      medicine is V. D. generally and Administrative Medicine.

      Q. Well, if you look back on the events that took place
24    about the time of the murder, did you have any reason to
      suspect that Dr. Hodel might have had something to do with it?

25    A. None whatever.
```

Exhibit #11: Dr. Hodel was the "wealthy Hollywood man" who was revealed to be a prime suspect in the murder.

It was leaked to the press that a "wealthy Hollywood man" had become a prime suspect and was being questioned by the 1949 Grand Jury. Steve Hodel maintains that the wealthy Hollywood man was his father, but the district attorney's Black Dahlia files reveal that Dr. Hodel was never questioned by the Grand Jury, nor was he a wealthy man. Dr. Hodel was undergoing financial reverses in 1949. The newspaper articles about his incestuous relationship with his daughter had destroyed his business, and his trial had been costly. While under surveillance, he was observed selling his belongings at auction. The district attorney's Black Dahlia files clearly establish that the "wealthy Hollywood man" who had become a prime suspect and was being questioned by the Grand Jury was Mark Hansen.

Exhibit #12: Shortly after the murder, Dr. George Hodel tried to silence Elizabeth's former Chancellor Apartments roommate, Sherryl Maylond.

On the evening of January 15, 1947, only hours after the remains of Jane Doe #1 had been discovered in Liemert Park, a man entered Boardner's Bar in Hollywood, where Elizabeth Short's former Chancellor roommate, Sherryl Maylond, was employed. The man was told by the bartender that it was Sherryl's night off. The same man returned the following night and asked to speak to Sherryl.

In *Black Dahlia Avenger*, Steve Hodel claims that the mysterious man was his father. Hodel states, "George Hodel returns to the same bar the next night and meets Sherryl Maylond, the ex-roommate of Elizabeth Short's at the Chancellor Hotel, room 501. Identifying himself as 'Clement,' George Hodel informs Sherryl he wants to talk to her about Betty Short."[23]

But in a *Herald Express* interview, Sherryl Maylond stated that when the man returned, she refused to talk to him, and she left the bar. She described the man as a "slight, dapper, olive-skinned man by the name of 'Clement.'" It was a description of Maurice Clement.

Demonstrably, there is no evidence to support Steve Hodel's claims in *Black Dahlia Avenger* that his father knew Elizabeth Short or had anything to do with her murder.

HODEL HYPOTHESIS NOTES

1 Steve Hodel, *Black Dahlia Avenger*, Arcadia Publishing, NY, 2003, p. 42.
2 "Black Dahlia Backlash," *Los Angeles Times*, July 11, 2003, p. 27.
3 Int., Mary Pacios, 2004.
4 CBS News.Com/Stories/2004/11/23/48Hours.
5 Steve Hodel, *Black Dahlia Avenger*, pp. 38, 299, and 3rd and 4th pages of photo insert.
6 Ibid., p. 239.
7 Ibid., pp. 239–56.
8 Ibid., p. 241.
9 Ibid., pp. 273–292.
10 Ordway Hilton, *Scientific Examination of Questioned Documents*, Callaghan, Chi, 1956, p. 305.
11 Steve Hodel, *Black Dahlia Avenger*, p. 275.
12 Ibid., p. 277.
13 *Los Angeles Examiner*, January 22, 1947, p. 2.
14 Steve Hodel, *Black Dahlia Avenger*, p. 277.
15 CBS News.Com/Stories/2004/11/23/48Hours.
16 Steve Hodel, *Black Dahlia Avenger*, p. 434.
17 Frank Jemison, List of Suspects, D.A.'s Black Dahlia files.
18 Ibid., pp. 158–9.

19 *Los Angeles Examiner*, January 22, 1947, p. 3.
20 Steve Hodel, *Black Dahlia Avenger* (paperback), pp. 496–7.
21 Ibid., p. 435.
22 *Herald Express*, January 18, 1947.
23 Steve Hodel, *Black Dahlia Avenger,* p. 435.

SOURCE NOTES

Note: References to other publications are indicated by authors and titles listed in the bibliography. Unless otherwise indicated, all interviews (int.) were conducted by the author.

Chapter 1

7   Bobby Jones, a young man . . . : John Gilmore, *Severed*, pp. 1, 2; int., Will Fowler, 2003.

8   Betsy Bersinger was pushing . . . : *Los Angeles Examiner*, January 17, 1947; Mary Pacios, *Childhood Shadows*, pp. 67–68.

9–10 At about 10:45 A.M. . . . : Will Fowler, *Reporters*, pp. 71, 72; int., Will Fowler, 2003.

10   "I'm a reporter on . . .": int. Fowler, 2003.

10   "Hell, someone's cut this girl . . .": Gilmore, *Severed*, p. 3.

10   The city room was . . . : Will Fowler, *Reporters*, p. 75.

10   "Take a good look . . .": Ibid.

11   By the time Fowler . . . : int., Fowler, 2003. The author had a number of interviews with Will Fowler, having first met him while researching a Marilyn Monroe biography in 1992. There were numerous conversations and interviews regarding the Dahlia case between 2002 and 2004.

11   "You could see the color . . .": Gilmore, *Severed*, p. 6.

11   "How come you let the *Times* . . .": Will Fowler, *Reporters*, p. 76.

11   Observing the condition of the body . . . : Haskins's observations are culled from his statements in the Coroner's Inquest. (See Appendix A, pages 327 to 338.)

12   Det. Sgt. Harry Hansen had been . . . : The chronology of the events at the crime scene on Norton are based on the LAPD Summary of the Crime Scene. (See Appendix A, pages 325 and 326.)

12   Reporters had been allowed . . . : Gilmore, *Severed*, p. 9.

12   "Homicide is a union that never . . .": Ibid, p. 9, 10.

13   "Get him over here!": Ibid, p. 10.

14   Hansen noted that there were . . . : The description of the corpse is based on the LAPD Summary of the Crime Scene. (See Appendix A, pages 325 and 326.)

14   When Pinker appeared at the scene . . .": Ibid.

15   Robert Meyer, who lived at . . . : *Examiner*, January 16, 1947; *Herald Express*, January 16, 1947.

16   "Police chemists were checking . . .": *Hollywood Citizen News*, January 18, 1947.

16   "This is the worst crime . . .": Gilmore, *Severed*, p. 11.

16   It was close to 2:00 P.M. . . . : LAPD Summary of the Crime Scene.

16   The *Examiner EXTRA* hit the streets . . . : Fowler int., 2003.

Chapter 2

20   The evening *Herald Express* referred . . ." : *Herald Express*, January 15, 1947.

20   The *Daily News* ran a four-column . . . : *Daily News*, January 16, 1947.

21   Frank Shaw had been elected . . . : Joe Domanick, *To Protect and to Serve*, p. 72.

21   The evidence of corruption was . . . : Ibid, p. 74.

22   "Buron Fitts had covered up enough crimes . . .": Marx and Vanderveen, *Deadly Illusions*, pp. 202, 210.

22   The Phaeton's motor had been left running . . . : Andy Edmonds, *Hot Toddy*, pp. 1–10.

22   The autopsy, however, disclosed that . . . : Ibid, pp. 11–12; Thelma Todd Inquest Report, 1935.

23 In 1932 Thelma Todd had a whirlwind romance . . . : Andy Edmonds, *Hot Toddy*, pp. 115–116.

23 Divorcing him in 1935 . . . : Ibid, p. 137.

23 Angry about the threats she . . . : Ibid, pp. 171, 172, 184.

24 On the night of Saturday, . . . : Ibid, pp. 186–196

24 When the Trocadero headwaiter . . . : Thelma Todd Inquest Report, 1935.

25 Bugsy and the Syndicate operated . . . ": Benjamin Bugsy Siegel's FOIA FBI File.

26 In December of 1946, Bugsy . . . : Jennings, *We Only Kill Each Other*, pp. 161–163.

27 The description of the Unknown Dead ledger . . . : The description is contained within the Inquest Files of Case #7569—Jane Doe #1.

27 According to Det. Finis Brown . . . : int., Will Fowler, 2002.

27 When Donahoe learned that *Examiner* artist . . . : Ibid.

27 Brown explained, "You can't tell much . . . : Gilmore, *Severed*, p. 13.

28 Newspaper reporters and police investigators . . . : int., Will Fowler, 2003.

29 "We have this new Soundphoto . . .": Fowler, *Reporters*, p. 77.

30 Undaunted, the *Examiner* photo lab . . . : Ibid.

31 This scoop put the *Examiner* . . . : Ibid, p. 78.

31 "Richardson shared William Randolph Hearst's . . .": Fowler, int., 2003.

31 On January 16, at 10:30 . . . : Coroner's Inquest documents. (See Appendix A, pages 327 to 338.)

31 Dr. Newbarr concluded . . . : Ibid.

32 Dr. Newbarr was quoted in the press . . . : *Examiner*, January 17, 1947.

32 While the mutilation and bisection of the body . . . : *See* FBI Reports in Appendix A, page 341; Harry Hansen's testimony to the Grand Jury is contained within the Black Dahlia files in the Los Angeles District Attorney's office.

32 The slashed mouth and the blows to the head . . . : Douglas and Olshaker, *The Cases That Haunt Us*, pp. 324–333.

33 An alleged copy of the Autopsy . . . : Knowlton and Newton, *Daddy Was the Black Dahlia Killer*, pp. 17–21.

34 Through the years various . . . : int., Fowler, 2003.

34 Fowler disclosed that Richardson . . . : Ibid.

Chapter 3

36 Where the underworld was connected to . . . : Gus Russo, *The Outfit*, pp. 126–133.

37 During the 1940's, Jack Dragna . . . : Rappleye and Becker, *All American Mafioso, The Johnny Rosselli Story*, p. 46–55..

37 Bugsy's mistress, Virginia "Sugar" Hill, was . . . : Gus Russo, The Outfit, pp. 152–153.

37 Johnny Rosselli, who had been a friend of Kennedy's . . . : Ibid, p. 66.

39 When the *Los Angeles Daily Examiner* identified . . . : int., Fowler, 2003.

39 ". . . reflected a sort of inquisitive innocence" . . . : Fowler, *Reporters*, p. 78.

40 "She was living in a bungalow . . .": *Examiner*, January 17, 1947.

41 Will Fowler recalled that the corpse had . . . : int., Fowler 2003.

41 When Will Fowler returned to the *Examiner:*. . . : The conversation between Sutton and Phoebe Short is based on the account in *Reporters*, p. 79, and Fowler's recollection during an interview with the author in 2003.

43 Reporters working for Richardson . . . : int., Fowler, 2003.

43 William Randolph Fowler was . . . : Wagner, *Red Ink—White Lies*, p. 196.

44 Hecht . . . once said, "A Hearst . . .": Hecht, *A Child of the Century*, p. 144.

44 Originally founded in 1923 . . . : Wagner, *Red Ink—White Lies*, p. 9.

44 Roy Ringer was a new . . . : Ibid, pp. 215–216.

45 Candidates for political office in Los Angeles . . . : Vincent Carter, *Rogue Cops*, pp. 22–49.

46 With the death of Harry Chandler in 1944 . . . : David Halberstam, *The Powers That Be*, pp. 94–122.

47 While Richardson, in his ruthless way . . . : int., Fowler 2003.

48 It was Aggie who was . . . : Agness Underwood, *Newspaperwoman*, p. 62.

48 "This is something you might like, Aggie . . .": Ibid, p. 67.

Chapter 4

50   "I want nothing to do with this . . .": *Herald Express*, January 20, 1947.

50   "I broke off with . . .": Ibid.

51   "She wouldn't stay home . . .": Ibid.

51   In 1930, Cleo had deserted . . . : Pacios, *Childhood Shadows*, p. 8.

51   "I didn't have a way of . . .": Gilmore, *Severed*, p. 18.

52   "She was happy one moment—sad the next . . .": *Examiner*, January 19, 1947.

52   Unable to pay the rent . . . : Pacios, *Childhood Shadows*, p. 9.

52   "I don't know why, but Betty . . .": int., Mary Pacios, 2004.

53   "Another Deanna Durbin . . .": Gilmore, *Severed*, p. 21.

53   "Betty had always been very friendly . . .": Ibid.

53   "by far the prettiest of the . . .": int., Bob Pacios, 2004.

53   Elizabeth began having asthma attacks . . . : Pacios, *Childhood Shadows*, p. 16.

54   Finis Brown went to Miami . . . : From the Black Dahlia case files of the Office of the Los Angeles District Attorney.

54   A former Miami police officer believes . . . : int., retired Miami officer, James Newton, 2003.

54   After her sophomore year . . . : int., Mary Pacios, 2004.

55   "I remember I hadn't seen Betty in a while . . .": Pacios, *Childhood Shadows*, p. 53.

55   "Betty had her legs crossed . . .": Gilmore, *Severed*, p. 22.

55   "I would like to . . .": Ibid., p. 26.

56   She was shocked to learn that Cleo . . . : Ibid, p. 23.

56   According to Muriel, Phoebe had . . . : Ibid, *Severed*, p. 26.

56   "I asked her if she was going to be a movie star . . .": int., Mary Pacios, 2004.

56   "They had their falling out in January . . .": *Examiner*, January 20, 1947.

57   "We knocked and knocked . . .": Quotes of Hansen's account of arriving at Cleo's apartment on Kingsley and his Cleo Short investigation are taken from his testimony for the 1949 Grand Jury, found within the Black Dahlia Case files of the Los Angeles District Attorney.

58   "We found that Mr. Short was working . . .": Ibid.

58   Inez Keeling, an employee of PX #1 . . . : *Examiner*, January 22, 1947.

58 Investigators learned that Elizabeth . . . : Information regarding "Chuck" was found within the Black Dahlia Case files of the Los Angeles District Attorney.

59 Will Fowler recalled that the *Examiner* was . . . : Fowler, *Reporters*, p. 81.

59 The building was managed by Glenn Wolfe . . . : Glenn Wolfe was also listed as a suspect within the Black Dahlia case files, which profiled his narcotics and procuring activities. The files indicate that the Chancellor was owned and managed by the Syndicate.

60 "She looked tired and worried . . .": *Examiner*, January 21, 1947.

60 "She had a lot of telephone calls . . .": *Oakland Tribune*, January 21, 1947.

60 "I've got to hurry! I've got to get out of here!": Ibid.

60 Elvera lived there with her . . . : *Examiner*, January 21, 1947.

61 "When she said, 'temporary' . . .": Gilmore, *Severed*, p. 96.

61 The next morning, Dorothy's younger brother . . . : Ibid, p. 97.

62 "I told her that was not necessary . . .": Ibid.

62 "There was a strong sweet-smelling flowery . . .": Ibid, pp. 97, 98.

63 One afternoon she had an appointment with . . . : Ibid, p. 98.

64 When *Examiner* reporters Devlin and O'Day . . . : Richardson, *For the Life of Me*, p. 300.

64 "Some people came to our door . . .": *Examiner*, January 20, 1947.

65 In checking at the San Diego . . . : Richardson, *For the Life of Me*, p. 302.

66 "Suspect described as . . .": from the LAPD All Points Bulletin of January 9, 1947.

Chapter 5

68 If Red had driven Elizabeth Short . . . : Richardson, *For the Life of Me*, p. 301.

68 Initially, Devlin and O'Day were unable . . . : Fowler, *Reporters*, p. 81.

68 Examining the Register . . . : Richardson, *For the Life of Me*, p. 302.

69 Without saying he was an officer . . . : Fowler, *Reporters*, pp. 81, 82.

70 "I know why you're here, but I didn't do it.": Ibid, p. 82.

70 *Examiner* photographer Ferde Olmo . . . : Ibid, p. 82; int., Fowler, 2003.

71 Manley was repeatedly questioned by Hansen . . . : *Examiner*, January 20, 1947.

71 I called my wife that night . . . : Ibid.

73 Knowing that he had been through a rough . . . : Agness Underwood, *Newspaperwoman*, p. 63.

73 Aggie recalled that she primed . . . : Ibid.

73 "I knew Beth Short—sure . . .": *Herald Express*, January 20, 1947.

74 "A week or ten days before . . .": Ibid.

75 But the truth was that Red . . . : Manley's service record and the notations regarding his "Section Eight" are included in the Black Dahlia case files at the Office of the Los Angeles District Attorney.

75 "After I left her . . .": *Herald Express*, January 20, 1947.

76 "When we got to the Hacienda Club . . .": Ibid.

77 "I went to my room . . .": Ibid.

77 "When I got home I didn't . . .": Ibid.

77 According to the Frenches . . . : *Examiner*, January 21, 1947.

78 As observed by Forrest Faith . . . : *Herald Express*, January 21, 1947.

78 "We went to a motel cabin . . .": *Herald Express*, January 20, 1947.

78 "En route, she wanted to stop . . .": Ibid.

80 Jemison: During the course of your . . . : From the Black Dahlia case files at the Office of the Los Angeles District Attorney.

81 "I asked where she was going to . . .": *Herald Express*, January 20, 1947.

82 "When we got to the Biltmore . . .": Ibid.

82 "That is the last time I ever . . .": Ibid.

82 Bellboy Captain, Harold Studholme told the police . . .": from the Black Dahlia case files at the Office of the Los Angeles District Attorney.

Chapter 6

84 After an exhaustive search, . . . : int., Fowler, 2002.

85 Richardson implored Donahue . . . : Richardson, *For the Life of Me*, p. 305.

85 Fowler remembers searching . . . : int., Fowler, 2002.

85 "You're welcome to the luggage . . .": Richardson, *For the Life of Me*, p. 305.

85 "Donahoe blew a fuse.": int., Fowler, 2003.

87 In *Black Dahlia Avenger*, . . . : Hodel, *Black Dahlia Avenger*, p. 156.

87 *My Darling Matt* . . . : Elizabeth Short's love letters were reproduced in the *Herald Express* and *Examiner* editions of January 20, 1947.

89 As Jim Richardson observed . . . : Richardson, *For the Life of Me*, p. 301.

90 Richardson had arranged for Phoebe . . . : Fowler, *Reporters*, 84–85.

90 "Betty always wanted to be an actress . . .": *Examiner*, January 20, 1947.

91 "I have suffered deeply.": Ibid.

91 When Phoebe returned to Los Angeles . . . : Gilmore, *Severed*, p. 146.

91 "I can't tell, Momma . . .": Ibid, p. 147.

93 The nine inquest jurors . . . : The account of the inquest is culled from the Coroner's Inquest documents. (See Appendix A, pages 327 to 338.)

94 Shortly after the murder was reported . . . : *Examiner*, January 20, 1947.

94 As in a lineup, . . . : *Examiner*, January 24, 1947.

95 "Those shoes have double heel caps . . .": Ibid.

96 Divorced by Harriet in the following . . . : Fowler, *Reporters*, p. 86.

96 Following the Inquest . . . : Pacios, *Childhood Shadows*, p. 37.

Chapter 7

98 A young man by the name of Daniel Voorhees . . . : *Examiner*, January 24, 1947.

99 The odds that a false suspect . . . : Gilmore, *Severed*, p. 155.

100 Dumais claimed to have been . . . : *Herald Express*, February 3, 1947.

100 "None of the confessors ever came close . . .": Gilmore, *Severed*, p. 155.

100 Among them were a Mr. and Mrs. Johnson . . . : *Herald Express*, January 23, 1947.

100 More than four hundred investigators and officers . . . : *Examiner*, January 22, 1947.

101 "No matter how questionable each lead . . .": Gilmore, *Severed*, p. 150.

101 Prior to Elizabeth Short's return to Los Angeles on . . . : The whereabouts and itinerary of Elizabeth Short between 1943 and 1947 is culled from the Elizabeth Short chronology found within the District Attorney's Black Dahlia files.

102 According to Vice Squad officer, Sgt. Charles Stoker . . . : Stoker, *Thicker'n Thieves*, p. 152.

102 Elizabeth's roommate at the Clinton, Lucille Varela . . . : Gilmore, *Severed*, p. 34, 35.

103 Syndicate Madam, Brenda Allen, . . . : Stoker, *Thicker 'n Thieves*, p. 78.

104 At that time she was Marie Mitchell . . . : Ibid, p. 79.

105 "She boasted to the girls who worked for her . . .": Ibid, p. 80.

106 He discovered that Brenda was working out of . . . : Ibid, p. 81.

106 "Then it struck me full-force . . .": Ibid, p. 84.

107 The Gangster Squad had a dark history . . . : Domanick, *To Protect and to Serve*, p. 70–79.

108 "Al Green" was Albert Louis Greenberg, a former . . . : int., Fred Otash, 1991.

108 In the 1940s the back room was a bookie joint . . . : The author worked at the Goldwyn Studio from 1957 through 1962, and the stories about Siegel and his Formosa office were legendary at the time. According to Fred Sawyer, the gate guard, who had been on the lot for many years, Siegel had an arrangement with the Goldwyn lot manager to park his car on the Goldwyn lot. He would then walk to the Formosa Street pedestrian entry, and walk across the street to his office above the Formosa Café.

108 Tone . . . he spotted the Black Dahlia sitting . . ." Gilmore, *Severed*, pp. 36–37.

108 "She said she was waiting for . . .": Ibid.

109 "I thought it was a pickup from . . .": Ibid.

109 During her stay in Hollywood in 1944 . . . : Ibid, p. 35.

110 Georgette's body had been found . . . : *Herald Express*, October 13, 1944.

110 She then returned to Miami for the winter season of 1944/45 . . . : Elizabeth Short chronology found in the District Attorney's Black Dahlia files.

110 It was at St. Clair's that . . . : Ibid.

111 Following her seasoned travel pattern . . . : Ibid.

111 Briefly returning to Medford . . . : Ibid.

111 During Elizabeth's five month stay . . . : Ibid.

112 "Elizabeth Short was always on . . ." : int., Vince Carter, 2004

112 When Elizabeth arrived in Los Angeles . . . : Elizabeth Short's chronology found in the District Attorney's Black Dahlia files.

112 "She lived down the street at the Washington . . ." : *Examiner*, January 21.

112 "One Army officer who saw her frequently . . .": *Herald Express*, January 21, 1947.

112 On finding that Fickling . . . : Suspect List, District Attorney's Black Dahlia files.

113 "I met Betty in 1944 before I . . ." : *Examiner*, January 22, 1947.

113 Fickling stated that he met her . . . : Suspect List, District Attorney's Black Dahlia files.

113 "Time and again I've suggested . . ." : *Examiner*, January 22, 1947.

113 "I do hope you find a nice . . .": Ibid.

114 "Do not write to me here . . .": Ibid.

114 It was on August 28 . . . : Suspect List, District Attorney's Black Dahlia files.

Chapter 8

115 When questioned by reporters . . . : *Herald Express*, January 20, 1947.

115 "Whenever we took the girls out . . .": Ibid.

116 After staying a month . . . : Elizabeth Short chronology, District Attorney's Black Dahlia files.

116 "Miss Short was always getting behind . . .": *Examiner*, January 22, 1947.

116 A multimillionaire . . . : Obit, *Los Angeles Times*, August 18, 1964.

116 Some of the showgirls and B-girls: int., Robert Slatzer, 2004.

116 In the ascendancy of Hollywood wannabees . . . : Ibid.

117 Judy Walters, a former prostitute: Ibid.

118 "Marilyn liked going to the Florentine Gardens and . . ." : int., Gilmore/Slatzer, 1989; int., Wolfe/Slatzer, 2004.

118 "Elizabeth Short and Marilyn spoke . . .": Ibid.

119 "We used to think the world of . . .": *Examiner*, January 21, 1947.

119 "She dated many different men while she was . . .": Testimony of Mark Hansen to Grand Jury investigator, Jemison, in 1949—District Attorney's Black Dahlia files.

119 "Short, dark complexioned man in his . . .": *Examiner*, January 21, 1947.

119 Witnesses at the Chancellor and the . . . : Maurice Clement's activities and his connection to the Brenda Allen call-girl ring were well known to a number of employees at Columbia Studios, where the author was employed in 1954.

120 Although Maurice was never publicly . . . : Suspect List, District Attorney's Black Dahlia files.

120 Former Columbia Studio employee . . . : int., Al Nolan, 2002.

121 "Beth had to be cautious . . .": Ann Toth's testimony for the 1949 Grand Jury—District Attorney's Black Dahlia files.

121 Finis was fully aware . . . : Forwarded to the district attorney's files from the LAPD are a number of references to Clement as an employee at Columbia Studios. Finis would have been fully aware of Clement's identity.

123 "A wealthy Hollywood man": *Herald Express*, October 13, 1949.

126 When Beth and Marjorie . . . : Marvin Margolis testimony, District Attorney's Black Dahlia files.

130 Clement had admitted he had seen . . . : Jemison notes, District Attorney's Black Dahlia files.

130 George Bacos, an usher at CBS . . . : George Bacos testimony, District Attorney's Black Dahlia files.

Chapter 9

133 "We believe that the killer may have been a woman . . .": *Herald Express*, January 21, 1947.

134 She had been last seen . . . : Ibid.

134 Lynn told the police . . . : *Herald Express*, January 22, 1947.

135 "I don't think so . . .": *Boston Globe*, January 22, 1947.

135 "I think a medical man was . . .": Harry Hansen Grand Jury testimony, 1949, District Attorney's Black Dahlia files.

136 "It was a fine piece of surgery . . .": Ibid.

136 "The murderer had some training in . . .": Elizabeth Short FBI report, February 25, 1947.

137 "There are a lot of girls in Hollywood . . .": *Herald Express*, January 23, 1947.

139 Her body had been discovered . . . : *Herald Express*, October 13, 1944.

139 "Miss Short's life in Hollywood . . .": int., Vince Carter, 2004.

141 "Is this the city editor?" . . . : Richardson, *For the Life of Me*, p. 307.

143 Mailed at the main branch of . . . : *Examiner*, January 25, 1947.

144 "This book is going to be dynamite . . .": *Examiner*, January 25, 1947.

145 "Once been sent to me from Denmark . . .": *Herald Express*, January 26, 1947.

145 "There were no entries in the book . . .": Ibid.

146 This message was sent . . . : *Examiner*, January 25, 1947.

146 "The fact that the postcard was . . .": *Examiner*, January 26, 1947.

147 "In signing the postcard, 'Black Dahlia Avenger' . . .": Ibid.

148 "If you want to surrender . . .": *Herald Express*, January 26, 1947.

148 At the same time, reporters from . . . : Richardson, *For the Life of Me*, p. 310.

148 "Get your boys away from here . . .": Ibid, p. 311.

148 "All that morning the City Room was . . .": int., Fowler, 2003.

148 "All that day I had a . . .": Richardson, *For the Life of Me*, p. 311.

Chapter 10

149 Richardson got his start in . . . : int., Fowler, 2003.

149 and the Governor's nephew . . . : Richardson's friendship with Mayor Bowron was confirmed by Richardson in his autobiography, *For the Life of Me*, pp. 224–225.

150 In 1937 he had been fired . . . : int., Fowler, 2003.

151 Carroll was a tenant when he looked after Marilyn Monroe: int., Slatzer, 2004.

151 Georgette's body was discovered . . . : *Herald Express*, October 12, 1944.

151 When the detectives from the sheriff's . . . : Ibid.

152 At the inquest it was . . . : Transcript of the Coroner's Inquest, October 17, 1944.

152 Three days later, Georgette's car . . . : *Herald Express*, October 15, 1944.

153 Her friend, June Ziegler, also a . . . : *Herald Express*, October 13, 1944.

153 "She was seated in her car . . .": *Examiner*, October 13, 1944.

153 Prints were also found on a light bulb . . . : Gilmore, *Severed*, p. 156.

154 And Aggie had heard through her contacts . . . : Ibid, p. 153.

154 According to Aggie's source . . . : Ibid, p.154; int., Underwood, 1964.

155 After Aggie wrote her article about . . . : Underwood, *Newspaperwoman*, p. 38.

156 "They kicked me up the ladder . . .": Ibid, p. 40.

157 "We are dealing with a homicidal maniac . . .": *Examiner*, January 26, 1947.

157 "Richardson suspected that Donahoe . . .": int., Fowler, 2004.

159 "It appears impossible . . .": *Herald Express*, February 1, 1947.

159 "May not have taken place in Los Angeles . . .": *Herald Express*, February 3, 1947.

160 The Frenches said they weren't certain . . . : *Examiner*, January 27, 1947.

160 "The old-line vice-payoff from . . .": Carter, *Rogue Cops*, p. 112.

161 "Donahoe had a reputation as a killer . . .": Ibid, p. 156.

161 "Donahoe and Chickie became . . .": Ibid, p. 158.

162 "Something in the autopsy . . .": int., Fowler, 2003.

162 It was a leak . . . : int., Fowler, Ibid.

162 Hearst reporter Sid Hughes was told . . . : Ibid.

162 "The manner in which the 'Black Dahlia' . . .": *Herald Express*, February 2, 1947.

164 "A second version of the crime . . .": Ibid.

164 "No lead had any conclusions . . .": Gilmore, *Severed*, p. 173.

165 "He was a brilliant detective . . .": Ibid, p. 142.

166 "I was personally concerned that Harry . . .": Ibid.

Chapter 11

169 The victim had been "kicked and stomped to death . . .": *Herald Express*, February 10, 1947.

169 While some deemed it a "copycat" killing . . . : *Herald Express*, February 11, 1947.

170 On February 19, he was summarily removed . . . : Carter, *Rogue Cops*, p. 189.

170 According to Vince Carter, Donahoe's problems . . . : Ibid; int., Carter, 2004.

170 "After that, things were never . . ." : Ibid.

171 According to the newspaper coverage . . . : *Herald Express*, February 22, 1947.

171 Deciding to attend the inquest . . . : Stoker, *Thicker 'n Thieves*, p. 91.

172 Several months later, Stoker learned . . . : Ibid, p. 104.

172 "Marilyn was convinced that . . .": Gilmore/Slater interview, 1989; author/Slatzer interview, 2004.

172 It was five months after the Black Dahlia . . . : *Examiner*, June 20, 1947.

Chapter 12

180 Born on February 28, 1905 . . . : Benjamin "Bugsy" Siegel's FBI Report.

180 Two of the early members . . . : Jennings, *We Only Kill Each Other*, pp. 22, 23.

180 By the time he had turned . . . : Siegel's FBI Report.

180 Some likened his murderous episodes . . . : Jennings, *We Only Kill Each Other*, p. 162.

181 "When we were in a fight . . .": Messick, *Lansky*, p. 112.

181 Not one to assign a murder . . . : Siegel's FBI Report. .

181 Unlike his brother, Maurice Siegel . . . : Ibid.

181 In the Spring of 1928 . . . : Jennings, *We Only Kill Each Other*, p. 23.

182 Lucky Luciano invited "Joe the Boss" Masseria . . . : Feder, *The Luciano Story*, pp. 77, 78.

183 His brother Maurice, along with his sister Bessie . . . : Siegel's FBI Report.

183 In his testimony before the Kefauver Committee . . . : Report of the Special Committee to Investigate Organized Crime (Kefauver), Vol. VI, p. 498.

184 Dewey was after organized crime, and . . . : Feder, *The Luciano Story*, pp. 135–166.

184 Returning to Los Angeles in the summer of 1936—Siegel's FBI Report.

185 While establishing a network of Syndicate . . . : Ibid.

186 According to the California Crime Commission . . . : Report of the Cal. Crime Com., 1950, Vol. II, p. 347.

186 At the instruction of Lansky . . . : Ibid, Vol. II, p. 426.

186 Born in Corleone, Sicily in 1891, Dragna . . . : Ibid. Vol. III, p. 520.

187 Although Dragna lacked . . . : Ibid, Vol. III, p. 522.

187 Dragna's Sotto Capo . . . : Rapplaye, *Johnny Rosselli Story*, pp. 58–66.

188 In 1938 Bugsy moved . . . into an elegant . . . : Jennings, *We Only Kill Each Other*, pp. 46–48.

188 The Countess Dorothy Denice Taylor di Frasso, was a . . . : Ibid, pp. 39–41.

189 A former goon for Murder, Inc. . . . : Ibid, pp. 82–85.

190 "We'll turn both cars around": Ibid, p. 84.

191 Big Greenie's murder remained . . . : Ibid.

191 Booked on September 14, 1940, for suspicion . . . : *Examiner*, September 17, 1940.

191 "There's something phony going on . . .": Jennings, *We only Kill Each Other*, p. 115.

191 Deciding it was worth investigating . . . : Richardson, *For the Life of Me*, pp. 16, 17.

193 There were investigations and reprimands, . . . : Jennings, *We Only Kill Each Other*, pp. 120–21.

193 Although Bugsy threatened Jim Richardson, and . . . : Richardson, *For the Life of Me*, p. 18

193 Esta Siegel's brother . . . : Siegel's FBI Report.

193 Bugsy sold his Holmby Hills mansion . . . : Jennings, *We Only Kill Each Other*, p. 133.

194 Succeeding in avoiding the draft . . . : Ibid, p. 139.

195 "The race-wire was the bookmakers only . . .": Report of the Special Committee to Investigate Organized Crime, Vol. VII, p. 208.

195 "Benny Siegel began pushing another wire . . .": Cohen, *In My Own Words*, p. 62.

195 "We tore that fucking office apart . . .": Ibid, p. 62.

196 Although Brenda was operating over . . . : Stoker, *Thicker 'n Thieves*, pp. 79–82.

196 It started with the gangland killing . . . : *Examiner*, May 3, 1940.

196 Then on October 3, . . . : *Examiner*, October 4, 1946.

197 Elizabeth Short returned to Los Angeles in July . . . : Elizabeth Short chronology, District Attorney's Black Dahlia files.

197 When her bisected . . . : Dragna's address in the 1946 telephone directory places him three short blocks from Thirty-ninth and Norton. His brother Louis T. Dragna, lived six blocks away at 702 West Forty-sixth Street.

Chapter 13

199 The Flamingo dream had been hijacked . . . : Wilkerson, *The Man Who Invented Las Vegas*, pp. 77–79.

200 "Moe, we're going to take this land, . . ." : Jennings, *We Only Kill Each Other*", pp. 149–50.

201 Deciding that the aisles . . . : Ibid, p. 152.

201 The construction budget was . . . : Wilkerson, *The Man Who Invented Las Vegas*, p. 99.

202 Al Greenberg ran narcotics traffic . . . : California Crime Commission: Vol VII, p. 179.

202 The McCadden Gang included . . . : *Examiner*, January 16, 1947; Gilmore int. with Jack Anderson Wilson, 1981; *L.A. Times*, January 15, 1947.

202 The theft of more than $150, . . . : *Herald Express*, November 12, 1946.

202 The jewels were fenced . . . : The Beverly Hills phone book of 1947 places Maurice Reingold's jewelry store at 218 N. Beverly Drive—two doors south of Jerry Rothchild's men's shop where Drucker's barbershop was located. Maurice Reingold was arrested on June 10, 1947 for complicity in the McCadden Gang jewel thefts, *L.A. Times*, June 15, 1947.

202 Although the hotel wasn't ready to open . . . : Wilkerson, *The Man Who Invented Las Vegas*, p. 102.

202 "The show was spectacular . . ." : Ibid, p. 102.

203 Accusing a dealer of cheating . . . : Jennings, *We Only Kill Each Other*, p. 172.

203 Westbrook Pegler had made some . . . : Ibid, p. 173.

203 With a $300, loss in the first ten days . . . : Benjamin Bugsy Siegel's FBI Report.

203 When he arrived in L.A.: Report of the Special Committee to Investigate Organized Crime (Kefeuver), Vol. VII, p. 279.

204 "I think she, too, is psychopathic . . ." : Ibid, p. 280.

204 The jewelry had been put on . . . : *Examiner*, January 7, 1947.

204 According to the FBI files . . . : Benjamin Bugsy Siegel's FBI Report..

205 On January 15, the day . . . : Ibid.

205 On January 16, the day after Elizabeth . . . : *Los Angeles Times*, January 16, 1947.

205 While Al Greenberg was identified . . . : Jennings, *We Only Kill Each Other*, p. 199.

206 By the time Bugsy Siegel returned . . . : Ibid, pp. 171–72.

206 When Siegel heard that Ray Kronsen . . . : Ibid, p. 183.

206 Paul Price, Siegel's publicist, recalled, "No one could . . ." : Ibid, p. 181.

206 On May 17, Hill was heard . . . : Ibid, p. 189.

206 Learning that Siegel's henchman . . . : *Herald Express*, June 18, 1947.

207 When Bugsy Siegel flew to Los Angeles . . . : The chronology of Siegel's whereabouts on Friday, June 20, is from Benjamin Bugsy Siegel's FBI Report.

207 Managed by Sonny Meyers, Jack's at the Beach . . . : Vandersteen's acquired interest in the Florentine Gardens and his gambling investments are chronicled in the District Attorney's Black Dahlia files.

207 Witnesses dining at Jack's at . . . : The witnesses were Alan and Jane Handler. Alan Handler, who was a partner of Vandersteen in several gambling enterprises, told the author of seeing Vandersteen and Siegel together at Jack's at the Beach on the night of the murder.

208 The first bullet smashed . . . : *Herald Express*, June 21, 1947.

210 Harry's brother Jack . . . : Accounts of Jack Drucker's association with the mob in New York can be found in: Turkus, *Murder, Inc.*, p. 147.

211 And in 1987, Eddie Cannizzaro . . . : int., Les Zoeller, 1998.

211 "Jack Dragna orchestrated it . . ." : Ibid.

212 "Dead": *L.A. Times*, October 26, 1952.

Chapter 14

215 According to Administrative Vice Officer Vince Carter . . . : int., Vince Carter, 1998, 2004.

215 "A lot of what was *not* printed . . .": Carter, *Rogue Cops*, pp. 47–48.

215 Although Norman Chandler wielded great power . . . : Halberstam, *The Powers That Be*, p. 100.

216 "I cannot find Norman! I cannot find Norman!": Ibid, p. 101.

216 "Everyone loved him, and no one knew him . . .": Carter, *Rogue Cops*, p. 48.

217 "Contrary to popular opinion . . .": Ibid, p. 49.

217 Police criminologist Ray Pinter was . . . : *Herald Express*, September 14, 1942.

217 "Chief Horrall wanted to know . . .": int., Otash, 1990.

217 Norman's marriage to Dorothy . . . : Halberstam, *The Powers That Be*, pp. 267–77.

217 Although the Chandlers had their own . . . : int., Vince Carter, 1998.

217 Before retiring from the LAPD . . . : int., Otash, 1990.

218 Arthur Lake had first met . . . : Gilmore, *Severed*, p. 154; int., Aggie Underwood, 1962.

219 During his Hollywood years . . . : Hecht, *Child of the Century*, pp. 610–613.

220 I came across a significant interview: *Herald Express*, January 24, 1947.

221 "He sped away with grinding . . .": Ibid.

223 One of the *Herald* stories . . . : *Herald Express*, July 2, 1947.

226 Aggie said she had . . . : int., Aggie Underwood, 1962.

227 "That was something I heard . . .": Ibid.

227 "I'm going to stick to my knitting . . .": Ibid.

Chapter 15

228 Jean Spangler was a statuesque . . . : *Examiner*, October 10, 1949.

230 "You sound happy . . .": *Herald Express*, October 11, 1949.

230 On Wednesday that evening, she had . . . : *Examiner*, October 11, 1949.

231 *"Kirk, Can't wait any longer . . ."*: Ibid.

231 The mother of film actress, . . . : *Daily News*, October 12, 1949.

232 The man was said to be . . . : from the confidential research files of the *Examiner*.

232 When questioned by detectives . . . : Ibid.

232 "Death by violence is indicated . . .": *Daily News*, October 14, 1949.

233 "I'm afraid that guy ain't living . . .": *Examiner*, October 22, 1949.

233 On the night that she disappeared . . . : *Examiner*, October 12, 1949.

233 . . . "appeared to be arguing with two . . .": Ibid.

233 "Sorry, you're not allowed in . . .": Douglas, *Rag Man's Son*, p. 149.

235 "When big city rackets and criminal elements . . .": Carter, *Rogue Cops*, p. 141.

235 On the night of August 19, 1948 . . . : Cohen, *In My Own Words*, pp. 120–122.

236 "When the guy with the pistol . . .": *Herald Express*, August 20, 1948.

236 "I laid myself down . . .": Cohen, *In My Own Words*, p. 121.

236 "The Mickey Cohen gangland shooting . . .": *Daily News*, August 22, 1948.

237 When Stoker received death threats . . . : Stoker, *Thicker 'n Thieves*, p. 127.

238 Among the subjects proposed to be . . . : *Examiner*, January 8, 1949.
238 Soon after the 1949 Grand Jury . . . : *Examiner*, January 11, 1949.
239 "There's no doubt in my mind . . .": *Herald Express*, January 11, 1949.
240 "We're not going to let anybody . . .": Ibid.
240 As chief of the so-called "Sex Offense Bureau . . .": Gilmore, *Severed*, p. 161.
240 According to Dillon, the charges . . . : *Herald Express*, January 22, 1949.
241 Former Homicide detective, Sgt. Stephan Bailey . . . : Gilmore, *Severed*, p. 163.
241 Initiating several telephone conversations . . . : Ibid.
242 "I flew to Las Vegas where . . .": Ibid.
242 "They kept me in the motel room . . .": Ibid., p. 164.
244 "It went on for about ten hours . . .": Ibid., p. 166.
245 The day after Dillon . . . : District Attorney's Black Dahlia files—Jemison's suspect summation.
245 Accusing Horrall of . . . : *Examiner*, January 24, 1949.

Chapter 16

247 To the average citizen . . . : Grand Jury Procedure, Los Angeles Grand Jury statutes.
248 Assigned to the case in October of 1949 . . . : District Attorney's Black Dahlia files—Jemison's notes.
248 Few people knew at the time that Finis Brown . . . : int., Vince Carter, 2004.
248 In the early weeks of his investigation . . . : District Attorney's Black Dahlia files—Jemison's notes.
249 His testimony was to include . . . : Stoker, *Thicker 'n Thieves*, pp. 200–201.
249 The Attorney General assigned . . . : Ibid.
249 "Every night that Mickey came in . . .": Kefauver Report, Vol. VII, p. 462.
251 The fusillade wounded Cohen in . . . : *Examiner*, July 21, 1949.
253 Stoker also disclosed that it was Brenda . . . : Stoker, *Thicker 'n Thieves*, p. 201.
253 The *Daily News* leaked Stoker's testimony . . . : *Daily News*, May 16, 1949.

254 When Brenda was escorted . . . : *Daily News*, August 5, 1949.

255 After the Grand Jury listened . . . : *Daily News*, August 17, 1949.

256 Ironically, the only officer publicly punished . . . : Stoker, *Thicker 'n Thieves*, pp. 285–338.

257 Among the revelations testified to by Stoker: Ibid, pp. 150–162.

257 When the detectives discovered that . . . : Ibid.

257 "Brown has an idea of who . . .": *Pasadena Star News*, January 15, 1987.

258 In the process of narrowing . . . : Ibid.

258 "This jury at this time . . .": Ibid.

259 In addition, on the night of January 14, 1947 . . . : Ibid.

259 "As of this date would you . . .": Ibid—Vandersteen testimony.

261 But after journeying to San Francisco . . . : Ibid—Jemison's notes, Suspect List.

261 Henry Hubert Hoffman was introduced . . . : Ibid—Jemison's notes, Suspect List.

261 The two detectives spent months . . . : Ibid—testimony of Case and Ahern.

262 "It was reported that the room . . .": *Herald Express*, September 13, 1949.

262 Hoffman submitted to a lie detector . . . : District Attorney's Black Dahlia files—Jemison's notes.

262 After thousands of man-hours spent . . . : Ibid.

262 On the morning of July 14, 1949 . . . : *Herald Express*, July 14, 1949.

263 "What was your involvement in . . .": District Attorney's Black Dahlia files—Finis Brown testimony.

266 "This jury has observed indications . . .": Report of the 1949 Grand Jury.

Chapter 17

267 In speaking to a former file clerk . . . : int., District Attorney's Office file clerk. The individual interviewed requested anonymity.

268 In examining Jemison's Dahlia files . . . ; D.A.'s Black Dahlia files—Jemison's notes.

270 The extensive memos and notations . . . : Ibid.

270 "What type of a doctor was . . ." : Ibid.

272 Jemison's notations included abortionists . . . who . . . : Ibid.

272 Dr. Leslie Audrain, who was identified by Sgt. Stoker . . . ; Stoker, *Thicker 'n Thieves*, pp. 150–152.

273 Dr. Audrain had died suddenly . . . ; obit, *Pasadena Star News*, September 12, 1949.

273 Jemison's notations also indicate . . . ; D.A.'s Black Dahlia files—Jemison's notes.

274 On District Attorney William Simpson's . . . : Ibid.

275 This also was an address Jemison found . . . : Ibid.

276 Another notation with the two names . . . : Ibid.

277 As the procurer who often . . . : int., Al Nolan, 2004.

278 and he may have arrived at . . . : D.A.'s Black Dahlia files—Jemison's notes. Clement had been placed as suspect #7 on Jemison's suspect list.

278 And *Examiner* reporter Will Fowler . . . : int., Fowler, 2003.

278 "There appeared to be a willful attempt . . .": Hodel, *Black Dahlia Avenger* (paperback), pp. 506–507.

279 According to Fred Otash, it was . . . : int., Otash, 1990.

279 Former Administrative Vice officers . . . : int., Carter, 2004.

280 The night before she left Hollywood . . . : D.A.'s Black Dahlia files—Mark Hansen testimony.

280 A Chancellor roommate said . . . : *Herald Express*, January 18, 1947.

280 She told her roommates, as well as . . . : D.A.'s Black Dahlia files—Mark Hansen testimony.

281 On the drive north . . . : Ibid, Robert Manley testimony.

282 But the Brenda Allen call-girl ring . . . : int., Carter, 2004.

282 Bugsy happened to be in town . . . : Benjamin "Bugsy" Siegel's FBI Report.

283 But these sightings were investigated . . . : D.A.'s Black Dahlia Files—Jemison's notes.

Chapter 18

286 Vince, I discovered, had been a . . . : int., Vince Carter, 1992.

285 After the resignation of Chief Horrall . . . : Carter, *Rogue Cops*, pp. 70–5.

286 At that time, Vince was . . . : Ibid.

287 "Hamilton continued his surveillance until . . .": Ibid.

288 Oblivious of his predicament . . . : Ibid.

288 I learned from Vince Carter . . . : int., Carter, 1992.

288 In the course of researching . . . : int., Vince Carter, 1992.

289 When they crossed Wilshire and . . . : Carter, *Rogue Cops*, p. 5.

289 "They're stopping up the block . . .": Ibid, p.6.

290 "Go ahead, turn it over . . .": Ibid, p. 8.

290 When questioned about the blood . . . : Ibid.

291 Grabbing the phone, Ahern called his partner . . . : Ibid, p. 9.

292 But Case and Ahern knew . . . : int., Ahern, 1997. In 1997, while researching the death of Marilyn Monroe, I located James Ahern, who had retired from the LAPD in 1974 and was living in Solvang, California, north of Santa Barbara.

292 Brenda Allen's bungalow court . . . : Ibid.

293 In profiling the Black Dahlia case . . . : Douglas, *The Cases That Haunt Us,* pp. 318–333.

294 "To do what he did to . . .": Ibid, pp. 326–327.

294 The UNSUB: Ibid, pp. 326–329.

296 "The washing is to eliminate . . .": Ibid, p. 325.

296 "There must have been some connection . . .": Ibid, p. 327.

Chapter 19

298 In *Severed,* the most respected of . . . : Gilmore, *Severed*, pp. 178–193.

298 The Wilson interviews, which are filed . . . : Ibid, p. 185.

299 An arrangement was made for Gilmore to . . . : Ibid, p. 179.

299 "The garage was filled with stuff that . . .": Ibid, p. 180.

300 "Smith told me there had been . . .": Ibid, p. 181.

300 Arnold Smith was the "tall, six-foot-four younger man with . . .": *Examiner,* January 7, 1947.

300 Gilmore expressed an interest in . . . : Gilmore, *Severed,* p. 179.

301 In reviewing the transcripts of . . . : The transcripts of their conversations, are maintained in the Black Dahlia files of the LAPD and the West Hollywood Sheriff's office, as well as the Gilmore Collection housed at the UCLA Library, Dept. of Special Collections.

301 In an interview that Slatzer recorded for Gilmore . . . : A tape recording of the Slatzer interview made in 1982 was discovered in the Black Dahlia Collection at the Medford Historical Society. Reinterviewed in 2003 by the author regarding his statements to Gilmore, Slatzer

reconfirmed his observations regarding Arnold Smith, Mark Hansen, Elizabeth Short, and Bugsy Siegel.

301 At one of their meetings . . . : Gilmore, *Severed*, p. 182.

301 Robert Slatzer . . . had also seen this photo of . . . : Gilmore int., Robert Slatzer, 1982; author's int., Robert Slatzer, 2003.

302 "He was one of those slick . . .": author's int., Slatzer, 2003.

302 In the course of his taped 1982 . . . : Gilmore, int., Slatzer, 1982. When interviewed by the author in 2004, Slatzer confirmed that he was told that Bugsy Siegel had been involved in the murder of Elizabeth Short by Bill Taylor, who was a friend of Johnny Rosselli. At the time, Bill Taylor, who had once been the studio manger of Columbia Pictures, managed the Taft Building at the corner of Hollywood and Vine where both Slatzer and Johnny Rosselli maintained offices in the 1950s. Bill Taylor was beaten to death in 1961.

302 During one of John Gilmore's interviews . . . : Arnold Smith transcript, UCLA Library, Dept of Special Collections.

309 "Smith's statements had the ring . . .": Elizabeth Short Collection, Medford Historical Society.

309 "Smith just had too much . . .": Ibid.

309 Although in *Severed* John Gilmore . . . : p. 202.

Chapter 20

312 By the time Hansen was brought . . . : D.A.'s Black Dahlia files—Harry Hansen testimony. In Hansen's testimony before the Grand Jury many questions were asked about the four prime suspects put before them—Cleo Short, Leslie Dillon, Mark Hansen, Henry Hubert Hoffman. But few questions went beyond those suspects.

313 "His reference to the others are . . .": Gilmore, *Severed*, p. 195.

313 "He may be the one we've . . .": Ibid, p. 196

314 The call came in late December . . . : Ibid.

314 "Smith seemed nervous and uncomfortable . . .": Ibid, pp 203–205.

314 Meanwhile, St. John had made . . . : Ibid, p. 196.

314 "I want to bust this guy so bad . . .": Ibid.

315 Wilson was lying on his bed . . . : Ibid, pp. 211–213.

316 "He wanted to do it ever since . . .": Arnold Smith transcript, UCLA Library, Dept. of Special Collections.

BIBLIOGRAPHY

Anger, Kenneth. *Hollywood Babylon*. San Francisco: Stonehill Publishing, 1975.

———. *Hollywood Babylon II*. New York: NAL, Penguin, 1984.

Blackman, Robin. *Scene of the Crime*. New York: Harry N. Abrams, Inc., 2004.

Bonelli, William G. *Billion Dollar Blackjack*. Beverly Hills: Civic Research Press, 1954.

Carpenter, Teresa. *Mob Girl*. New York: Simon & Schuster, 1992.

Carter, Vincent A. *LAPD's Rogue Cops*. Lucerne Valley, CA: Desert View Books, 1993.

Cavendish, Marshall. *Crimes & Punishment*. New York: Angus Hall, 1985.

Cohen, Mickey. *In My Own Words*. Englewood Cliffs, NJ: Prentice-Hall, 1975.

Corrina, Joe, *Mobsters*. San Francisco: World Publications Group, 2003.

Demaris, Ovid. *The Last Mafioso*. New York: Times Books, 1981.

———. *The Lucky Luciano Story*. New York: Tower Books, 1969.

De River, J. Paul, M.D. *The Sexual Criminal: A Psychoanalytical Study*. Burbank, CA: Bloat Publishing, 1949; rev. ed., 2000.

Domanick, Joe. *To Protect and to Serve: The L.A.P.D.'s Century of War in the City of Dreams*. New York: Pocket Books, 1994.

Douglas, John, and Mark Olshaker. *The Cases That Haunt Us.* New York: Lisa Drew Books/Scribner, 2000.

———. *Mind Hunter.* New York: Lisa Drew Books/Scribner, 1995.

Douglas, Kirk. *The Ragman's Son.* New York: Simon & Schuster, 1988.

Edmonds, Andy. *Bugsy's Baby: The Secret Life of Mob Queen Virginia Hill.* New York: Birch Lane Press, 1993.

———. *Hot Toddy.* New York: William Morrow and Co., 1989.

Eisenberg, Dennis, Uri Dan, and Eli Landau. *Meyer Lansky: Mogul of the Mob.* Paddington Press, 1979.

Feder, Sid, and Joachim Joesten. *The Luciano Story.* New York: David Mckay Co., Inc., 1954.

Fetherling, Doug. *The Five Lives of Ben Hecht.* Toronto: Lester & Orpen, 1977.

Finney, Guy W. *Angel City in Turmoil.* Los Angeles: Amer Press, 1945.

Fowler, Will. *The Young Man from Denver.* Garden City, NY.: Doubleday & Co, 1962.

———. *Reporters: Memoirs of a Young Newspaperman*: Malibu, CA: Roundtable, 1991.

Freed, Donald, and Raymond Briggs. *Killing Time.* New York: MacMillan, 1996.

Gates, Daryl. *Chief: My Life in the LAPD.* New York: Bantam Books, 1992.

Giesler, Jerry, and Pete Martin. *The Jerry Giesler Story.* New York: Simon & Schuster, 1960.

Gilmore, John. *Severed: The True Story of the Black Dahlia Murder.* CA: Amok Books, 1998.

Granlund, Nils T. *Blondes, Brunettes, and Bullets.* New York: David McKay, 1957.

Halberstam, David. *The Powers That Be.* New York: Alfred A. Knopf, 1979.

Hecht, Ben. *A Child of the Century.* New York: Primus, 1954.

Heimann, Jim. *Sins of the City: The Real L.A. Noir.* San Francisco: Chronicle Books, 1999.

Henderson, Bruce, and Sam Summerlin. *The Super Sleuths.* New York: MacMillan, 1975.

Henstell, Bruce. *Los Angeles, an Illustrated History.* New York: Alfred A. Knopf, 1980.

Hodel, Steve. *Black Dahlia Avenger.* New York: Arcade Publishing, 2003.

Jennings, Dean. *We Only Kill Each Other: The Life and Bad Times of Bugsy Siegel.* Englewood Cliffs, NJ: Prentice-Hall, 1967.

Keppel, Robert D. *Signature Killers.* New York: Pocket Books, 1997.

Knowlton, Janice, and Michael Newton. *Daddy Was the Black Dahlia Killer.* New York: Pocket Books, 1995.

Lacey, Robert. *Little Man: Meyer Lansky and the Gangster Life.* Boston: Little Brown and Co., 1991.

Larkin, Rochelle. *Hail Columbia.* New York: Arlington House, 1975.

Martinez, Al. *Jigsaw John.* Los Angeles: J.P. Tarcher, 1975.

Marx, Samuel, and Joyce Vanderveen. *Deadly Illusions.* New York: Random House, 1990.

Messick, Hank. *Lansky.* New York: Putnam & Sons, 1971.

Morton, James. *Gangland International: An Informal History of the Mafia and Other Mobs in the Twentieth Century.* London: Little, Brown & Company, 1998.

Muir, Florabel. *Headline Happy.* New York: Henry Holt & Co., 1950.

Otash, Fred. *Investigation Hollywood.* Chicago: Regnery, 1976.

Pacios, Mary. *Childhood Shadows: The Hidden Story of the Black Dahlia Murder.* Downloaded and printed via electronic distribution from the World Wide Web. ISBN 1-58500-484-7, 1999.

Rappleye, Charles, and Ed Becker. *All American Mafioso: The Johnny Rosselli Story.* New York: Doubleday, 1991.

Reid, David. *Sex, Death and God in L.A.* New York: Random House, 1992.

Reid, Ed. *The Grim Reapers: The Anatomy of Organized Crime in America.* Chicago: Henry Regnery, 1969.

Richardson, James H. *For the Life of Me: Memoirs of a City Editor.* New York: G.P. Putnam's Sons, 1954.

Roeburt, John. *Get Me Giesler.* New York: Belmont Books, 1962.

Rothmiller, Mike, and Ivan G. Goldman. *L.A. Secret Police: Inside the L.A.P.D. Elite Spy Network.* New York: Pocket Books, 1992.

Rowan, David. *Famous American Crimes.* London: Frederick Muller, 1957.

Russo, Gus. *The Outfit.* New York: Bloomsbury, 2001.

Slatzer, Robert. *The Life and Curious Death of Marilyn Monroe.* New York: Pinnacle, 1974.

———. *The Marilyn Files.* New York: SPI, 1992.

Smith, Jack. *Jack Smith's L.A.* New York: McGraw-Hill, 1980.

Starr, Kevin. *Inventing the Dream: California through the Progressive Era.* New York: Oxford University Press, 1985.

———. *The Dream Endures: California Enters the 1940s.* New York: Oxford University Press, 1997.

Sterling, Hank. *Ten Perfect Crimes.* New York: Stravon, 1954.

Stoker, Charles. *Thicker 'n Thieves.* Santa Monica: Sidereal, 1951.

Tejaratchi, Sean, *Death Scenes: A Homicide Detective's Scrapbook.* Portland: Feral House, 1996.

Thomas, Bob. *King Cohn.* New York: G. P. Putman's Sons, 1967.

Turkus, Burton B., and Sid Feder. *Murder Inc.: The Inside Story of the Mob.* New York: Farrar, Straus & Giroux, 1951.

Tygiel, Jules. *The Great Los Angeles Swindle.* New York: Oxford University Press, 1994.

Underwood, Agness. *Newspaperwoman.* New York: Harper & Brothers, 1949.

Vaus, Jim. *Why I Quit Syndicated Crime.* New York: Communication, Inc., 1951.

Wagner, Rob Leicester. *Red Ink—White Lies.* Upland, CA: Dragon Flyer Press, 2.

Walker, Clifford James. *One Eye Closed the Other Red: The California Bootlegging Years.* Barstow, CA: Back Door Publishing, 1999.

Webb, Jack. *The Badge.* Greenwich, CT: Fawcett, 1958.

Wilkerson III, W. R. *The Man Who Invented Las Vegas.* Los Angeles: Ciro's Books, 2000.

Wilson, Colin. *Murder in the 1940s.* New York: Carroll & Graf, 1993.

Wolf, George, and Joseph DiMona. *Frank Costello, Prime Minister of the Underworld.* New York: William Morrow, 1974.

Wolf, Marvin J., and Katherine Mader. *Fallen Angels: Chronicles of L.A. Crime and Mystery.* New York: Facts on File, 1986.

INDEX

abortionists. *See also* Audrain, Dr. Leslie C.
(Dr. Morris)
Brenda Allen girls and, 280
in Elizabeth address book, 270, 272, 274,
275, 278, 311
Elizabeth and, 120, 122, 214, 227,
257–58, 270–72, 273, 278–79, 280
investigation of, 122, 257–58, 270–72,
273
Jean Spangler death and, 231, 232, 234
Mark Hansen on, 129
surgical bisection of body and, 32–33, 34,
135–36, 167, 169, 259, 341–42
as suspects, 120, 272–74
Syndicate/police protection, 235, 238,
257, 273
Abrams, Louis, 202, 205
Abrams, Marty, 202, 205
address book
abortionist names in, 270, 272, 274, 275,
278, 311
Arthur Lake and, 226
discovered, 143, 144
Dr. Faught and, 270, 271
father of child and, 279
Gangster Squad pre-interviewing leads in,
170

Jemison suspects from, 273–75
Mark Hansen and, 144–45, 259
Maurice Clement address in, 275
names cut out of, 144, 279, 282
photograph, 145
prominent names in, 144
Administrative Vice. *See also* Carter, Vince
call-girl ring connection, 105, 106–7, 253
Syndicate pay-off knowledge in, 160–61
tracing Elizabeth movements, 111–12
Ahern, James. *See* Case, Archie and James
Ahern
Al Green's Nightspot
Elizabeth frequenting, 108, 202
as robbery operations center, 202
Albro, Mrs. Curtis, 287–88
Allen, Brenda (Marie Mitchell)
arrest, 237–38
attempted murder of, 171–72
call-girl ring, 103–8, 120, 194, 196,
253–54, 282
Catalina Street bungalow of, 106, 171–72,
289–92, 297, 309–10
customers, 107
Elizabeth murder and, 171–72, 280, 282
Grand Jury investigation of, 253–56
in hiding, 172

INDEX